Global Perspectives on Contemporary Marketing Education

Brent Smith
Saint Joseph's University, USA

Amiram Porath
AmiPorCon Ltd, Israel

A volume in the Advances in Marketing, Customer
Relationship Management, and E-Services
(AMCRMES) Book Series

An Imprint of IGI Global

Published in the United States of America by
> Business Science Reference (an imprint of IGI Global)
> 701 E. Chocolate Avenue
> Hershey PA, USA 17033
> Tel: 717-533-8845
> Fax: 717-533-8661
> E-mail: cust@igi-global.com
> Web site: http://www.igi-global.com

Library of Congress Cataloging-in-Publication Data

Names: Smith, Brent, 1973- editor. | Porath, Amiram, editor.
Title: Global perspectives on contemporary marketing education / Brent Smith
  and Amiram Porath, editors.
Description: Hershey, PA : Business Science Reference, [2016] | Includes
  bibliographical references and index.
Identifiers: LCCN 2015042006| ISBN 9781466697843 (hardcover) | ISBN
  9781466697850 (ebook)
Subjects: LCSH: Marketing--Study and teaching.
Classification: LCC HF5415 .G566 2016 | DDC 658.80071--dc23 LC record available at http://lccn.loc.gov/2015042006

This book is published in the IGI Global book series Advances in Marketing, Customer Relationship Management, and E-Services (AMCRMES) (ISSN: 2327-5502; eISSN: 2327-5529)

British Cataloguing in Publication Data
A Cataloguing in Publication record for this book is available from the British Library.

For electronic access to this publication, please contact: eresources@igi-global.com.

Advances in Marketing, Customer Relationship Management, and E-Services (AMCRMES) Book Series

Eldon Y. Li
National Chengchi University, Taiwan &
California Polytechnic State University, USA

ISSN: 2327-5502
EISSN: 2327-5529

MISSION

Business processes, services, and communications are important factors in the management of good customer relationship, which is the foundation of any well organized business. Technology continues to play a vital role in the organization and automation of business processes for marketing, sales, and customer service. These features aid in the attraction of new clients and maintaining existing relationships.

The Advances in Marketing, Customer Relationship Management, and E-Services (AMCRMES) Book Series addresses success factors for customer relationship management, marketing, and electronic services and its performance outcomes. This collection of reference source covers aspects of consumer behavior and marketing business strategies aiming towards researchers, scholars, and practitioners in the fields of marketing management.

COVERAGE

- Relationship marketing
- CRM in financial services
- Legal Considerations in E-Marketing
- Social Networking and Marketing
- Cases on CRM Implementation
- CRM and customer trust
- Web Mining and Marketing
- Customer Retention
- B2B marketing
- Database marketing

IGI Global is currently accepting manuscripts for publication within this series. To submit a proposal for a volume in this series, please contact our Acquisition Editors at Acquisitions@igi-global.com or visit: http://www.igi-global.com/publish/.

Titles in this Series

For a list of additional titles in this series, please visit: www.igi-global.com

Competitive Social Media Marketing Strategies
Wilson Ozuem (University of Gloucestershire, UK) and Gordon Bowen (Regent's University London, UK)
Business Science Reference • copyright 2016 • 317pp • H/C (ISBN: 9781466697768) • US $195.00 (our price)

Product Innovation through Knowledge Management and Social Media Strategies
Alok Kumar Goel (CSIR Human Resource Development Centre, India) and Puja Singhal (Amity University, India)
Business Science Reference • copyright 2016 • 421pp • H/C (ISBN: 9781466696075) • US $205.00 (our price)

Fuzzy Optimization and Multi-Criteria Decision Making in Digital Marketing
Anil Kumar (ABV-Indian Institute of Information Technology & Management, India) and Manoj Kumar Dash (ABV-Indian Institute of Information Technology & Management, India)
Business Science Reference • copyright 2016 • 368pp • H/C (ISBN: 9781466688087) • US $200.00 (our price)

Trends and Innovations in Marketing Information Systems
Theodosios Tsiakis (Alexander Technological Educational Institute of Thessaloniki, Greece)
Business Science Reference • copyright 2015 • 454pp • H/C (ISBN: 9781466684591) • US $225.00 (our price)

Capturing, Analyzing, and Managing Word-of-Mouth in the Digital Marketplace
Sumangla Rathore (Sir Padampat Singhania University, India) and Avinash Panwar (Sir Padampat Singhania University, India)
Business Science Reference • copyright 2016 • 339pp • H/C (ISBN: 9781466694491) • US $200.00 (our price)

Strategic Customer Relationship Management in the Age of Social Media
Amir Khanlari (University of Tehran, Iran)
Business Science Reference • copyright 2015 • 332pp • H/C (ISBN: 9781466685864) • US $200.00 (our price)

Maximizing Commerce and Marketing Strategies through Micro-Blogging
Janée N. Burkhalter (Saint Joseph's University, USA) and Natalie T. Wood (Saint Joseph's University, USA & Edith Cowan University, Australia)
Business Science Reference • copyright 2015 • 380pp • H/C (ISBN: 9781466684089) • US $225.00 (our price)

Analyzing the Cultural Diversity of Consumers in the Global Marketplace
Juan Miguel Alcántara-Pilar (University of Granada, Spain) Salvador del Barrio-García (University of Granada, Spain) Esmeralda Crespo-Almendros (University of Granada, Spain) and Lucia Porcu (University of Granada, Spain)
Business Science Reference • copyright 2015 • 403pp • H/C (ISBN: 9781466682627) • US $200.00 (our price)

www.igi-global.com

701 E. Chocolate Ave., Hershey, PA 17033
Order online at www.igi-global.com or call 717-533-8845 x100
To place a standing order for titles released in this series, contact: cust@igi-global.com
Mon-Fri 8:00 am - 5:00 pm (est) or fax 24 hours a day 717-533-8661

Table of Contents

Detailed Table of Contents

Vivian Faustino-Pulliam, University of San Francisco, USA
Carlos Ballesteros Garcia, Universidad Pontifica Comillas, Spain
Mirjeta Beqiri, Gonzaga University, USA

In a world, increasingly confronted with conflict and various social issues, universities play a larger role in regards to understanding how education can be best deployed to advance social justice, freedom, equality, and human development. This chapter aims to share with readers - students and educators - valuable insights gathered from the online teaching experience of three educators based in various parts of the globe, who have come together "virtually" to teach a global markets course to refugees and indigenous people of diverse cultural backgrounds from various refugee camps in Africa- Kakuma, Kenya and Dzaleka, Malawi, and Amman in Jordan. The chapter provides insights into how digital pedagogy, culturally relevant curriculum design, support from community partners and commitment from volunteer educators can sustain the goal of educating those at the margins and promote social change towards sustainable human development.

Ana Estima, University of Aveiro, Portugal
Paulo Duarte, University of Beira Interior, Portugal

The debate on what should be offered by universities concerning their marketing education curricula in order to serve the market needs, specifically the employers' has been widely present in the literature. Its relevance derives from the fact that employers are one of the most important stakeholders of higher education institutions, given their responsibility in the career of graduate students. In this chapter we intend to contribute to the understanding of the state of undergraduate marketing education offered by Portuguese universities and assess whether there is a mismatch between marketing education and market needs. A better understanding of the mismatch and its implications can lead to better marketing education programs, increasing not only the acceptance and employability of students but also the transfer of innovative marketing knowledge to companies. The findings show that there is indeed a gap between what is being offered by the academia and what is requested by the job market, in terms of marketing, that could be higher than 50% of the requirements expected by employers.

This chapter outlines the pathway to advanced marketing education by students in a developing country. We begin by contrasting the similarities and differences in undergraduate marketing education in Saudi Arabia versus the U.S. The analysis includes the typical markers of language and access to secondary sources, and culture-specific differences in the perception of time and various cultural influences using Hofstede's cultural dimensions. This is followed with a description of the pathway students from Saudi Arabia take to pursue a Master's and/or Doctorate in marketing in the U.S. The chapter concludes with the unique insight - unlike a sizeable number of foreign students in the U.S., most students from Saudi Arabia return to Saudi Arabia and in so doing stem the 'brain drain' so many other countries face when their brightest head to the U.S. for advanced study.

This chapter considers the appropriateness and importance of including the natural environment (i.e., nature and geography) as part of the external business environment featured in marketing textbooks. Based on myriad examples from industry, the natural environment is regarded as an uncontrollable force that constantly affects decisions about markets and marketing activities. Thus, it deserves some (greater) mention next to economic, competitive, regulatory, and other variables typically featured in most marketing textbooks. Based on a review of business news, industry concerns, and marketing textbooks, this chapter considers the current listing of uncontrollable environment forces typically discussed within twenty-five popular marketing textbooks. It is observed that nature and geography, common priorities for business decision makers, are conspicuously absent from mention within most of these textbooks. This chapter shows that the natural environment is mentioned in only five of twenty-five marketing textbooks: two introductory marketing; one marketing management; and two international marketing. Based on scholarly definitions and industry examples, nature and geography are, in fact, uncontrollable influential forces that affect markets and marketing activities. Consequently, there is reasonable cause for including them in more marketing textbooks. Textbook authors and instructors can provide students a more complete picture of how domestic and international markets and marketing activities are affected by the natural environment. In practice, business people acknowledge that the natural environment affects and is affected by markets and marketing activities in virtually all industries. Alas, marketing textbooks seldom little, if ever, acknowledge that nature and geography (e.g., topography, climate, weather, solar flares, natural disasters) affect how companies think about their markets and marketing mix. This chapter offers simple, actionable steps for discussing the natural environment in marketing textbooks and courses.

Homer B. Warren, Youngstown State University, USA

David J. Burns, Kennesaw State University, USA

The complex realities of the increasingly global nature of business require managers who are able to see and comprehend the multiple interrelationships of factors in the environment to optimize decision making. This paper offers a mental model used by the authors to help students better understand the heuristic thinking processes that successful strategic marketing managers use in decision making and problem solving. The authors argue that seeing the "whole" marketing system and understanding how to integrate marketing knowledge is a key ingredient in heuristic thinking. To this end, the paper details the foundation for and the construction of a mental model for a strategic marketing management course. An application is discussed.

Krittinee Nuttavuthisit, Chulalongkorn University, Thailand

This chapter discusses the learning of consumption and marketing within the context of social-related issues. The objectives are to expand dimensions of marketing education into a wider perspective beyond the economic focus to the social domain. Exploring the different contexts can help uncover a deeper perspective beyond general concepts of consumption and marketing. Moreover, considering the social aspect can enhance a longer perspective of business beyond current profit maximization, particularly in the 21st century with its emphasis on sustainability. The learning process can follow the four main steps of understanding the problem, introducing the solution, engaging participation (with real actions to support the project or organization), and evaluating output and outcome. These processes are elaborated together with examples of real practices and summarized learning derived from the classes conducted in Thailand. Not only can this benefit the students, but also the overall business and the society by turning marketing students into active citizens.

Stephanie A. Tryce, Saint Joseph's University, USA

As we move toward 2050, the United States will become a country of minorities. These changing demographics have tremendous implications for the way marketers understand both the marketplace and consumer behavior. Intentionality, specificity, and intersectional approaches to diverse sport's history are key in successfully providing millennial students with the cultural competence required to become first-rate global marketers. Sport provides marketing educators and students a unique opportunity to examine cultural diversity in a way that ameliorates diversity fatigue from underexposed students. This chapter details relevant diversity and inclusion language and terminology, provides individual lesson plan examples, and details outcomes and instruction for developing cultural competence in millennial student populations.

Chapter 8

The state of Sarawak is the biggest among the 13 states in Malaysia. It is strategically located in South East Asia in the island of Borneo. In the state of Sarawak, Marketing education has seen a tremendous growth over the years. Marketing is one of the most sought-after business courses by many school leavers. In Sarawak, Marketing education is provided by public and private universities and institutions of higher education in the form of degree and diploma courses. Marketing education views marketing as a discipline that can be learned through the classroom (off the job). However the employers' perspectives differ as they prefer hands on (on the job). The main challenge confronting the Sarawak institutions of higher learning is to produce marketing graduates capable of being competent marketing practitioners serving in public and private sectors. The question that remains unanswered is whether the marketing education curriculum content matches the trends and major forces in our external environment as proper attention to these dimensions will enable the institutions to produce graduates equipped with the relevant skills in the workforce or whether the curriculum content has been designed in recognition of the fact that students will need to cope with the complex nature of today's business planning and decision-making. The literature on marketing education in Sarawak, is limited and very few research articles are found exploring the effectiveness. The authors have contributed to the field of Marketing education in Sarawak in one of their previous article published five years ago. Therefore this chapter is an attempt by the authors to explore the effectiveness of marketing education in meeting the organizational needs in Sarawak from the perspectives of employers. This study uses qualitative methods which includes interview (face-to-face and telephone), informal discussions, email communications with managers, personal observations by the authors, and a review of literatures in the area of Marketing education. Marketing education, like marketing practice, is dynamic. Marketing education should continually evolve in such a manner to accommodate and satisfy various stakeholders such as government, business and industry, academics as well as students. The findings reveal several issues and challenges of Marketing education from the employers' perspectives in Sarawak. These findings will be useful for curriculum design of marketing courses. It will also assist marketing educators in understanding the organizational needs of marketing knowledge, skills and abilities required of a graduate. Future marketing students will also be able to know the industrial and organizational expectations required of them as a marketing graduate. This chapter clearly identifies some of the deficiencies in the area of practical skills required by marketing graduates in the context of Sarawak. This chapter is expected to provide the framework and prospect for conducting an in-depth quantitative research in Marketing education in future in Sarawak (Borneo).

Chapter 9

With the assistance of new computing technologies and consumer data collection methods, advertising professionals are capable of generating better targeted advertising campaigns. Big Data analytics are particularly worth noticing and have presented ample opportunities for advertising researchers and practitioners around the world. Although Big Data analytic courses have been offered at major universities, existing advertising curricula have yet to address the opportunities and challenges offered by Big Data. This chapter collects curricular data from major universities around the world to examine what Big Data has posed challenges and opportunities to existing advertising curricula in an international context. Curricula of 186 universities around the world are reviewed to describe the status of integrating these developments into better preparing advertising students for these changes. Findings show that only selected advertising programs in the U.S. have begun to explore the potential of the data analytics tools and techniques. Practical and educational implications are discussed.

Chapter 10

The role of technology in marketing education can be described from two different points of view, the role of the technology as a tool for marketing education and the role of technology in marketing as part of the curriculum of marketing education. We begin with a description of the role of technology in education in general. That has been a focal point for research for the last two decades and in that aspect marketing education is no exception, in fact it is even more relevant for marketing education as marketing uses communication as a major tool. Alternatively, the changing world of communication changes how marketing is viewed, opening new venues for opportunities but also exposing new threats, one cannot be called a marketing expert without understanding the new rules of communication. The chapter will than present two cases one of a threat and another of an opportunity to demonstrate that point while also discussing the role of technology in education in an effective way for marketing education. It ends with a suggestion for electives for marketing education curriculum.

Chapter 11

Organizations have increased expectations for expertise in data analytics by marketing students. The chapter describes the change taking place in business in general and in marketing specifically and the disconnect between demand and supply. While tools have been available to teach marketing research using survey, experimental, and qualitative methodologies. However, a lack of materials and a huge learning curve are major reasons for methodologies for analyzing digital data, big data, or social media data not being used. Teradata, Inc., worked with Marketing Information Systems academics to create TeradataUniversityNetwork.com (TUN) as a place for sharing tools, software, articles, and data so analytics can be taught in the classroom. As of August 2014, (TUN) is a resource for sharing tools, software, articles, and videos that focus on marketing analytics. This chapter describes the range of materials available and how they can be used in the classroom.

This chapter addresses those fundamentals and ethical issues related to the profession of marketing, as well as indirectly to other decision makers in companies, to guide human action in a moral sense. The main objective will be to provide different insights to business and marketing professionals to identify and analyze ethical problems in the various elements of a marketing strategy to propose alternatives, so that they may adjust their behavior according to the set of life and judging human acts (own and externals) according to the accepted norms and values. The chapter leads readers to an open invitation to reflect about his/her professional field: how I can contribute from an ethical perspective? From the ethics of marketing, how I can make decisions based on principles such as confidentiality, truthfulness, loyalty, transparency, fairness and accountability?

Chapter 13

This chapter presents a peace-centered process of teaching marketing that the author has implemented during 2002-2015 academic years with undergraduate and graduate business students in various marketing courses at two Christian Universities in the United States. The peace-centered process is related to the development of a unified world view about human life in a culture of peace and culture of healing and the development of virtues in a marketing career. The chapter discusses (1) the manifestation of violence in marketing, (2) the concept of a peace-centered process of teaching marketing, (3) the responsibility of marketing educators, and (4) the seven pedagogical strategies for this approach.

Cultural diversity in society, the workplace and classrooms is more or less is a global phenomenon. The multi-cultural classroom provides an opportunity for students from different cultures to bring their enormous range of experiences, knowledge, perspectives and insights to the learning – if the process is enabled. Many firms around the globe are expanding their businesses beyond domestic markets. These trends indicate that many individuals are likely to study or work in multicultural environments domestically and abroad. Research suggests that faculty and trainers adapt their teaching style and classroom policies to accommodate multicultural learners. Disconnections may arise, however, regarding the willingness to include these accommodations. This chapter explores various issues which faculty and students face regarding adjustments in teaching style, content, and policies to adapt to multicultural learners. Specific recommendations to meet the challenges of multicultural learning are also provided.

Educational organizations have to face logistic hurdle when introducing remote learning using mobile devices. Unlike the introduction of a new textbook, the introduction of e-learning into educational environment requires adaptation, on the physical as well as the human infrastructure levels. The case study below describe such a move in a regional high school in Israel and presents the major logistic question the move presented to the school and other interested parties. The answers may differ from country to country but the questions seem to be more generalize, and therefore should at least be considered when preparing for the move. The paper ends with some of the lessons learnt, and recommendations for the future.

Preface

According to the Associate to Advance Collegiate Schools of Business (AACSB International, 2015), there are an estimated 16,484 schools worldwide granting business degrees at the bachelors level or higher. 21st Century marketing professionals operate in a very sophisticated, dynamic, and hypercompetitive global environment. Thus, they must maintain constant awareness of key factors that can shape markets, direct trends, and, in turn, influence marketing activities. Given the need to develop market offerings that acknowledge people, planet, and profit, leaders of market-driven and market-driving organizations will need human talent that is competent not only in the marketing mix but also in cultural literacy, ethics, analytics, and sustainability.

Global Perspectives on Contemporary Marketing Education is focused on the development and education of future marketing professionals in an age of shifting markets and heightened consumer engagement. A compendium of innovations, insights, and ideas from marketing professors and professionals around the world, this title explores the need for students to be prepared to enter the sophisticated global marketplace. This book will be invaluable to business students, educators, administrators, and professionals who value the infusion of fresh globally-sourced ideas into their courses. This book also will be of use to a broad international and multicultural audience of business academics hoping to improve their approaches to teaching and assurance of learning. The reader should appreciate how this work brings together content from contributors of various ethnic origins working in a variety of countries, such as the United States of America, Spain, Portugal, Taiwan, Israel, Malaysia, Mexico, Pakistan, and Thailand.

If you would thoroughly know anything, teach it to others.
Tryon Edwards, Theologian (1809-1894)

For generations, the marketing community has helped organizations improve their market offerings, value propositions, and relationships with key markets. As academics and practitioners, we have a keen interest in advancing the marketing knowledge that students learn in classrooms, and ultimately apply in the field, office, or boardroom. Edmund Jerome McCarthy, a recently deceased pioneer in the Marketing discipline, offered up 4Ps–product, promotion, price, and place of distribution–which have been absorbed deeply into the mainstream lexicon of business. Acknowledging both our past and present, we conceived this book project as a way to broaden views on what marketing means and how marketing education can be brought to life around the world.

As countries compete to become stronger players in the global market, they have emphasized the need to foster homegrown efforts that develop business professionals with well-rounded experience, exposure, and education. As evidence of this fact, nearly 30% of AACSB's membership is based outside of the United States of America. (AACSB International, 2015). We will continue to see more business schools and programs of all sizes trying to achieve, or maintain, the outcomes required for accreditation by AACSB, Accreditation Council for Business Schools and Programs (ACBSP), European Quality Improvement System (EQUIS), International Assembly for Collegiate Business Education (IACBE), and other comparable bodies. Beyond accreditation issues, concerns persist from governments, consumer advocacy groups, and others regarding business' ability to create value responsibly and sustainably within our increasingly diverse, inclusive, and ever-sophisticated society. Indeed, this book aims to highlight the work and insights of business academe's teacher-scholars to ensure that marketing students around the world are educated in ways that meaningfully integrate diversity, ethics, analytics, and sustainability, among other topics. In that vein, the book focuses on contribution from some of today's best marketing teachers in the Americas, Africa, Asia, Europe, and Oceania.

The mere imparting of information is not education.
Carter G. Woodson, Historian (1875-1950)

This book features innovations, insights, and ideas from globally minded marketing educators who emphasize effective teaching and learning in their pedagogy. Targeted in its scope and broad in its sources, we hope that this book will become a key reference for marketing and business educators looking for quality literature about how to foster excellence among students in the 21ˢᵗ Century.

We realize that higher education's stakeholders expect us to assess and improve our teaching. Moreover, the public-at-large expects that we will take greater initiative in addressing marketing's intersections with timeless concerns such as ethics, sustainability, social responsibility, social justice, service learning, and so forth.

We now accept the fact that learning is a lifelong process of keeping abreast of change. And the most pressing task is to teach people how to learn.
Peter Drucker, Management consultant (1909-2005)

ORGANIZATION OF THE BOOK

In this book, the reader will find a diverse array of chapters that can help advance our understanding of what it means to educate business students whose training can help them become better decision makers, colleagues, team players, and leaders (Smith, 2011). These chapters are produced by people hailing from different cultural backgrounds, national origins, disciplinary expertise, and institutional profiles. We all have something to learn from our fellow teachers regarding utilization of technology, integration of ethics, cross-cultural engagement, curriculum enhancement, as so on. Representing over ten different countries, the contributors in this book provide examples of what they have done and learned in the process of teaching people about marketing.

In order, the chapters are listed below and, thereafter, described in greater detail.

- **Chapter 1: Reflections on Teaching a Global Markets Course at Jesuit Commons Higher Education at the Margins** by Vivian Faustino, University of San Francisco; Carlos Ballesteros Garcia, Universidad Pontifica Comillas; and Mirjeta Beqiri, Gonzaga University.

- **Chapter 2: The Mismatch between Undergraduate Marketing Education and Employers' Requirements in Portugal** by Ana Estima, University of Aveiro and Paulo Duarte, University of Beira Interior.
- **Chapter 3: From Marketing Education in a Developing Country to a U.S. Master's and/or Doctoral Degree in Marketing** by Matt Elbeck, Troy University – Dothan.
- **Chapter 4: Nature and Geography – Tragic Voids within Marketing Textbooks and the External Business Environment** by Brent Smith, Saint Joseph's University.
- **Chapter 5: A Mental Model for Teaching Strategic Marketing Management** by Homer Warren, Youngstown State University, and David Burns, Kennesaw State University.
- **Chapter 6: Turning Marketing Students into Active Citizens – The Learning of Consumption and Social-Related Marketing in Thailand** by Krittinee Nuttavuthisit, Sasin Graduate Institute of Business Administration, Chulalongkorn University.
- **Chapter 7: Using Sport's History to Develop Cultural Competence in Millennial Marketers – Title IX, Stadium Development, and Post-Apartheid Rugby** by Stephanie Tryce, Saint Joseph's University.
- **Chapter 8: Marketing Education in Sarawak – Looking at it from the Employers Viewpoint** by Balakrishnan Muniapan, Wawasan Open University; Margaret Gregory, Universiti Teknologi MARA; and Edith Lim, Swinburne University of Technology.
- **Chapter 9: Integrating Big Data Analytics into Advertising Curriculum – Opportunities and Challenges in an International Context** by Kenneth C.C. Yang, University of Texas – El Paso, and Yowei Kang, Kainan University.
- **Chapter 10: Two Different Aspects of Technology Regarding Marketing Education** by Amiram Porath, AmiPorCon Ltd, Israel.
- **Chapter 11: Preparing Students to Use Marketing Technology for Decision-Making** by Camille Schuster, California State University San Marcos.
- **Chapter 12: Ethical Marketing** by Carlos Ballesteros, Universidad Pontificia Comillas, and Dulce Saldaña, Tecnologico de Monterrey.
- **Chapter 13: Teaching Peace and Marketing Education – From Pieces to Peace** by Maria Lai-Ling Lam, Point Loma Nazarene University.
- **Chapter 14: Promoting Effective Learning in Diverse Classrooms** by Amir Manzoor, Bahria University.
- **Chapter 15: Logistic Issues in Introducing Remote Learning Devices – Case Study** by Amiram Porath, AmiPorCon Ltd, Israel.

In the first chapter, "Reflections on Teaching a Global Markets Course at Jesuit Commons Higher Education at the Margins," authors Vivian Faustino (University of San Francisco), Carlos Ballesteros Garcia (Universidad Pontifica Comillas), and Mirjeta Beqiri (Gonzaga University) detail their development and delivery of an online course for refugees in Kenya, Malawi, and Jordan. Their experience reflects a strong mission-driven effort to deploy education virtually as means to advance social justice, freedom, equality, and human development. This chapter provides insights into how digital pedagogy, culturally relevant curriculum, and collaborative partnerships can sustain the goal of educating persons at the margins.

In the second chapter, "The Mismatch between Undergraduate Marketing Education and Employers' Requirements in Portugal," Ana Estima (University of Aveiro) and Paulo Duarte (University of Beira Interior) examine the debate about how universities can develop marketing education curricula that can address market needs of employers. The authors take a closer look at the state of undergraduate marketing education offered in Portugal per key outcomes, such as employability of students and transfer of innovative marketing knowledge to companies.

In the third chapter, "From Marketing Education in a Developing Country to a U.S. Master's and/or Doctoral Degree in Marketing," Matt Elbeck (Troy University – Dothan) compares and contrasts undergraduate marketing education in Saudi Arabia versus the United States. He then describes a pathway taken by students from Saudi Arabia to pursue a Master's and/or Doctorate in marketing in the United States. The chapter concludes with a rather the unique insight on "brain drain" that distinguishes Saudi Arabian graduate students from other international students.

In the fourth chapter, "Nature and Geography: Tragic Voids within Marketing Textbooks and the External Business Environment," Brent Smith (Saint Joseph's University) presents a critique of mainstream marketing textbooks that lack specific inclusion of nature and geography ("natural environment") within discussions of dimensions comprising the external business environment. Citing myriad examples from industry, Smith argues that industry, more so than business academe, recognizes that nature and geography are uncontrollable forces that affect decisions about markets and marketing activities. Thus, the natural environment deserves (greater) mention next to economic, competitive, regulatory, and other variables typically featured in most marketing textbooks. By making such a change, textbook authors and marketing instructors can provide students a more complete picture of factors that actually impact domestic and international markets and marketing activities.

In the fifth chapter, "A Mental Model for Teaching Strategic Marketing Management," Homer Warren (Youngstown State University) and David Burns (Kennesaw State University) put forward a mental model to help students understand the heuristic thinking processes that successful strategic marketing managers use in problem solving. The authors argue that this model addresses industry's demand for managers who can see and comprehend multiple interrelationships of factors in the environment to optimize decision-making. The authors also discuss an application related to seeing the "whole" marketing system and understanding how to integrate marketing knowledge into heuristic thinking.

In the sixth chapter, "Turning Marketing Students into Active Citizens: The Learning of Consumption and Social-Related Marketing in Thailand," Krittinee Nuttavuthisit (Chulalongkorn University) discusses the learning of consumption and marketing within the context of social-related issues. By turning students into active citizens, she suggests that business and society can be enriched not only by achievement of profit maximization but also emphasis on sustainability.

In the seventh chapter, "Using Sport's History to Develop Cultural Competence in Millennial Marketers: Title IX, Stadium Development, and Post-Apartheid Rugby," Stephanie Tryce (Saint Joseph's University) notes that sport provides marketing educators and students a unique opportunity to examine cultural diversity in a way that ameliorates diversity fatigue from underexposed students. As the United States approaches 2050, it will become a country of minorities. Thus, millennial students must have – possess, acquire, or develop -- the cultural competence required to become first-rate global marketers. The chapter provides relevant diversity language, inclusion terminology, and examples of individual lesson plans.

In the eighth chapter, "Marketing Education in Sarawak: Looking at it from the Employers' Viewpoint," Balakrishnan Muniapan (Wawasan Open University), Margaret Gregory (Universiti Teknologi MARA), and Edith Lim (Swinburne University of Technology) examines the past, present, and future potential of marketing education in Sarawak, the largest of Malaysia's thirteen states. While marketing has garnered greater respect as a discipline, employers and new graduates still struggle to implement it most effectively in professional practice. Thus, marketing educators must evaluate and improve curriculum design of marketing courses. They also must make efforts to understand what public sector and private sector organizations require of graduates in terms of marketing knowledge, skills, and abilities required of a graduate.

In the ninth chapter, "Integrating Big Data Analytics into Advertising Curriculum: Opportunities and Challenges in an International Context," Kenneth C.C. Yang (University of Texas – El Paso) and Yowei Kang (Kainan University) contend that advertising professionals can utilize new computing technologies to producing better targeted advertising campaigns. While Big Data and analytics courses have been offered by many colleges and universities, they authors find that existing advertising curricula have yet to integrate such courses or related concepts in a significant way. The chapter brings together curricular data from nearly 190 universities around the world to examine how Big Data has posed challenges and opportunities for existing advertising curricula. Findings show that proportionally few advertising programs in the United States have begun to explore the potential of the data analytics tools and techniques.

In the tenth chapter, "Two Different Aspects of Technology Regarding Marketing Education," Amiram Porath (AmiPorCon Ltd, Israel) states that the role of technology in marketing education can be described from two different points of view: (1) as a tool for marketing education and (2) as part of the curriculum of marketing education. His chapter begins with a general description of the role of technology in education. Porath argues that one cannot be called a marketing expert without understanding the new rules of communication. Given the changing world of communication, marketing educators should consider how marketing practices may be viewed, what new opportunities may be created, and what new threats may manifest. The chapter presents two cases, one involving a threat and another involving an opportunity to illustrate these points while highlighting the role of technology. It ends with recommendations for elective in a marketing curriculum.

In the eleventh chapter, "Preparing Students to Use Marketing Technology for Decision-Making," Camille Schuster (California State University - San Marcos) looks at how organizations have increased their expectations for new marketing hires, particularly in the area of data analytics. Her chapter describes overall changes occurring in business, and more specifically in marketing, highlighting a longstanding disconnect between demand and supply. Despite the availability of existing tools for teaching marketing research (e.g., survey, experimental, and qualitative methodologies), marketing educators desire to integrate analytics lessons seem to be thwarted by a lack of materials and a huge learning curve. Schuster details how Teradata, Inc., working in cooperation with Marketing Information Systems academics, created TeradataUniversityNetwork.com (TUN) as a place for sharing tools, software, articles, and data so that analytics can be taught in classroom settings. This chapter describes TUN's range of marketing analytics materials (e.g., software, articles, and videos) available to marketing educators and offers recommendation on how those materials can be used in the classroom.

In the twelfth chapter, "Ethical Marketing," Carlos Ballesteros (Universidad Pontificia Comillas) and Dulce Saldaña (Tecnologico de Monterrey) address some fundamental ethical issues related to the profession of marketing. They also discuss how these issues may relate indirectly to other decision makers in companies, ultimately guiding organization-wide human action in a moral sense. The main objective of their chapter is to provide different insights for identifying and analyzing ethical problems across various elements of a marketing strategy. The chapter leads the reader to an open invitation to reflect about his/her professional field: How I can contribute from an ethical perspective? From the ethics of marketing, how I can make decisions based on principles such as confidentiality, truthfulness, loyalty, transparency, fairness and accountability?

In the thirteenth chapter, "Teaching Peace and Marketing Education: From Pieces to Peace," Maria Lai-Ling Lam (Point Loma Nazarene University) presents a *peace-centered* process of teaching marketing that she implemented during 2002-2015 academic years undergraduate and graduate business students at two Christian universities in the United States. She describes her pedagogical approach as one related to the development of a unified worldview about human life in a culture of peace, healing, and virtue. In her chapter, she discusses four main topics, including: (1) the manifestation of violence in marketing, (2) the concept of a peace-centered process of teaching marketing, (3) the responsibility of marketing educators, and (4) the seven pedagogical strategies for this approach.

In the fourteenth chapter, "Promoting Effective Learning in Diverse Classrooms," Amir Manzoor (Bahria University) discusses how the multicultural classroom provides an opportunity for students from different cultures to bring and benefits from a range of experiences, knowledge, perspectives and insights to the learning. It is no secret that successful, striving, and even struggling firms are moving increasingly to expand their reach beyond domestic markets. Paralleling this activity, more individuals–students, recent graduates, and new hires–are likely to study and/or work in multicultural environments domestically and internationally. In this chapter, Manzoor explores some issues faced by faculty and students regarding possible adjustments in teaching style, content, and policies to accommodate multicultural learners. Specific recommendations are provided to address these issues.

In the fifteenth chapter, "Logistic Issues in Introducing Remote Learning Devices: Case Study," Amiram Porath (AmiPorCon Ltd, Israel) describes logistical hurdles that educational organizations face when trying to introduce remote learning with mobile devices. Porath argues that unlike the introduction of a new textbook, the introduction of e-learning may require special adaptations at the physical and human infrastructure levels. He offers a case study that highlights how such a move presented major questions for a regional high school and its stakeholders in Israel. While the answers may differ from country to country, the questions are relevant enough for consideration by any educator or administrator when preparing for the move. The chapter ends with lessons learned and recommendations for the future.

CONCLUSION

Global Perspectives on Contemporary Marketing Education offers a diversity of teaching approaches for helping students understand how to apply, augment, and assess marketing paradigms and functions. A successful marketing department has the power to make or break a business. Today, successful marketing professionals must have broad knowledge and actionable skills that enable themselves, and their firms, to remain competitive in the global market.

As companies compete for international standing, the value of marketing professionals with well-rounded experience, exposure, and education will not subside. The contributions featured in this book capture good examples of how Marketing educators aim to develop the teaching and learning within and across cultural, geographic, national, and other boundaries.

Brent Smith
Saint Joseph's University, USA

Amiram Porath
AmiPorCon Ltd, Israel

REFERENCES

AACSB International. (2015). *Business school data guide 2015*. Author.

Smith, B. (2011). Who shall lead us? How cultural values and ethical ideologies guide young marketers' evaluations of the transformational manager–leader. *Journal of Business Ethics, 100*(4), 633–645. doi:10.1007/s10551-010-0701-0

Acknowledgment

We, the editors, wish to acknowledge the work of all persons who played an important role in taking this book project from its beginning to its completion. We thank the authors for contributing their perspectives, observations, and insights on many facets of marketing education. We are grateful to the reviewers who volunteered their time and service to help improve the content, scope, and quality of materials in this book. We are most appreciative of those authors who also doubled their contributions as reviewers.

Brent Smith
Saint Joseph's University, USA

Amiram Porath
AmiPorCon Ltd, Israel

Chapter 1

Reflections on Teaching a Global Markets Course at Jesuit Commons:
Higher Education at the Margins

Vivian Faustino-Pulliam
University of San Francisco, USA

Carlos Ballesteros Garcia
Universidad Pontifica Comillas, Spain

Mirjeta Beqiri
Gonzaga University, USA

ABSTRACT

In a world, increasingly confronted with conflict and various social issues, universities play a larger role in regards to understanding how education can be best deployed to advance social justice, freedom, equality, and human development. This chapter aims to share with readers - students and educators - valuable insights gathered from the online teaching experience of three educators based in various parts of the globe, who have come together "virtually" to teach a global markets course to refugees and indigenous people of diverse cultural backgrounds from various refugee camps in Africa- Kakuma, Kenya and Dzaleka, Malawi, and Amman in Jordan. The chapter provides insights into how digital pedagogy, culturally relevant curriculum design, support from community partners and commitment from volunteer educators can sustain the goal of educating those at the margins and promote social change towards sustainable human development.

INTRODUCTION

Education plays an integral role in promoting change due to its transformational impact on humans. Education provides knowledge which, in turn, empowers people. It allows humans to acquire the knowledge and skills, as well as to cultivate the attitudes and values, necessary to shape a sustainable future.

DOI: 10.4018/978-1-4666-9784-3.ch001

According to the Report to UNESCO of the International Commission on Education for the Twenty-first Century, also known as the Delors Report, sustainable education should consist of four pillars: "learning to know", "learning to do", "learning to live together, learning to live with others", and "learning to be" (Delors et al., 1996, p. 5). Along similar lines, the authors argue that education is a transformative experience and a powerful tool for ensuring sustainable human development. Education allows for the expansion of human choices and human capabilities. As stated by Nelson Mandela, "Education is the most powerful weapon which you can use to change the world" (Washington Post, 2013).

Education is transformational and life changing. It not only provides opportunities for individuals to find gainful employment and become productive members of society, but beyond these economic benefits, there is also a more important aspect that education brings forth: it develops minds and enables individuals to question, explore, and analyze the situations around them.

In this chapter, the authors present a compelling narrative of how education – similar to many other factors of production, such as labor and capital – can easily cross borders in today's increasingly globalized world. While it is an enormously challenging task, delivering higher education to those at the margins can be accomplished.

BACKGROUND

Jesuit Commons: Higher Education at the Margins (JC:HEM) is an initiative of the Society of Jesus that brings Jesuit higher education to individuals at the margins of society. Its services include:

1. Bringing together those who would normally be unable to access higher education, with institutions seeking a practical way to provide education where it is needed most.
2. Enabling collaboration to fully and freely create a global, virtual, and immersive learning environment through which Jesuit higher education can be delivered in a manner that is scalable, sustainable, and transferable.
3. Promoting human dignity and gender equality among educators and learners.
4. Giving life to the principles of Ignatian pedagogy by offering higher education that is capable of resulting in transformational learning.
5. Sharing the common human and spiritual values of all religions and cultures ("JC:HEM," n.d. para. 1-3)

Access to Higher Education

Higher education is the strongest, sturdiest ladder to increase socio-economic mobility. – Drew Faust, President Harvard University, Davos WEF, January 2015

In today's borderless society, where every economy strives to achieve a deeper level of integration while benefitting from evolving globalization, it is no longer impossible to provide access to higher education to those who need it most. Many parts of Africa, Asia, and other less developed nations are struggling with poverty, inequality, and other social issues. To alleviate these ills, many supranational institutions, such as United Nations' UNICEF, UNDP, UNIDO, the World Health Organization, the World Bank, and ILO, among many other organizations, have focused their attention on these issues. Numerous studies have reflected on and argued that education is a ticket to social mobility. Open to people of all faiths, the JC:HEM program draws on the rich and centuries-long Jesuit tradition of higher education and mobilizes the resources of the worldwide network of Jesuit educational institutions.

There are two programs that JC:HEM offers: a diploma in Liberal Studies and a non-credit certificate in the Community Learning Service Track. The authors have taught in the diploma program, which is granted by Regis University. Under this setup, courses are donated by various Jesuit universities and are taught by different volunteer faculty members.

Technology as Enabler

Delivering a course in the Liberal Studies program requires the innovative application of technology. To accomplish this undertaking, the underlying technology is similar to those used in the massive open online courses, or MOOCs, offered by an increasing number of select colleges in the U.S. These courses are touted for their potential to expand the reach of higher education. Online course offerings in higher education have increased enormously in the last 10–15 years (Beqiri, Chase, & Bishka, 2010). In the case of JC:HEM, delivering online courses was made possible through a dynamic partnership with various Jesuit universities, such as Regis University, Georgetown University, the University of San Francisco, and Gonzaga University, among many others across the world. In its early stage, Gonzaga University provided the learning management platform, Blackboard, for the Global Markets course; however, in 2015, the course was migrated to a proprietary JC:HEM platform through the generosity of Georgetown University; the same educational platform, Blackboard, is being used as well.

For these camps, the technology infrastructure consists of a number of computers for each classroom, local Internet providers, power sources, and the software required to run the program. To provide a more vivid description of the situation in one of the camps, here is an excerpt from its current on-site coordinator, Joseph Slaven, Project Director JRS – JC:HEM (February 18, 2015):

In Malawi, we have two power sources: the solar panels on our roof and ESCOM (the standard Malawian utility provider). The solar power is dedicated to powering our computers and IT system while ESCOM powers the lighting, electrical sockets, etc.

Malawi has one rainy season (January through March). In January there was massive flooding in the country that damaged much of the electricity infrastructure, meaning that electricity was often rationed while they worked to repair everything. This is pretty typical from what I understand - ESCOM is noto-riously unreliable (colloquially it is referred to as Electricity Sometimes Comes on Mondays), and thus we are often without lights and charging capability in the center (most students charge their cell phones from our sockets because there aren't many other opportunities in camp).

This became an issue over one weekend in January when our inverter (the device that converts our solar power to a usable frequency) broke and we could not simply fall back onto ESCOM due to the power rationing. The center was unusable for several days while we scrambled to fix/replace the inverter.

We have wireless Internet (though most of the computers are also connected by Ethernet cable because the wireless signal often wavers) provided by a company called Skyband. It is not government owned. Skyband is more reliable than the company we previously used, although there are frequent issues. Once or twice a week we will have to call in to their customer service and have them test/reset the connection. Usually it's a one-hour fix of that nature. On occasion there will be larger issues - a couple of weeks ago somebody cut a cable that was running into Mozambique from the ocean and that meant we didn't have wireless for several days.

With regards to the computers that are available to students, the on-site coordinator added:

We have 45 Lenovo laptops, though there are always some that are in various stages of disrepair at any one time. There are also three MacBooks and about 20 desktop computers that are separated into five computer stations. The laptops operate on one small server and the desktops operate on another. In addition to the computers we also have a supply of headphones, a few projectors, and a couple of printers though students have a very meager printing allowance due to the high cost of printing.

The Volunteer Team

The facilitators of every course within the Liberal Studies diploma program include volunteers from various Jesuit universities around the world. Many of them became aware of this opportunity through their colleagues, or through a special invitation sent via university emails. Though these facilitators are subject matter experts, some of them have never taught online, which was a common fear among those who would like to take on the job. Basic online training was provided by JC:HEM for new volunteers, which consisted of orientations to Blackboard's functionalities, and some further introduction on JC:HEM was also provided. After this basic training, the academic lead (the faculty member who designed the course) met virtually with the other course facilitators to discuss course materials, design, deliverables, and the other items necessary to facilitate the course.

In the spring of 2012, a team of volunteer faculty members from across the globe taught the newly designed course (Global Markets) at various JC:HEM learning sites. The faculty members – or facilitators, as they are referred to at JC:HEM – are as diverse as the students themselves. They originate from Jesuit universities in various parts of the globe – Southeast Asia, Europe, and the United States. The team of facilitators is comprised of full-time academics with one adjunct or part-time lecturer. The one great commonality that is observable among this team is that they share a united view of and advocate the provision of access to higher education to those who have very limited opportunities to receive it.

Student Profiles

JC:HEM students are unique in their outlooks and perspectives. They are refugees from various parts of Africa, specifically the civil strife-torn and economically challenged areas of the continent. The majority of students work full-time to provide for themselves and their families. Refugee camps consist of a conglomerate of races, ethnicities, and religions. Several languages and dialects are spoken in these camps. Refugees arrive with few possessions, and often run into members from opposing warring tribes. They must find a way to live peacefully, side-by-side, leaving behind old prejudices while wondering about the fate of their homes, families, and friends. In addition, camp life has its own struggles. Basic human needs, such as quality sanitation, plentiful food, and safe, potable water, are not successfully met. Refugees face overwhelming odds, both physically and mentally (Byrd, 2014).

In Malawi alone, and in partnership with the Jesuit Refugees Service (JRS), primary education is provided to over 4,500 refugee and asylum-seeking children. Approximately 500 children receive secondary education. Malawian nationals also benefit from the educational facilities in the camp. As of June 2014, 20 refugees have been granted scholarships to study in Canada in 2013. An interesting description of these students is captured by the following statement: "If I had to describe these students in one word, it would be *hopeful*. [*Italics added*]. They know this is opening doors for them and all they want to know is what they can do next" (Laclede, 2013).

As of January 2015, in Dzaleka, the camp population is around 20,000, which is relatively smaller than those of other camps like Kakuma. The buildings and houses are all relatively compact, and outside the perimeter of the camp there are several acres of maize crops tended by refugees (H. Godefroid, personal communication, February 2015). Some of the students work as teachers for JRS' primary and secondary schools. Similar to any traditional Western students, these students vary in their abilities; some are quick learners, some are good students, some coast along, and many struggle with managing their time while juggling family, illnesses (a common occurrence), work, and school. Though there are many similarities, these students face tremendous challenges that impede their learning.

Despite the challenges these students have to overcome, there is a large number of graduates who have shown significant progress in various areas. Since completing CSLTs, in Communication and Performing Arts, at JC:HEM in Dzaleka, Tresor Nzengu Mpauni has been progressively rewriting the rules of what a refugee can achieve in Malawi. He has recently delivered an inspiring talk at TedX, Lilongwe, sharing his own experience and the experiences of others in refugee camps. His talent for music and poetry was used as an instrument to share the plight of refugees with the world outside the camps. Tresor stresses that his journey to this point started with his involvement in the CSLTs, and that this program provided a turning point in his life in Malawi. "If you run away from your dreams, they will run after you till they catch you again. After completing a Community Service Learning Track, I was involved in volunteering in the community. Through doing this I made new friends who connected me with people and venues outside of camp to perform"("JC:HEM," personal communication, n.d.).

Each graduate has a different story, Muzabel Welongo, another graduate noted "The Muzabel I was before the JC:HEM is a very different person now. I think, act, communicate, and relate differently from before I joined the program. This program exposed me to intensive reading that I think has improved my English proficiency and eloquence. The courses I have taken have changed my critical thinking, and transformed the way I make decisions or argue about things. Before I make any decision, I am able to use proper supporting evidence or ideas before I express my point." On another positive note, the facilitators were very pleased that educating women led to another transformative experience for this often overlooked/underrepresented segment. As Muriel Ilunga eloquently expressed "To be a woman in the camp is hard as women are exposed to a number of challenges.(…) As a woman I can say JC-HEM helps women in a number of ways. First, JC-HEM encourages women to apply for diploma and track programs. The education gained transforms our thinking and we see the world in a better way. Secondly, the gardening group is a source of income for the women involved as they grow vegetables and fruits in the JC:HEM compound and sell the products" ("JC:HEM," personal communication, n.d.).

Global Markets Course

The Global Markets course is part of the JC:HEM diploma program in Liberal Studies, which started in 2012. It is one of the courses offered under the Business concentration. Students are given an option to choose between education and business, as their area of concentration, once they complete the ten core courses under the Liberal Studies program.

The course offers a basic level of understanding of the core theories in the study of global markets. Emphasis is given on providing a marketing framework that transcends domestic economy and transforms the marketing discipline within a global context, where global risk, profit, competition, and ownership are redefined. Recent global events have proven that traditional, nationally confined trade regulations are no longer adequate; yet, international accords over trade, intellectual property, labor standards, and a host of other issues are frequently criticized by various interest groups.

The course integrates the evolving global customer in the borderless economy and emphasizes relevant linkages and current social issues that affect the marketing discipline, such as curative marketing, social responsibility, ethics, and sustainability. The rise of the new world economic powerhouse and the importance of developing and emerging economies are taken into account when analyzing the entry and participation of Multinational Corporations (MNCs) and small-to-medium-sized firms.

Global markets consist of four primary focus areas: the international marketing environment, the global customers, the global marketing mix, and the global marketing manager. Throughout the course, students are required to partake in relevant discussions while applying the concepts learned about the four focus areas of the contemporary global business enterprise. The course builds upon the introductory course in the study of global business that the students must complete prior to taking this course. The concepts that students learned in the introductory marketing and global business courses contribute to their knowledge base and the analytical framework necessary for this course. Through this marketing course, students should be able to spot the opportunities around them, especially in this exciting time for Africa, given its improved performance and increased participation in global trade.

Online Pedagogical Design

Designing a new course in a traditional learning environment has always been challenging, as curriculum design and instruction need to be adapted to meet the learners' rapidly evolving attitudes and behaviors. The pedagogical design of this course makes it an extremely challenging task. First, it is delivered online to a culturally, politically, and socially diverse body of students. Second, the course is facilitated by volunteers of equally diverse backgrounds who have different degrees of commitment to the program, and who are from different universities featuring varying academic policies. Third, the camp is situated in a country or location where the technological infrastructure is raw. Fourth, the entire program is led by a newly formed agency, JC:HEM. Though JC:HEM is doing its best, it is still in its pilot phase where it is currently forming its structure and building its capacity for long-term growth. All of the aforementioned factors pose a big challenge to anyone who is designing a course for this program. The pedagogical design of the course has taken into account several key factors:

1. **Instructional Strategy and Digital Design for an Online Course:** Students have to be trained on how to use the Learning Management System (LMS) or the educational platform. Each of the courses is hosted by different donating universities that use different educational platforms; these pose another challenge for both the students and faculty who need to learn how to use them. Another daunting task is for JC:HEM to plan, manage, and allocate limited resources within the camp, such as offering access to the Internet, as well as providing tutors and equipment. As noted earlier, there is a modest number of desktop computers in each camp that students can use. However, it seems that

the greatest challenge is the intermittent power connection that hampers students' schedules while working on their assignments and completing other research-related tasks. It is important to also point out that most of these students do not have their own personal computers. In addition to the limited bandwidth and intermittent connectivity, video streaming and very large files are limited. It is worth mentioning that, in a learning environment where the facilitator's physical presence is absent, the use of engaging images and related videos is indispensable to supplement the reading materials; they also render the understanding of the theories and concepts much easier.

2. **Contextualization of the Theories and Concepts:** This posed a major hurdle for the faculty since the textbook was written by Western authors, for Western students; hence, case studies and other learning materials must be carefully selected to match and meet the socio-cultural and economic contexts of the students. Cases pertaining to Africa and other similar economies were used to ensure that the students could relate to each topic, warranting its localization and relevance to the students' degree of understanding and their limited exposure to such issues. It is imperative that the content fits within the realm of the learners. Group projects, as well as other tools and methods that are intended to make the learning process a rewarding, creative, and productive experience for students were at first applied, only to find out that group work would bring additional challenges.

3. **Course Structure, Facilitation, and Delivery:** In a setting where students struggle to cope with concepts and ideas that may be foreign to them, a subject expert who can actualize these theories through the work they do within the students' current environment was an exciting enhancement to the course/program. The course design included the invitation of a prominent marketing practitioner from the Lilongwe Wildlife Preservation Center to present at its marketing forum. Based on the feedback collected from students through reflection papers, students found the experience to be highly rewarding and indicated that it was something they could relate to. Additionally, on-site tutors are also available to support students and address their various concerns, ranging from Internet connectivity and site navigation, to follow-ups with some technical concepts that need clarification. Furthermore, the program engages online writing tutors, who are also students in various U.S. universities; these are individuals to whom JC:HEM students can send their work for proofreading and editing prior to final submission to the facilitator. This process seems to work fairly well, and instructors see a tremendous increase in the quality of the work submitted by the students who seek out those services.

The first time the course was offered, students were asked to work in self-selected groups for all the course assignments, including the final project. The intention was to enable them to become immersed with various ethnic groups, to learn new ways of thinking outside their own group, and to build on each other's strengths. It was also meant to foster cooperation and teamwork – skills and traits that are essential in today's workplace. Working in teams also tends to encourage effective time management and task prioritization. Moreover, collaboration can enhance core ideas that can lead to more concrete and sound strategies, which are useful to real-life situations; yet, the facilitators discovered that this approach had its own challenges due to students residing in various locations.

4. **Course Prerequisite:** It would have been helpful to offer a course discussing the principles of marketing as a prerequisite prior to taking an international marketing course. However, JC:HEM decided that offering a marketing course featuring a global context would be a better approach. The rationale behind this option was to prime students for foreign market entry given the vast

opportunities brought about by global market integration. It is about time that Africa veers away from its usual role of exporting only primary commodities that are highly vulnerable to market shocks and volatile demand. With the Internet becoming more cost-effective, a larger number of the population in Africa is gaining online access. This technological breakthrough provides vast opportunities to engage in e-commerce. Increasing consumer awareness and support for fair trade products from the least developed countries (LDCs) increases opportunities for Africans to start producing and selling manufactured goods, while harnessing their local talents and indigenous materials to produce unique African products that will compete with other ethnic products available from various online retailers (i.e., Etsy) ("The Economist, Special Report", 2014). African manufacturers can also capitalize on existing trade agreements with the USA and the EU to capture a sizeable manufacturing or subcontracting business from China for ready-to-wear items of clothing and other durable goods. Currently, a number of refugees are running businesses that include selling crops and farming; operating tearooms, restaurants, hairdresser salons, barbershops, bars, shops, and Internet cafés; and performing tailoring, carpentry, and shoe as well as car repair. All of these small businesses can benefit from applying the concepts introduced in this course; their numbers can increase, making it possible to subsequently participate in global trade, which can be facilitated by other community partners.

Growing Pains and Challenges

Course development started in late 2011 by a volunteer faculty member who designed the course in its entirety, in a very unique way, as it was the only course that was not taken off-the-rack (i.e., part of a list of existing courses) from other donating universities. After the course was designed, it was sent to the donating university's curriculum committee for approval, which proved to be a much more daunting task. After a couple of months of navigating through the approval process, the course was finally approved and was ready to be uploaded into the learning platform of another hosting institution. Finally, the course was officially offered in January of 2012.

Four faculty members volunteered to serve as facilitators, in collaboration with the course developer, who served both as the academic lead to support the other three volunteers and as a facilitator. During this spring semester, there were four course sections offered with eight to ten students per section. Students were mainly from DRC, Rwanda, Burundi, Somalia, Ethiopia, Kenya, and Sudan. Kiswahili is the language used by almost every refugee to communicate in the camp. To communicate with Malawians, students use either English or Chichewa. Inside each community, there are various subcultures – i.e., in the Congolese community, there is the Babembe, the Bafuliru, the Bakasai, and the Bashi, Barega. The camp consists of about 90% Christians and the rest of the population practices Islam. The students exhibit similar characteristics (H.Godefroid, personal communication, November 2014).

Highlights from the first run of the Global Markets course offering are detailed below.

1. There were a number of major concerns, such as students' limited access to textbooks, intermittent Internet connectivity, and time management issues, since many of the students were juggling different roles as students, parents, and spouses in between their actual jobs. Another major concern pertained to their health. Students became sick with malaria, diarrhea, and high fever, which is still a regular occurrence in these camps (while the real scare happened in 2014, at the time of writing this chapter, when Ebola was ravaging West Africa).

2. On the pedagogical side, the course was delivered online. While offering online courses is a challenge in itself, a highly critical issue in this case pertained to the course's delivery across national boundaries, as there are significant differences in cultural (including language), social, political, and economic conditions. The course used a Western textbook that was written in English. To most students, English is only their second or third language. However, beyond language, the contextualization of the cases and readings was a much deeper concern. The students' day-to-day activities were limited within their respective communities. After they were displaced and subsequently placed or relocated in the refugee camps, their lives revolved around the camps; they were limited to its nearby communities and had rare opportunities to travel to another city. Their understanding of marketing concepts was influenced by their exposure to their immediate marketing environment. Their knowledge and appreciation of business ideas were based on their limited experiences and the information gathered from various media, such as radio, TV, Internet, and print.

3. There is little to no awareness among students regarding ethics and codes of conduct in education, particularly pertaining to the risk of plagiarism. Students needed to be frequently alerted and warned that there would be consequences for copying another classmate's work (even partly) or plagiarizing. Students need to be aware, right from the beginning of the semester, of the importance of academic honesty and its implications.

4. Students also mentioned the fast-paced nature of the course. The usual eight-week structure offered by the donating institution does not seem to work successfully at JC:HEM. Students felt that it was too fast, which made it hard to appreciate, understand, and embrace the very nature of the subject being taught. Having more time to grasp the material would allow them to better understand the concepts and reflect upon them in order to find applications for their final paper. This will result in a more substantial and relevant output.

5. For some students, the major challenge had to do with the difficulties experienced when trying to understand the various concepts; they also faced an inability to express their ideas given their difficulty with the English language. The frustration of not being able to express what they intended seemed to consume them. Facilitators had to spend a tremendous amount of time providing feedback to the students, not only with regards to the course, but also in relation to grammatical errors, misspelled words, and sentence structure. For this reason, it would help if the course takes on a different pace or adopts some preparatory work or steps to address these concerns as soon as students have been accepted into the program.

6. The facilitators' unique teaching styles brought about their own challenges. The course facilitators were informed that all four sections should be taught in a similar manner, with more or less the same content, using the same discussion questions, and featuring the same cases, which curtailed some of the facilitators' own styles in delivering a similar course. It is important to note that facilitators are accustomed to academic freedom and they expect the same in this setting as well.

7. Another area that needed reinforcement was communication. It seemed that students were not accustomed to regularly reading their emails or course announcements posted on Blackboard which, at times, contained information related to their assigned work. This caused delays that led to 'hanging issues', which made it time consuming and counterproductive.

8. As was mentioned earlier, it turned out that group work was a major hurdle for many students. Working online was not a proper venue given the intermittent outages in power and connectivity. The actual group meetings were quite a challenge given the dispersed locations of the students.

Transportation was not very friendly and it would require much effort for students to meet in a common place that was convenient for every member of the group.

With respect to the cultural dimensions, it is important to take into consideration that the cohort of students consists of individuals facing various difficult situations that led them to the camps. The students are mainly refugees and other indigenous people (accounting for 13% out of the total group) from Africa and the Middle East. Many ethnic and cultural issues present additional challenges that the facilitators must be mindful about. An excellent point brought up by all facilitators regarding students' comments and posts in the discussion forums was that they are consistently very polite, courteous, and thoughtful. Oftentimes, students' responses to their classmates' comments must begin with a long sentence of thankfulness, gratefulness, and politeness. This sometimes makes it difficult for the instructor to follow the discussion, as the students get caught up with the ongoing pleasantries – a sense of gratefulness and appreciation that Western students rarely display. Similarly, when responding to messages or providing feedback to students, the facilitators need to be very cautious about choosing the appropriate words and expressions to avoid any misunderstanding or cultural insensitivity issues.

Gender is another important variable to consider. Most of the students were male. Females were underrepresented in the virtual classroom; only 29% of the total students were females. It is interesting that there was a difference in regions with regards to the involvement of females in the student population; while Kakuma and Dzaleka students were largely male, Amman had more female students.

REDESIGNING THE COURSE

With an effective feedback mechanism and strong collaboration among the teaching team, the course was redesigned when it was offered the second time. The course designer reflected on what was really important for these types of learners. The facilitators should not classify these students as refugees; they are not indigenous, they are simply students whose goal is to learn. As Jesse Stommel (2014) stated in his work, "Pedagogy, on the other hand, starts with learning as its center, not students or teachers".

The following changes were recommended to the existing offerings, although many of them have already been implemented as of this writing:

1. *Replace group work with individual work.* Students work on their papers and assignments at their own pace while adhering to the set deadlines. Knowing that access to resources varies for different students, depending on their location, assigning individual assignments makes the process more efficient.
2. *Use more local cases or small business cases that students can easily relate to.* This is ideal to provide examples that are within our students' reach in order for concepts to be grasped more quickly. It is best if we could find business cases from other developing or transitioning countries, similar to those of Africa's status.
3. *Include in the course syllabus a paragraph on plagiarism and emphasize its importance right from the beginning.* Ask the students to submit their papers via Turnitin. Explain the consequences of plagiarism and take necessary steps should there be any signs of copying or plagiarizing. Rubrics in regards to assessing the coursework must be emphasized; they should be posted along with the

course syllabus at the start of the course. The online tutors should also inform students regarding these matters during their initial encounters with them.

4.   *Return students' papers with detailed comments and feedback.* Remarkable improvements are noted with students' papers when the facilitator provides detailed comments and feedback. However, as noted earlier, the facilitator also needs to provide critiques not only regarding the content, but also with respect to grammar, syntax and spelling; this ultimately translates into more work for the facilitators. Services by the writing tutors must be continued. Another key point to mention here is that many of the students do not submit their work on time; this delays grading papers, as the facilitators need to grade the papers and projects once everyone has turned them in to ensure fairness and consistency in grading.

5.   *Encourage students to use local examples when contributing to the discussion forums.* Students tend to post replies to a student's work that deals with some of the issues, places, persons, or products they can relate to. This also helps the facilitator gain a better understanding of the students' personal situations and living conditions. As a result, the interaction becomes a two-way learning venue that will be helpful to both the learner and the educator. This is the part that facilitators find truly enlightening.

6.   *Include videos to demonstrate difficult concepts and make the experience more interesting.* If the technology allows this, such methods as "live online lecture", "webinar session", or online chat forums could be scheduled to provide students with an opportunity to engage in an interactive learning activity, and facilitators would have the ability to measure students' understanding of the subject matter directly and immediately.

7.   *Seek frequent feedback from students.* In most cases, students appear to be quiet and focused only on the questions provided for the week. However, it has been observed that when the facilitator becomes more consistent and persistent in asking for feedback, the real picture may emerge.

8.   *Encourage analytical thinking by posting challenging questions that will make students process the concepts beyond what is presented, and have the students apply these concepts to real-world examples.* Students must respond with proposed solutions. Emphasize the importance of creativity, and critical as well analytical thinking. Students are held responsible for any announcements that are made via the learning education platform. They should frequently check for emails, announcements, and so on. Students must reply to the facilitator's questions, as they relate to their submitted work, so they will be given appropriate advice or guidance on how to proceed with the next steps. Any pending matters must be addressed right away in a timely manner to avoid any delays.

9.   *Too much structure can be overpowering and could potentially stifle creativity; not enough structure can lead to unmanageable chaos.* Having an appropriate structure with enough room for maneuverability is the best approach to follow. The course syllabus must provide the right amount of structure, leaving ample room for flexibility for the students and for the individual facilitator. Having the choice to pick one of two discussion forum questions offers some flexibility to the students and the facilitator. Keep revisiting the question of using structure as a positive force (there is less complexity to deal with) and not as an inhibiting force (it disallows freedom of thinking), as perceived by both the students and facilitators (Cinta, Beatty, Faustino-Pulliam, 2012).

10. *Conduct students' assessments towards the fifth week to identify any challenges encountered in the course, and to provide recommendations on how to address them to further improve course delivery.* Early assessment will greatly aid the facilitator in changing and mitigating any content or methodological issues that the students might face.

NEW FRONTIERS

Volunteer Faculty

The program thrives on volunteer faculty to deliver the course; they are a critical resource for JC:HEM. Having an established framework on how to recruit, train, retain and acknowledge the volunteers would be valuable for the organization as it expands its programs and the number of its volunteer faculty increases. Additionally, the students' faculty evaluation results must be provided to the faculty members by JC:HEM at the end of the course. This evaluation would help facilitators improve their work. Lastly, a simple email signifying the course's closure will be an ideal way to officially conclude the course while letting the faculty team know that the virtual classroom will be unavailable for students and faculty after a stated period of time. Overall, simple reminders and an effective system of communications will be indispensable tools for faculty and the onsite team.

To attract new volunteers, or to speed up recruitment and training, allowing a new or prospective volunteer to visit the 'virtual classroom' of an ongoing class would help them acquire a sense of how the actual 'virtual classroom' works. This 'shadowing' experience prepares the newcomer by allowing them to gain an idea of the site, its functionalities, and other technical concerns that need to be addressed prior to starting his/her own class. This also allows the volunteer to adjust or redesign his/her own style and teaching materials according to the new platform. The 'shadowing' activity will further address future volunteers' fears or level of intimidation about teaching online. It was determined that many interested volunteers had never taught an online course, and as such, this is a major showstopper for them. Lastly, facilitators sharing the transformative power of teaching in this program with the potential volunteers would prove very beneficial. As one of the facilitators of this course notes: "I feel blessed to be part of a community that dedicates itself to caring for others. It's been a pleasure devoting myself to guiding our students along their learning journey, hoping to shape their skills and help them become tomorrow's business leaders. Despite its own challenges, the experience has been truly rewarding."

Research Opportunities

Several interesting research opportunities can arise from this initial paper. From an economics perspective, one interesting avenue for further research could be to investigate the impact of education on a particular segment: refugees and indigenous groups. From a development studies point of view, there are certainly interesting new challenges, but also opportunities, associated with this program. Nevertheless, these are some themes that may need to be considered when extending this research.

1. **Education at the Frontiers:** As a comparative study of other initiatives, what can be learned that is transferable? One could identify best practices, key success factors, obstacles, challenges, and so on. It is an extraordinary undertaking to serve such a dedicated group of learners; however, these programs should take into account other marginalized groups that are in need of higher education.
2. **Global Market Course in a Non-Market Context:** How can educators teach marketing concepts to people or learners that do not have a well-developed business market perspective due to their unique situation and living context?
3. **Explore Relationships between Students' Completion of the Program and Human Development:** This measure should be encompassing and not limited to social and economic mobility. It must

cover longer and healthier life spans, better standards of living (measured in non-economic terms), and include such attributes as students' influence on social change, their participation in resolving conflicts, and their facilitation of peaceful transitions within the community.

Jesuit Commons' Branding

JC:HEM should establish a strong presence with other Jesuit universities across the world to generate heightened awareness of the program. It has to improve its brand equity to gather more media space and support, and to further build its reputation. Having a unique and powerful brand will attract donors and provide other opportunities that could bring about new revenue streams. As it is now, JC:HEM can leverage its name, as it is associated with the Jesuit brand. However, JC:HEM has to be distinct from other programs. It should not be confused with any other Jesuit initiatives that are connected to refugees, but it has to stand out as an agency that deals with educating those at the margins, which includes other less privileged people from around the world.

Jesuit Commons: Higher Education at the Margins and Its Various Stakeholders

Since the authors started with the program, there has been a lot of progress that has taken place from its pilot run all the way to where it is now. The capacity building efforts are ongoing within JC:HEM and between its partners. The authors identified the following areas that can help ensure the sustainability of this program:

1. JC:HEM must establish a strong global presence and leverage its Jesuit connections across the world. This is so it can solicit local Jesuit and non-Jesuit universities to assist in granting diplomas to JC:HEM's local graduates. This will provide immediate utility to the graduates who came from the same country, ensuring that the credits are transferable to another local college or university.
2. JC:HEM must leverage its connections with Jesuit graduates from all over the world who are working with MNCs that are possible benefactors (e.g., DHL to deliver textbooks and the Maersk shipping company to transport the learning equipment, such as PCs and any other heavy machinery needed in the camps).
3. It must get exposure in other academic publications, networks, and groups to encourage volunteerism and invite donors.
4. It should recruit local professors and lecturers from local Jesuit universities as volunteers for the in-country program.

JC:HEM provided the impetus to both students and faculty to get involved in this life-changing experience. The authors are grateful for such a great opportunity; yet, the program must be strongly supported to allow it to move forward and achieve a level of sustainability. Fragmented efforts rarely yield success; collaboration and continuous cohesive effort is undoubtedly needed. The effort to educate does not end with students completing this course; it is only the beginning of a life-long journey that will shape worldviews about this continent.

To the rest of the JC:HEM stakeholders, their efforts to build human capital could bring about huge economic opportunities that will lead foreign direct investors and non-profit groups to change their perceptions of Africa; that it is not only a market where they can practice marketing at the bottom of the pyramid and engage in other fair trade initiatives that many are advocating in the developed world. Rather, it is important to view the rest of Sub-Saharan Africa as a supplier of goods and services that will transform not only the graduates' lives, but also the society as a whole.

As of this writing, the authors are still tracking the progress of this cohort (within the first 2 years of the program) and where they are now in the program. Future studies will hopefully be carried out to explore how educating those at the margins will ultimately impact the graduates, their families, as well as their communities in the long term.

Donated Course Approval or JC:HEM Proprietary Courses

The initial course approval was viable only for one semester; the donating university would like to go through another round of course approval prior to the next offering. This process has taken its toll on the faculty members involved and has posed a major constraint for JC:HEM, as students' progression leads them closer to taking the course. If the course has not yet been approved, students will have to wait for one or two semesters until the course is approved. This delay will affect students' plans and will create some programmatic issues within its curriculum. Moving forward, JC:HEM can address this issue by developing a structure to seek approval from donating universities once the course has been designed by a volunteer faculty member. After the course has been approved, JC:HEM and the faculty member who designs the course share ownership of the course. This approach will result in cost savings by eliminating the need to go through the process of establishing a team of academic experts, and it can assure that the course has met all the accreditation standards that are important to the institution granting the diploma.

Another option would be that JC:HEM comes up with its own set of courses designed by academic experts in the various subject matters using the course design framework and the standards of the diploma-granting institution which, in turn, will grant the final approval. This way, JC:HEM could focus on managing and running the program, rather than dealing with the specifics and issues surrounding course design, development, and approval.

CONCLUSION

The Global Markets course is one of the various business courses offered by JC:HEM, but the authors believe that it should not be taken simply as a marketing course that students will have to complete to fulfill program requirements. It is the facilitators' hope that the course extends far beyond that. Given the economic conditions in these regions, such as limited job opportunities, coupled with the legal restrictions that refugees face when trying to obtain paying jobs and re-settlement, the onus is on the students to apply the fundamental knowledge learned in this course to various situations, such as working as a peace worker, teaching in local elementary schools, and engaging in many other meaningful jobs that fall beyond simple economic activity. It is important for graduates to be the agents of social change and for this learning experience to be a transformative one. It also offers hope that Africa – particularly, its less developed countries – has a lot to offer, which needs to be explored. This is similar to what students were being exposed to when performing an environmental scan as part of their final project. Students need to identify the unique opportunities and threats, as well as the strengths and weaknesses that those regions and countries possess. Students need to appreciate the global marketing landscape, as it offers not only a huge window of opportunity for the African continent, but it can also change the habits of consumers, as was learned from the Global Markets course.

The facilitators view and treat these camps as another place and space where people live their lives and engage in various transactions like everybody else. There should be no distinction between being a refugee and a traditional college student in the U.S., Spain, Albania, or the Philippines; they are all learners who need to acquire knowledge and eventually contribute to sustainable human development. In today's globalized world, there are conflicting interests among nations; hence, leaders and governments play a crucial role in providing governing institutions to ensure that the gains made from economic development are equally distributed to and accrued by society at large. Furthermore, students can play a large role in making this happen.

It is important that other courses within the Liberal Studies program align with the objectives of JC:HEM; this program attempts not only to educate those at the margins, but also to provide sustainable means to get these students and their families out of poverty and offer them an opportunity for economic mobility. As noted earlier, it is central to JC:HEM's mission that education is geared towards developing minds; it should equip people with transferable skills and provide basic frameworks to allow humans to develop to their full potential.

On a broader scale, it is also ideal to collaborate with other African universities and multinational companies that have a presence in Africa to provide students with access to an immersion program and other initiatives that facilitate real-life practice. The limitation or absence of an internship program within JC:HEM can be addressed via strategic collaboration and partnership. The local government and business community should be able to provide training skills that will encourage entrepreneurship in an inclusive manner. Funding will always be an issue for those who want to start a small business. After being motivated to get into entrepreneurship from this program, students lose their "steam", thinking that there are not enough resources available to them. Social entrepreneurs who have a presence in Africa could offer a solution. Time and time again, it has been illustrated that those in Sub-Saharan Africa need less aid; however, they do need more opportunities to help them sustain their newfound economic and financial freedom. Tapping into micro-lending programs offered by local banks or specialized banks (like Grameen Bank), as well as other non-profit agencies (such as ACCION), might offer a solution.

One agenda that Jesuit Business Education (JBE) must prioritize is to incorporate initiatives to re-shape the attitudes and values underpinning human behavior, one that veers toward being socially responsible and away from a singular focus on economics results alone. JBE must produce well-informed graduates who are confident and empowered to challenge the political culture that perpetuates social injustices. This means placing a strong emphasis on research, teaching, and curriculum development to ultimately focus on issues that cater to the core values of human development – equality, empowerment, diversity, and sustainability. This also means collaborating with other institutions to influence social and political reforms that will enable every refugee regardless of race, religion, and social class to participate fairly and equally in a well-functioning market economy, which lays the foundation for sustainable human development.

The role of educational institutions in sustainable human development and nation building cannot be diminished or ignored. One institution whose power could be considered as a force for more humane and sustainable human development is the university. Educators need to take this commitment to heart. Social responsibility, immersion, social justice, and service learning courses or initiatives are not merely prerequisites or buzzwords; they must be a core part of every program, and they should result in actionable projects with measurable results. Our role is not only limited to finding what the issues are but, most importantly, to offering solutions to commonly identifiable problems that are beseeching the marginalized and underprivileged. The Global Markets course must be delivered in a manner that is meaningful to its learners without sacrificing academic rigor. This requires far-reaching changes in the way education is often practiced, delivered, and measured today.

REFERENCES

Beqiri, M. S., Chase, N. M., & Bishka, A. (2010). Online course delivery: An empirical investigation of factors affecting student satisfaction. *Journal of Education for Business*, *85*(2), 95–100. doi:10.1080/08832320903258527

Byrd, K. (2014). *Bringing the five practices to life*. Retrieved from http://www.leadershipchallenge.com/leaders-section-articles-stories-detail/bringing-the-five-practices-to-life-kenya-jesuit-commons-kareena-byrd.aspx

Cinta, R., Beatty, M., & Faustino-Pulliam, V. (2012). Lessons from the Field: Teaching a Completely Online "Global Business" Course to African Refugees in Northern Kenya and Malawi. *Jesuit Higher Education Journal*, *1*(1), 144–147.

Commons, J. Higher Education at the Margins. (2014). *About Us*. Retrieved from http://www.jc-hem.org

Commons, J. Higher Education at the Margins. (2015). Retrieved from http://alumni.jc-hem.org/story?TN=PROJECT-20150220014952

Delor, J., Al Mufti, I., Amagi, I., Carneiro, R., Chung, F., Geremek, B., & Nanzhao, Z. (1996). *Learning the treasure within: Report to UNESCO of the International Commission on Education for the Twenty-first Century* (pp. 1–46). Paris: UNESCO publishing.

Laclede, A. (2013, August 6). *JRS intern reports. Independent Catholic News*. Retrieved from http://www.indcatholicnews.com/news.php

Pyle, J. L., & Forrant, R. (2002). *Globalization, universities and sustainable human development*. Cornwall: MPG Books Ltd. doi:10.4337/9781843767398

Sharp, A. M., Register, C. A., & Grimes, P. W. (2013). *Economics of social issues*. New York: McGraw-Hill.

Stommel, J. (2014). *Critical digital pedagogy*. Retrieved from http://www.hybridpedagogy.com/journal/critical-digital-pedagogy-definition

Strauss, V. (2013). *Nelson Mandela on the Power of Education*. Retrieved from http://www.washingtonpost.com/blogs/answer-sheet/wp/2013/12/05/nelson-mandelas-famous-quote-on-education

The Economist. (2014, December). *Africa rising*. Retrieved from http://www.economist.com/news/special-report/21572377-african-lives-have-already-greatly-improved-over-past-decade-says-oliver-august

KEY TERMS AND DEFINITIONS

Externalities: A consequence of an activity that benefits those beyond the original primary intended beneficiary of the act.

Facilitator: A volunteer faculty member who facilitates the online course delivery in various camps across the JC:HEM network.

Ignatian Pedagogy: Jesuits' approach to teaching and learning based on the dynamics and principles of the Spiritual Exercises of St. Ignatius.

Online Courses: Courses in which the materials are delivered entirely online, and students have access to the instructor only electronically.

Online Tutors: Graduate students from various U.S. Jesuit universities helping students improve their writing skills.

On-Site Coordinator: A JC:HEM staff member who manages the day-to-day operations in the camp and who tends to students' needs; he or she serves as point of contact for students and facilitators.

Sustainable Human Development: Growth that is measured by overall improvements in the standard of living and the quality of life, which extends beyond economic progress and focuses on the richness of human life.

Transferable Skills: Knowledge acquired from a certain discipline or other life experiences that can be applied to a broader set, such as employment, entrepreneurship, politics, social work, and so on.

Chapter 2
The Mismatch between Undergraduate Marketing Education and Employers' Requirements in Portugal

Ana Estima
University of Aveiro, Portugal

Paulo Duarte
University of Beira Interior, Portugal

ABSTRACT

The debate on what should be offered by universities concerning their marketing education curricula in order to serve the market needs, specifically the employers' has been widely present in the literature. Its relevance derives from the fact that employers are one of the most important stakeholders of higher education institutions, given their responsibility in the career of graduate students. In this chapter we intend to contribute to the understanding of the state of undergraduate marketing education offered by Portuguese universities and assess whether there is a mismatch between marketing education and market needs. A better understanding of the mismatch and its implications can lead to better marketing education programs, increasing not only the acceptance and employability of students but also the transfer of innovative marketing knowledge to companies. The findings show that there is indeed a gap between what is being offered by the academia and what is requested by the job market, in terms of marketing, that could be higher than 50% of the requirements expected by employers.

INTRODUCTION

It is universally accepted that higher education plays a fundamental role in the development of a region or country (Cox & Taylor, 2006; Thanki, 1999). This is due to the fact that universities contribute largely to increase knowledge and productivity (Andrews & Higson, 2008), to create new business opportunities, to leverage entrepreneurship and, in general, to encourage competitiveness (Pestonjee, Spillan, Song,

DOI: 10.4018/978-1-4666-9784-3.ch002

& Virzi, 2010). To be able to participate more successfully in this process, universities should have a deep understanding of the community in which they operate. This harmonious integration is not easy to achieve. One possible way to achieve it would be by allowing the participation of civil society in the university life, reinforcing the interaction with external actors, the so-called *stakeholders* (Bjørkquist, 2008). Employers are a major stakeholder (Mainardes, Alves, & Raposo, 2010, 2013). Therefore, universities should look at employers as clients of the "product" emerging from the education process. The acceptance of this particular perspective would compel universities to take into account employers' needs and requirements when designing the program curriculum. If what is taught to students does not meet the expectations and needs of the labor market, the cooperation will be more difficult and there will be problems to solve at different levels.

Although this question seems quite clear from the outset, it is important to note that the primary goal of education, in any area, is to train people so that they can develop their professional activity and face the market as prepared as possible (Sampson & Betters-reed, 2008). Several authors from different areas have reported in previous studies the existence of a gap between what students learn in their academic journey and what employers expect of them in terms of knowledge and skills (Breen, 2014; Fechheimer, Webber, & Kleiber, 2011; Hunt, 2002; Stringfellow, Ennis, Brennan, & Harker, 2006; Wellman, 2010).

Marketing is no exception, and in order to bring universities and employers closer, it is very important to understand the needs, requirements, and objectives of both parties and find solutions to overcome the mismatch between employers' expectations and the learning outcomes provided by undergraduate marketing programs.

The debate between the marketing taught at the academia and the companies' practice is not new (e.g. Done, 1979) and has been widely discussed by several studies (Finch, Nadeau, & O'Reilly, 2012; D. M. Gray, Peltier, & Schibrowsky, 2012; Harrigan & Hulbert, 2011). The main issues being discussed are the concerns related to the development of marketing curricula and its adequacy to labor market needs, given the constant change and evolution (Harvey, 2000). As a result, "'closing the gap' or 'bridging the divide' between marketing taught in academia and in practice marketing has been one of the most discussed items in marketing" (Hunt, 2002, p. 385). A simple literature review reveals numerous authors who have conducted research aiming to better understand this gap and find ways to overcome it (Hunt, 2002; Stringfellow, Ennis, Brennan, & Harker, 2006; Wellman, 2010).

Another concern arising frequently in the literature is how to provide marketing students, by means of the curriculum, with the necessary knowledge, skills and tools to cope with the market demands in the best possible way (Burger & Schmidt, 1987; Miller, Holmes, & Mangold, 2007; Miller, 1985; Pefanis Schlee & Harich, 2010). The extensive discussion focuses primarily on a set of issues, such as: determining which subjects are fundamental to students (Wellman, 2010), what they should know, what skills they should have when they graduate, what learning levels they must demonstrate, what future employers may expect from these graduates (Sampson & Betters-reed, 2008), if the curricula should be more pragmatic and professional or more academic and intellectual and if marketers should be educated or trained (Clarke, Gray, & Mearman, 2006).

This discussion raises questions about the strategy that should be followed and who should contribute to the development of curricula in highly dynamic areas such as marketing, which is constantly being influenced by what happens in the market. Burns (2011), Hunt (2002), Stringfellow et al. (2006), and Wellman (2010), are some of the authors that emphasize the idea that more research is needed to reduce the gap between academia and the effective working practice in the area of marketing. In this sense, it is necessary to identify the dimensions that academics consider relevant when designing an undergraduate marketing program and, at the same time, also identify what is important to employers, in order to try to match both positions.

A better understanding of the gap between undergraduate marketing education and employers' requirements was the major drive for the development of the current analysis. A deeper understanding of these dimensions and their implications can lead to the development of better marketing programs, increase students' employability, and produce better synergies between companies and universities.

Taking into account the growth of marketing education in Portugal and also the increasing importance that is given by companies to marketing, as well as the fact that there is no similar study in Portugal, this chapter's main objectives are to:

1. Characterize the marketing curricula in Portugal at the undergraduate level;
2. Characterize the market requirements; and
3. Identify and discuss the differences between what is taught by universities and what is required by the labor market.

In order to achieve these objectives, a methodology composed by three stages was designed and implemented. In the first stage, the offer of undergraduate marketing programs in Portugal was characterized. All the degree programs containing the word "marketing" in the designation were registered and their respective courses analyzed. In the second stage, the job market requirements for marketing professionals were analyzed based on a total of 220 job offers posted between July 2011 and March 2014 in the employment section of Expresso, a well-known and reputable Portuguese newspaper. For each offer, the requirements were analyzed and a profile representing the marketer outline expected by Portuguese employers was generated according to the following requirements: language knowledge, technical knowledge, interpersonal skills and Information Technologies (IT) knowledge.

Finally, in the third stage, demand and offer were matched to determine the gap between marketing degree programs and job market demands.

This chapter is organized as follows: the next section will focus on a literature review, in order to present the research conducted in this area and the conclusions reached. Next, we will describe the methodology adopted in this study. The results will be presented and discussed in the subsequent section and the chapter will finish with some conclusions and future research directions.

BACKGROUND

This section explores what has been reported in the literature about the mismatch between education and market needs, emphasizing the marketing area, but not limited to it. The concepts of Marketing Education and Marketing Practice are also examined, in order to understand the vision of different authors, as well as what they have been arguing as being essential in any Marketing curriculum.

Marketing Education vs. Marketing Practice

The divergences between market needs and marketing education provided by universities have been part of a long-running debate and the interest of the scientific community over this issue has been constant, as it touches upon larger fundamental questions (Harrigan & Hulbert, 2011; Harvey, 2000; Hunt, 2002;

Stringfellow et al., 2006). Some authors even suggest that there is a "fight" between what the marketing skills and knowledge really are and what they should be (Finch et al., 2012). This debate is rather important, because all disciplines, at any given point in time, should discuss their nature, scope and objectives to better understand their purpose and to achieve a sustainable growth (Hunt, 2002). The need to continuously adapt to the markets where their professionals operate justifies the need for a permanent discussion about what is relevant to any marketing curriculum (Brennan, 2004).

On the other hand, universities have been urged to provide students with transferable skills that fit the labor market and not only with theoretical concepts (Andrews & Higson, 2008), on the grounds that "the possession of the skills, knowledge, attitudes and commercial understanding will enable new graduates to make productive contributions to organizational objectives soon after commencing employment" (Mason, Williams, & Cranmer, 2009, p. 1).

According to Wellman (2010), the apparent mismatch between the academia and the practice is based on the following arguments:

- Most marketing curricula are based on teaching strategy and high-level decision making when, in fact, most professionals are involved in operational and tactical roles;
- The marketing planning, as taught, does not seem to reflect reality;
- Marketing theory is a miscellany that, whilst important, does not reflect a link to practical application;
- Marketing degree programs are designed around familiar and comfortable theories, most of which do not solve the practical marketing management problems, but result in an easy way of developing programs and courses;
- Despite the importance of the business-to-business sector, programs are still too focused on the business to consumer and fast moving consumer goods (FMCG) market.

Other authors have reported gaps caused by a so-called myopia of education (Cunningham, 1999) as a result of teachers being much more focused on theoretical issues and research. Several authors suggest that this myopia is mostly caused by the pressure of universities' quality evaluation systems that are based on the number of PhDs, the "publish or perish" culture and other academic tasks of administrative nature, which force the relationships with companies and professionals to be left behind (Bacellar & Ikeda, 2011; Boddy, 2007; Brennan & Ankers, 2004). Boddy (2007, p. 217) even argues that it is necessary "to question the research foundations on which modern universities have built themselves". The fact that much of the produced marketing research is based on complex quantitative models with a language considered inaccessible by professionals represents another issue often used to justify the existence of a fracture between the academic theory and the professional practice (Brennan & Ankers, 2004).

Leaving aside the possible causes of the identified gaps, Clarke, Gray, & Mearman (2006) suggest the division of marketing education into two different perspectives: intrinsic and instrumental. The first perspective is more focused on teaching towards the free choices and the ability to be independent, autonomous, and courageous when taking decisions, as well as acting based on beliefs. The second perspective is more directed towards providing the development of skills such as communication, teamwork, leadership, task management, among others. Thus, according to the authors, while in an instrumental perspective the use and implementation of techniques is enough, an intrinsic perspective requires that students are also able to critically evaluate such techniques, make moral judgments and actively participate in debating the evolution of marketing as a professional career.

Regardless of the educational perspectives, a lower gap between the theory and the practice would increase the performance of students as marketing professionals. Thus, it is believed that better synergies between universities and companies would improve the quality of the training programs, resulting in more capable and competent graduates (Harrigan & Hulbert, 2011).

According to Hunt (2002, p. 306) marketing should be seen "as a university discipline that aspires to be a professional discipline." Therefore, marketing education actors have responsibilities towards different categories of stakeholders:

1. Society as a whole, by training students with technical knowledge and social responsibility;
2. The students themselves, by providing them with the necessary training to allow them to grow as marketing experts and responsible citizens;
3. The employers, by supplying them with competent and responsible human resources; and, ultimately,
4. The academy itself, by supporting its mission of promoting and producing knowledge capable of developing and improving society (Hunt, 2002).

Perspectives on Marketing Curricula and Teaching Methodologies

The responsibilities described in the previous section lead, undoubtedly, to a new approach to the marketing discipline. Several researchers (e.g. Beggs, 2011; N. Borin & Metcalf, 2010; Cadwallader, Atwong, & Lebard, 2013; Kurthakoti, Boostrom, Summey, & Campbell, 2013; Purushottam, 2013; Ueltschy, 2001) suggest different perspectives concerning the marketing curriculum and even recommend the incorporation of new areas of knowledge and innovative teaching methodologies.

Among the proposals are areas as diverse as: interactive technology (Ueltschy, 2001); sustainability (Borin & Metcalf, 2010; Nicholls, Hair, Ragland, & Schimmel, 2013; Purushottam, 2013); history (Witkowski, 1989); Geographic Information Systems (GIS) (F. L. Miller et al., 2007); information management (Burger & Schmidt, 1987); database marketing (DBM) (Teer, Teer, & Kruck, 2007); quality improvement tenets (Marshall, Lassk, Kennedy, & Goolsby, 1996); ethics (Beggs, 2011; Ferrell & Keig, 2013; Nicholls et al., 2013); cross-cultural research (Taylor & Brodowsky, 2012); writing skills (Bacon, Paul, Johnson, & Conley, 2008); creativity (Titus, 2007); reflection and critical thinking (Peltier, Hay, & Drago, 2005; A. Roy & Macchiette, 2005) and professional and career development skills (Tymon, 2013).

Similarly, other authors (e.g. Brennan, 2009; Cadwallader et al., 2013; Čančer, 2012; Kennedy, Lawton, & Walker, 2001; von der Heidt & Quazi, 2013) mention that including new disciplines is not enough and that teaching paradigms also have to change, in order to incorporate new methodologies that can help marketing students increase their personal and professional skills. These authors suggest that the teaching process should move from a teacher-centered to a student-centered approach, so that students can truly experience learning (Kennedy et al., 2001). Some of the proposed methodologies are: community service and service learning (CS&SL) (Cadwallader et al., 2013); case studies (Brennan, 2009); experiential learning (Cunningham, 1999; Pollack & Lilly, 2008; D. P. Roy & Tennessee, 2006); traditional learning to action learning (Cunningham, 1999); situated learning (Ardley, 2006); marketing simulations (Kirpalani & College, 2009); creative problem solving methods (Čančer, 2012); student-centered learning (von der Heidt & Quazi, 2013). Other authors have suggested less orthodox approaches, such as Weinrauch's (2005) music-based learning metaphors or a methodology that inspires students to organize their own funeral, reported by Butler (2007). Schiller, Goodrich, and Gupta (2013) suggest using the Second Life platform to increase interest and knowledge retention. Furthermore, the literature presents other tested methodologies based on games, theatre, challenges, images, sounds, written assessment, as well as group and individual work.

Different Visions on Marketing Education and Marketing Practice

For some authors, marketing professionals should completely ignore academia (e.g. November, 2004). This particular author clarifies that the objective is not to say that research in marketing should be ignored by professionals, but rather the way it is currently taught. To support this position, November (2004) divides the arguments into seven categories: customers, structure, causality, reductionism, precision, generalizations and replication. Despite the justifications provided, this vision is often considered too radical. Although there might be some real basis, at least to some of the arguments, it is understood that the discussion of practical problems without the support of a solid theoretical foundation can lead to imperfect solutions. In this sense, a marketing degree curriculum, prepared with useful tools and framed according to the reality of the market can be a decisive success factor for future marketing professionals and organizations. This success could help to overcome the idea, shared in some literature, that a number of areas within organizations often do not acknowledge the role of the marketer, as referred by Baker and Holt, (2004, p. 560): "marketers are perceived to be "unaccountable" by the rest of the organization; they are seen as unable to demonstrate a return on investment in the activities they have control over".

Therefore, it is important to note that, although the university has much knowledge to offer, "we are at a stage where marketing academia has a lot to learn from marketing practice" (Harrigan & Hulbert, 2011, p. 33). One of the reasons often presented as the cause of the gap is the fact that universities are closed in on themselves, providing students with more analytical and strategic perspectives but failing to transfer core competencies that are vital to high-level professionals (Hutt & Speh, 2007).

However, other opinions arise in the literature, challenging "the orthodox view that academics themselves are responsible for the failure of practitioners to engage in dialogue with them" (Southgate, 2006, p. 547).

This author, a professional who has been an academic, suggests new understanding levels that, disregarding the "who should do what", would help entrepreneurs use the knowledge provided by academics. Exploring the problems that have promoted this gap, Southgate (2006) emphasizes the idea that academics often try to approach professionals but they do not follow up with the contacts, claiming that they lack time due to a demanding workload. Therefore, he proposes that the next challenge is to engage with practitioners to make them believe that their involvement with the academia will save them time today, tomorrow and for the rest of their careers, which could be a promising way to cross the great divide (Southgate, 2006).

Regardless of the causes, it seems obvious that the gap is real. To better understand this problem and try to find ways to overcome it, multiple studies have been conducted to obtain the perception of the various stakeholders involved in the marketing education process: students (Leite, Santiago, Sarrico, Leite, & Polidori, 2006; Peltier & Scovotti, 2010; Tymon, 2013); alumni (Piercy, 2002); faculty (Gibson-Sweet, Brennan, Foy, Lynch, & Rudolph, 2010; Hopkins, Raymond, & Carlson, 2011; Tregear, Dobson, Brennan, & Kuznesof, 2010); professionals (Cunningham, 1999; Finch et al., 2012) and employers/managers (Walker et al., 2009).

These studies demonstrate that there are not many areas motivating such an interest among the research community in different sectors, mostly because marketing techniques, knowledge and skills might be applied to almost any area, in a wide range of industries and services, complementing and enhancing their efficiency and effectiveness. This poses considerable challenges to the training of students that need to be provided with the necessary skills in order to be hired (Walker et al., 2009).

Given the meaning of all the solutions proposed, it seems very difficult to incorporate all of them in only one curriculum, as some of them are actually more appropriate for post-graduate rather than for graduate programs. Therefore, it seems clear that cooperation bridges are essential to overcome the existing gap. It seems also clear that marketing is mostly seen as a professional subject (M. J. Baker, 2013; Clarke et al., 2006; Hunt, 2002). Finally, teachers, universities, research and businesses are facing a challenge that seems easier to identify than to solve (Barnett, Dascher, & Nicholson, 2004). On this regard, Stringfellow et al. (2006, p. 247) outline the problem in this way:

It is this: how can marketing academics get closer to, and contribute to, the world of marketing practice, and yet maintain sufficient independence and objectivity so as to retain the fundamental integrity that defines their unique contribution to knowledge production and dissemination? Too close, and research becomes consultancy, students become trainees. Too distant, and marketing education becomes irrelevant, students learn nothing of value to their future careers.

THE MISMATCH IN THE PORTUGUESE MARKETING EDUCATION CONTEXT

To analyze the gap in the Portuguese context, we will now describe the functional organization of the Portuguese marketing degree programs, the courses offered and the demand of the labor market in the analyzed period. The data from the universities' programs and the profile of marketing professionals requested by the market were compared in order to assess and evaluate the gap between marketing education and employers' requirements.

Undergraduate Marketing Programs Offered in Portugal

Higher education in Portugal is based on a binary system that includes university and polytechnic education. University education is provided in public and private institutions comprising universities, university colleges and other higher education institutions, and is driven by a perspective of promoting research and knowledge. On the other hand, polytechnic education is also taught by public and private institutions, with an approach oriented towards applied research and development, and aimed at understanding and supplying solutions to concrete and practical business problems and needs.

Marketing undergraduate programs in Portugal possess different designations depending on the intended focus and on the institution. Some institutions focus their programs on a specific area of activity, whereas other institutions design their programs within a broader scope, training students with key marketing competencies without focusing on any particular area of professional activity.

It is also assumed by the institutions that the designation of the programs might have a decisive influence on the students' choice. This is particularly relevant in a recruitment process, where students might be preferred due to the graduate program or school they have attended. Firstly, we have examined the offer of undergraduate marketing programs in Portugal. All the marketing degree programs containing the word "marketing" in the designation were registered and their courses analyzed.

The different programs in Portugal are distributed among universities and polytechnics, but there is no apparent reason that objectively justifies why some of them are taught at Universities and others at

Table 1. Distribution of marketing undergraduate programs offered in Portugal

	Universities	Polytechnics	Total
Public sector	3	19	22
Private sector	10	6	16
Total	13	25	38

Polytechnic institutions. Table 1 presents the marketing degree programs being offered by Portuguese higher education institutions for the academic year of 2013/2014, divided by universities and polytechnic institutes, both public and private.

According to the Table 1, the distribution of marketing programs in Portugal is as follows:

- There are 38 undergraduate programs officially registered. It should be noted that 8 of these programs are duplicated, being offered by the same institutions but in different regimes, namely through part-time and e-learning options;
- 16 graduate programs, corresponding to 42%, have the general designation of "Marketing", making it the most common designation;
- 22 graduate programs (58%) are taught at public institutions, and 16 at the private sector;
- The polytechnic institutions almost double the number of graduation programs taught at universities;
- Regarding the public sector, only 13.6% of graduation programs are taught at universities. A large majority are taught at polytechnic institutions, providing a more practical orientation to the students;
- In what concerns the private sector, the situation is reversed, although the difference is not significant: 10 graduate programs are taught at universities and 6 at polytechnic institutions.

As stated before, eight of the undergraduate programs offered are duplicated. In these cases, where the same institution offers the same program in different regimes, only one was analyzed.

To have a concrete idea of what is being offered in terms of marketing degree programs, all the courses in all programs, both mandatory and optional, were registered. For the purpose of this analysis, only mandatory courses were taken into account, given the fact that optional courses may not be offered every year and frequently change according to the institution's convenience and student demand.

From the 30 marketing undergraduate programs analyzed, 536 mandatory unique courses were identified, from which 381 courses (71.1%) are only offered in one program, 73 courses (13.6%) are offered in 2 programs and 32 courses (5.97%) are offered in 3 programs.

Together, these categories represent 90.7% of the total courses offered. Such scattering effect might lead to confusion and misunderstandings when employers need to recruit a new marketing employee.

Another important aspect that should be mentioned is related with the curricular internship, offered only by nearly 50% of the programs. This very important experience might make a difference in the future integration of recent graduates in the job market, by providing them with a real work contact and experience.

Figure 1 presents the list of the most common courses offered in Portuguese marketing undergraduate programs. There are three particular courses offered by more than 50% of the programs. Consumer behavior is the most frequent and therefore the most consensual course among all marketing programs, being offered by 21 programs, followed by international marketing and market research, both offered by 17 programs. Very close to 50% are services marketing, human resources management, and statistics, courses offered by 12 programs.

Figure 1. Most frequent courses offered in marketing undergraduate programs

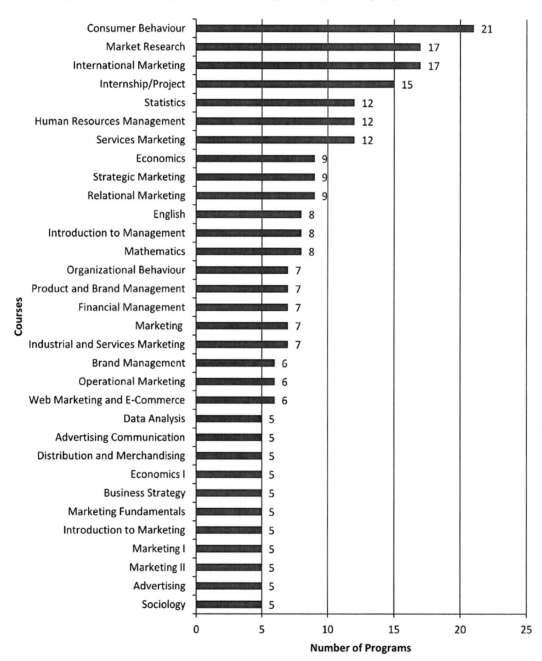

Characterization of the Marketer Profile in Portugal

In a second stage, the market requirements in the field of marketing were gathered, organized and examined. Between July 2011 and March 2014, 220 job offers requesting marketing professionals were collected from the Expresso employment section, a well-known and reputable Portuguese newspaper. For each offer, the requirements were analyzed and a profile representing the marketer outline expected by Portuguese employers was generated. This profile embodies four categories referring to knowledge and skills that are of interest for the current analysis:

1. **Language Knowledge:** That includes all the different languages required;
2. **Technical Knowledge:** Comprising all the knowledge directly related to the area of marketing;
3. **Interpersonal Skills:** Containing all the social/behavioral characteristics and competences, more closely related with the personal development of each individual and the ability to deal with different people in diverse situations; and
4. **Information Technologies Knowledge:** Covering all the requirements directly related with the information and communication technology field.

The offers were analyzed and divided into categories and the most common aspects are presented in Table 2.

As can be observed in Table 2, in terms of job titles, 156 different positions were identified, with Marketing Assistant, Key Account Manager, Marketing Manager, Product Manager, Commercial Assistant, Marketing Director and Responsible of Marketing, being the most requested. Regarding the line of business, around 25% of the positions did not provide any specific information, with the remaining 75% showing a lot of dispersion, the most common being the Retail Sector, Pharmaceutical, Automobile, Fashion, Banking and the Wine Sector.

Concerning the degree, 96.4% of the positions specifically require a general degree in "marketing" without any further specification, followed by other designations such as Marketing Management, Marketing and Advertising, Digital Marketing, Marketing and Communication and Operational Marketing. In terms of age, 190 job offers (86.4%) did not make any specific reference to this and the remaining asked for people between 20 and 45 years old. In terms of previous experience, 89 positions, representing 40.5%, did not mention this requirement, whereas 13.6% asked for 2 years of experience, 23.6% required at least 3 years and 14.1% asked for 5 years.

Regarding the knowledge of languages, for the positions specifying this requirement (73.6%), English was clearly the most highly demanded language, present in 71.4% of the job offers, followed by Spanish, French, German and Mandarin, with 22.3%, 15.0%, 5.0% e 0.5%, respectively. Moreover, 3.2% of the job offers simply required "knowledge of a foreign language", without specifying any particular language.

Technical knowledge was specified by 50.9% of the offers. As far as this attribute is concerned, we have identified Negotiation Techniques as the most common skill, being referred to in 28 offers and representing 12.7%, followed by Capacity for Business Development, Market Analysis, New Product Development and Implementation of Business Plans, present in 8.6%, 6.8%, 6.4% and 5.9% of the offers, respectively.

The number of offers requiring Interpersonal Skills was very high, with 76.8% of the offers demanding at least one of these skills. In this category, Communication was clearly the most required skill with

Table 2. Most common requirements, separated by category, from the total job offers analyzed

Categories	Most Common Requirements	Num. Offers
Designation of the position	Marketing Assistant	10
	Key Account Manager	10
	Marketing Manager	9
	Product Manager	8
	Commercial Assistant	5
	Marketing Director	5
	Responsible of Marketing	9
Business Sector	Retail	7
	Fashion	6
	Automobile	5
	Pharmaceutical	5
	Banking	4
	Wine	4
Program designation	Marketing	212
	Marketing Management	3
	Marketing and Advertising	2
	Digital Marketing	1
	Marketing and Communication	1
	Operational Marketing	1
Age	>30	4
	>35	3
	<=30	2
	22 e 35	2
Minimum experience	3 years	52
	5 years	31
	2 years	30
	4 years	10
	10 years	8
Language knowledge	English	157
	Spanish	49
	French	33
	German	11
	One foreign language	7
	Mandarin	1
Technical knowledge	Negotiation	28
	Business development capacity	19
	Market Analysis	15
	Conception of new products	14
	Implementation of business plans	13
Interpersonal Skills	Communication	78
	Teamwork	52
	Dynamism	49
	Interpersonal relationships	45
	Proactivity	44
IT Knowledge	Basic Computer Knowledge	55
	Advanced Office Knowledge	43
	Excel	29
	Word	20
	PowerPoint	19

35.5%, followed by Team Work with 23.6%, Dynamism with 22.3%, Interpersonal Relationships with 20.5% and Proactivity with 20%.

In 104 job offers, at least one knowledge in the Information and technology area was required. The most demanded was Basic Computer Knowledge (25.1%), followed by Advanced Office Knowledge, with 19.5%. The remaining IT knowledge requirements demanded were Excel, Word and PowerPoint, with 13.2%, 9.1% and 8.6%, respectively.

The Mismatch between Marketing Education and Employers' Requirements

Based on the education and market analyses, we proceed to assess the gap between the offer and demand by determining and evaluating the level of agreement between the job market requirements and what is being offered by the academia. Not all the requirements identified in the professional profile developed can be compared with the learning outcomes of undergraduate marketing programs. This is due to various reasons. For example, some of the requirements are not acquired within the academic journey and others are more related with an individual's personal characteristics. Therefore, only those requirements that can be directly acquired within the academia, namely language, technical, and IT knowledge skills, were extracted and compared with marketing programs in order to produce a matching chart. The result of this process is presented in Figure 2, which shows the level of agreement between each marketing undergraduate program and the marketer profile according to the job offer requirements.

Figure 2 shows quite an impressive mismatch between what is offered by the academia and what is being required by the job market. All the marketing undergraduate programs are more than 50% away from the demanded requirements. This mismatch is clear at the main level but also in each of the three compared categories in particular.

Looking at each of these categories separately, there are six programs that do not offer any course related to foreign languages, therefore not providing any skills and learning outcomes to the students

Figure 2. Comparison between the marketer profile and the marketing undergraduate programs

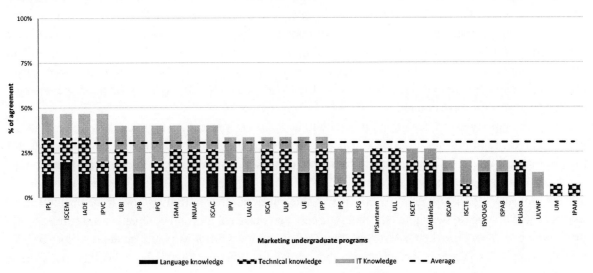

in this category. All the other programs offer one foreign language and only one program includes two language courses.

Regarding the technical knowledge requirement, seven programs do not offer any course on this and only two programs offer four of these requirements. Moreover, these two programs are currently among the top-ranked degrees. In terms of IT knowledge requirements, five programs do not offer any course providing related learning outcomes and only two programs actually include four of the five requirements on this matter.

Globally, the best score belongs to four programs that provide courses which comply with 46.67% of the knowledge required by the job market. At the other end of the scale, there are two programs that only cover 6.67% of the job market requirements, not responding at all to the required language and IT knowledge.

These results show that the profile of marketing graduates, in what concerns the attributes studied, is significantly different from what is expected by the employers.

FINAL REFLECTIONS AND FUTURE RESEARCH DIRECTIONS

Studies focusing on the importance of further adapting marketing programs to the reality and needs of the job market indicate that the current priorities are oriented towards providing students with knowledge in the areas of return of investment and strategic marketing (Finch et al., 2012). These authors also argue that "the ability to creatively identify, formulate, and solve problems; the ability to write in a business environment; and the ability to set priorities" will be some of the future priorities in terms of meta-skills (Finch et al., 2012, p. 54). Kennedy et al. (2001) also suggest problem solving capacity, creativity, and interpersonal skills as priorities for educational programming efforts, which is in line with the conclusions of the present study on the most required skills by the Portuguese job market for marketing professionals.

On the other hand, the dynamic evolution of the markets makes it very difficult, if not impossible, to promptly respond to all the challenges, from both the academic and industry point of view (Day, 2011). This may be one of the causes of the mismatch between what is being offered by the academia and the job market requirements, in terms of marketing knowledge and skills, which has also been confirmed in this study. Portuguese undergraduate marketing programs are currently missing more than 50% of the requirements expected by employers, suggesting that the academia is far behind in terms of fulfilling the job market needs and it needs to find a way to quick and effectively respond to an increasingly challenging working environment.

The literature review showed that this problem does not only affect Portugal but it is rather a global problem crossing almost all areas of knowledge. However, there are some changes happening at this precise moment that should contribute to overcome this issue. For instance, the inclusion of internships in the academic programs seems to be a helpful solution towards bridging the gap between the academia and the industry. Internships are only one face of the solution; other initiatives have to be promoted and implemented in order to strengthen the dialogue between the academia and companies and subsequently bridge the gap. Therefore, better levels of cooperation amongst employers and academia must be promoted, to achieve a tighter balance between theoretical and practical knowledge. Together, the various stakeholders have to identify the important skills that are required and incorporate them, as much as possible, in marketing programs.

This research suggests that abilities like language knowledge and IT knowledge are essential, but also that the offer of other capabilities, such as knowledge on Negotiation Techniques, Capacity for Business Development, Market Analysis, New Product Development and Implementation of Business Plans must be increased. Moreover, it is very important to mention that the existence of a mismatch may, to a certain degree, be healthy and desirable, given the role of universities in the advance of science, e.g. universities need to be always in the upfront of science development, yet they cannot ignore the job market because employers are the "consumers" of their "product".

The current findings and reflections should be seen as a contribution to the discussion on how to reduce the mismatch between the academia and the industry, and a contribution to the future development of marketing programs by bringing them closer to market expectations in terms of knowledge. This would help universities improve their performance by enhancing the marketability of their students and increasing the employability rate of their graduates, ensuring that companies would have employees trained to face daily challenges.

Given that this field is characterized by being a never-ending and open debate, the development of a longitudinal study would be both very interesting and important to understand the evolution of the mismatch over time, as well as to find trends for the future. Ultimately, this would help organizations and institutions to anticipate changes and make the necessary adjustments even before critical mismatch problems emerge.

Similarly to what is being implemented in Scotland by the project "Marketing in a Smart Successful Scotland" (Scottish Executive, 2004), aimed to discover what is happening with more than one thousand marketing graduates in Scotland every year, it would be interesting to implement such a project in Portugal and compare the employability rate with the mismatch in order to establish a correlation between these two variables.

Another interesting advance would be to determine the perception of the different stakeholders on this matter, e.g. students, faculty, and employers, among others, to explore and try to understand the differences between them. Alumni also might be, to some extent, a very interesting source of information on this topic, since they were already students, they are very likely employees now, and some may also be employers, which gives them a more precise perception of the mismatch and its impact on various domains.

REFERENCES

Andrews, J., & Higson, H. (2008). Graduate Employability, "Soft Skills" Versus "Hard" Business Knowledge: A European Study. *Higher Education in Europe, 33*(4), 411–422. doi:10.1080/03797720802522627

Ardley, B. (2006). Situated learning and marketing: Moving beyond the rational technical thought cage. *Marketing Intelligence & Planning, 24*(3), 202–217. doi:10.1108/02634500610665682

Bacellar, F. C. T., & Ikeda, A. A. (2011). Evolução do ensino de marketing: Um breve histórico. *Organizações & Sociedade, 18*(58), 487–511. doi:10.1590/S1984-92302011000300008

Bacon, D., Paul, P., Johnson, C., & Conley, T. (2008). Improving Writing Through the Marketing Curriculum: A Longitudinal Study. *Journal of Marketing Education, 30*(3), 217–225. doi:10.1177/0273475308322643

Baker, M. J. (2013). Michael J. Baker: Reflections on a career in marketing. *Journal of Historical Research in Marketing, 5*(2), 223–230. doi:10.1108/17557501311316842

Baker, S., & Holt, S. (2004). Making marketers accountable:a failure of marketing education? *Marketing Intelligence & Planning, 22*(5), 557–567. doi:10.1108/02634500410551932

Barnett, S. T., Dascher, P. E., & Nicholson, C. Y. (2004). Can School Oversight Adequately Assess Department Outcomes? A Study of Marketing Curriculum Content. *Journal of Education for Business, 79*(3), 157–162. doi:10.3200/JOEB.79.3.157-162

Beggs, J. M. (2011). Seamless Integration of Ethics. *Marketing Education Review, 21*(1), 49–56. doi:10.2753/MER1052-8008210107

Bjørkquist, C. (2008). Continuity and Change in Stakeholder Influence Reflections on Elaboration of Stakeholder Regimes. *Reflecting Education, 4*(2), 24–38.

Boddy, C. R. (2007). Academia marketing myopia and the cult of the PhD. *Marketing Intelligence & Planning, 25*(3), 217–228. doi:10.1108/02634500710747734

Borin, N., & Metcalf, L. (2010). Integrating Sustainability Into the Marketing Curriculum: Learning Activities That Facilitate Sustainable Marketing Practices. *Journal of Marketing Education, 32*(2), 140–154. doi:10.1177/0273475309360156

Breen, J. (2014). Exploring criticality in management education through action learning. *Action Learning Research and Practice, 11*(1), 4–24. doi:10.1080/14767333.2013.874328

Brennan, R. (2004). Should we worry about an "academic-practitioner divide" in marketing? *Marketing Intelligence & Planning, 22*(5), 492–500. doi:10.1108/02634500410551879

Brennan, R. (2009). Using case studies in university-level marketing education. *Marketing Intelligence & Planning, 27*(4), 467–473. doi:10.1108/02634500910964038

Brennan, R., & Ankers, P. (2004). In search of relevance: Is there an academic-practitioner divide in business-to-business marketing? *Marketing Intelligence & Planning, 22*(5), 511–519. doi:10.1108/02634500410551897

Burger, K. J., & Schmidt, S. L. (1987). Integrating Information Management Skills into the Marketing Curriculum: An Example Using the Marketing Research Course. *Journal of Marketing Education, 9*(1), 12–18. doi:10.1177/027347538700900103

Burns, D. (2011). MBA Marketing Curriculum for the 21st Century. *Journal of Marketing.* doi:10.1300/J050v10n02

Butler, D. D. (2007). Planning your own funeral: A helpful pedagogical tool. *Marketing Education Review, 17*(1), 95–100. doi:10.1080/10528008.2007.11488993

Cadwallader, S., Atwong, C., & Lebard, A. (2013). Proposing Community-Based Learning in the Marketing Curriculum. *Marketing Education Review, 23*(2), 137–150. doi:10.2753/MER1052-8008230203

Čančer, V. (2012). Teaching creative problem solving methods to undergraduate economics and business students. *Journal of Further and Higher Education, 38*(4), 485–500. doi:10.1080/0309877X.2012.726968

Clarke, P., Gray, D., & Mearman, A. (2006). The marketing curriculum and educational aims: Towards a professional education? *Marketing Intelligence & Planning, 24*(3), 189–201. doi:10.1108/02634500610665673

Cox, S., & Taylor, J. (2006). The Impact of a Business School on Regional Economic Development: A Case Study. *Local Economy, 21*(2), 117–135. doi:10.1080/02690940600608069

Cunningham, A. C. (1999). Commentary: Confessions of a reflective practitioner: meeting the challenges of marketing's destruction. *European Journal of Marketing, 33*(7/8), 685–697. doi:10.1108/03090569910274311

Done, A. (1979). Matching the Marketing Curriculum To Market Needs. *Journal of Marketing Education, 1*(1), 4–12. doi:10.1177/027347537900100103

Fechheimer, M., Webber, K., & Kleiber, P. B. (2011). How well do undergraduate research programs promote engagement and success of students? *CBE Life Sciences Education, 10*(2), 156–163. doi:10.1187/cbe.10-10-0130 PMID:21633064

Ferrell, O. C., & Keig, D. L. (2013). The Marketing Ethics Course: Current State and Future Directions. *Journal of Marketing Education, 35*(2), 119–128. doi:10.1177/0273475313491498

Finch, D., Nadeau, J., & O'Reilly, N. (2012). The Future of Marketing Education: A Practitioner's Perspective. *Journal of Marketing Education, 35*(1), 54–67. doi:10.1177/0273475312465091

Gibson-Sweet, M., Brennan, R., Foy, A., Lynch, J., & Rudolph, P. (2010). Key issues in marketing education: The marketing educators' view. *Marketing Intelligence & Planning, 28*(7), 931–943. doi:10.1108/02634501011086508

Gray, D. M., Peltier, J. W., & Schibrowsky, J. (2012). The Journal of Marketing Education: Past, Present, and Future. *Journal of Marketing Education, 34*(3), 217–237. doi:10.1177/0273475312458676

Harrigan, P., & Hulbert, B. (2011). How Can Marketing Academics Serve Marketing Practice? The New Marketing DNA as a Model for Marketing Education. *Journal of Marketing Education, 33*(3), 253–272. doi:10.1177/0273475311420234

Harvey, L. (2000). New realities: The relationship between higher education and employment. *Tertiary Education and Management, 6*(1), 3–17. doi:10.1080/13583883.2000.9967007

Hopkins, C., Raymond, M. A., & Carlson, L. (2011). Educating Students to Give Them a Sustainable Competitive Advantage. *Journal of Marketing Education, 33*(3), 337–347. doi:10.1177/0273475311420241

Hunt, S. D. (2002). Marketing as a profession: On closing stakeholder gaps. *European Journal of Marketing, 36*(3), 305–312. doi:10.1108/03090560210417138

Hutt, M. D., & Speh, T. W. (2007). Undergraduate Education: The Implications of Cross-Functional, Relationships in Business Marketing–The Skills of High-Performing Managers. *Journal of Business-To-Business Marketing, 14*(1), 75–94. doi:10.1300/J033v14n01_08

Kennedy, E. J., Lawton, L., & Walker, E. (2001). The Case for Using Live Cases: Shifting the Paradigm in Marketing Education. *Journal of Marketing Education, 23*(2), 145–151. doi:10.1177/0273475301232008

Kirpalani, N., & College, L. I. M. (2009). *Developing Entrepreneurial Self-Efficacy in Marketing Students by Using Simulation-Based Pedagogy*. Society for Marketing Advances Proceedings.

Kurthakoti, R., Boostrom, R. E., Summey, J. H., & Campbell, D. (2013). Enhancing Classroom Effectiveness Through Social Networking Tools. *Marketing Education Review, 23*(3), 251–264. doi:10.2753/MER1052-8008230304

Leite, D., Santiago, R., Sarrico, C., Leite, C., & Polidori, M. (2006). Students' perceptions on the influence of institutional evaluation on universities. *Assessment & Evaluation in Higher Education, 31*(6), 625–638. doi:10.1080/02602930600760264

Mainardes, E., Alves, H., & Raposo, M. (2010). An Exploratory Research on the Stakeholders of a University. *Journal of Management and Strategy, 1*(1), 76–88. doi:10.5430/jms.v1n1p76

Mainardes, E., Alves, H., & Raposo, M. (2013). Identifying stakeholders in a Portuguese university : A case study. *Revista de Educación, 362*, 429–457. doi:10.4438/1988-592X-RE-2012-362-167

Marshall, G. W., Lassk, F. G., Kennedy, K. N., & Goolsby, J. R. (1996). Integrating Quality Improvement Tenets into the Marketing Curriculum. *Journal of Marketing Education, 18*(2), 28–38. doi:10.1177/027347539601800204

Mason, G., Williams, G., & Cranmer, S. (2009). Employability skills initiatives in higher education: What effects do they have on graduate labour market outcomes? *Education Economics, 17*(1), 1–30. doi:10.1080/09645290802028315

Miller, F. (1985). Integrating the Personal Computer into the Marketing Curriculum: A Programmatic Outline. *Journal of Marketing Education, 7*(3), 7–11. doi:10.1177/027347538500700302

Miller, F. L., Holmes, T. L., & Mangold, W. G. (2007). Integrating Geographic Information Systems (GIS) into the Marketing Curriculum. *Marketing Education Review, 17*(3), 49–63. doi:10.1080/10528008.2007.11489013

Nicholls, J., Hair, J. F., Ragland, C. B., & Schimmel, K. E. (2013). Ethics, Corporate Social Responsibility, and Sustainability Education in AACSB Undergraduate and Graduate Marketing Curricula: A Benchmark Study. *Journal of Marketing Education, 35*(2), 129–140. doi:10.1177/0273475313489557

November, P. (2004). Seven reasons why Marketing Practitioners should ignore Marketing Academic Research. *Journal of Marketing Research, 12*(1991), 39–50. doi:10.1016/S1441-3582(04)70096-8

Peltier, J. W., Hay, A., & Drago, W. (2005). The Reflective Learning Continuum: Reflecting on Reflection. *Journal of Marketing Education, 27*(3), 250–263. doi:10.1177/0273475305279657

Peltier, J. W., & Scovotti, C. (2010). Enhancing entrepreneurial marketing education: The student perspective. *Journal of Small Business and Enterprise Development, 17*(4), 514–536. doi:10.1108/14626001011088705

Pestonjee, D. D., Spillan, J. E., Song, H., & Virzi, N. D. (2010). A Comparative Analysis of Curriculum in International Marketing and Business Between Peruvian and Guatemalan University Students. *Journal of Teaching in International Business, 21*(4), 282–306. doi:10.1080/08975930.2010.526027

Piercy, N. F. (2002). Research in marketing: Teasing with trivia or risking relevance? *European Journal of Marketing*, *36*(3), 350–363. doi:10.1108/03090560210417165

Pollack, B. L., & Lilly, B. (2008). Gaining Confidence And Competence Through Experiential Assignments: An Exploration Of Student Self-Efficacy And Spectrum Of Inquiry. *Marketing Education Review*, *18*(2), 55–66. doi:10.1080/10528008.2008.11489039

Purushottam, N. (2013). Sustainability and marketing education: Emerging research themes. In *Vision 2020: Innovation, Development Sustainability, and Economic Growth - Proceedings of the 21st International Business Information Management Association Conference, IBIMA 2013* (Vol. 2, pp. 600–605).

Roy, A., & Macchiette, B. (2005). Debating the Issues: A Tool for Augmenting Critical Thinking Skills of Marketing Students. *Journal of Marketing Education*, *27*(3), 264–276. doi:10.1177/0273475305280533

Roy, D. P., & Tennessee, M. (2006). *Enhancing Marketing Curriculum Through Experiential Education*. Marketing Management Association.

Sampson, S. D., & Betters-reed, B. L. (2008). Assurance of Learning and Outcomes Assessment: A Case Study of Assessment of a Marketing Curriculum. *Marketing Education Review*, *18*(3), 25–36. doi:10.1080/10528008.2008.11489045

Schiller, S., Goodrich, K., & Gupta, P. (2013). Let Them Play! Active Learning in a Virtual World. *Information Systems Management*, *30*(1), 50–62. doi:10.1080/10580530.2013.739891

Schlee, R., & Harich, K. (2010). Knowledge and Skill Requirements for Marketing Jobs in the 21st Century. *Journal of Marketing Education*, *32*(3), 341–352. doi:10.1177/0273475310380881

Scottish Executive. (2004). A Smart, Successful Scotland - Strategic direction to the Enterprise Networks and an enterprise strategy for Scotland. Author.

Southgate, N. (2006). The academic-practitioner divide: Finding time to make a difference. *Marketing Intelligence & Planning*, *24*(6), 547–551. doi:10.1108/02634500610701645

Stringfellow, L., Ennis, S., Brennan, R., & Harker, M. J. (2006). Mind the gap: The relevance of marketing education to marketing practice. *Marketing Intelligence & Planning*, *24*(3), 245–256. doi:10.1108/02634500610665718

Taylor, R. L., & Brodowsky, G. H. (2012). Integrating Cross-Cultural Marketing Research Training in International Business Education Programs: It's Time, and Here's Why and How. *Journal of Teaching in International Business*, *23*(2), 145–172. doi:10.1080/08975930.2012.718706

Teer, H. B., Teer, F. P., & Kruck, S. E. (2007). A Study of the Database Marketing Course in AACSB Accredited Business Schools. *Journal of Marketing Education*, *29*(3), 245–253. doi:10.1177/0273475307306891

Thanki, R. (1999). How do we know the value of higher education to regional development? *Regional Studies*, *33*(1), 84–89.

Titus, P. (2007). Applied Creativity: The Creative Marketing Breakthrough Model. *Journal of Marketing Education*, *29*(3), 262–272. doi:10.1177/0273475307307600

Tregear, A., Dobson, S., Brennan, M., & Kuznesof, S. (2010). Critically divided?: How marketing educators perceive undergraduate programmes in the UK. *European Journal of Marketing*, *44*(1/2), 66–86. doi:10.1108/03090561011008619

Tymon, A. (2013). The student perspective on employability. *Studies in Higher Education*, *38*(6), 841–856. doi:10.1080/03075079.2011.604408

Ueltschy, L. C. (2001). An Exploratory Study of Integrating Interactive Technology into the Marketing Curriculum. *Journal of Marketing Education*, *23*(1), 63–72. doi:10.1177/0273475301231008

Von der Heidt, T., & Quazi, A. (2013). Enhancing learning-centeredness in marketing principles curriculum. [AMJ]. *Australasian Marketing Journal*, *21*(4), 250–258. doi:10.1016/j.ausmj.2013.08.005

Walker, I., Tsarenko, Y., Wagstaff, P., Powell, I., Steel, M., & Brace-Govan, J. (2009). The Development of Competent Marketing Professionals. *Journal of Marketing Education*, *31*(3), 253–263. doi:10.1177/0273475309345197

Weinrauch, J. D. (2005). An Exploratory Use of Musical Metaphors to Enhance Student Learning. *Journal of Marketing Education*, *27*(2), 109–121. doi:10.1177/0273475304273353

Wellman, N. (2010). Relating the curriculum to marketing competence: A conceptual framework. *The Marketing Review*, *10*(2), 119–134. doi:10.1362/146934710X505735

Witkowski, T. H. (1989). History's Place in the Marketing Curriculum. *Journal of Marketing Education*, *11*(2), 54–57. doi:10.1177/027347538901100209

KEY TERMS AND DEFINITIONS

Knowledge: Understanding of theories and practices related with a particular field or area.

Marketer: Someone who works in the field of marketing on a professional level.

Marketing Education: Related to the formal curricula, at both the undergraduate and post-graduate levels, specifically created to teach the theories and practices related with the professional activity of marketing.

Marketing Practice: Related to the activity developed by marketers, e.g. all the activity developed by marketing professionals, within any organization.

Mismatch: Difference between two or more realities.

Skill: Ability to produce solutions acquired by training.

Stakeholder: Any person or group interested in or concerned about an organization.

Chapter 3
From Marketing Education in a Developing Country to a U.S. Master's and/or Doctoral Degree in Marketing

Matt Elbeck
Troy University – Dothan, USA

ABSTRACT

This chapter outlines the pathway to advanced marketing education by students in a developing country. We begin by contrasting the similarities and differences in undergraduate marketing education in Saudi Arabia versus the U.S. The analysis includes the typical markers of language and access to secondary sources, and culture-specific differences in the perception of time and various cultural influences using Hofstede's cultural dimensions. This is followed with a description of the pathway students from Saudi Arabia take to pursue a Master's and/or Doctorate in marketing in the U.S. The chapter concludes with the unique insight - unlike a sizeable number of foreign students in the U.S., most students from Saudi Arabia return to Saudi Arabia and in so doing stem the 'brain drain' so many other countries face when their brightest head to the U.S. for advanced study.

INTRODUCTION

As a marketing educator in the U.S., have you ever wondered about the educational pathway your non-U.S. born marketing faculty colleagues took? You will likely discover that most earned an undergraduate degree and perhaps a Master's degree from their home country, with the vast majority earning their Doctorate in business administration or marketing from the U.S. This journey is a result of a number of factors that includes a major influence from completing an undergraduate marketing course or a marketing major. The purpose of this chapter is to compare undergraduate marketing education in a developing country versus the U.S., and second, to explain how this might lead to an earned Master's and/or Doctorate in marketing from the U.S.

DOI: 10.4018/978-1-4666-9784-3.ch003

Compared to all other countries, we are spoilt in the U.S. when it comes to access to a college or university. In the U.S. there are there are some 4,599 degree granting institutions (U.S. Department of Education, 2013) with some 21 million enrolled students (National Center for Education Statistics, 2013) or 4,566 students per college. In contrast, all other countries have 23,887 universities (Webometrics, 2015) with a total 131 million students (Maslen, 2012) or 5,484 students per college. Most telling is the ratio of colleges per capita. For the U.S. with a population of 318.88 million (U.S. Census, 2015) the number of colleges and universities per capita is 69,837 people. For the world with a population of 7.24 billion (U.S. Census, 2015), the number of colleges and universities per capita is 303,093. The difference is a factor of 4.34 or the greater than four-fold availability of colleges and universities for the U.S. population versus the rest of the world.

The relatively higher number of university seats and the prestige associated with a high quality U.S. education is not lost on the rest of the world. Some 4% or 886,052 of the total U.S. college and university student population is represented by foreign students, of which 50% come from China, India and South Korea, and 6.1% (54,000) from Saudi Arabia (Institute of International Education, 2014)

Initial Cultural Orientation

Prior to entering a foreign nation to live and contribute as a marketing faculty member, it is essential to orient oneself to that nation's culture beyond a review of the school's website. Two sources come to mind. For a broad overview, the best would be the *The World Factbook* (Central Intelligence Agency, 2015) that is updated on a weekly basis offering short two to three page summaries on the nation's history, geography, demographics, government, economy, energy, communications, energy, military, and transnational issues for 267 countries. The second, and perhaps more important source particularly for marketing faculty is the website based on Hofstede's cultural dimensions (Hofstede Centre, 2015) that offers a contrast along six dimensions (power distance, individualism, masculinity, uncertainty avoidance, long-term orientation and indulgence).

The following sections offer insights from teaching undergraduate marketing courses in a developing country based on five-years teaching at Saudi Arabia's AACSB accredited King Fahd University of Petroleum and Minerals' business school where all classes are taught in English and the curriculum is based on the U.S. model.

Notable Cultural Influences

When contrasting Saudi Arabian culture to the U.S., the remarkable differences relate to power distance and individualism. Practically speaking, Saudi Arabia's relatively high power distance underscores that society "accept a hierarchical order in which everybody has a place and which needs no further justification... a collectivistic society (Hofstede Centre, 2015). However, Saudi Arabia's relatively low score for individualism results in "a close long-term commitment to the member 'group', be that a family, extended family, or extended relationships. Loyalty in a collectivist culture is paramount, and over-rides most other societal rules and regulations" (Hofstede Centre, 2015). The implications for the marketing faculty member are (a) in the classroom you are considered the equivocal and sole boss – what you say and require is met with no resistance, though the challenge is to foster and environment conducive to class discussion, and (b) high regard for tribal and family loyalties means that when it comes to group work and projects, take care assigning students to groups.

INITIAL OBSERVATIONS

As with most countries, high school students are well aware of the two most desirable professions; medicine and engineering. Business is middle ranked as a desirable profession, though the similarity with the U.S. stops there. Unlike most US business schools where the brightest students tend to migrate toward majors in accounting and/or finance, in Saudi Arabia the marketing major draws very bright students because of their profound interest in entrepreneurship based on their family's' trading background. In developing nations such as Saudi Arabia, students are keen learners of marketing primarily because their family's success is based on risk taking and negotiation.

Students in Saudi Arabia may be segmented into two basic groups, the sophisticated urban types who are well versed with the western world and are quite open minded and keen to learn. In contrast, students from rural and remote areas (typically of Bedouin heritage) are relatively less sophisticated and rather more conservative. The challenge teaching marketing to the Bedouin students is to emphasize that marketing involves understanding the target market and developing the offer without introducing personal opinions about customer excesses and materialistic tendencies.

The segregation of male and female students into universities catering to a specific gender means that the instructor's gender dictates the gender of their students. There are a few cases where a male instructor will teach female students behind an opaque screen with all verbal communication with the students via an elderly female chaperone. Although visual interaction is not possible, female students are typically far more diligent and motivated than their male counterparts, which leads to some spirited discussions fostering a deep learning of the topic at hand.

Finally, the vast majority of students are full-time and are typically not distracted with a part-time job, though the instructor should be mindful that the primary distraction is family and to a lesser extent, tribal membership.

Native Saudi Arabian faculty (most with PhDs from highly respected U.S. business schools) follow a strict didactic pedagogy characterized as "instruction and immutable facts, of authority and telling, and of right and wrong answers," (Kalantzis & Cope, 2015, line 2). In contrast, western (including U.S.) expatriates engage in participatory and experiential pedagogies such as active learning and problem-based learning. This contrast is not unnoticed by the students who are intrigued by the way we try to engage the students and our willingness to listen to their personal and professional ambitions. Instead of the typical dry lecture, the western expatriate's pedagogy in marketing education is both refreshing and empowering to the students. One of the major (and universal) in-class subcultural hurdles is to introduce students to critical thinking versus the traditional rote style of learning. Achieving a higher order thinking (HOT) class environment (National Research Council, 1987) includes seeking reasons and causes, justifying solutions, revealing assumptions in reasoning, and identifying bias or logical inconsistencies (Anon, 2011) requires work on the part of the professor that is rather more challenging than usual given the didactic-based instruction the students are used to, together with the default question, "will it be on the exam?" That is, any type of highly directed cookie-cutter style of instruction (e.g., definitions-based learning) will be met with minimal resistance. Moving too rapidly toward a more reflective type of instruction (e.g. cases with open-ended questions) is likely to be met with dismay and fear.

TEACHING MARKETING

- **Marketing Curriculum:** The curriculum is typically no different from what one might find at a teaching, or balanced teaching and research school in the U.S. This is typically reflected in the use of textbooks written by U.S. authors. Often times, especially for the developed nations (e.g., Australia, U.K., Canada, Western Europe), local marketing educators of high repute join as co-authors to shift the examples away from the U.S. and to the local nation. The implications are that students are exposed to the U.S.-based materials and come to learn that the center of the marketing world is the U.S.

As is the case for any country or region, the influence of culture directly influences marketing instruction and the case is no different for Saudi Arabia. The following sections introduce cultural influences summarized in Table 1 to a framework of marketing core concepts developed by LaFleur et al (2009).

- **Marketing Fundamentals:** Explaining the various fundamentals (e.g., positioning, segmentation, exchange, marketing mix) is relatively straightforward though care must be taken given the students are non-native English speakers (though they have all taken a one or two-year English college level immersion program) and the liberal use of local examples.
- **Understanding the Customer:** Explaining the consumer decision process is straightforward, though factors influencing the purchase decision and buying center roles is perfect for student discussion and the opportunity to develop student projects to investigate the local or regional influence on influences and the buying center.
- **Product Concepts:** In general, the various elements such as product life cycle, brand equity, services and branding strategies are best presented using locale examples and well-known western brands. There are related issues to be aware of such as the commonality across most less developed and developing nations is the requirement to touch a product before purchase. In class this lends itself well to discussions about product packaging. The country of origin is very well entrenched in the student's minds. For example, when purchasing a TV, buyers will check whether the TV is made in Malaysia, China or Japan – with the latter attracting a price premium. One of the challenges facing instructors in any foreign country is to try and use local examples whenever possible, and Saudi Arabia is no exception. The author has at times forgotten this and from time to time even well-known examples such as *Nike* are meet with puzzlement, particularly by the less sophisticated Bedouin students.
- **Pricing Concepts:** The typical computations associated with pricing (e.g., breakeven, fixed and variable costs, price elasticity and margins) are clear-cut to the students. Challenges relate to pricing strategies, especially the objective and task method primarily because the data that might be used to explain the concept are not available. A unique topic would be fixed prices that are an anathema due to the cultural passion to haggle. This leads to great inefficiencies in a business model where time is required to reach a final price. The exception to this are the western style shopping malls where fixed process are the norm. Clearly, the situational context matters.
- **Place Concepts:** Again, most of the concepts are easily explained such as distribution intensity, title taking, channel levels and intermediary types. Perhaps the greatest challenge is related to the non-linear approach to time when talking about logistics customer service and just-in-time inventory models. The easiest way to explain the urgency of time is to ask students whether they

Table 1. Relevant cultural differences for marketing education between the US and Saudi Arabia

Cultural Influence	Description	Influence on Marketing Core Concept, Pedagogy and Courses	Marketing Education Challenge
Language	Non-native English speakers	All; requires a focus on clarity and connection with local examples	Must connect with local examples and be mindful of society's conservative nature
Power Distance	The paramount influence of hierarchy	All; may impede student self-empowerment and expression	Encourage discussion starting with the most outspoken students
Individualism	Default loyalty is to the family and tribe	Group work; student group rosters should be assigned with family names in mind	Harmonious and constructive groups must avoid groups containing tribes in conflict with one another
Segregation	Classes are not coed	More of a career issue	Introduce the possibility of working with and for females.
Professional Aspirations	Tendency to expect a senior position upon graduation	All; a tendency to assume career success.	Emphasize the importance of career progression
Entrepreneurial	Risk takers		
Heritage	Urban sophisticated versus rural practicality	All; examples used in class may not be understood.	Organize field trips to large corporations and shopping malls.
Negotiation	Haggle and delay decision making for a better deal.	Pricing. Difficult to comprehend a fixed price policy.	Expose students to western franchises and shopping malls reflecting a fixed pricing scheme
Professional experience	Full-time students will have more time to study	All; primarily because the benefit of part-time jobs to gain experience.	Focus on signing up for an internship course.
Privacy	A keen sense of respect for privacy	Marketing research and selling.	Focus on face-to-face data collection
Secondary Sources	Lack of national buyer behavior data infrastructure	All; especially marketing research.	Expose students to the richness of US sources and introduce studies on the national/local market.
Tangibles	Tendency to handle goods prior to purchase decision	Services marketing	Spend time explaining and demonstrating the importance of non-tangibles to marketing success.
Conservatism	Devoted to tradition and modesty.	All, especially promotion;	Avoid salacious and sensationalist examples and focus on word-of-mouth.
Conformance	Adherence to tradition	All; the primary instructional method is rote memorization that defeats critical thinking.	Introduce 'blue-book' short essay type questions.
Time	Multi-active where the present trumps all	All; especially homework and project deadlines	Introduce deadlines based on events (before the weekend) versus clock time or calendar date.

would like their soft drinks in the air conditioned cafeteria or placed outside in the hot sun. Similar examples and perhaps experiential exercises make for appreciation for at least how time influences marketing decisions.

- **Promotion Concepts:** Explaining the various promotional methods, pull and pull strategies, role of promotional strategies and steps in the selling process are similar to the approaches in the U.S. Though Saudi Arabia has commercial media and the availability of satellite TV channels, one needs to be sensitive to the cultural norms and hence modesty trumps all. As in the rest of the world, word-of-mouth communication is extremely powerful and easily understood by students. An interesting challenge concerns personal selling. If the approach is cold calling, then resistance will be met due to the high regard for individual privacy. However, if the selling process is presented as ways mangers compete for resources or selling in a business to business setting, then the students absorb all.

- **Analyzing Marketing Problems:** This topic typically results in the construction of a Strengths, Weaknesses, Opportunities and Threats (SWOT) table. Unlike U.S. undergraduate students who have a hard time motivating themselves to read assigned materials, the Saudi students will read materials, though the instructor must be prepared to explain even the simplest tem. For example, during one class the author discovered that some of the Bedouin students did not know what 'hamburger' meant. More importantly, the importance of critical thought necessities the need to orient the class with a carefully constructed detailed example together with rubrics to ease the students into the mindset of careful analysis, problem identification and the construction of an actionable SWOT table.

- **Role of Information:** Again, teaching process and procedures such as the steps in marketing research, types of data, data collection method and simple research designs are straightforward. The key challenges relate to sampling and data collection problems, data describing corporate performance and the need for longitudinal studies given the fast pace of growth in developing nations (Hoskisson et al, 2000) such as Saudi Arabia.

Perhaps the most influential challenge to managing information are secondary sources and the perception of time. The absence of data sources common-place to the U.S. (e.g., U.S. Census, Department of Commerce) shifts reliance from secondary to primary sources of data. A key impediment are the high levels of privacy that make telephone surveys next to impossible, especially if a male students calls a home where a lady may answer the telephone. The path of least resistance is to conduct face-to-face interviews at shopping malls or encourage students to tap into their large families. As importantly is the impact of time where in the West we are familiar with time-sensitive delivery of goods and services. This linear-active approach to time is fundamentally different in developing nations such as Saudi Arabia where the concept of time is multi-active (Lewis, 1996) such that schedules or punctuality are of minimal importance though students will pretend to observe them if the professor's orientation is linear-active. Nonetheless the 'here and now' emphasis of time leads instructors to offer flexible office hours and a willingness to spend extensive time (versus short sequential meetings) meeting students to fully discuss a project, advising or personal matters. Abruptly cutting off a meeting to rush to the next is not positively received. The smart professor will work with this issue and use artifacts to implement some delivery deadline such as "let's try to finish this project before the weekend for you to have time with your family."

Ethics and Assessment

Though not central to core concepts in marketing, a note on ethics and assessment help develop an even deeper understanding of teaching marketing in Saudi Arabia.

- **Ethics:** Though not a core subject, the introduction of ethics in an entry level marketing course seems to be the norm. Although most of the students will understand the difference between legal and illegal practices, the concept of ethics is best presented in terms of the societal respect for modesty and above all, honesty. Well-known to students are grey marketing and counterfeit products that segues easily into discussions about ethics, intellectual property, product quality and market segment preferences.

- **Assessment:** A critical component of any course or program is discovering the degree of student learning. Naturally, the preferred method is direct assessment (Elbeck & Bacon, 2015) versus self-reports by students about their learning. In this regard, students in Saudi Arabia are no different from students across the world where some are brighter than others and the use of direct assessment methods (e.g., observations of student performance, blue-book exams) are effective and revealing of student learning. It goes without saying that communication may at times be awkward for the non-native English speakers, though it is remarkable how grammatically correct and clearly written communications are compared to the 'typical' US student.

The challenge for Saudi Arabian students is a direct outcome of their primary and secondary school educational experiences based on rote memorization. If the method of assessment focuses on objective type multiple-choice and true/false questions then there is no problem. However, if a portion of learning is based on critical thinking, then the instructor faces a major challenge to wean away students from rote memory and toward reflection and creativity that are best understood by using the case study approach (use short cases at first).

In summary, teaching and conducting research in the developing nation of Saudi Arabia offers a number of perspectives for contemporary marketing education as follows.

- **Standardization vs. Customization of Curriculum:** The five years spent teaching in Saudi Arabia makes clear that the scope and depth of a U.S.-based marketing curriculum does result in student learning. This outcome is supported given all the marketing and business textbooks used are 'international' editions of what U.S.-based students use. For other universities whose language of instruction is Arabic, these textbooks are translated either by the publisher or locally.
- **Pedagogy:** As with students from across the world, pedagogy matters in developing a sustained interest in the discipline of marketing, perhaps best express by the generally accepted Confucian phrase "I hear and I forget, I see and I remember, I do and I understand."
- **Culture:** The immutable influence of national culture and subcultures play a role in marketing education from a communications perspective. That is, the less noise (being respectful of cultural norms in discussions, textbook selection, projects) there is, the more likely the student will appreciate the remarkable benefits of a marketing education as it applies to their self, and their career.
- **Connecting with Students:** This point is particularly important in marketing education and forces the instructor to become familiar with current events in the local, regional and national marketing environment because currency and relevance of marketing examples is a great way to attract student attention, wherever one may be.
- **Critical Thinking:** It is this author's belief that the students who emerge as successful leaders in the marketing discipline are strong critical thinkers, a style of problem solving essential to the success of marketing education that may be in the hands of our university colleagues outside the business school.

The preceding has summarized the context and challenges of teaching marketing in a developing nation (Sadia Arabia) that in terms of material coverage is no different to teaching marketing at universities in the U.S. It is simply a function of the instructor's enthusiasm and interest in disseminating his or her knowledge in a manner that results in maximal student learning.

FROM STUDENT TO PROFESSOR

We now return to the initial question posed at the start of this paper, "have you ever wondered about the educational pathway your non-US born marketing faculty colleagues took?"

The cache that U.S. schools offer the best graduate business education is supported with 50% of the top hundred MBA programs in the world located in the U.S. (Financial Times, 2015). Furthermore, in spite of the significant inroads marketing doctoral programs in Germany, Netherlands, France, England and Canada have achieved, the top-flight marketing doctoral programs by sub-area are all in the U.S. (Elbeck & Vander Schee, 2014). The world-wide prestige of U.S. universities (Atkinson & Blanpied, 2008), the contribution of western expatriate instructors and their pedagogies, exposure to reputable US authored textbooks and the internet's unending source of valuable college information makes the journey to a U.S. university's marketing program a well-grounded advancement, particularly at the doctoral level.

Related to a desire for a U.S. doctoral program is funding where a major factor contributing to state sponsorship is AACSB accreditation. Out of approximately 14,540 business schools in the world, 727 are accredited by the AACSB from which 71% or 513 AACSB accredited business schools are located the U.S., and 214 outside the U.S. (AACSB, 2015). These facts are not unnoticed such that 21% of all foreign students are enrolled in a U.S. business program (Institute of International Education, 2014)

The question of funding for doctoral programs in marketing (and other disciplines) is not as large a challenge as one might expect given that developing countries are cognizant of the long term contribution of higher education to developing countries as "essential to national social and economic development" (World Bank, 2000, p.14).

As with any student body, whether from a developing nation or the U.S., large numbers pursue the MBA degree (some with a concentration in marketing) and even fewer enter the exacting demands of a doctoral program, with a handful enrolling in a marketing doctoral program. With doctorate in hand, most Saudi students will head back to Saudi Arabia drawn by both family demands and government scholarship requirements. This emotional draw has a major benefit to a developing nation, as a powerful disincentive to a national brain drain. Perhaps one or two a decade might stay on and join the marketing faculty ranks in the U.S. In either case, they represent the catalyst for change and the introduction of materials and pedagogies to enhance marketing education. The journey is long and arduous that with a bit a patience results in change for the better.

CONCLUSION

The universality of marketing (a.k.a., business) is appealing to students from all developing countries as a means to personal and career success. The adjustments to undergraduate and Master's level marketing education in a developing country are for the most part culturally-based that do not take away from the principles, theories and models that help shape marketing thought. After all, one of those students might develop a paradigm shift to what we in the U.S. consider contemporary marketing education.

REFERENCES

Anon. (2011). *Learning Theory, Teaching Higher-Order Thinking*. Teach for America. Retrieved from http://teachingasleadership.org/sites/default/files/Related-Readings/LT_Ch5_2011.pdf

Atkinson, R. C., & Blanpied, W. A. (2008). Research universities: Core of the US science and technology system. *Technology in Society*, *30*(1), 30–48. doi:10.1016/j.techsoc.2007.10.004

Census, U. S. (2015). *U.S. and World Population Clock*. United States Census Bureau. Retrieved from http://www.census.gov/popclock/

Central Intelligence Agency. (2015). *The World Factbook*. Central Intelligence Agency. Retrieved from https://www.cia.gov/library/publications/the-world-factbook/

Elbeck, M., & Bacon, D. (2015). Toward Universal Definitions for Direct and Indirect Assessment. *Journal of Education for Business*, *90*(5), 278–283. doi:10.1080/08832323.2015.1034064

Elbeck, M., & Vander Schee, B. (2014). Global benchmarking of marketing doctoral program faculty and institutions by subarea. *Journal of Marketing Education*, *36*(1), 45–61. doi:10.1177/0273475313514234

Financial Times. (2015). *Global MBA Ranking 2015*. The Financial Times Ltd. Retrieved from http://rankings.ft.com/businessschoolrankings/global-mba-ranking-2015

Hofstede Centre. (2015). *Country Comparisons*. The Hofstede Centre. Retrieved from http://geert-hofstede.com/countries.html

Hoskisson, R., Eden, L., Lau, C., & Wright, M. (2000). Strategy in emerging economies. *Academy of Management Journal*, *43*(3), 249–267. doi:10.2307/1556394

Institute of International Education. (2014). *Report on International Educational Exchange*. Institute of International Education, 2014 Open Doors Presentation, November 17. Retrieved from http://www.iie.org/Research-and-Publications/Open-Doors

Kalantzis, M., & Cope, M. (2015). Didactic. *New Learning*. Retrieved from http://newlearningonline.com/learning-by-design/glossary/didactic

LaFleur, E. K., Babin, L. A., & Burnthorne, L. T. (2009). Assurance of Learning for Principles of Marketing Students: A Longitudinal Study of a Course-Embedded Direct Assessment. *Journal of Marketing Education*, *31*(3), 131–141. doi:10.1177/0273475309335242

Lewis, R. D. (1996). *When Cultures Collide: Leading Across Cultures*. Nicholas Brealey International.

Maslen, G. (2012). Worldwide student numbers forecast to double by 2025. *University World News*. Retrieved from http://www.universityworldnews.com/article.php?story=20120216105739999

National Center for Education Statistics. (2013). *Digest of Education Statistics*. National Center for Education Statistics. Table 105.20. Retrieved from http://nces.ed.gov/programs/digest/d13/tables/dt13_105.20.asp

National Research Council. (1987). *Education and Learning to Think*. National Research Council Committee on Research in Mathematics, Science, and Technology Education.

U.S. Department of Education. (2013). *Digest of Education Statistics, 2012*. National Center for Education Statistics. (NCES 2014-015), Chapter 2. Retrieved from https://nces.ed.gov/fastfacts/display.asp?id=84

Webometrics. (2015). *Countries arranged by Number of Universities in Top Ranks*. Webometrics. Retrieved from http://www.webometrics.info/en/node/54

World Bank. (2000). *Higher education in developing countries: Peril and promise*. Washington, DC: The International Bank for Reconstruction and Development, World Bank.

Chapter 4
Nature and Geography:
Tragic Voids within Marketing Textbooks and the External Business Environment

Brent Smith
Saint Joseph's University, USA

ABSTRACT

This chapter considers the appropriateness and importance of including the natural environment (i.e., nature and geography) as part of the external business environment featured in marketing textbooks. Based on myriad examples from industry, the natural environment is regarded as an uncontrollable force that constantly affects decisions about markets and marketing activities. Thus, it deserves some (greater) mention next to economic, competitive, regulatory, and other variables typically featured in most marketing textbooks. Based on a review of business news, industry concerns, and marketing textbooks, this chapter considers the current listing of uncontrollable environment forces typically discussed within twenty-five popular marketing textbooks. It is observed that nature and geography, common priorities for business decision makers, are conspicuously absent from mention within most of these textbooks. This chapter shows that the natural environment is mentioned in only five of twenty-five marketing textbooks: two introductory marketing; one marketing management; and two international marketing. Based on scholarly definitions and industry examples, nature and geography are, in fact, uncontrollable influential forces that affect markets and marketing activities. Consequently, there is reasonable cause for including them in more marketing textbooks. Textbook authors and instructors can provide students a more complete picture of how domestic and international markets and marketing activities are affected by the natural environment. In practice, business people acknowledge that the natural environment affects and is affected by markets and marketing activities in virtually all industries. Alas, marketing textbooks seldom little, if ever, acknowledge that nature and geography (e.g., topography, climate, weather, solar flares, natural disasters) affect how companies think about their markets and marketing mix. This chapter offers simple, actionable steps for discussing the natural environment in marketing textbooks and courses.

DOI: 10.4018/978-1-4666-9784-3.ch004

Nature does not hurry, yet everything is accomplished. – Lao Tzu

Nature is a mutable cloud which is always and never the same. – Ralph Waldo Emerson

INTRODUCTION

Textbooks continue to serve as primary course material for undergraduate and graduates studying marketing principles, marketing strategy, and international marketing. Elbeck et al. (2009) state, "An instructor's decision to adopt a particular textbook will influence the marketing knowledge, business major selection, and career choices of tens, if not hundreds of students" (p. 49). In their early chapters, marketing textbooks generally provide established frameworks for understanding the external business environment and its relationships to markets and marketing activities. The external business environment, or marketing environment, is a multidimensional set of uncontrollable forces that can influence how companies and consumers might behave. Marketing textbooks generally identify five dimensions of the external business environment (see Tables 1-3) with slightly varying terms, including:

1. Economic,
2. Competitive,
3. Political/legal/regulatory,
4. Sociocultural, and
5. Technological.

The External (Business) Environment

In *Principles of Marketing, 15th ed.*, Kotler and Armstrong (2013) state that the company's macro environment shapes both opportunities and threats for companies. In *Marketing, 12th ed.*, Lamb, Hair, and McDaniel (2013) agree that marketers generally cannot control elements of the marketing environment, but rather must understand how they change and can potentially impact target markets. In *Marketing Channels, 8th ed.*, Rosenbloom (2012) notes that channel managers must take into account how the uncontrollable environment can influence the activities of their member and nonmember participants. In their text, *Marketing Strategy, 5th ed.*, Ferrell and Hartline (2011) say the following:

The final and broadest issue in a situation analysis is an assessment of the external environment, which includes all the external factors — competitive, economic, political, legal/regulatory, technological, and sociocultural — that can exert considerable direct and indirect pressures on both domestic and international marketing (p. 101).

Emphasizing the importance of these factors, Lamb, Hair, and McDaniel (2013) assert that marketing managers cannot plan intelligently if they fail to understand the environment and its impact on how firms work and compete. In fact, they suggest the following:

Table 1. Textbook coverage of nature/geography within external business environment

Textbook Title	Elements Of External Business Environment					
	Competitive	Economic	Natural	Political/ Legal	Sociocultural	Technological
Focus: Marketing Principles						
Marketing: An Introduction, 11ᵗʰ ed. Armstrong and Kotler (2012) Publisher: Pearson/Prentice Hall ISBN-13: 978-0132744034	+	+	*	+	+	+
Contemporary Marketing, 15ᵗʰ ed. Boone and Kurtz (2012) Publisher: South-Western/Cengage ISBN-13: 978-1111221782	+	+		+	+	+
Marketing, 3ʳᵈ ed. Grewal and Levy (2011) Publisher: McGraw-Hill Irwin ISBN-13: 978-0078028830	+	+		+	+	+
Marketing, 11ᵗʰ ed. Kerin, Hartley, and Rudelius (2012) Publisher: McGraw-Hill Irwin ISBN-13: 978-0078028892	+	+		+	+	+
Principles of Marketing, 15ᵗʰ ed. Kotler and Armstrong (2013) Publisher: Pearson/Prentice Hall ISBN-13: 978-0133084047	+	+	*	+	+	+
MKTG, 7ᵗʰ ed. Lamb, Hair, and McDaniel (2014) Publisher: South-Western/Cengage ISBN-13: 978-1285091860	+	+		+	+	+
Marketing, 12ᵗʰ ed. Lamb, Hair, and McDaniel (2013) Publisher: South-Western/Cengage ISBN-13: 978-1111821647	+	+		+	+	+
Marketing 2012, 16ᵗʰ ed. Pride and Ferrell (2012) Publisher: South-Western/Cengage ISBN-13: 978-0538475402	+	+		+	+	+
Marketing: Real People, Real Choices, 7ᵗʰ ed. Solomon, Marshall, and Stuart (2011) Publisher: Pearson/Prentice Hall ISBN-13: 978-0132176842	+	+		+	+	+

If there is one constant in the external environment (outside the firm) where firms work and compete, it is that things are constantly changing. If the organization doesn't understand or fails to react to the changing world around it, it will soon be a follower rather than a leader (p. 87).

Generally speaking, the external business environment can be characterized as one that:

- Is uncontrollable and constantly changing;
- Imparts difference influences on different industries, companies, and business units;

Table 2. Textbook coverage of nature/geography within external business environment

Textbook Title	Elements of External Business Environment					
	Competitive	Economic	Natural	Political/ Legal	Sociocultural	Technological
Focus: Marketing Management / Marketing Strategy						
Marketing Planning: Strategy, Environment, and Context Blythe and Megicks (2010) Publisher: Financial Times Management ISBN-13: 978-0273724711	+	+		+	+	+
Marketing Management: A Customer-Oriented Approach Clow and Baack (2009) Publisher: Sage ISBN-13: 978-1412963121	+	+		+	+	+
Marketing Strategy, 5th ed. Ferrell and Hartline (2010) Publisher: South-Western/Cengage ISBN-13: 978-0538467384	+	+		+	+	+
Strategic Marketing Problems, 13th ed. Kerin and Peterson (2012) Publisher: Pearson/Prentice Hall ISBN-13: 978-0132747257	+	+		+	+	+
Marketing Management, 14th ed. Kotler and Keller (2011) Publisher: Pearson/Prentice Hall ISBN-13: 978-0132102926	+	+	*	+	+	+
Focus: Marketing Channels/Retailing						
Retail Management: A Strategic Approach, 12th ed. Berman and Evans (2013) Publisher: Pearson/Prentice Hall ISBN-13: 978-0132720823	+	+		+	+	+
Retailing Management, 8th ed. Levy and Weitz (2012) Publisher: McGraw-Hill Irwin ISBN-13: 978-0073530024	+	+		+	+	+
Marketing Channels, 8th ed. Rosenbloom (2012) Publisher: South-Western/Cengage ISBN-13: 978-0324316988	+	+		+	+	+

- Has short-term and long-terms effects on marketing activities;
- Affects and is affected by marketing activities;
- Creates and shapes opportunities, challenges, and threats for companies;
- Exerts direct and indirect pressures on domestic and international marketing.

Without question, marketing strategists must constantly scan the business environment to identify threats or opportunities that could affect industries, companies, products, brands, and consumers. For instance, international market entry decisions should take into account the political risk and regulatory

Table 3. Textbook coverage of nature/geography within external business environment

Textbook Title	Elements of External Business Environment		
	Competitive	Economic	Natural
Focus: International/Global Marketing			
Global Marketing: Contemporary Theory, Practice, and Cases Alon and Jaffe (2012) Publisher: McGraw-Hill Irwin ISBN-13: 978-0078029271	+	+	
International Marketing Baack, Harris, and Baack (2012) Publisher: Sage ISBN-13: 978-1452226354		+	+
International Marketing, 16ᵗʰ ed. Cateora, Gilly, and Graham (2013) Publisher: McGraw-Hill Irwin ISBN-13: 978-0073529974		+	+
International Marketing, 10ᵗʰ ed. Czinkota and Ronkainen (2012) Publisher: South-Western/Cengage ISBN-13: 978-1133627517		+	
Global Marketing, 3ʳᵈ ed. Gillespie and Hennessey (2010) Publisher: South-Western/Cengage ISBN-13: 978-1439039434	+	+	
Global Marketing: A Decision-Oriented Approach, 5ᵗʰ ed. Hollensen (2010) Publisher: Pearson/Prentice Hall ISBN-13: 978-0273726227	+	+	
Global Marketing: Foreign Entry, Local Marketing, and Global Management, 5ᵗʰ ed. Johansson (2008) Publisher: McGraw-Hill Irwin ISBN-13: 978-0073381015	+	+	
Global Marketing, 7ᵗʰ ed. Keegan and Green (2012) Publisher: Pearson/Prentice Hall ISBN-13: 978-0132719155	+	+	

climate within a given country since these factors could help or hinder operations. Economic recession may compel luxury product manufacturers to offer more value-conscious merchandise to their portfolios. Ongoing competitive pressures from generic drugs and expiring patents drive leading pharmaceutical companies to innovate in order to stay competitive.

Marketing Education: A Need for Continuous Improvement

In our discipline's history, we have valued continuous improvement regarding our paradigms, metrics, pedagogy, and textbooks (the focus of this article). For example, Dickinson (2002) argued for the need to revamp textbook presentations of price elasticity. Hubbard and Armstrong (2006) have examined why we — scholars and students — do not really know what statistical significance means. Others have performed comparative reviews of consumer behavior textbooks (Finn 1985) or examined the readability of marketing textbooks (Shuptrine & Lichtenstein, 1985; Spiro, Kossack, & Kossack, 1981) have examined the readability of marketing textbooks. Myriad examples of our critical self-assessment indicate that we aim to improve how marketing education speaks to the realities and challenges faced by students and practitioners of different cultures, societies, and industries (Catterall, Maclaran, & Stevens, 2002; Peltier, Hay, & Drago, 2006; Petkus, 2007; Rosa, 2012; Sheth, 2011).

Nature and Geography Matter: Missing Topics in Marketing Textbooks and Discussions of the Business Environment

Nature is just enough; but men and women must comprehend and accept her suggestions. – Antoinette Brown Blackwell

In business, nature and geography matter. This fact has been made evident and underscored repeatedly throughout human history in all parts of the world. Thus, strategic marketing planning should take into account how nature and geography can impact and be impacted by industries, markets, companies, and consumers (Cateora, Gilly, & Graham, 2013; Kotler & Armstrong, 2013; Pattison, 1964).

As noted above, the call to improve our marketing textbooks, curricula, and pedagogy is constant and never-ending. In fact, it is as unrelenting as the dynamic, omnipresent forces of the business environment that affect markets and marketing activities. Indeed, Achtenhagen's (1979) exhortation still drives us: "Submit your ideas; ideas that will have the impact of enhancing the effectiveness of teaching marketing" (p. 2).

From a historical perspective, marketing education boasts an impressive record of responsiveness to developments in communications, lifestyle changes, technology, and more (Petkus, 2010). However, less can be said for marketing education's acknowledgement of nature and geography as elements of the uncontrollable external marketing environment. This fact is rather puzzling, since in practice, proprietors, managers, and laborers are keenly aware of the nature's importance to their businesses. Marketing is about meeting needs, providing utility, and fostering exchange relationships. As will be shown in this article, nature and geography *can* and *do* affect all of these.

Farmers understand that soil, weather, and other factors directly impact the volume, quality, perishability, salability, and distribution of their crops. Atop high-altitude mountain slopes, viable seasons for ski lodges depend on cold temperatures and ample snow to attract patrons (Burki, Elsasser, & Abegg, 2003; Hamilton et al., 2003; Spector et al., 2012). Stoddart (2012) notes that the quality and quantity of snow can shape how skiers interact with mountain environments. In the international flower markets, growers in Ecuador and Kenya enjoy natural advantages of good climate, high altitude, and quality sunlight (Alvaro, 2006; Orton-Jones, 2008). Tropical tourist destinations in the Caribbean can leverage the attractiveness of their geographic locations and climate for much of the year, except hurricane season (Hudson, 1986). These examples reflect how producers tap into the natural resource-based view and compete effectively (Hart, 1995). Even today's communications companies monitor how space weather (e.g., solar flares), magnetic fields, and sub-oceanic earthquakes might affect their satellites' ability to broadcast television shows, stream videos online, or support two-way voice communications around the world (Hayward, 1999; Smith, 2010). In 2010, Japan suffered catastrophic losses to homes, infrastructure, and industry as a direct result of a series of natural events (i.e., undersea earthquake, tsunami, and flooding) (Chrysler, 2011). Japanese automakers faced many competitive setbacks and struggled to serve their global customers. In areas prone to hurricane and tornadoes, insurance companies manage product portfolios to address various causes of loss — wind, flood, hail, lightning, acts of god — to a homeowner's or farmer's property (Bel & Churchill, 2012; Williams, 1994). The very innovations in artificial lighting (e.g., candle, lamp, light bulb) exemplify a human response to natural conditions that *once* imposed significant limits on labor, productivity, and transportation. The natural environment can also influence daily work schedules and quality of shipping/traffic routes (Read & Bentz, 2011). For example, the Eyjafjallajökull volcanic eruptions in Iceland produced such an awesome scale of volcanic ash that it consequently halted all major trans-Atlantic and Western European air traffic (Ulfarsson & Unger, 2011). The passenger airline industry alone was estimated to have lost over $1 billion (US).

Marketing managers in industry have shown serious concerns about the potential, and sometimes predictable, impact of the natural environment on marketing activities and outcomes (see Figure 1). For example, companies such as Planalytics, AWIS Weather Services, and other competitors, provide business weather intelligence services to a diverse array of clients (e.g., Wal-Mart, Black & Decker, Subway) that strategically use information about the natural environment to manage product inventories, shift distribution allocations, plan sales promotions, calibrate pricing, and more.

Alas, in light of examples such as those above, it is rather ironic that nature and geography — the first and most omnipresent aspects of the *environment* — have been noticeably absent from marketing textbook's and the external business environment. These omission reveal in plain sight how current marketing curricula and pedagogy fall short in recognizing the realities of merchants and consumers everywhere (Rosa, 2012; Sheth, 2011), particularly, but not limited to, those in subsistence economies. Considering that the advancement of human society has always required people to study, submit and

Figure 1. Companies whose marketing planning is impacted by the natural environment (Source: Planalytics)

react to elements and events of nature, it would seem necessary for marketing textbooks to acknowledge nature's role in the marketing environment. Looking back in time and beyond the discipline's predominantly Western authors and publishers, one finds significant insight about nature and the natural world from other cultures (Smith, 2010). For example, in the *Art of War* (Sawyer, 1994), a major reference text for business strategists, Sun Tzu identifies heaven (i.e., weather, climate, seasons) as one pivotal strategic factor to consider when making situational assessments. He stresses that heaven includes uncontrollable, dynamic forces which can, if studied carefully, reveal opportunities to seize competitive advantages.

Analysis of Marketing Textbooks: The Status Quo

In attempting to learn the status quo of marketing education on nature and geography, the author performed an analysis of 25 marketing textbooks geared towards undergraduate and graduate students. These textbooks represented the work of over 40 authors, ranged in edition from first to sixteenth and included 5 well-known international textbook publishers: South-Western/Cengage; Financial Times; McGraw-Hill/Irwin; Pearson/Prentice Hall; and Sage. The entire group of textbooks covered marketing principles, marketing management, marketing strategy, retail management, and international/global marketing (see Tables 1-3).

An examination of the most recent editions of leading marketing principles textbooks reveals that most textbooks do not explicitly cite the natural environment as a factor. Interestingly, the natural environment (i.e., nature, geography) received little to no coverage in the textbooks. *International Marketing, 16th ed.* by Cateora, Gilly, & Graham (2013) devoted the clearest attention to the natural environment, namely through geography (e.g., climate, topography, resources). They also acknowledge that "the study of geography is important in the evaluation of markets and their environment," and it is "an element of the uncontrollable environment that confronts every marketer but which receives scant attention" (p. 62). Armstrong and Kotler (2012) and Kotler and Armstrong (2013) explicitly mention the natural environment as part of the company's macro environment along with demographic, economic, technological, political, and cultural forces. Unfortunately, their definitions are quite narrow, vague, and limited exclusively to natural resources that are needed by marketers or affected by marketing activities (e.g., raw materials, pollution, government intervention). Baack, Daniel, and Baack (2013) provide a brief two-page description of geography and its relationship to culture (e.g., lifestyles, occupations, clothing). Virtually, none of the textbooks mentions *nature*, *geography*, *natural environment*, or related terms in the table of contents or index. In many instances, the textbooks say little to introduce, define, or characterize the external business environment before discussing its dimensions/elements, which typically include competitive, economic, political/legal/regulatory, sociocultural, and technological. For example, Solomon, Stuart, and Marshall (2012) lead into these elements with the following:

Whether or not you've decided to venture into a foreign market, it's essential to understand your external environment. For firms that choose to limit themselves to their domestic market, having a sharp picture of the marketing environment allow them to make good decisions about marketing strategies. If you've decided to go global, understanding local conditions in potential new country or regional markets helps you figure out just where to go. In this section, we'll look at the economic, competitive, technological, political/legal, and sociocultural factors in the external environment that we need to think about" (p. 73).

Changes to Marketing Textbooks: Encouraging Signs

There are some encouraging indications that marketing textbook authors recognize the importance of the natural environment as a factor and force that acts upon human society, business, and industry. Thus, as a factor/force, the natural environment can be understood as more than merely something that we act upon, but that can, and *does*, affect the existence, prosperity, and behavior of our industries big and small. In addition to Cateora, Gilly, and Graham (2013), Czinkota and Ronkainen (2013) updated the latest edition of their text, *International Marketing*, producing a first-chapter appendix that directly addresses relationships between geography and international marketing.

These developments are encouraging; however, they are too few and, thus, not sufficient to fill the "nature gap" still obvious in our discipline's textbooks. Clearly, not every marketing student will have the opportunity to enroll in an international marketing class and/or be assigned one of the cited textbooks. Therefore, one cannot be satisfied that any international marketing (or green marketing) textbook would actually compensate for material omissions of the natural environment from gateway textbooks in marketing principles. As the business community becomes more attuned to the metrics of the triple bottom line, overlooking the factors of natural environment could yield significant shortcomings for MBA marketing students relying on information from textbooks in marketing management or marketing strategy. Might they not understand how nature can affect the activities of suppliers, distributors, or customers? Could they develop less intelligent plans that require adaptive responses to challenges or opportunities resulting from natural events? Might they not adequately comprehend how nature and geography affect barriers to entry, industry rivalry, and Porter's other forces of industry attractiveness?

Marketing education's present concerns about nature and geography are almost exclusively directed towards social responsibility, sustainability, and green marketing (see Boone & Kurtz, 2012; Pride & Ferrell, 2012; and others). However, these areas represent only a fraction of nature's importance to business. Referencing questionably skewed developments in the study of the human-environment relationship, Robinson (1976) even cautioned his geographer colleagues on this matter:

In the past decade, the pendulum has swung to another extreme, with the emphasis on man rather than land. Now many young geographers, and particularly the students in our geography classrooms, are deeply concerned with man's impact or influence upon his environment. No longer do students think about how the environment controls man's activities; they are worried about how man is destroying his environment. As is too often the case in the media, the middle view of man-land relationships is lost. There may now be just as many extreme, enthusiastic, ill-informed "eco-freaks" who want to protect the environment for no use as there formerly were serious prophets of doom who warned that people would be confined only to certain places on the earth because of the inhospitable environments elsewhere (p. 527).

While protecting the natural environment is important discussion of myriad business opportunities and challenges created by that environment are almost entirely absent from today's marketing textbooks. Indeed, Robinson (1976) reinforces this article's position that natural environment can affect and be affected by our markets and marketing activities:

That man works with, adapts to, uses, or abuses his environment are pertinent concepts (p. 528).

Course Integration

Textbooks provide the most common medium through which marketing students are introduced to or learn about the formal principles of the discipline. Thus, wherever a particular textbook introduces the multiple dimensions of marketing environment, the natural dimension (i.e., nature and geography) should be included. While the cited international marketing textbooks do mention geography and relate it to markets, they present the topic in narrow sections devoted mainly to culture. Given the importance of the external business environment (Ferrell & Hartline, 2011; Solomon, Stuart, & Marshall, 2011; and others), forces/factors of the natural environment must be presented with, not separated from, the other dimensions.

As a starting point for properly integrating the nature and geography into marketing textbooks, it may be useful to consider the meaning of both terms. Not surprisingly, definitions can be legion and may possibly share (lack) a singular focus. The *point* of this article is really to help marketers grasp the importance of nature and geography in business. In sum, the definitions below suggest that nature and geography can, but do not necessarily, overlap. Thus, this article identifies them together to ensure proper acknowledgement in the marketing education.

The Oxford English Dictionary (2013) defines nature as:

1. *The phenomena of the physical world collectively; esp. plants, animals, and other features and products of the earth itself, as opposed to humans and human creations.*
2. *In wider sense: the whole natural world, including human beings; the cosmos.*

According to Merriam Webster (2013), geography is defined as:

A science that deals with the description, distribution, and interaction of the diverse physical, biological, and cultural features of the earth's surface.

The Oxford English Dictionary (2013) defines geography as:

1. *The field of study concerned with the physical features of the earth and its atmosphere, and with human activity as it affects and is affected by these, including the distribution of populations and resources and political and economic activities; also as a subject of educational study or examination.*
2. *The geographical features or topography of a place or region; a place or region, or terrain, as characterized by such features. Also: the range or extent of what is known geographically.*

The origins of the term can be traced to the Latin *geographia,* and Greek *geōgraphia,* both derived from *geōgraphein* (from *geō- + graphein), meaning* "to describe the earth's surface" (Merriam Webster, 2013)

Pattison (1964) identified four traditions of geography, namely:

1. Spatial/locational tradition;
2. Area studies/regional tradition;
3. Man-land/human-environmental tradition; and
4. Earth science tradition.

The basic elements of each tradition are summarized below.

- **Spatial/Locational Tradition:**
  - Areal distribution; location of and distance between things;
  - Spatial arrangements of cities and patterns of land uses;
  - Movement and transportation;
  - Quantitative methods for mapping and measuring.
- **Area Studies/Regional Tradition:**
  - Description of physical geographic areas/regions;
  - Relationships between areas/regions;
  - Comparisons and contrasts of differences areas/regions.
- **Man-Land/Human-Environmental Tradition:**
  - Impact of human beings on nature;
  - Impact of nature of human beings;
  - Natural events/hazards.
- **Earth Science Tradition:**
  - Physical geography of the Earth;
  - Interactions between the Earth;
  - Atmosphere, biosphere, and other spheres.

For marketing education, the human-environmental tradition is probably the most intuitively germane to the external business environment, since its elements deal directly with:

1. The impact of humans on nature;
2. Impact of nature on humans;
3. Natural hazards; and
4. Human perceptions of the natural environment.

Elements of the Natural Environment

The natural environment arguably provides the most basic context for all humans to understand how their life, work, and interactions are impacted by forces beyond their control. All societies, whether agricultural, industrial, or otherwise, are rather familiar with the many aspects and impacts of the natural environment.

The natural environment includes, but is not limited to: weather, land, natural resources, climatic conditions (e.g.. weather), topography (e.g., rivers, seas, soil, passages), solar and lunar activity, and natural events/disasters (e.g., earthquakes, floods). Certain items, though not all, can be categorized with geography (Cateora, Gilly, & Graham, 2013). However, they are presented separately here to help ensure clarity and broader understanding of nature's ubiquitous role in the uncontrollable external environment. Ultimately, this author would contend that the natural environment satisfies the same criteria of other forces — competitive, economic, political/legal/regulatory, sociocultural, and technological — within the external business environment. Specifically, like its would-be counterparts, it:

- Is an uncontrollable and constantly changing force;
- Imparts difference influences on different industries, companies, and business units;

- Has short-term and long-terms effects on marketing activities;
- Affects and is affected by marketing and consumer activities;
- Creates and shapes opportunities, challenges, and threats for companies;
- Exerts direct and indirect pressures on domestic and international marketing.

Given the sheer absence of the natural environment (i.e., nature and geography) from most marketing textbooks, the following definition of the natural environment is suggested:

The natural environment includes climate, topography, resources, disasters and other uncontrollable elements that affect or are affected by marketing and consumer activities. These factors have the potential to influence directly and indirectly the existence, prosperity, and practices of companies and their markets.

The above definition is not a perfect one, yet it reflects a starting point to underscore the idea that nature is an independent, multifaceted, ubiquitous, and significant force in any business environment. Indeed, this idea has received very little coverage in textbooks that have been, and still are, read by millions of students in business and marketing classes around the world. For instance, Cateora, Gilly, and Graham (2013) acknowledge, "Geography, the study of the Earth's surface, climate, continents, countries, peoples, industries, and resources" (p. 62).

It must be noted that the term 'geography' has been defined and described in various ways by different people from different backgrounds, era, and geographies (Pattison, 1964; Pattison, 1990; Robinson, 1976). For sake of simplifying its inclusion in marketing textbooks, it is recommended that authors focus generically on geography, rather than on specialized strands, such as cultural geography, economic geography, or transportation geography.

Recommendations for Including Nature and Geography in the Marketing Environment

By including nature and geography in marketing textbooks, professors and students will be able to discuss a range of topics and stakeholders in the value creation process. As shown above, nature and geography can and do affect myriad subjects of interest in marketing: natural resources, location of suppliers, threats to service delivery, bases of competitive advantage, etc. Indeed, tomorrow's marketing professionals must understand how nature and geography shape and condition a company's macro environment. These factors are not limited to endangered lands, habitats, and creatures. Moreover, they should not be limited to a handful of textbooks on international marketing, green marketing, or sustainable marketing that students may never get to read. As stated by Lamb, Hair, and McDaniel (2013), if marketing managers do not understand that the environment, in its fullness, can impact firms and how they compete, then they cannot plan intelligently for the future. In addition to the examples already mentioned, the following paragraphs provide some topics for discussing the natural environment and its relationship with markets and marketing activities. The topics reflect the definitions of nature and geography noted earlier. Per Ferrell and Hartline's (2011) criterion, these examples show how nature, like other aspects of the external environment, can "exert considerable direct and indirect impact on both domestic and international marketing" (p. 101).

Factor: Climate, Weather, and Temperature Conditions

Factors such as altitude, temperature, humidity, and exposure to elements often have a foreseeable direct or indirect impact on products, prices, inventories, and other marketing related matters. In many cases, companies often can or cannot do develop methods and responses for dealing with these factors.

- **Example:** Industries and products impacted by climate, weather, and seasons.
  - Sufficiently cold temperatures to produce snowfall at skiing resorts;
  - Weather conditions for theme parks, outdoor concerts, and festivals;
  - Frosts that disrupt or terminate growing/harvesting of oranges, strawberries, etc.;
  - Hurricanes, hail, and floods that require specific types of property insurance;
  - Devastating tsunamis that limited production operations of Japan's auto industry;
  - Climate-controlled containers to prevent spoilage of fruits, vegetables, and meats in trucks, warehouses, or retail spaces;
  - Promotional discounts on foods and food products nearing expiration date.

Factor: Geography: Topography and Climate

Topography and climate can help (hinder) a region's potential to participate or compete effectively in markets that require access to location-specific natural resources related to sourcing, distribution, logistics, and communication.

- **Example:** Impact on location of infrastructure; shipping/transportation options.
  - Proper sunlight and altitude for growing flowers in Kenya or coffee in Guatemala;
  - Abundance (lack) of coastal ports and inland water routes for shipping;
  - Viability and vitality of Lowell and Lawrence textile mills along the Merrimack River during the Industrial Revolution;
  - Production of wind energy for land-based and sea-based wind turbines;
  - Soil quality, temperature, and rainfall affecting production of wheat (e.g., corn) or grapes (e.g., champagne, ice wine);
  - Trade winds (e.g., attractiveness of Aruba as tourist destination);
  - Accessible plant/animal habitat for research and development of pharmaceuticals.

Factor: Natural Processes, Natural Disasters, and Cosmic Events

Cateora, Gilly, and Graham (2013) state, "Mountains, oceans, seas, jungles, and other geographical features can pose serious impediments to economic growth and trade" (p. 63). In addition, various non-geographic natural events (e.g., cosmic, natural aging processes, time) can affect markets and marketing activities.

- **Example:** Impact on raw materials, transportation routes, and communications.
  - Natural perishability of flowers, fruits, and vegetables after being picked/harvested;
  - Scheduling shipping/logistics services to deliver fresh flowers and produce from Latin America to international markets;

- ○ Volcanic ash from Eyjafjallajökull eruptions blocking airplane traffic and disrupting passenger/shipping service;
- ○ Hardware stores selling disaster-relief products (e.g., power generators, flashlights) before and after hurricanes;
- ○ Solar flares interrupting telephone, broadcast media, and other communications.

Improving Marketing Textbooks and Pedagogy: Questions for Reflection and Analysis

One's first step in wisdom is to question everything — and one's last is to come to terms with everything.
– Georg Christoph Lichtenberg, Scientist, 1742-1799

While geography is important, it does not represent the fullness of the natural environment. As noted and described in various examples (e.g., solar flares, floods, forms of precipitation), the natural environment includes, but is not limited to, geography.

Taking cues from Ferrell and Hartline (2011), textbooks can provide a framework for helping students analyze basic, but important questions about factors of the external environment. With regard to the natural environment, possible questions to help marketing students might include, for example:

1. **Insurance:** Are we offering an appropriate set of insurance products for homeowners, farmers, ranchers, or renters in locations frequently affected by particular weather events and/or natural disasters? How much risk can/should we accept in providing insurance products to consumers in certain geographic areas?
2. **Tourism/Resorts:** How can nature and geography affect the attractiveness of a tourist destination? What natural environmental factors can make certain tourist destinations more attractive than others during particular seasons or times of year?
3. **Agriculture/Horticulture:** Could rainfall, pests, or crop diseases affect growers' ability to generate revenue or profit? Might these factors lead growers to increase prices or request government aid? Could these factors affect our nation's absolute or comparative advantages in global markets? Do lack of altitude and sunlight create any entry barriers to would-be rivals?
4. **Logistics/Retail/Food Products:** Could weather, climate, or topography at any time threaten our ability to manufacture, supply, or distribute products to domestic or international markets? What can be done to prevent spoilage of perishable food products in transit to local or distant markets?
5. **Banking/Education:** How much could adverse weather conditions, geographic distance, and other natural factors affect our ability to serve our consumer base?
6. **Pharmaceuticals/Medicine:** How could the number, size, location, and vitality of tropical rainforests affect our ability to discover/innovate future drugs or nutritional products?
7. **Energy:** What are the world's best geographical locations and methods for harvesting solar, wind, and magnetic energy sources?
8. **Communications/Distribution/Trade:** Does the natural environment impose limits on the ability to facilitate communications, product distribution, or trade within or between countries?
9. **Sport Training and Competitive Events:** Do altitude, climate, and topography make particular cities more attractive locations to host entertainment events or sport competitions?

Table 4. Clients of planalytics' business weather intelligence services

Company	Industry	Company	Industry
Coca-Cola	Beverages	Johnson & Johnson	Consumer goods
Debenhams	Apparel/Accessories	Middle TN Natural Gas	Natural gas/oil
DSM Chemicals	Chemicals	Orscheln Farm and Home	Retail
Dreyer's Ice Cream	Foods	Perry Ellis	Apparel/Accessories
Haier	Home appliances	Petsmart	Specialty Retail
Hanes Brands Inc.	Apparel/Accessories	Procter & Gamble	Consumer goods
Hozelock Ltd.	Retail	Shaw Industries	Textile
Illinois Tool Works	Manufacturing	Sonic Corporation	Restaurants
Jamba Juice	Restaurants	Tween Brands	Retail

Source: Planalytics.com (2013).

CONCLUSION

Marketing decisions makers cannot plan intelligently without properly considering how all elements of the business environment affect their industry, rivals, and consumers. Nature and geography dynamically shape the conditions under which markets exist and marketing activities occur. Indeed, nature and geography have always affected how human beings live, work, and interact. Myriad examples presented in this article show that small farmers, passenger airlines, insurance companies, and others clearly recognize that the natural environment affects their business. Alas, most of our discipline's popular textbooks have offered little education on such issues. While we have come to acknowledge the importance of protecting the natural environment via green marketing and sustainability programs, we have yet to address the telling voids — nature and geography — in our current conceptualization of the external business environment. Future marketing students and professionals must learn how to scan that environment more carefully. They will need to understand and respond to the influences of topography, inflation, culture, legal regulation, and natural disaster on their suppliers, markets and marketing activities. Thus, marketing textbook authors and publishers have an opportunity to respond to this call for expanding the external business environment to include its most enduring and omnipresent factors, nature and geography.

REFERENCES

Achtenhagen, S. H. (1979). Letter from the editor. *Journal of Marketing Education, 1*(1), 2–2. doi:10.1177/027347537900100101

Alon, I., Jaffe, E., & Vianelli, D. (2013). *Global marketing: contemporary theory, practice, and cases.* New York, NY: McGraw-Hill/Irwin.

Alvaro, M. (2006, Feb 22). Deal sought for Ecuador flower exports. *Wall Street Journal*. Retrieved from http://search.proquest.com/docview/398970029

Armstrong, G., & Kotler, P. (2013). *Marketing: an introduction.* Boston, MA: Prentice Hall.

Baack, D., Harris, E., & Baack, D. (2013). *International marketing*. Thousand Oaks, CA: Sage.

Bel, S., & Churchill, C. (2012). Using insurance to drive trade. *International Trade Forum*, (1), 24-26.

Berman, B., & Evans, J. (2013). *Retail management: a strategic approach*. Boston: Pearson.

Blythe, J., & Megicks, P. (2010). *Marketing planning: strategy, environment and context*. Harlow, UK: Financial Times / Prentice Hall.

Boone, L. E., & Kurtz, D. L. (2011). *Contemporary marketing*. Mason, OH: South-Western/Cengage.

Burki, R., Elsasser, H., & Abegg, B. (2003). Climate change and winter sports: environmental and economic threats. *5th World Conference on Sport and Environment*.

Cateora, P., Gilly, M., & Graham, J. (2013). *International marketing*. New York, NY: McGraw-Hill Irwin.

Catterall, M., Maclaran, P., & Stevens, L. (2002). Critical reflection in the marketing curriculum. *Journal of Marketing Education*, 24(3), 184–192. doi:10.1177/0273475302238041

Chrysler, M. (2011). Japanese auto industry faces somber market. *WardsAuto.Com*. Retrieved from http://search.proquest.com/docview/926925346

Clow, K., & Baack, D. (2010). *Marketing management: a customer-oriented approach*. Thousand Oaks, CA: Sage.

Czinkota, M., & Ronkainen, I. (2013). *International marketing*. Mason, OH: South-Western/Cengage.

Dickinson, J. R. (2002). A need to revamp textbook presentations of price elasticity. *Journal of Marketing Education*, 24(2), 143–149. doi:10.1177/027753024002007

Elbeck, M., Williams, R., Peters, C. O., & Frankforter, S. (2009). What marketing educators look for when adopting a principles of marketing textbook. *Marketing Education Review*, 19(2), 49–62. doi:10.1080/10528008.2009.11489074

Ferrell, O. C., & Hartline, M. (2011). *Marketing strategy*. Mason, OH: South-Western/Cengage.

Finn, A. (1985). Consumer Behavior Textbooks: A Comparative Review. *Journal of Marketing Education*, 7(3), 46–54. doi:10.1177/027347538500700308

Geography. (2013). In *Merriam-Webster Collegiate Dictionary*. Retrieved March 28, 2013, from http://www.merriam-webster.com/dictionary/geography

Geography. (2013). In *OED Online*. Oxford University Press. Retrieved March 28, 2013, from http://www.oed.com/view/Entry/77757

Gillespie, K., & Hennessey, H. (2011). *Global marketing*. Mason, OH: South-Western/Cengage.

Grewal, D., & Levy, M. (2012). *Marketing*. New York, NY: McGraw-Hill/Irwin.

Hamilton, L. C., Rohall, D. E., Brown, B. C., Hayward, G. F., & Keim, B. D. (2003). Warming winters and New Hampshire's lost ski areas: An integrated case study. *The International Journal of Sociology and Social Policy*, 23(10), 52–73. doi:10.1108/01443330310790309

Hart, S. L. (1995). A natural-resource-based view of the firm. *Academy of Management Review*, *20*(4), 986–1014.

Hayward, G. (1999). Sun-burned. *Airman*, *43*(10), 46–48.

Hollensen, S. (2011). *Global marketing: a decision-oriented approach*. Harlow, UK: Financial Times / Prentice Hall.

Hubbard, R., & Armstrong, J. S. (2006). Why we don't really know what statistical significance means: Implications for educators. *Journal of Marketing Education*, *28*(2), 114–120. doi:10.1177/0273475306288399

Hudson, B. (1986). Landscape as resource for national development: A Caribbean view. *Geography (Sheffield, England)*, *71*(2), 116–121.

Johansson, J. (2009). *Global marketing: foreign entry, local marketing, & global management*. Boston, MA: McGraw-Hill Irwin.

Keegan, W., & Green, M. (2013). *Global marketing*. Boston, MA: Pearson.

Kerin, R., Hartley, S., & Rudelius, W. (2013). *Marketing*. New York, NY: McGraw-Hill/Irwin.

Kerin, R., & Peterson, R. (2013). *Strategic marketing problems: cases and comments*. Boston, MA: Pearson.

Kotler, P., & Armstrong, G. (2013). *Principles of marketing*. Boston, MA: Pearson.

Kotler, P., & Keller, K. (2012). *Marketing management*. Upper Saddle River, NJ: Prentice Hall.

Lamb, C. W., Hair, J. F., & McDaniel, C. (2013). *Marketing*. Mason, OH: South-Western/Cengage.

Lamb, C. W., Hair, J. F., & McDaniel, C. (2014). *MKTG 7*. Mason, OH: South-Western/Cengage.

Levy, M., & Weitz, B. (2012). *Retailing management*. New York, NY: McGraw-Hill/Irwin.

Mooradian, T., Matzler, K., & Ring, L. (2012). *Strategic marketing*. Boston, MA: Pearson Prentice Hall.

Nature. (2013). In *OED Online*. Oxford University Press. Retrieved March 28, 2013, from http://www.oed.com/view/Entry/125353?rskey=LWvDsZ

Ormrod, R. P., Henneberg, S., & O'Shaughnessy, N. (2013). Political marketing: Theory and concepts. *Sage (Atlanta, Ga.)*.

Orton-Jones, C. (2008). Bloom and bust. *Financial Management*, (Feb): 18–21.

Pattison, W. D. (1964). The four traditions of geography. *The Journal of Geography*, *63*(5), 211–216. doi:10.1080/00221346408985265

Pattison, W. D. (1990). The four traditions of geography. *The Journal of Geography*, *89*(5), 202–206. doi:10.1080/00221349008979196

Peltier, J. W., Hay, A., & Drago, W. (2006). Reflecting on reflection: Scale extension and a comparison of undergraduate business students in the United States and the United Kingdom. *Journal of Marketing Education*, *28*(1), 5–16. doi:10.1177/0273475305279658

Petkus, E. (2007). Enhancing the relevance and value of marketing curriculum outcomes to a liberal arts education. *Journal of Marketing Education, 29*(1), 39–51. doi:10.1177/0273475306297384

Pride, W., & Ferrell, O. C. (2012). *Marketing*. Australia: South-Western/Cengage.

Read, B., & Bentz, B. (2011, Sep 29). Preparing for the panama canal. *Journal of Commerce*. Retrieved from http://search.proquest.com/docview/894806986

Robinson, J. L. (1976). A new look at the four traditions of geography. *The Journal of Geography, 75*(9), 520–530. doi:10.1080/00221347608980845

Rosa, J. A. (2012). Marketing education for the next four billion challenges and innovations. *Journal of Marketing Education, 34*(1), 44–54. doi:10.1177/0273475311430802

Rosenbloom, B. (2013). *Marketing channels: a management view*. Cincinnati, OH: South-Western/Cengage.

Sawyer, R. D. (1994). *Sun Tzu: the art of war*. Boulder, CO: Westview Press, Inc.

Sheth, J. N. (2011). Impact of emerging markets on marketing: Rethinking existing perspectives and practices. *Journal of Marketing, 75*(4), 166–182. doi:10.1509/jmkg.75.4.166

Shuptrine, F. K., & Lichtenstein, D. R. (1985). Measuring readability levels of undergraduate marketing textbooks. *Journal of Marketing Education, 7*(3), 38–45. doi:10.1177/027347538500700307

Smith, B. (2010). Gazelle, lion, hyena, vulture, and worm: A teaching metaphor on competition between early and late market entrants. *Marketing Education Review, 20*(1), 9–16. doi:10.2753/MER1052-8008200102

Smith, J. N. (2010). Sci-fi supply chain innovations. *World Trade, WT 100, 23*(5), 50-50.

Solomon, M., Marshall, G., & Stuart, E. (2012). *Marketing: real people, real choices*. Boston, MA: Prentice Hall.

Spector, S., Chard, C., Mallen, C., & Hyatt, C. (2012). Socially constructed environmental issues and sport: A content analysis of ski resort environmental communications. *Sport Management Review, 15*(4), 416–433. doi:10.1016/j.smr.2012.04.003

Spiro, R. L., Kossack, S., & Kossack, E. (1981). The introductory marketing text: An examination of readability. *Journal of Marketing Education, 3*(2), 41–51. doi:10.1177/027347538100300209

Stoddart, M. C. (2012). *Making meaning out of mountains: the political ecology of skiing*. UBC Press.

Ulfarsson, G. F., & Unger, E. A. (2011). Impacts and responses of Icelandic aviation to the 2010 Eyjafjalla-jokull volcanic eruption case study. *Transportation Research Record, 2214*, 144–151. doi:10.3141/2214-18

Williams, G. F. (1994). Another disaster, another market crisis. *American Agent & Broker, 66*(2), 18–18.

Chapter 5

A Mental Model for Teaching Strategic Marketing Management

Homer B. Warren
Youngstown State University, USA

David J. Burns
Kennesaw State University, USA

ABSTRACT

The complex realities of the increasingly global nature of business require managers who are able to see and comprehend the multiple interrelationships of factors in the environment to optimize decision making. This paper offers a mental model used by the authors to help students better understand the heuristic thinking processes that successful strategic marketing managers use in decision making and problem solving. The authors argue that seeing the "whole" marketing system and understanding how to integrate marketing knowledge is a key ingredient in heuristic thinking. To this end, the paper details the foundation for and the construction of a mental model for a strategic marketing management course. An application is discussed.

INTRODUCTION

Colleges of business, particularly those in the U.S., are under a societal microscope. Corporate America has concerns about the function-based approach colleges of business use to teach students who will become management-level employees (Stevens, 2000). Taxpayers demand accountability through value-added analysis (Greene & Bao, 2009). The AACSB's accreditation guidelines include outcome assessments and clear competencies (Moskal, Ellis, & Keon, 2008). Seemingly, stakeholders' concerns center around whether colleges of business are going beyond content-based, rote memorization instruction to developing graduates with the cognitive skills necessary to effectively function within a dynamic business environment.

DOI: 10.4018/978-1-4666-9784-3.ch005

Marketing researchers and theorists have done their part in producing a large body of knowledge about marketing strategy development and the management skills needed for algorithmic tasks (the straightforward mundane situations) and heuristic tasks (problems for which managers need to find new and/or imaginative solutions). To their credit, marketing educators have regularly explored methods to bring to the classroom the created body of knowledge. In the face of these efforts, however, stakeholders' concerns remain. The graduates of colleges of business are entering an increasingly complex and interrelated global business environment, but, in the views of several, without the skills and abilities necessary to contribute to their employers and society (e.g., Bennis & O'Toole, 2005). Waddock and Lozano (2013) state "we face a world in which management education is by many assessments in crisis for too narrowly and analytically orienting future managers who will need to lead in a complex, socially and ecologically fraught world, where simple answers just do not work" (p. 265). It may very well be that marketing education needs to place increased emphasis on the cognitive processes that operate when successful marketers deal with complex decisions (Smith, 2004). To wit, cognitive processes need to be modeled to aid students in implementing the body of marketing knowledge in the "real world."

Although the need for college graduates to be able to critically and strategically think globally is widely recognized (Bok, 2006) and although such thinking skills are often prominently included in the stated objectives and goals of most colleges of business (Bigelow, 2004), the success of colleges of businesses in successfully building these abilities in students is questionable (Waddock & Lozano, 2013). If colleges of business seek to improve their students' thinking skills, there may be a need to develop new pedagogical approaches to accomplish this. Smith (2014) suggests that strategic thinking skills involve drawing on the outputs of what he calls lower-order mental activities (e.g., perception, attention, memory, affect) as inputs into higher-order mental activities (e.g., problem solving, decision making). By developing strategic thinking skills, students become able to cognitively analyze multiple inputs to arrive at appropriate solutions. Research appears to indicate that most students do not possess these abilities (e.g., Arum & Roksa, 2011). Smith (2014) suggests the problem may lie in the way that thinking skills are addressed in colleges of business today – "we allow students to get by with a superficial mental competence that will not produce rigorous, insightful thought in practical situations" (p. 401).

This paper proposes a cognitive (mental) model for a strategic marketing management course. The mental model's main objective is to help students conceptualize and visualize the thinking behavior operating when successful marketing managers undertake heuristic marketing decision making and problem solving. First, a discussion about the nature of mental models and their appropriateness to a strategic marketing management course is presented. Next, the operational features of the proposed mental model are presented and illustrated. Finally, its application is explored.

STRATEGIC MATRIX

Mental Models

The discussion of marketing systems and general theories was elevated to formal debate by a *Journal of Marketing* article titled "Towards a Theory of Marketing" (Alderson & Cox, 1948). The debate helped trigger the development of the current body of strategic marketing management literature that legitimized marketing as discipline with its own language structure, classification schemes, scientific methodology, and practical applications. Another result is that many marketing educators have relied on content-based pedagogy to convey this information to students.

The debate and resulting literature also included a discussion of marketing systems and the implications of the interrelationships within and among the language structure and the classification schemes (Menon, Bharadwaj, Adidam, & Edison, 1999; also see Sheth, Gardner, and Garrett's (1988) chapter on the interactive-noneconomic schools of marketing). Many marketing educators, however, have arguably been lax in developing a pedagogy centered around teaching students methods to think about the marketing system holistically and integratively (i.e., using mental models). To this point Van Doren and Smith (1999) state:

The objective of academia in general, and marketing faculty specifically, must be to enhance the strategic thinking skills of individual managers and to assist them in developing the ability to help their organizations adapt to the future in a competitively superior way. Developing strategic thinking means building and updating mental models (p.147).

To think about marketing systems holistically and integratively, marketing students' education must go beyond a simple analytic approach to problem solving (Waddock & Lozano, 2013). An analytic approach is suitable for well-defined and constrained problems, such as those addressed in many business cases, rather than the situations typically encountered in the actual business world (Glen, Sucin, & Baughn, 2012). Indeed, in their analysis of popular MBA cases, Liang and Wang (2004) observed a persisting reliance on a limited analytic approach despite repeated calls for a deeper holistic approach. Reliance on an analytic approach to decision making has been viewed to be detrimental to preparing students for their careers (Clinehall & Clinehall, 2008; Pfeffer & Fong, 2002).

Mental models represent the way individuals structure their knowledge of a specific area (Xu & Yang 2010). They represent how individuals organize and view a specific knowledge area. Mental models are used in the business world as a means to capture increasingly complex market realities (Karakayo & Yannopoulis, 2010) by structuring and cognitively representing the business environment (Gary & Wood, 2011). Their purpose is to describe, explain, and predict within specified environments (Palmuen, Pelto, Peelumäki, & Lainema, 2013), simplifying and improving decision making by providing a basis for considering relevant and important information (Karakayo & Yannopoulis, 2010). The use of mental models have been shown to be advantageous – Gary and Wood (2011), for instance, report that managers with more accurate mental models achieve higher performance outcomes. Nowhere are the complexities in the business world greater than in the global arena. Mental models, therefore, seem to be particularly useful in global business settings. Mental models, for instance, have been used to holistically view offensive (Maignan & Lucas, 1997) and defensive (Karakayo & Yannopoulis, 2010) market entry strategies.

The importance of mental models in the context of learning is also being recognized (Nadkarni, 2003). Mental models affect how students analyze specific problem situations (Nadkami, 2003). Wang, Chiu, Lin, and Chou (2013) argue that correction and expansion of students' mental models is essential for learning to take place. A mental model in which students organize and view a knowledge area holistically permits students to perceive and incorporate interrelationships between constructs that otherwise may be overlooked or ignored in an analytic perspective. Holistic mental models have been observed to help students develop thinking and problem-solving skills by permitting them to see and synthesize diverse perspectives (Xu & Yang, 2010). Consequently, a holistic mental model for teaching strategic marketing management is presented.

A HOLISTIC MENTAL MODEL FOR TEACHING STRATEGIC MARKETING MANAGEMENT

Holistic thinking maintains that the whole is primary, that the parts are logically secondary but are not separate and distinct, and that the structure (e.g., the marketing system) is not the summation of the parts but has emergent properties. Integrative thinking may be defined as the process of linking (integrating) any one conceptual part of the structure (e.g., a single marketing concept or idea) with any other conceptual part of the structure. Consequently, the proposed Strategic Matrix has three pedagogical components. The first is a content itemization scheme to portray holistically the concepts and ideas of strategic marketing management. In this component, each of the marketing parts (concepts and ideas) is identified. The second is the use of a 3-dimensional SWOT (strengths, weaknesses, threats, and opportunities) mapping scheme to facilitate the conceptualization and visualization of heuristic tasks that involves thinking about the concepts and ideas presented in the itemization scheme. The third is the incorporation of integrative thinking into the SWOT mapping scheme.

The Strategic Matrix's Holistic Depiction of Strategic Marketing Management

The tables of contents in popular strategic marketing management textbooks present major and sub-headings that cover hundreds of concepts and ideas. To instill in students the idea that strategic marketing management is to be viewed as a "whole" system of interrelated parts, the Matrix presents an itemized outline of the concepts and ideas contained in the textbooks. To further instill in students the "whole" system and interrelated parts proposition, the Matrix substitutes the term "marketing parts" for marketing concepts and ideas. In an unscientific study of the tables of contents, glossaries, and indexes of five popular strategic marketing management textbooks, an average of 450 distinct concepts and ideas (marketing parts) were identified (Warren, 1992).

The Strategic Matrix's SWOT Mapping

Discussing strengths, weaknesses, opportunities, and threats (SWOT) has become a mainstay in teaching strategic marketing management. The use of SWOT as a component of the Strategic Matrix is based on the work of Piercy (1992). The benefits of SWOT have been identified to be simplicity (no extensive training or technical skills needed to use it); flexibility (can be used without extensive marketing information); allows the integration and synthesis of diverse qualitative and quantitative information; and fosters collaboration between managers responsible for different marketing parts. Usually, as a content-based learning tool, SWOT analysis is reduced to identifying the strengths of, weaknesses of, opportunities for, and threats to the marketing parts of a product. In case studies, SWOT analysis is often used to compile a list of determinants or causal elements related to the problem areas of a case.

SWOT, however, is not without shortcomings. Valentin (2005) and Panagiotou and van Wijen (2005) provide summaries of the critiques. Pickton and Wright (1998), for instance, critiqued SWOT and conclude that it is often used as a static analytical tool that is "mechanistic." The realities of strategy formulation, however, are more likely to be incremental, non-rational and irregular (i.e., more "organic" than "mechanic"). Everett (2014) and Yüksel and Dağdeviren (2007) suggest that many of the critiques of SWOT lie in misunderstanding the tool and/or misusing it. Similarly, Hill and Westbrook (1997) state "it could be argued that there is perhaps no reason why SWOT could not still be valuable" (p. 51).

Consequently, Yüksel and Dağdeviren (2007) suggest a means by which several of the shortcomings of SWOT can be overcome to improve strategy development. In the Strategic Matrix, SWOT is employed as a platform to stimulate thought in a means which overcomes several of the SWOT shortcomings identified. It is not used as a static tool to provide lists of items or "the answer," but it is used as the basis of an organic holistic process. SWOT also has a long history of being employed in global settings (e.g., Ng & Bloemraad, 2015; Hayat, 2014).

The Strategic Matrix's 1-D SWOT Map

Under the Strategic Matrix, students are instructed to view SWOT "organically." SWOT analysis is an ongoing thinking process. Tautologically, simply thinking about or discussing any of the marketing parts for a product is, in fact, a SWOT analysis. Cognitively, marketing managers are in an ongoing SWOT analysis mode by the very nature of their responsibilities. Contrary to the formal mechanistic reference to SWOT as a periodic tool to be called upon when needed, a SWOT analysis of marketing parts is naturally built within the manager's ongoing planning, implementing, and controlling strategies. In an attempt to conceptualize and visualize the 'organic' proposition of SWOT being a natural cognitive component of strategic marketing management, the Strategic Matrix begins with three (3) ordinal continuums to capture the degree of a marketing part's SWOT and then creates a 3-D SWOT mapping scheme to portray holistic strategic decision-making.

The first SWOT continuum reflects the marketing part's relative strengths and weaknesses. One extreme (+3) represents the assessment that the marketing part's internal strengths far outweigh any internal weaknesses it may have. The other extreme (-3) represents the assessment that the marketing part's internal weaknesses far outweigh any internal strengths it may have. The second continuum reflects the external opportunities associated with the marketing part. One extreme represents many actionable opportunities (+6) and the other represents no opportunities (0). The final continuum represents external threats with one extreme representing many serious threats (-6) and the other representing minimal or no threats (0). The primary purpose of the three ordinal continuums is to encourage students to recognize the dimensionality of SWOT. Locating a marketing part on each continuum obliges students to verify (with data and/or intuitive analysis) the location and to realize that a marketing part is not static – that its location may change dramatically within a short period of time.

In preparations for the 3-D SWOT mapping of marketing parts, students are instructed to consider the fact that marketing parts do not have equal importance to a product's success. Importance weights are used to indicate the perceived importance of any one marketing part. A marketing part receiving a zero is not subjected to SWOT analysis. A weight of 1 indicates that the marketing part has very little real contribution to the success (or failure) of a product, while a 5 represents a very strong contribution.

The Strategic Matrix's 3-D SWOT Map

To advance the study, the three continuums form a 3-D mapping of the marketing parts (see Figure 1). The Strategic Matrix uses the term "Status Coordinate" to identify a marketing part's 3-D location in any one of the eight (8) sections. The Status Coordinate is the marketing part's importance weight multiplied by its scale value on each of the three SWOT continuums. The absolute best 3-D location for a marketing part is +3 for strengths, +6 for opportunities and 0 for threats (located in Section #1). If this marketing part is given an importance weight of 5, its Status Coordinate is (+15, +30, 0). The

Figure 1. The strategic matrix 3-D SWOT map and status coordinates for each marketing part

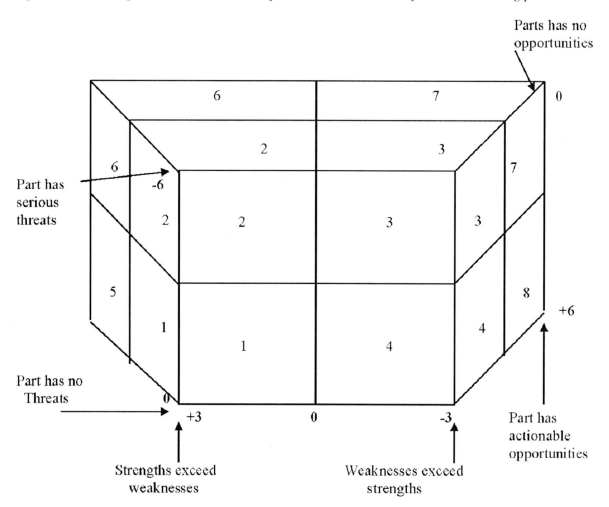

absolute worst 3-D Status Coordinate for a marketing part with an importance weight of 5 is (-15, 0, -30) located in Section #7.

The marketing parts do not exist in isolation, however. Instead, they dynamically interact with each other. In many situations, changing the Status Coordinates of one marketing part becomes a function of the past, present, and even forecasted nature of the Status Coordinates of other marketing parts. Decision-making involving the Status Coordinate for any one marketing part becomes an exercise in identifying and assessing its impact on the Status Coordinates of other marketing parts.

To facilitate the student's assessment of the relationships between (among) marketing parts, associative (integrative) thinking is used. As an introductory exercise, students are asked to think of any conceivable association between any two objects (e.g., a pencil and a blank sheet of paper). This exercise has produced results from the obvious statements that the pencil and paper are made from wood and are instruments in communication to the clever construction of pinwheels and paper airplanes using the pencil as a bomb. After this exercise, students perform free association between the Status Coordinates of two marketing parts (the instructor randomly selects a pair from the marketing parts in the Strategic Matrix's itemization scheme). Obviously, some pairings of marketing parts will not produce clear associations, but through the effort to find relationships, students come to realize that the thinking process is more important than the outcome. This is in accord with Beroggi's (2001) argument that policy decision making is a process, rather than a means to an end, stretching over a long time span in a dynamic environment. The possible permutations plus the many associations that may result between any two marketing parts overwhelms the imagination. Herein, students can consciously recognize the true dynamics of marketing and, in turn, articulate those dynamics to others.

The integration of the Status Coordinates of marketing parts helps students to address the notion of how making decisions for any one marketing part (i.e., changing its Status Coordinates) has accompanying costs and benefits. Beyond calculating the resource cost, the manager must judge (by research, experience, or intuition) the costs by way of negative effects that an action taken for one marketing part may have on the Status Coordinates of other marketing parts. This is weighed against judging the benefits to be achieved to changing the Status Coordinates of the targeted marketing part and any positive effects to the Status Coordinates of other marketing parts.

Referring back to the importance weights (0 to 5) assigned to each marketing part, students are informed that such weights can be determined by performing the above integration of marketing parts and cost/benefit judgments. Hence, a rule of thumb for assigning an importance weight is: the larger the number of marketing parts affected by the change in one marketing part, the higher the weight assigned to the marketing part.

Applications of the Strategic Matrix

The Strategic Matrix's itemization scheme, Status Coordinates, and the integration process may be used to broaden intellectual understanding of specific marketing issues raised in the strategic marketing management course. Through marketing issues such as portfolio analysis, market-entry analysis, cross-functional team decision-making, relationship marketing, diversity, mergers, and product life cycle analysis, students are to think about these marketing issues within the context of the Strategic Matrix's Status Coordinates and the integration process. The level of analysis used in the proposed matrix is flexible, broadening its usefulness. Instead of focusing on marketing parts, for instance, a product itself and/or a particular country or market can also be located within the 3-D SWOT map. Locating a product in any one section of the map essentially represents an analysis of the marketing parts that comprise a product, particularly for the marketing parts with high importance weights. To illustrate, an abstract of product portfolio analysis of a product within a selected market is offered.

Assume students are analyzing Product A in Market X. First, students are responsible for analyzing the marketing parts which comprise the product to be able to determine the position of the product within the selected market on the Matrix. Assuming that students determine the product/market to reside in section #7 of the 3-D SWOT map (the most disadvantaged section), two highly related alternatives may be suggested:

1. Dropping Product A from the portfolio of offerings in Market X; and
2. Proposing appropriate actions to save/reposition Product A in Market X.

For the first alternative, using Status Coordinates and integration work, students do a cost/benefit analysis of Product A's marketing parts within the context of Market X. A major part of the argument is that if dropped, resources used to support Product A in Market X can be redistributed to the marketing parts of other products in Market X or to the marketing parts of Product A or other products in other markets. On the other hand, dropping Product A from Market X also may adversely affect the sales of other products offered in that market. Hence, dropping Product A triggers an analysis of the 3-D SWOT locations of the other products and the Status Coordinates of each product's marketing parts. The main questions become which product(s) and which of the product's marketing parts should receive the freed up resources if Product A is dropped from Market A if this is deemed to be the optimal choice, and whether this action will adversely affect the sales of the company's other products in Market X.

The analysis for the first alternative (dropping Product A from Market X) is not complete at this point. The choice to drop Product A from the product portfolio in Market X may affect the success of Product A in other markets. Even if there are no marketing implications (which is most likely untrue), the choice to drop Product A in Market X may disrupt the manufacture of the product or adversely affect the cost of manufacture (e.g., lower production volume). Hence, it will be important for students to use the Strategic Matrix to explore the effects that dropping Product A may have on the Status Coordinates of Product A in other markets.

The second alternative involves saving Product A. Saving Product A raises the initial question of whether opportunities exist to permit the saving of the product and whether adequate strengths exist to take advantage of the opportunity(ies). (Given that few opportunities were regarded as existing for the product, students may determine that the product cannot be saved and that this alternative may not be feasible). If a viable opportunity does exist, how can it be pursued? Hence, attempting to save Product A in Market X also triggers an analysis of the 3-D SWOT locations of the other products and the Status Coordinates of the product's marketing parts. What would be required to save the product in this market? In other words, which marketing part(s) will need to receive additional resources to permit the saving of the product? Even if it is feasible to save the product, what will be the effect of this course of action the company's other products/markets? For instance, given that the supply of resources available to a company is typically finite, what will be the effect of investing additional resources into Product A in Market X? In other words, from which other product(s) or markets(s) will the additional resources come? Ideally, a resource reallocation will not negatively affect the Status Coordinates of the marketing parts of the "donor" product, but this is usually not the case. Students must analyze each of the other firm's other products and markets to gauge the resulting effect and to permit of a cost-benefit analysis on the effects of saving the product.

The above very brief overview illustrates how the Strategic Matrix may be used to a company's product portfolio and, by doing so, should raise several additional ideas of how the Strategic Matrix may be applied for other marketing issues.

FUTURE RESEARCH DIRECTIONS

In spite of the favorable anecdotal evidence from applying the Strategic Matrix to a classroom setting, the Strategic Matrix has yet to be empirically tested. Such testing will include the following research questions: Does the use of the Matrix affect how well students recall and recognize marketing concepts and ideas? Does use of the Matrix aid in understanding that marketing knowledge is best understood in a holistic and integrative context? Does it improve actual workplace marketing decision-making? Does it enhance the quality of a marketing manager's thinking processes? Even without empirical support, the authors' claim of validity rests in the fact that the body of strategic marketing management knowledge is not neglected in the classroom. If nothing else, the Strategic Matrix can be considered a delivery system that any marketing instructor can incorporate into his/her lesson plan to ensure an analysis of strategic marketing issues and to build students' ability to think strategically.

CONCLUSION

The importance of the use of appropriate mental models in the business world is recognized. "With appropriate models, managers should be able to improve their capacity to deal with dynamically complex environments in order to achieve long-term success" (Capelo & Dias, 2009, p. 629). Given the added complexities inherent in global markets, mental models seem to be play an important role in global marketing. Consequently, marketing educators need to be dedicated to pedagogy that prepares students for the complexities of the global business environment. This paper argues that mental models should be given more attention in this effort. Van Doren and Smith (1999) are adamant about the need to build and update mental models as a bridge to enhancing marketing managers' strategic thinking skills. The Strategic Matrix, a proposed mental model, was presented with this in mind.

The Strategic Matrix's pedagogical components were designed to help students conceptualize and visualize the heuristic thinking that contributes to successful marketing decision making and problem solving. The purpose of the Matrix is to add complexity to student's thinking processes – Nadkarni (2003) states "complexity of mental models is an important indicator of learning because it reflects the ability of a student to identify key issues and make dense connections between these issues in solving complex problems" (p. 335). Furthermore, students are instructed in using the Strategic Matrix as a self-teaching tool to give intellectual depth to marketing issues which are often, because of time constraints, superficially covered in the classroom.

One of the authors of this paper has used the Strategic Matrix exclusively in graduate strategic marketing management classes and EMBA classes. The author has also used a variation of the Strategic Matrix (i.e., far less usage of the 3-D SWOT mapping) in undergraduate marketing courses including business to business marketing and personal selling classes. Though anecdotal, comments from a number of former graduate and undergraduate students have attested to the model's success in providing them with valuable business skills. Specifically, they have informed the authors that the Strategic Matrix vastly enhanced their ability to see their own organization's marketing efforts more holistically and integratively and improved their decision making and problem solving skills. A number of students stated during their organization's decision making and/or problem solving sessions, the Strategic Matrix's 3-D SWOT mapping gave them decided advantages over their colleagues. Furthermore, after the final was given in an EMBA class, the authors requested that they allow a taping of their analysis of the Strategic Matrix. These 14 executives unanimously stated that they never thought about the products (and services) offered by their organizations in the manner forwarded by the Strategic Matrix. They noted an initial difficulty in "getting out of the box" to understand how Status Coordinates of two or more marketing parts can be examined holistically and integratively and how the Strategic Matrix could be used to elaborate marketing issues. Once they overcame earlier mindsets, however, the Strategic Matrix was found by them to be quite intellectually stimulating and very easy and profitable to apply to their own environments.

REFERENCES

Alderson, W., & Cox, R. (1948). Towards a theory of marketing. *Journal of Marketing, 13*(2), 137–152. doi:10.2307/1246823

Arum, R., & Roksa, J. (2011). *Academically adrift: Limited learning on college campuses.* Chicago, IL: University of Chicago Press.

Bennis, W., & O'Toole, J. (2005). How business schools lost their way. *Harvard Business Review, 83*(5), 96–104. PMID:15929407

Beroggi, G. E. G. (2001). Visual-interactive decision modeling (VIDEMO) in policy management: Bridging the gap between analytic and conceptual decision modeling. *European Journal of Operational Research, 128*(2), 338–350. doi:10.1016/S0377-2217(00)00076-X

Bigelow, J. D. (2004). Using problem-based learning to develop skills in solving unstructured problems. *Journal of Management Education, 28*(5), 591–609. doi:10.1177/1052562903257310

Bok, D. C. (2006). *Our underachieving colleges: A candid look at how much students learn and why they should be learning more.* Princeton, NJ: Princeton University Press.

Capelo, C., & Dias, J. F. (2009). A feedback learning and mental models perspective on strategic decision making. *Educational Technology Research and Development, 57*(5), 629–644. doi:10.1007/s11423-009-9123-z

Clinebell, S. K., & Clinebell, J. M. (2008). The tension in business education between academic rigor and real-world relevance: The role of executive professors. *Academy of Management Learning & Education, 7*(1), 99–107. doi:10.5465/AMLE.2008.31413867

Everett, R. F. (2014). A crack in the foundation: Why SWOT might be less than effective in market sensing analysis. *Journal of Marketing and Management, 1*(1), 58–78.

Gary, M. S., & Wood, R. (2001). Mental models, decision rules, and performance heterogeneity. *Strategic Management Journal, 32*(6), 569–594. doi:10.1002/smj.899

Glen, R., Suciu, C., & Baughn, C. (2014). The need for design thinking in business schools. *Academy of Management Learning & Education, 13*(4), 653–667. doi:10.5465/amle.2012.0308

Greene, S., & Boa, Y. (2009). Addressing AACSB global and technology requirements: Exploratory assessment of a marketing management mssignment. *Journal of Teaching in International Business, 29*(4), 272–292. doi:10.1080/08975930903405043

Hayat, S. A. (2014). Indonesian global expansion: A case study. *International Journal of Global Business, 7*(2), 9–32.

Hill, T., & Westbrook, R. (1997). SWOT analysis: It's time for a product recall. *Long Range Planning, 30*(1), 46–52. doi:10.1016/S0024-6301(96)00095-7

Karakaya, F., & Yannopoulos, P. (2010). Defensive strategy framework in global markets: A mental models approach. *European Journal of Marketing, 44*(7/8), 1077–1100. doi:10.1108/03090561011047535

Liang, N., & Wang, J. (2004). Implicit mental models in teaching cases: An empirical study of popular MBA cases in the United States and China. *Academy of Management Learning & Education, 3*(4), 397–413. doi:10.5465/AMLE.2004.15112545

Maignan, I., & Lukas, B. A. (1997). Entry mode decisions: The role of managers' mental models. *Journal of Global Marketing, 10*(4), 7–23. doi:10.1300/J042v10n04_02

Menon, A., Bharadwaj, S. G., Adidam, P. T., & Edison, S. W. (1999). Antecedents and consequences of marketing strategy making: A model and a test. *Journal of Marketing, 63*(2), 18–40. doi:10.2307/1251943

Moskal, P., Ellis, T., & Keon, T. (2008). Summary of assessment in higher education and the management of student-learning data. *Academy of Management Learning & Education, 7*(2), 269–278. doi:10.5465/AMLE.2008.32712624

Nadkarni, S. (2003). Instructional methods and mental models of students: An empirical investigation. *Academy of Management Learning & Education, 2*(4), 335–351. doi:10.5465/AMLE.2003.11901953

Ng, E., & Bloemraad, I. (2015). A SWOT analysis of multiculturalism in Canada, Europe, Mauritius, and South Korea. *The American Behavioral Scientist, 59*(6), 619–636. doi:10.1177/0002764214566500

Palmunen, L.-M., Pelto, E., Paalumäki, A., & Lainema, T. (2013). Formation of novice business students' mental models through simulation gaming. *Simulation & Gaming, 44*(6), 846–868. doi:10.1177/1046878113513532

Panagiotou, G., & Wijen, R. (2005). The telescopic observations framework: An attainable strategic tool. *Marketing Intelligence & Planning, 23*(2), 155–171. doi:10.1108/02634500510589912

Pfeffer, J., & Fong, C. (2002). The end of business schools? Less success than meets the eye. *Academy of Management Learning & Education, 1*(1), 78–95. doi:10.5465/AMLE.2002.7373679

Pickton, D. W., & Wright, S. (1998). What's SWOT in strategic analysis? *Strategic Change, 7*(2), 101–109. doi:10.1002/(SICI)1099-1697(199803/04)7:2<101::AID-JSC332>3.0.CO;2-6

Piercy, N. (1992). *Market-led strategic change.* Oxford, UK: Butterworth-Heineman.

Sheth, J. N., Gardner, D. M., & Garrett, D. E. (1988). *Marketing theory: Evolution and evaluation.* New York, NY: John Wiley & Sons.

Smith, G. F. (2014). Assessing business student thinking skills. *Journal of Management Education, 38*(3), 384–411. doi:10.1177/1052562913489028

Stevens, G. E. (2000). The art of running a business school in the new millennium: A dean's perspective. *S.A.M. Advanced Management Journal, 65*(3), 21–28.

Valentin, E. (2006). Away with SWOT analysis: Use defensive/offensive evaluation instead. *Journal of Applied Business Research, 21*(2), 91–104.

Van Doren, D. C., & Smith, D. B. (1999). Scenario planning: A new approach to teaching marketing strategy. *Journal of Marketing Education, 21*(2), 146–155. doi:10.1177/0273475399212008

Waddock, S., & Lozano, J. M. (2013). Developing more holistic management education: Lessons learned from two programs. *Academy of Management Learning & Education, 12*(2), 265–284. doi:10.5465/amle.2012.0002

Wang, T.-H., Chiu, M.-H., Lin, J.-W., & Chou, C.-C. (2013). Diagnosing students' mental models via the web-based mental models diagnosis system. *British Journal of Educational Technology, 44*(2), E49–E48. doi:10.1111/j.1467-8535.2012.01328.x

Warren, H. (1992). Implementing holistic education in marketing courses. *Marketing Education Review, 2*(2), 21–24. doi:10.1080/10528008.1992.11488361

Xu, Y., & Yang, Y. (2010). Student learning in business simulation: An empirical investigation. *Journal of Education for Business, 85*(4), 223–228. doi:10.1080/08832320903449469

Yüksel, İ., & Dağdeviren, M. (2007). Using the analytic network process (ANP) in a SWOT analysis – A case study for a textile firm. *Information Sciences, 177*(16), 3364–3382. doi:10.1016/j.ins.2007.01.001

KEY TERMS AND DEFINITIONS

Analytic Thinking Process: Thinking that involves choosing a solution from a set of given alternatives.

Heuristic Thinking Process: Thinking that involves developing new and/or imaginative solutions to problems.

Holism: The idea that the whole is greater than the parts.

Integrative Thinking: The idea that concepts and constructs are interrelated.

Marketing Part: Marketing concepts and ideas.

Mental Model: The way individuals structure their knowledge of a specific area.

Status Coordinate: A marketing part's 3-D location on the Strategic Matrix.

SWOT: A tool involving identifying strengths, weaknesses, opportunities, and threats.

Chapter 6
Turning Marketing Students into Active Citizens:
The Learning of Consumption and Social-Related Marketing in Thailand

Krittinee Nuttavuthisit
Chulalongkorn University, Thailand

ABSTRACT

This chapter discusses the learning of consumption and marketing within the context of social-related issues. The objectives are to expand dimensions of marketing education into a wider perspective beyond the economic focus to the social domain. Exploring the different contexts can help uncover a deeper perspective beyond general concepts of consumption and marketing. Moreover, considering the social aspect can enhance a longer perspective of business beyond current profit maximization, particularly in the 21st century with its emphasis on sustainability. The learning process can follow the four main steps of understanding the problem, introducing the solution, engaging participation (with real actions to support the project or organization), and evaluating output and outcome. These processes are elaborated together with examples of real practices and summarized learning derived from the classes conducted in Thailand. Not only can this benefit the students, but also the overall business and the society by turning marketing students into active citizens.

INTRODUCTION

The 21st century demands people who can understand and manage the balance of people, planet, and profit realities. To create business people who have a good grounding in understanding beyond business knowledge to appreciate cultural literacy, ethics, analytics, and sustainability, it is better to begin early with education. With today's focus on more collaborative efforts, it is crucial to develop people who can become active citizens. For business school students, this means their contribution not only in donating allocated profits (aka philanthropy), but also incorporating social development into their everyday

DOI: 10.4018/978-1-4666-9784-3.ch006

practices. Furthermore, society has recognized the need and called for action from the business sector to take part in improving social conditions.

"Consumption and Marketing" is the subject fundamental to most businesses, particularly marketing, since it involves analysis of consumer behavior and its implications for developing marketing strategies. Overall, the topic includes how to explore and interpret consumer psychology, sociocultural influences, and consumer decision-making. With its essence of understanding relevant groups and delivering values matching their demands, this subject of Consumption and Marketing is in fact applicable to many other contexts such as international relations, technological advancement, and social development. For instance, many countries have been focusing on acquiring soft power through the promotion of cultural values, entertainment, or commercializing products and services in other countries. This concept is based on the ability to influence others by way of cooperating rather than the traditional coercion (aka hard power) (Nye, 2004). Thus, understanding Consumption and Marketing is central to the programs. Another example is the technological advancement of alternative energy, which relates to the way in which people consume and save energy as well as success of marketing efforts in breaking into the dominant fossil fuel market. For social development, Consumption and Marketing can be utilized to stimulate changes in people's behaviors, for instance, bike riding and recycling to reduce global warming.

Realizing the importance of Consumption and Marketing and its implications in different contexts, this chapter aims to connect the subject to the goal of developing business school students who seek to generate meaningful initiatives beyond achieving business profits to creating real benefits to society. Particularly, the chapter features summarized concepts of how to organize the learning and engage students' participation in social development projects. Based on the classes conducted in Thailand, where active citizenship has become a principle concern, this specific case approach demonstrates both overview perspectives of Consumption and Social-related Marketing and example practices related to the country's contextual situations.

CONSUMPTION AND MARKETING IN SUPPORT OF SOCIAL DEVELOPMENT

Social development refers to the need to put people first in attaining sustainable growth and a better quality of life. With its central role to address complex relationships between societies, states and communities, social development requires collective efforts of all stakeholders where all can contribute according to their interests and capabilities. In the past, the business sector was generally viewed as the source of donations since business operations tended to be disconnected from social development activities. Therefore, their allocated resources were mainly contributions, in cash or in kind. In the early days, the concept of corporate social responsibility (CSR) began with the goal of upholding ethical practices in managing business and later extended to the acquisition of resources and production of products and services with considerations of public benefit. Table 1 explains the development of CSR. Over time the practice has become integral to the corporate strategy. Therefore, it is evident that more businesses are now organizing their own initiatives to support social development while there has been increased use of business knowledge in a variety of social development projects.

Consumption and Marketing is one of the areas in business practice that can directly yield benefits in support of social development. The subject involves an interrelated relationship between analyses of consumption behaviors and development of marketing to satisfy the needs, wants, demands, or desires of target consumers and hence produce returns (e.g. sales, profits). The focused topics include understanding

Table 1. The development of CSR

Though it is claimed that CSR is not a new development, the publication of Howard R. Bowen's book, Social Responsibilities of the Businessman in 1953 seemed to mark the beginning of this concept. Bowen explicitly called on business leaders to always uphold ethical principles in making business plans and decisions. In 1954, Peter Drucker stated in his widely recognized book, The Practice of Management, that the practice of public responsibility must be considered as one of the major goals of business development.

From the firm basis initiated previously, CSR in the 1960s continued to be extensively discussed, mainly in terms of the meaning of CSR and its relevance to the economy. This extended the notion of CSR beyond general ethics. William C. Frederick, in his article "The growing concern over business responsibility" (1960), referred to the responsible use of society capitals (e.g. natural resources, cultural assets) in furthering the business and the economy. Joseph Mcquire, supported this broader view of CSR in his book, Business and Society (1963) and suggested that business should take into account the general public beyond the markets and matters related to the specified business only. Others, such as Milton Friedman, the author of Capitalism and Freedom (1962), argued that the responsibility of business is to maximize profit for the shareholders. This is consistent with the comment by T. Leavitt from the Harvard Business School who emphasized that corporate welfare makes good sense as long as it makes good economic sense. In this period, CSR was mostly analyzed at the macro socioeconomic level, and there were some questions about the economic value of CSR since it could not be calculated directly as could other business transactions.

Entering the 1970s, the debates continued with some attempts to reach a compromise. While Milton Friedman insisted in his 1970 article titled "the social responsibility of a business is to increase its profits", he remained open to the possibility that some acts of social responsibility could lead to long-term profit for the company. On the contrary, Keith Davis, stressed the "Iron law of responsibility" (1967) and explained that when the company does not adhere to social responsibility, it will lose its considerable position in society to the other businesses who will assume such responsibility instead. Despite the opposite standpoints, it is observed that both recognize that benefits for business can simultaneously yield benefits to the society. This is regarded as the enlightened self-interest model that demonstrates the transformation of CSR from normative ethics to a concrete understanding of its causes and effects.

With the more specific approach, CSR in the 1980s moved towards more micro-analytical perspectives with a focus on stakeholder engagement. Thomas M. Jones proposed in the article, "Corporate social responsibility revisited, redefined," to emphasize the process of CSR rather than the input and output as illustrated earlier. During that time, Peter Drucker revisited his view from the 1950s and wrote the article, "The new meaning of corporate social responsibility" (1984), suggesting the shift from viewing CSR as a general principle to a strategy that can enhance better returns for business. Subsequent research supported the concept with evidence of a direct relationship between social contribution and business performance.

Tangible and clear benefits led to the expansion of CSR from the 1990s until now with continued studies in both academic and practical aspects which suggest that CSR is essential to business profitability. Thus, CSR has now become one of the core business functions central to the corporate strategy rather than being a separate, additional unit.

of "consumer psychology" which refers to the internal influences (i.e. motivation, perception, learning, attitude, personality) that affect consumers' decision-making processes. Motivation is the driving force within individuals that impels them to consume. Next, consumption is based on what consumers perceive to be reality including information from both sensory input and subconscious perception. During consumption, consumers continually learn or acquire knowledge that serves as feedback and provides the basis for future, related behavior. Consumers then form an attitude or a learned predisposition to behave in a consistently favorable or unfavorable way with respect to a given object in a specific situation. The inner psychological characteristics both determine and reflect consumer personality, which explains how a person responds to the external environment, for instance, marketing strategies.

Besides the internal influences, there is a wide range of external factors in "consumer sociocultural backgrounds" such as culture, cross-culture, subculture, and social class. Culture represents the sum total of learned beliefs, values, and customs that serve to direct the consumer behavior of members of a particular society. However, globalization drives the impact of cross-culture which describes the similarities and differences between the consumers of different societies or nations. Next, members of the same society may be segmented based on subcultures such as generation, gender, ethnicity, and religion. Consumer society may also be categorized according to different social classes which indicate consumers with relatively similar social status and lifestyle.

Consumer sociocultural backgrounds and consumer psychology both play important roles in "consumer decision-making." During the process of decision-making, consumers must recognize that a need exists, make a pre-purchase search, and evaluate alternatives before deciding to try, and later repeat purchases if they are satisfied in the post-purchase evaluation. This information becomes consumers' experience and serves to influence their future behaviors.

Though theories of consumer behavior, with the three major aspects of consumer psychology, sociocultural background, and consumer decision-making, are mainly developed based on the business perspectives, learning this subject can also support the other missions. In this case, it can help identify target a group of people to engage in social development, analyze their behaviors and prepare strategies that can persuade them to take action. These implementations of Consumption and Social-related Marketing are demonstrated in initiatives ranging from charity-based activities (e.g. fundraising) to more business-oriented functions (e.g. selling merchandise to raise funds for social causes) and finally the development of a new model such as social enterprise, which combines a business practice with social development concept.

Fundraising is one of the major means of gathering support from people who want to help further social development. From a business perspective, soliciting donations can be quite challenging and different from normal selling practices because donors must be sold on supporting the causes rather than the benefits of any products or services. The strategy must engage learning of the social issues, which can sometimes be too distant and complicated, and persuade belief in the efforts to realize some additional benefits beyond the good deeds. Fundraising strategy has been extensively studied by the non-profit sector. But recently it has been extended to integrate learning of other relevant subjects, e.g. consumption and marketing, and digital marketing, which can promote advancement of both social administration programs and marketing education. An example from a world-famous campaign in 2014, the ice bucket challenge, demonstrates how awareness of the Amyotrophic Lateral Sclerosis (ALS) disease was raised via direct learning i.e. dumping a bucket of ice water on one's head to experience numbness caused by the disease. Additionally, by filming one's own act, donating, and sending a clip to challenge other nominated participants to do the same, this strategy, combining altruistic, entertaining, self-congratulatory, and social motives, has become one of the most successful viral marketing and crowd funding campaigns. It was reported that the ALS Association received almost 80 million USD from 1.7 million donors in one month, while the organization raised only 64 million USD funds in the whole of 2013 (TIME, 2014).

Next, the subject of Consumption and Marketing can be used in more applied business initiatives such as selling merchandise as part of fundraising strategies. Currently many social development organizations are trying to become more independent and sustainable by not relying solely on donations or grants but selling products or services to generate income. An example is the sale of UNICEF cards and products which reached a historical high performance of 77 Million USD in 1995 (UNICEF, 2014). But with the change of consumption (e.g. on-line communications), this business has declined and UNICEF has decided to change the business model from centralized, in-house operations to third-party licensing and local sourcing. This helps increase the variety of products that suit local consumer interests, and brings better returns on investment, while leveraging the brand equity. A similar idea can be observed in cause-related marketing when a business sells specific items (e.g. limited editions) with the communicated objective of raising funds for some identified social cause. An example is Product Red launched in 2006 that has since become one of the largest cause-related marketing campaigns with a number of global companies (e.g. Apple, Nike, Coca-Cola, Starbucks, Gap) featuring their products with the red color and licensed brand, (PRODUCT)RED, stating the portion of their profits to be donated to the Global Fund to help eliminate HIV/AIDS in Africa. It was reported that Product Red has contributed 150 Million USD to the Fund (Global Fund, 2010).

Finally at the business model level, Consumption and Marketing can be applied in operating a social enterprise that is a business, either for-profit or non-profit by its structure, working to achieve the goal of social development rather than maximizing returns for shareholders. The definition of social enterprise remains quite broad, from running a normal business but allocating a major part of profit to address social causes to running a business operating with the goal of addressing social causes at the same time. An example is Grameen Bank, the Nobel peace prize-winning microfinance organization in Bangladesh working to provide small loans to the underserved people who do not have access to formal sources of finance to be used in pursuing normal livelihoods, such as self-employment. Unlike the conventional financial institutes, Grameen Bank does not require collateral but utilizes mutual trust among community members to drive success of high repayment. This social enterprise was recognized for its efforts to create economic and social development from grass roots with the performance of more than seven million borrowers averaging 100 USD each in 2006, when the award was received (Nobel prize, 2014).

With the greater impact of understanding and applying Consumption and Marketing in support of the broader contexts such as social development, business schools are therefore responsible for promoting such knowledge and skills among their students in order for them to become meaningful human resources in society. However, despite the significance of this subject, it is not always easy to engage business schools students, or any other people, to become active citizens. Based on the continual efforts in conducting Consumption and Marketing classes in Thailand and attempts to engage students' participation in social development, this chapter discusses how to facilitate such learning with the objectives of expanding *dimensions* of marketing education into a *wider* perspective beyond the economic focus to the social domain. Exploring the different contexts can help uncover a *deeper* perspective beyond general concepts of consumption and marketing. Considering the social aspect can enhance a *longer* perspective of business beyond current profit maximization to the emphasis on sustainability. It is necessary to clearly communicate these objectives to students in order to promote real and strong interest in advancing their studies while, at the same time, contributing to the development of active citizenship.

LEARNING CONSUMPTION AND SOCIAL-RELATED MARKETING: THE CASE OF THAILAND

Thailand is a Southeast Asian country with a population of approximately 67 million. The country was an absolute monarchy for over seven centuries until the 1932 Revolution that led Thailand into the era of democracy with a constitutional monarchy. The movement towards Western modernity (e.g. in politics and economics) was criticized as being abrupt and alien to most people at that time. Hence, during the early phase of democratization, the country still depended on the authorities while ordinary people were not much involved in the country's development as they believed that the government could exercise power in their best interests. It was the civil uprisings against oppression in the 1970's that gave rise to the power of the people. Though people's participation was given more emphasis, barriers in the Thai political context still resulted in rather inefficient bureaucracy with the domination of entrenched interest groups (Rigg, 1991) such as the army, politicians, civil servants, and business tycoons. Most efforts were aimed at advancing the country's economic growth capitalizing on the country's abundant resources and its strategic location in the region.

In spite of the growth of Thailand's economy, this approach seemed to disregard human and social development. Like many emerging countries, Thailand is facing the problem of the increasing gap between the rising growth of economy and the lagging improvement of social standards. Evidently the advancement of the business sector and economic expansion does not translate into better quality of life for most people but in fact creates further problems of inequality. In Thailand, the problem of income distribution seems to be enduring, with the top 20% earning more than half of the income share (54% in 1998 and 55% in 2007) and the bottom 20% earning less than 5% (4.58% in 1998 and 4.3% in 2007). In terms of social inequality, there exist variations in the quality of the social services (e.g. education, healthcare) provided to Thais depending on their socioeconomic status. Some disadvantaged groups, especially the poor, have restricted access to the judicial system, administration process, and public resources. While those who can earn more seek better opportunities to improve their standard of living, those at lower levels of the pyramid are left with minimal welfare benefits. This can potentially cause separations and breakdowns not only on a national, but also on a global scale in today's interconnected world.

Nevertheless, the economic progress of Thailand continued until the financial collapse in 1997 leading to the major Asian economic crisis. Realizing the need to focus on sustainability, subsequent programs were redirected towards incorporating all aspects of political, social, and economic development. Unfortunately, though this effort was intended to engage all relevant stakeholders, only a few influential groups (particularly from the business sector) participated still with the aim to take advantage of the country's policy at large. To gain support from the general public, more emphasis was placed on short-term returns in relation to some political agendas (aka populism). The mismanagement has yielded disorder and fragmentation in the country as witnessed in the continual civil unrest over the past few years until the military government took control in 2014.

Currently the major sentiment in Thailand is that everyone is accountable for the country's development. From the business perspective, many businesses have now taken serious steps to advance their efforts in CSR. Prayukvong and Olsen (2009) suggested that many companies in Thailand are involved in philanthropy and there is a dramatic increase in CSR discussions, initiatives, awards, and workshops, as well as institutes such as the Corporate Social Responsibility. Wellbeing research involving 100,000 people in Thailand (Khon Thai Monitor, 2012) revealed a lack of satisfaction with business involvement, specifically in the creation of substantial and long-term benefits for society. Comments suggested the need for businesses to reevaluate their approaches such as changing from event-based CSR activities organized by the CSR department to engaging everyone in the company and combining CSR into their everyday practices. Thus, it is crucial to let business people become aware, prepare, and collaborate to tackle challenges in other aspects such as social development. Particularly with the rather close-knit, collectivistic society of Thailand, business and other sectors are quite interrelated. As witnessed, many business persons have become key opinion leaders in matters of sociopolitical development and they are compelled to join forces in solving multiple problems in the country. Moreover, with the less structured establishment of social welfare and benefits, well-designed socially and environmentally responsible products and services can to a great extent influence the wellbeing of the general public. Therefore, promoting business engagement in improving the social conditions can significantly contribute to the better development of the country. These various efforts represent a good platform to learn about Consumption and Social-related Marketing in Thailand.

Additionally, due to unique characteristics of Thai culture, learning from this specific context can help advance descriptive understanding of the subject. For instance, one of the most important cultural values, inculcated in the dominant influence of Buddhism, is to be considerate and try to help people who are suffering (Vichit-Vadakan, 2002). Merit making is widely practiced through philanthropy, charity, sponsoring, volunteering, or sharing. It is believed that this might help improve conditions in the future of this or the next life. Thus, it is evident that Thai people can be quite generous in giving, from small-scale responses to begging, to large-scale disaster donations, with no doubt or query about the cause and how the money is being handled. When interacting with other people, it is important to maintain smooth relationships and avoid causing inconvenience or trouble (aka *kreng-jai*) to others (e.g. by asking for detailed information or monitoring processes). The prompt willingness to share can help speed the initial efforts but at the same time inhibit the continued cooperation because of less concrete engagement. As a result, Thailand is ranked in the top 5 countries according to the 2012 World Giving Index, averaging 76% of people in the country donating money in the month prior to interview, but achieves a lower level of active citizenship with only 18% of people engaged in volunteering (Charities Aid Foundation, 2012).

This leads to intertwined problems such as dependence on the authorities and corruption because people rely on the materialistic means (e.g. money) rather than volunteering which requires more understanding and engagement in the development process. It is stressed that civic participation can help promote greater efficiency, more accountability and transparency of resource allocation and development in society (Fung & Wright, 2001). Hence, increasing active citizenship is the key to genuine and sustainable poverty alleviation, as it can enhance ownership and commitment among diverse groups of people (Chambers, 1983), promote collaborative networks, and finally help reduce the mounting problem of inequality that has been present strongly among communities with passive citizens.

TURNING MARKETING STUDENTS INTO ACTIVE CITIZENS OF THAILAND

Realizing the importance of promoting active citizenship in Thailand, it seems quite natural that the youth would be the right target because they are more open and full of energy. Similarly at the global level, Youth and active citizenship are widely discussed as the young people are perceived as 'citizens in the making' (Marshall, 1950, p. 25) and therefore they have become the main target of policies to increase active citizenship over the past decade. The recent research of 4,000 young people, aged 18-25 years, in Thailand illustrated that more than half expressed their desire to see change in society and specifically demanded that the country's leaders practice good governance with no corruption for the people's benefit (Khon Thai Youth Monitor, 2014). Interestingly, while the youth in Thailand are aware of the problem as well as the need to improve the nation, when asked about their contribution, more than half mentioned passive roles such as not causing problems to others and being a good student, explaining that they are too young to make a difference.

From a business school perspective, there is a serious need to foster students' (who represent the leaders of the younger generation) active engagement. However, it is recognized that learning must be carefully designed so that students become motivated and engaged in understanding and applying the subject (i.e. Consumption and Marketing in this case) in support of the broader context such as social development. As proposed by Jansen, Chioncel, and Dekkers (2006), educating active citizenship can be achieved by linking the context of practice to the content of learning. Students should learn to critically analyze information about the particular context in conjunction with overall situations. Next, they should be facilitated opportunities and access to experience a wide range of citizenship activities as well as how to monitor and evaluate the practices. This chapter proposes that the learning process can follow the four main steps of understanding the problem, introducing the solution, engaging participation (with real actions to support the project or organization), and evaluating output and outcome.

In the following section, these processes are elaborated together with examples of real practices and summarized learning derived from the Consumption and Marketing classes conducted at the Sasin Graduate Institute of Business Administration, Thailand (AACSB, EQUIS). The main approach for this course is to facilitate opportunities for students to attain hands-on experience from group assignments to in-class exercises, fieldwork, and projects. These various initiatives present broader opportunities to explore the different pedagogical approaches. Moreover, with a mixture of local students (half of whom have been educated in Western countries) and foreign full-time and exchange MBA students, the discussion also sheds light on the topic of cultural diversity.

Step 1: Understanding the Problem

Understanding the social problem is fundamental to any further development. A deeper view of the issue can lead to more opportunities to overcome the challenges while producing more active citizens who can identify the options and limitations inherent in social development practices. But how to connect with business/marketing students who may not be familiar with, or have little interest in, many social subjects can be difficult. To elaborate on current situations and explain major causes of the problem, both macro perspectives (e.g. impact on relevant stakeholders) and micro perspectives (e.g. personal stories of the affected group) are needed. The macro view can help emphasize the importance of the matter and bring it closer to students' lives, while the micro stories can help move them emotionally.

An example is derived from the case of Yaowawit School described in Table 2. Yaowawit is a boarding school founded to care for orphans from the Tsunami in 2004 and later expanded to include other disadvantaged children. When discussing the case, students were first provided with macro information about the large-scale troubles that many unfortunate children are currently facing in the country, ranging from poverty to low quality of education, psychical and mental health problems. These have consequently led to a multiplicity of entangled social concerns such as drug addiction, violence, crime, all of which can eventually affect everyone's lives. Like most case studies, many claimed solutions to these problems lie in education. Yet there has never been enough support from government welfare alone. Looking closer at the micro perspectives of Yaowawit children's backgrounds, all have been subjected to various kinds of trauma from a young girl being abused by family members to a homeless boy wandering around to find food from garbage. Hearing so many of these stories (with due respect to the children's privacy and confidentiality) immediately engages students into serious concern about the situation and the need to take part in tackling the problems of this vulnerable group in society.

Learning from the Yaowawit case suggested that it is important to make students feel involved and accountable for the situation. While both macro and micro perspectives are needed, cultural differences among students could also play an important part. It was observed that students with Western backgrounds (e.g. growing up or studying in Western countries) seemed to pay attention to learning about the overview (macro) information such as inquiring about education policies, and foster care systems while those of the Asian (i.e. Thai) background seemed to be moved by the individual (micro) stories. With regard to CSR perspectives, it was suggested that the Western ideas seemed to focus on laws and disciplines whereas Thai concepts are based on the individual's spirit (Prayukvong & Olsen, 2009). Nevertheless, both perspectives have their limitations as the macro information can be too distant and create the perception of the problem being too large to handle while the micro, emotional information can be too personal and susceptible to change. Therefore, to gain thorough understanding of the problem both perspectives must be combined in order to reach both cognitive and emotional commitment.

Table 2. Yaowawit School case

The Tsunami of December 2004 caused widespread devastation in the southern part of Thailand. The tidal wave swept away lives, properties, and hope. Many people were left homeless after 58,550 homes were destroyed and another 6,824 homes were damaged. In addition, 882 children were orphaned. But just as these unfortunate victims were sinking down under the devastating effects of the tidal wave, they were pulled back to life by many helping hands. One of the efforts was through the kindness of the Children's World Academy Foundation which aims to provide education, (food and shelter) and living support to children in need between four and eighteen years of age. Mr. Philipp Graf von Hardenberg, an entrepreneur and the founder of this organization, initiated the Yaowawit public welfare boarding school opened in April 2006.

I believe that the most important parts of my vision were and are ...one, the children must be able to break out of the vicious circle of poverty by receiving a fundamentally first class school and vocational education. Two, Yaowawit School must be a project mainly run and supervised by Thai people. And lastly, Yaowawit School must be able to generate its own income so all people involved feel responsible for the future of the project. – Philipp Graf von Hardenberg, Founder

Hardenberg's attempts, together with support of several friends and partners, made possible the realization of the Yaowawit School project. The school, situated on a large 22 hectare plantation in the village Kapong, is approximately 125 km north of the city Phuket and about 65 km east of the tourist spot KhaoLak. The school is located in an orchard outside Kapong village with a unique landscape of hills and valleys, tropical forests, creeks, lakes, and gardens.

Yaowawit School was originally designed to support children and orphans who suffered from the tsunami aftermath. Later it was extended to include disadvantaged children living in poverty or tolerating unacceptable social circumstances, e.g., being forced into a life of begging or prostitution. The school mission is to provide a community of well being and care where children can obtain a first class education and practical training. The curriculum is designed to meet Thai educational standards, the students' needs, and the regional situation. Children will not only learn the required academic subjects but also acquire practical skills, craftsmanship as well as entrepreneurial spirit and knowledge. Students will grow up and learn bilingually, in Thai and English, as well as learning from an early age how to use computers and the internet. To provide a firm foundation for the future, students of Yaowawit will receive practical training in areas that complement Southern Thailand's businesses such as farming and tourism.

Currently, the Yaowawit School has about 130 children and is accepting around fifteen kindergarten children every year. Each month, the school has to bear expenses of approximately at 30,000 USD, of which fifty percent is for salaries and the other fifty percent is used for food, gas, electricity, etc. To date, the school has relied mainly on income from fund raising. However, an ever increasing scarcity of resources and many unfortunate events around the world has made it more difficult for the Yaowawit School to rely solely on international donations.

Realizing the need to stand on its own, the foundation and the school started, as planned from the beginning, projects that can help reduce costs and have the potential to generate income. Among these, farming is a high priority because it is one of the most important businesses in southern Thailand. In the school plantation, children learn about agricultural ecology and at the same time produce food to supply the school's meals. These agricultural products such as latex from rubber trees and palm oil are expected to provide financial returns in the future. Yet the school is concerned that an abundant supply and competitive market will make it difficult to bring profit particularly the school is located far from the downtown leading to heavy transportation costs. While the school is struggling to find more sources of income, its expenses soar because more children are accepted and the older ones are entering the level of education which the school is not yet ready to provide. Sending them to other secondary schools nearby requires additional funding for transportation, food, and personal expenses.

Because PhangNga province is well known for its beautiful national parks, islands, and beaches, the tourism business attracted Hardenberg's interest because it can not only generate income but will provide the children with lucrative jobs in the future. Before the tsunami, over two million people per annum visited the province with the peak at 2.89 million people in 2004. Almost 65% of these visitors were foreigners, 53% from Europe (particularly Scandinavians, Germans, and Swiss) and 33% from Asia. For international visitors, the main purpose of their visit was pleasure (about 95%) while the domestic visitors' ratio was pleasure (70%) and business (30%) e.g., meetings, seminars, company visits, exhibitions. Most tourists who choose PhangNga prefer seclusion and a peaceful time with their families. With the significant effort of both private and public sectors to rebuild tourism businesses after the tsunami, the situation has improved remarkably with more domestic tourists traveling to PhangNga. Most international visitors are still Europeans with many from Germany, Scandinavia, and the UK, while the Asians are mainly from China, Hong Kong, and Taiwan.

Early in 2007, Yaowawit School initiated a small hotel project, Yaowawit Lodge, with two mutual objectives; to provide practical training for their children in the hospitality business and to generate income to cover the school's running costs. Because tourism is a significant business sector in the southern part of Thailand, it is good to support young Thais to find career opportunities in this field. The first phase of this business had four buildings with a total of twelve guest rooms as well as a guest lounge and a lobby with a restaurant located in the school's commons building. Currently students participate in the hotel operation as part of their education on a voluntary basis. Trained staffs instruct them in English communication, manners, and service. Children also learn directly from practice in the housekeeping, laundry, and kitchen units. For other activities, hotel guests can walk to the school's plantation and orchard. They can also take an excursion tour with children guiding them to visit neighboring villages only 5 km away. Guests can also visit the two temples in the village that cooperate with Yaowawit School.

Adapted from Nuttavuthisit, K. (2008). Yaowawit School Kapong, Kellogg School Case 5-308-500.

It should also be recognized that there might be different segments of business/marketing students who have different degrees of interest in social issues. Thus, in the initial stage some students may show hesitation or even resistance to participation. However, all must be encouraged with the underlying belief that everyone wants to be a good active citizen when opportunity allows. Additionally, true learning about consumption and social-related marketing requires real practice or first-hand experience beyond conceptual analyses in the classroom.

Step 2: Introducing the Solution

After contemplating the social problem, the students should then be introduced to selected development projects with supporting information such as background, vision, mission, main tasks and responsibilities. Besides this general information, the discussion must also incorporate the management aspect of the project or organization such as strengths and weaknesses, opportunities and threats, strategy development, implementation (marketing/communications, operations, human resources, financial management), and performance evaluation. Organizing this in the form of case discussion with specified challenges can stimulate dialogue with students and lead to more engaging questions (Ackerman, Gross, & Perner, 2003). While content about the social interventions is important, it should be emphasized here that the purpose of learning for this group of business/marketing students is in the implication of consumption and marketing to support such an approach. Therefore, the focus is not on discussing social work but the relevant management, specifically marketing, areas such as how to communicate the program in order to attract interest and gain collaboration from stakeholders, and how to generate more revenue from donations and businesses.

Examples derived from the classes indicate that there can be quite a few challenging issues stemming from students' investigation of the management of social projects or programs. Business school students particularly can be goal-oriented and focus on effectiveness and efficiency (Vansteenkiste, Lens, & Deci, 2006). while many social development organizations are running with the goal to promote other aspects (e.g. wellbeing) regardless of high operating expenses and low returns on investment. For instance, when discussing the management and operation of Yaowawit, many students directly or indirectly criticized the school's premium offerings from resort-like facilities to extra learning of English, sports, and computer training. Such dialogue is in fact quite helpful as it can lead to better understanding of the school's concept, which believes that basic education is not enough for these disadvantaged children to find their own ways of breaking out of the vicious cycle of problems. They need extra qualifications to move forward so they can hold their own in the future.

This process also helps highlight concerns or reservations that students may have regarding the social development project, while the Q&A provides opportunities for students to learn about any queries they may encounter and how to handle them in the next step. Jansen, Chioncel, and Dekkers (2006) stressed the need to promote communicative interaction in resolving conflicts of interest and interpretation as it helps building participatory competencies of active citizens, while learning to question any rationales behind the current practices can raise awareness of the context-bound nature of the social developments. In this case, arranging discussion in the dialogue format can serve as a platform to exchange different and constructive perspectives. As an example in the abovementioned case of Yaowawit, the vision of the German founder, Mr. Philipp Graf Von Hardenberg, was that every child deserves to receive the best possible chance and the school should foster a positive attitude in the children to strive for a quality life so they can maximize their potential and eventually can lend a hand to others in need. Yet, in the eyes of many people living in the developing countries, they see many more children who can barely make ends meet each day and they are familiar with projects running at minimal cost. Such a difference between helping children to survive versus to thrive must be addressed because it involves the different business models and management/marketing strategies. The group discussion concluded that Yaowawit School must project clear positioning of being a place to create social change agents who can not only lift themselves up but create a ripple effect on others. This would then justify the need to engage premium services. But it was found that such a distinct concept would be well accepted only among certain groups of people in Thailand, as reflected in almost 100% of donations coming from abroad. This can be explained by the social psychology theory which indicates that individuals from collectivistic cultures are motivated to avoid failure while those from individualistic cultures are motivated to pursue success in life (Lockwood, Marshall, & Sadler, 2005). Though this understanding can help plan segmentation and targeting of potential donors, to achieve sustainability it is necessary for social development projects to also promote local involvement and contribution (Greensmith, 2002). This leads to further discussion on how to respond to such issues. The next process explains one of the efforts to engage participation among business school students and other relevant stakeholders.

Step 3: Engaging Participation

Though the sharing of ideas about how to tackle challenges of project management can already be considered a good contribution to social development, the matter still requires concrete action beyond thinking and making plans. Thus, in this stage students are engaged in activities with platforms designed to facilitate their learning and the implications of consumption and marketing, while at the same time producing results (e.g. raising funds) to support the social project or organization. Examples are activities to solicit donations or applied business practices such as selling souvenirs prepared by the organization and taking part in social enterprise projects with opportunities to learn the total business process.

From the case of Yaowawit School, prior discussion illustrates the need to promote more local involvement and contribution. At the basic level of donations, students are engaged to plan and activate fundraising activities with reference to strategies such as friend raising, special events, direct marketing, sponsorship, and customer (i.e. donor) relationship marketing. Realizing the need to overcome some reservations among the locals who may not buy into the school's concept (i.e. to thrive rather than to merely survive), the students thought that direct experience would be one of the main mechanisms to enhance learning of this different model and to encourage support. With the chosen target segment of business people in their networks, students decided to organize a charity event to bring the group to join various activities at the school ranging from touring the site and its neighboring community, to farming, and teaching children extracurricular subjects. The event resulted not only in significant funds raised but also future opportunities to invite business groups to interact with the school.

Summarized learning from the activity was that students seemed to be uncomfortable with soliciting donations particularly with the tough proposition of Yaowawit School and no urgent circumstances (e.g. natural disaster) to endorse the activity. This is congruent with the current situation worldwide of lacking good personnel, resources, and management systems in the field of fundraising (Bell & Cornelius, 2013). Hence, most strategies implemented (at least in Thailand) are through personal networking. Though this approach may produce fast and easy returns, it is mostly restricted to interpersonal relationships rather than the real causes and the projects. Additionally, this method makes it difficult for new organizations with limited connections to successfully reach donors, and cannot yield long-term benefits. Students came to the conclusion that in this context it was good to begin with personal networks but then to continue through some other systematic approaches to fundraising.

Next, besides asking for donations, students were encouraged to practice selling items or merchandise from the social development organizations to generate additional revenue. While Yaowawit School was still in the early stages of product development (e.g. lemongrass tea from the farm), students were introduced to other projects from UNICEF (selling souvenirs such as stationary and greeting cards) and the Thai Red Cross (selling commemorative coins to raise funds for the new building of the King Chulalongkorn Memorial Hospital), both of which have a variety of products and price ranges. Each group of students would begin by selecting and analyzing their target segments before planning and conducting marketing strategies. To enhance learning of diversity, students were assigned to work with different groups of consumers, arrange a different mix of products (souvenirs) and pricing, and sell products at different venues. In all cases, supporting materials (e.g. official brochures, banners, receipts) were provided to endorse credibility of the activities and avoid students incurring expenses.

Summarized learning from these activities is mainly derived from opportunities to directly interact with real markets and customers, particularly those whom students may not be familiar with such as the lower income group, or the older people who can become supporters of these projects. From their experience of being in the market students, particularly those with an international background, could observe cultural differences. Amusingly, those students who could not speak Thai became magnets through their attempts to communicate the good will. Here, students could see the different consumption behaviors and how to approach the target market. For example, students mentioned that they could reach the baby boomers early in the morning at the park and it was critical to attract the opinion leader because they could easily persuade others in their peer group to contribute via their social media networks. In this case, products serve as a medium to open up and connect the social issues with the general public's attention and eventually this could lead to further donations which remain the major source of income for most social development organizations. To apply this to the case of Yaowawit, it was suggested that this approach could help tackle challenges of the school being too premium to attract donations, but support through the buying of merchandise would be possible.

Finally in the more business-oriented state, students were engaged in the social enterprise projects which provided them with direct opportunities to make use of business knowledge and skills in support of social development. At Yaowawit, there is Yaowawit Lodge created for students to gain professional training in the hospitality sector and for the school to generate additional revenue. The goal is for the school to eventually become sustainable and be less dependent on donations. Students learned from the real case that this hotel, situated far from the beach and tourism areas, could attract very little interest among tourists on vacation. Therefore, they suggested targeting different groups such as businesses and other school communities who might be interested in organizing activities (e.g. bonding trip, camping) at Yaowawit and, with its mission to support disadvantaged children, it could also be incorporated into their social responsibility projects. This idea has been realized and has successfully raised a continuous stream of income for the school up until today. Students also learned about focusing on subsegment of schools or academic-related groups because they have shared common interests in organizing activities that can be easily combined with the school's arrangements. It also promotes Yaowawit children's interactions with friends and teachers from other school communities. Interestingly, most partner schools are international schools in Thailand or from abroad, probably due to the common approach regarding children's development. An example of continued relationship is the Hong Kong International School's summer camp organized every year as a part of their social conscience education program.

Besides Yaowawit Lodge, students were introduced to another social enterprise project, Pan Kan, a charity shop developed to sell donated items to raise funds for scholarships for needy children under the care of the Yuvabadhana foundation. Established in 1993, this organization has sponsored more than 5,000 children to finish high school, vocational school, or university. For this project, students had a chance to operate their own pop-up retail shops in designated venues during the specified period (with permission to use the space free of charge as part of the University's activity). Here, they had to work through the whole process from market identification and consumption analysis to sourcing (e.g. asking for donations of used items), arranging products, pricing, displays, logistics, promotions, and more. Here, students learned how to solve problems and adapt their strategies accordingly, which can help connect creativity with social responsibility as well as generate identification and commitment to the causes (Wildemeerschet al., 1998). One student group, assigned to work at a busy fresh market, saw that despite the high traffic most people were not paying attention to anything other than food and groceries. So they tried to walk around calling interest to their shop, but they learned that this would interrupt the other vendors' businesses. Later, they changed their approach to introduce this business to the other vendors and gained collaboration from them to help invite customers to visit the shop.

For students, it is crucial to highlight that the primary objective of these organized exercises is learning and engaging students in planning and conducting activities, rather than measuring the end results (e.g. amount of money raised). The group mentioned earlier could not achieve high sales performance at the end, but gained impressive involvement from the community which can also serve as a significant mechanism to promote social development projects.

Step 4: Evaluating Output and Outcome

After the exercises, students were asked to evaluate output according to their prior analyses and strategic plan. Each team needed to give a presentation on their selected target segment, how they analyzed this segment's behavior, planned and performed strategies leading to their outputs. Importantly, evaluation would be based on their own plan and performance rather than comparing the returns across different groups. In fact, students might collect a small amount of donations from the low-income group but achieve high success regarding their plan to promote participation with no boundary. In this stage, management teams from the social development organizations would be invited to share their views with students and collect new ideas for their future development. They could assist in the process of connecting the outputs with possible outcomes such as analyzing to what extent these efforts could become scholarships for disadvantaged students under support of the organization, or how the activities conducted could help broaden the organizations' collaborative networks. The management teams must be open and acknowledge that engaging volunteers, specifically the business school students, could lead to greater and longer lasting impact despite some imperfect results and the extra effort needed. As Wenger (1998) suggested, learning of social practices enhances how to participate rather than the end result. Such perspective must be emphasized as some NGOs might prefer to gain only resource support, especially from the business sector, instead of collaborating with students, as they might be concerned about the complex nature of the social issues or want to control management and operations internally. There might also be some doubts about the sincerity of business entities which need to be clarified.

To summarize the learning process, all proceeds from students' activities were then combined into the class donation to the organizations, and for their future reference and engagement every student would be presented with a certificate from the organization to acknowledge their contribution. For example, the recent activity to sell commemorative coins for the Thai Red Cross raised 32,500 USD within ten days. This will contribute to the expansion of the King Chulalongkorn Hospital, a public tertiary hospital serving about 1.4 million patients a year. The other pop-up retailing for Pan Kan totaled 4,000 USD sales in one day, or scholarships for 20 underprivileged children.

Finally, each student would submit a short essay to reflect on individual experiences. This reflection process is important after any activity since it allows opportunities for students to review and integrate their learning. Moreover in promoting active citizenship, this process can help connect awareness of social conditions and developments with personal life themes and bring students to attain underlying meanings of experiences. Examples from the real practices are shown in students' feedback after class (and even after graduation). Many of them still recall and talk about such experiences while some have become supporters of these and/or other social projects. For instance, one Japanese alumnus has brought a group of people from his organization to visit Yaowawit every year. Other alumni said these activities (stated in their CVs) are normally discussed in job interviews and the experience could bring quite insightful conversations with the companies. Those who felt reluctant at the beginning even noted (in the evaluation) that the initiative had given them new perspectives in making a difference and they felt proud to have taken part. This is consistent with Jansen, Chioncel, and Dekkers (2006) who suggested that the sense of communality could arise from encountering experience of togetherness and sharing of symbolic meanings or emotional events.

CONCLUSION

Business and society are interdependently related as business is initiated from the ability to analyze and promote opportunities to fulfill the needs of people in the society. Such an approach yields better satisfaction for the people as well as producing higher returns for business. In our modern economy with its forces of capitalism and globalization, it is ever more evident that society is being driven by business progress. Thus, in today's more complex world with its serious and fragmented issues, further involvement of business in tackling and preventing problems is needed in order to promote shared happiness and sustainability. As CSR has become increasingly emphasized, the concept has become the common reference point for individuals and organizations who want to contribute to society.

The movement is quite apparent in the case of Thailand, an emerging country with a positive growth of economy which has, at the same time, faced serious sociopolitical problems due to mismanagement and the lack of contributing efforts from the people. Particularly, the business sector has benefited significantly from the country's resources and economic expansion but contributed further problems of inequality and separation. This has led to a call for the responsibility of business people to play a bigger role in social development. This concern is quite apparent and the best and most fundamental way to begin is to start from education. Many business schools around the world have responded accordingly, to the extent that some schools announce the vision to produce business leaders who can make a positive difference in society. Nevertheless, despite the desire to see change, it is not always easy to make the change especially among the business school students who will have to manage a balance of other expectations such as making returns on investments of shareholders.

This chapter features the summarized learning from examples of MBA classes conducted in Thailand. While the subject of Consumption and Marketing can connect with the goal because it enhances better understanding of the target group of people and devising of strategies to persuade them to take action in support of social development projects, the subject also requires care in the design of processes to facilitate the integrated learning. Here, the four main steps from understanding the problem to introducing the solution, engaging participation, and evaluating output and outcome are discussed together with the use of techniques such as problems, practices, and projects. In each class, students are introduced to problems from various sectors (business, social, etc.) at both domestic and international levels and they are encouraged to practice tackling the multiple challenges with focuses on analyses of target customer/donor behaviors and development of marketing strategies. Finally, students will be able to apply knowledge and experiences into their projects or activities. Through this process, students can learn about relevant theoretical concepts but in a more engaging and pragmatic manner. As a result, students will be able to further develop their analytical, creative, and theoretical skills. Analytical skill denotes the ability to collect, analyze, and present information in a logical and coherent manner. Creativity includes, for example, innovative and thought-provoking ideas, fresh and different viewpoints, and unique techniques or styles. Theoretical skill is the ability to employ or engage some concrete concepts/theories of consumption and marketing.

Besides learning the subject, Consumption and Marketing, this process can enhance students' understanding of the wider, deeper, and longer (sustainable) perspectives as it expands the boundary of marketing education from a business/economic focus to the social issues, and from class-based to experiential-based learning. Empirical evidence from the real practice demonstrates such effort being well received because unlike some businesses which may be limited to specific interest groups, social problems are close to the heart and lie in the hands of everyone. Not only can this benefit the students, but also the overall business sector and economy, to move in the direction of sustainability. The learning from the case of Thailand can bring insights into the 21st century marketing education and emphasize ongoing initiatives promoted by various business schools to integrate diversity, ethics, analytics, and sustainability into their programs. Ultimately, this learning can impact on society by turning marketing students into active citizens of the country and the world.

REFERENCES

Ackerman, D. S., Gross, B. L., & Perner, L. (2003). Instructor, Student, and Employer Perceptions on Preparing Marketing Students for Changing Business Landscapes. *Journal of Marketing Education*, *25*(1), 46–56. doi:10.1177/0273475302250572

Bell, J., & Cornelius, M. (2013). *Underdeveloped: A National Study of Challenges Facing Nonprofit Fundraising*. San Francisco, CA: CompassPoint Nonprofit Services & the Evelyn and Walter Haas, Jr. Fund.

Bowen, H. R. (1953). *Social responsibilities of the businessman*. New York: Harper.

Chambers, R. (1983). *Rural development: putting the last first*. London: Longman.

Charities Aid Foundation. (2012). *World Giving Index 2012*. Retrieved January 26, 2015, from http://www.cafonline.org/PDF/WorldGivingIndex2012WEB.pdf

Davis, K. (1967). Understanding the social responsibility puzzle: What does the businessman owe to society? *Business Horizons*, *10*(4), 45–50. doi:10.1016/0007-6813(67)90007-9

Drucker, P. (1984). The New Meaning of Corporate Social Responsibility. *California Management Review, 26*(2), 53–63. doi:10.2307/41165066

Drucker, P. F. (1954). *The Practice of Management.* New York, NY: Collins. (reprinted 2006)

Frederick, W. C. (1960). The growing concern over business responsibility. *California Management Review, 2*(4), 52–61. doi:10.2307/41165405

Friedman, M. (1962). *Capitalism and Freedom.* Chicago: University of Chicago Press.

Friedman, M. (1970, September 13). The social responsibility of a business is to increase its profits. *The New York Times Magazine.*

Fung, A., & Wright, E. O. (2001). Deepening Democracy: Innovations in Empowered Participatory Governance. *Politics & Society, 19*(1), 5–41. doi:10.1177/0032329201029001002

Global Fund. (2010). *(PRODUCT)RED generates landmark US$150 million.* Retrieved January 26, 2015, from http://www.theglobalfund.org/en/mediacenter/newsreleases/2010-06-01_PRODUCT_RED_generates_landmark_USD_150_million_for_the_Global_Fund/

Greensmith, J. (2002). Trends in Fundraising and Giving by International NGOs. *Global Policy Forum.* Retrieved January 26, 2015, from https://www.globalpolicy.org/component/content/article/176/31462.html

Jansen, T., Chioncel, N., & Dekkers, H. (2006). Social Cohesion and Integration: Learning Active Citizenship. *British Journal of Sociology of Education, 27*(2), 189–205. doi:10.1080/01425690600556305

Jones, T. M. (1980). Corporate social responsibility revisited, redefined. *California Management Review, 22*(3), 59–67. doi:10.2307/41164877

Khon Thai Monitor. (2012). *Research Report sponsored by the Khon Thai Foundation.* Bangkok, Thailand: Khon Thai Foundation.

Khon Thai Youth Monitor. (2014). *Research Report sponsored by the Khon Thai Foundation.* Bangkok, Thailand: Khon Thai Foundation.

Levitt, T. (1958). The dangers of social responsibility. *Harvard Business Review, 36,* 41–50.

Lockwood, P., Marshall, T. C., & Sadler, P. (2005). Promoting success or preventing failure: Social comparisons across cultures. *Personality and Social Psychology Bulletin, 31,* 379–394. doi:10.1177/0146167204271598 PMID:15657453

Marshall, T. H. (1950). *Citizenship and Social Class and Other Essays.* Cambridge: University of Cambridge Press.

McGuire, J. (1963). *Business and Society.* New York, NY: McGraw-Hill.

Nobel Prize. (2014). Grameen Bank – Facts. *Nobel Prize.* Retrieved January 26, 2015, from http://www.nobelprize.org/nobel_prizes/peace/laureates/2006/grameen-facts.html

Nuttavuthisit, K. (2008). *Yaowawit School Kapong.* Kellogg School Case 5-308-500.

Nuttavuthisit, K., Jindahra, P., & Prasanpanich, P. (2015). Participatory Community Development: Evidence from Thailand. *Community Development Journal: An International Forum, 50*(1), 55–70. doi:10.1093/cdj/bsu002

Nye, J. (2004). *Soft Power: The Means to Success in World Politics*. New York: Public Affairs.

Prayukvong, P., & Olsen, M. (2009). *Research paper on Promoting Corporate Social Responsibility in Thailand and the Role of Volunteerism*. The NETWORK of NGO and Business Partnerships for Sustainable Development, commissioned by UNDP.

Rigg, J. (1991). Grass-roots development in rural Thailand: A lost cause? *World Development, 19*(2/3), 199–211. doi:10.1016/0305-750X(91)90255-G

Thailand Development Research Institute. (2005). Bangkok: Economic Impact of Tsunami on Thailand.

TIME. (2014, August 25). Ice Bucket Challenge Nears $80 Millions Mark. *TIME*. Retrieved January 26, 2015, from http://time.com/3173833/als-ice-bucket-challenge-fundraising-total/

UNICEF. (2014). *Private Fundraising and Partnerships. 2013 Annual Report*. Retrieved January 26, 2015, from http://www.unicef.org/about/annualreport/files/Private_Fundraising_and_Partnerships_AR_2013. pdf

Vansteenkiste, M., Lens, W., & Deci, E. L. (2006). Intrinsic versus Extrinsic Goal Contents in Self-determination Theory: Another Look at the Quality of Academic Motivation. *Educational Psychologist, 41*(1), 19–31. doi:10.1207/s15326985ep4101_4

Vichit-Vadakan, J. (2002). Part One: The Country Report. In Investing In Ourselves: Giving and Fund Raising in Thailand (pp. 3-27). Manila: Asian Development Bank.

Wenger, E. (1998). *Communities of practice: Learning, meaning, and identity*. Cambridge University Press. doi:10.1017/CBO9780511803932

Wildemeersch, D., Jansen, T., Vandenabeele, J., & Jans, M. (1998). Social Learning: A New Perspective on Learning in Participatory Systems. *Studies in Continuing Education, 20*(2), 251–265. doi:10.1080/0158037980200210

KEY TERMS AND DEFINITIONS

Active Citizen: A person who actively takes responsibility or participate in the area of public or social development.

Consumption: An act of consuming product, service, idea, or concept influenced by psychological factors (e.g. motivation, perception, learning, attitude, self-concepts and personality) and sociocultural factors (e.g. family, social class, culture, cross-culture, subculture).

Fundraising: An effort to gather money for social development projects.

Social Development: A process to benefit people and the society.

Social Enterprise: An organization that applies business strategies for the benefit of public or social development.

Social-related Marketing: A strategic process of identifying demands and exchanging values in support of social development.

Sustainability: An ability to sustain itself and to continue in the future.

Chapter 7
Using Sports History to Develop Cultural Competence in Millennial Marketers:
Title IX, Stadium Development, and Post–Apartheid Rugby

Stephanie A. Tryce
Saint Joseph's University, USA

ABSTRACT

As we move toward 2050, the United States will become a country of minorities. These changing demographics have tremendous implications for the way marketers understand both the marketplace and consumer behavior. Intentionality, specificity, and intersectional approaches to diverse sport's history are key in successfully providing millennial students with the cultural competence required to become first-rate global marketers. Sport provides marketing educators and students a unique opportunity to examine cultural diversity in a way that ameliorates diversity fatigue from underexposed students. This chapter details relevant diversity and inclusion language and terminology, provides individual lesson plan examples, and details outcomes and instruction for developing cultural competence in millennial student populations.

INTRODUCTION

I recently attended a sporting event where Hispanic Heritage was being celebrated in synchronicity with the United States' month-long celebration. Music by El Gran Combo, a Puerto Rican Salsa orchestra, played in the arena while the starting lineup was announced in Spanish to complement the Spanish translations of the player's event-specific uniforms. As team advertisements played throughout the evening, I noticed the singular usage of the term Hispanic to refer to the largely Puerto Rican attending population. I noticed too the announcement of half-priced tacos during half-time as a continuation of the celebration. The questionable confabulation of Hispanic, Latino, and Chicano cultural heritages given the probable

DOI: 10.4018/978-1-4666-9784-3.ch007

singularity of the targeted audience, led me to question the cultural competency of the host team's marketing department. While no expert, as a Black American woman educated in diverse spaces, I know anecdotally that many of my Puerto Rican friends tend to refer to themselves collectively as Latinos rather than as Hispanics and that tacos likely date back to 18th century Mexico rather than Puerto Rico. I take access to this sort of knowledge for granted, but what happens when there is no access to this type of cultural information? This example makes clear that when lacking culturally specific information or the wherewithal to ask appropriate questions, marketers devoid of cultural competence can unwittingly alienate the very consumers a specific marketing campaign is seeking to target. As an educator I am determined to create students who will be equipped to do better.

What is the best way to accomplish this? To answer this question, I turn to the work of Dr. Ronald Takaki, who was a professor at the University of California, Berkeley, who wrote extensively about cultural diversities in the United States (Adams & Welsch, 2009). Professor Takaki believed in multicultural education. He implored us to reject what he called the "master narrative" of American history that America was settled by European immigrants and that Americans are white or European in ancestry. He believed it is the responsibility of educators to be aware of the master narrative, but construct new, more accurate narratives. Professor Takaki's approach to teaching was interdisciplinary, believing it is important to integrate knowledge. He insisted that by understanding our individual and collective histories we help to integrate knowledge across disciplines. As America moves swiftly toward being a "country of minorities" as Dr. Takaki stated, we have to keep in mind that "culture" is not static but fluid. The "holistic, humanistic view of culture synthesized by Kroeber and Kluckhohn includes too much and is too diffuse either to separate analytically the twisted threads of human experience or to interpret the designs into which they are woven" (Keesing, 1974). These words are truer today and will be truer in the coming years as America becomes more and more diverse. We must remain open to rethinking and redefining culture.

I create lesson plans in support of and as a result of theories like that of Professor Takaki. Intentionality, specificity, and intersectional approaches to diverse sport's history are key in successfully providing Millennials students with the cultural competence required to become first-rate global marketers. In what follows you will find a series of lessons designed to combat the glaring absences in both outcomes and instruction for developing cultural competence in millennial student populations. This chapter describes and articulates relevant diversity and inclusion language and terminology, provides individual lesson plan examples on approaches to teaching Title IX, Stadium Development, and Nelson Mandela's rebranding of Rugby in post-apartheid South Africa.

Americans, like many global citizens, are heavily socialized to engage in sport as both participants and spectators. To say that sport is a big business is not cliché; it's accurate. IEG, LLC, a leading provider of sponsorship analytics, projects 70% of the North American sponsorship market in 2015 will be sport sponsorships, followed by entertainment sponsorship at a distant 10%. It is no wonder then that sport references like: team player, game plan, hardball, and leveling the playing field have made their way into business parlance. The expression and concept of "leveling the playing field" likewise found welcome space within the U.S. Civil Rights Movement. Given this intersection, educators and students find a unique area where these ideas meet in order to produce culturally competent global marketers. Doing this type of work in the classroom creates the space to ameliorate "narrative[s] that non-white success is purposefully engineered at the expense of white sacrifice" (Hughey, 2013). With lessons designed around rich contextual historical knowledge, students learn not just the specifics around a given diverse issue within sport, but what sorts of questions to pose as they become future marketers.

Sport operates "[a]s a collection of social practices and relations that are deeply rooted in the society of which it is a part analytical accounts of sport must be grounded in a historical and socially critical examination of the larger political, economic, social and ideological configurations within society" (as cited in Brooks & Althouse, 2007). Educators can prepare the next generation of marketing leaders to understand the business imperative for cultural diversity and inclusion in marketing strategies. And it is incumbent upon educators to do so as far too often business success can rest on the cultural competence of an organization's employees. Lacking cultural competence is no longer excused with a simple apology as is evidenced by the recent sale of the LA Clippers.

No industry is forced to so publicly manage diversity and inclusion (race, gender, sexuality, ability, religion, ethnicity, etc.) successes and foibles as sport, making its rich data collection particularly ripe for pedagogical use. Notwithstanding the product or service to be marketed, sport plays an important role for connecting brands with consumers. Well beyond box scores and shooting percentages, by law and for team use, sport organizations collect information around almost every aspect of play including coaching staff and front office executive changes, sponsors, player positions, and player productivity. This data has been mined for a wide variety of uses and has been particularly useful in ascertaining factual information around diverse leadership in Major League Baseball (Rimer, 1996) and the development of the NFL's Rooney Rule (Maske, 2009). In the lesson plan section, I will take this up again in more detail.

Future marketing professionals will be required to navigate an increasingly diverse world in which sport marketing figures prominently; the lack of pedagogical instruction made available to them in this area continues to leave them ill-equipped to do business. While they lack a contextual historical understanding of today's diversity and inclusion business challenges, they are not necessarily prepared to receive the information they need. Examining the intersectionality of the difficult gender and race relationships in both the United States and South Africa, does not generally engender widespread enthusiastic responses in majority classrooms, particularly with students who have had primarily homogenous cultural experiences. Sport and its history prove to be a particularly useful salve in this respect. Couching difficult discussions in the context of sport provides a space for student engagement, which is not immediately gendered or racialized. Students have been socialized to talk about sport and thus sport becomes the frame for stimulating discussions around cultural diversity and as educators, we can use this socialization to our advantage to create avenues to cultural competence.

According to the Pew Research Center, the population of the United States will rise to 438 million in 2050. The largest part of that increase, 82%, will be the result of immigration. The Latino population, which currently represents the largest minority group in the United States, will triple in size by 2050. In the same year whites will become a minority representing 47% of the total U.S. population. This change in demographics has tremendous implications for how we do and will conduct business into the future. If for no other reason, the next generation of marketing/business leaders will be required to understand, internalize, and manage diverse human capital and projects with a sophisticated level of cultural competence. The business imperative to do so is clear.

BACKGROUND

"Our identities shape our inquiries." These five words spoken by Joyce E. King, immediate past President of the American Educational Research Association resonate deeply with me. They implore me to reflect on how my identity influenced my choice to practice civil rights law and shapes my current academic interests at the intersection of sport, law and social justice. I identify collectively as Black, female, and American. I consider myself neither black first, then female, nor female first, then black. For me, these two identities are intricately and permanently interwoven; it is the lens through which I experience the world. I do not have the luxury or freedom to experience life outside the social constructs of race and gender. My lived experience teaches me that my very fair complexion and straightened long hair grants me access to spaces, which my more richly pigmented brothers and sisters are often not invited. It is from this unique perspective that I conclude how essential it is for all of my students to have access to the knowledge that comes from allowing other identities to impact and enrich our academic inquiries.

Discerning that the multicultural marketplace is no longer a niched space also influences my curricular strategies for developing future culturally competent global marketers. I use sport to develop lesson plans, which challenge students to solve real-world problems around cultural diversity and social justice. In doing so, students are required to research deeply in order to understand how history shapes current circumstances. This knowledge serves as the foundation for creative, respectful, and inclusive marketing strategies. Aside from sport marketing learning objectives, the very nature of culturally focused projects and class activities is to give students an opportunity to reflect on what they have learned about others in my classroom which often runs counters to their previous knowledge. Students personal reflections from these culturally centered lesson plans reveal that the project or activity helped improve their critical analysis of stakeholders' positions, cultural awareness, and sensitivity to factors that can help and hinder brand meaning (Tryce & Smith, 2015).

Teaching with Inclusion and Diversity Language and Terminology

Culture

Culture is as rapidly changing and as difficult to pin down as its definition. In an early attempt to create a holistic definition, anthropologists Arthur Kroeber and Clyde Kluckhohn in 1952 analyzed 164 existing definitions of culture. From these definitions they devised that culture: "is a product; is historical; includes ideas, patterns, and values; is selective; is learned; is based upon symbols; and is an abstraction from behavior and the products of behavior." It is a shared set of values and beliefs and understanding by members of a society (Deshpande & Webster, 1989). Much of their definition is dependent on a collected set of beliefs held by a community consisting of members in agreement. In communities where members are not in agreement about the conditions of membership, when membership is in flux and/or under contestation, this definition meant to be inclusive, is pressurized (Deshpande & Webster, 1989).

Diversity

In a manner similar to Kroeber and Kluckhohn, George Cunningham (2011) considers several definitions in his attempt to provide a holistic approach to understanding diversity. His four primary conclusions are: 1) diversity requires interaction between at least two individuals; 2) it can relate to in-group differences 3) the perception of difference has greater effect on outcome over the fact of it; 4) diversity is associated with a myriad of work outcomes ranging from the individual to the group level. These four conclusions led Cunningham (2011) to define diversity as, "the presence of differences among members of a social unit that lead to perceptions of such differences and that [they] impact work outcomes." Cunningham asserts that understanding the power of diversity and inclusion is fundamental in creating and maintaining well-balanced and well-run organizations.

Multiculturalism

"Multiculturalism…is a reform movement that seeks to equalize educational opportunities for students by diversifying the curriculum to include and teach about the contributions of individuals and cultures that are outside of the dominant Euro-centric Christian cultural frameworks in U.S. and Canadian schools" (Meyer, 2010). While there are a number of different schools of thought driving multiculturalism's influence and effect, in business, multicultural operational approaches contribute to an organization's overall success. Simply stated, one of the key factors in the ultimate success of an organization rests with the multicultural diversity of any given team.

Intersectionality

Intersectionality is a theoretical framework formalized by Columbia University and UCLA law professor Kimberlé Crenshaw meant to address the limitations of individual subject positions and the law. Through her work in antidiscrimination law, particularly the DeGraffenreid v. General Motors case, she readily observed the law's inability to see the full scope of a person's multiple subject positions. Clients could seek redress because of race or gender, but what if they were attempting to account for the harm created at the intersections of gender and race, either acting concurrently and/or sequentially (Crenshaw,1989)? While this theory was formalized through the observations of Black American women and US law, its influence and application have been far reaching with a recent article in the *Journal of Public Policy and Marketing* making a strong case that "traditional diversity research is typically positioned as providing value-neutral contributions [while] intersectional research is typically positioned as 'critical' or 'transformative' (Gopaldas, 2013).

Lesson Plans

The goal of each lesson plan described here is to engage students in passive, active and interactive learning methods designed to encourage student to student and educator to student collaboration.

Title IX Lesson Plan

1. **Learning Objectives:**
   a. To understand the athletic and non-athletic benefits of athletic scholarships.
   b. To analyze the experiences of athletic scholarships for men and women to determine if gender discrimination exists.
   c. To perform consumer research and to critically analyze to what degree Title IX has reached its goal, particularly with marginalized communities.
2. **Materials:** The Title IX statute.
3. **Procedure or Lecture Format:**
   a. Initiate a 10-15 minute discussion to determine the students' everyday understanding of gender discrimination in sport.
   b. To test student synthetization of information discussed ask three key questions:
      i. What is the purpose of Title IX?

ii.   Analyze and explain the relationship between America's adoption of Victorian ideals of femininity and woman's absence from sport.

iii.   Compare and contrast the impact that Title IX provides to White American women and Black American women regarding sport, athletic scholarships and the benefits that flow therefrom.

c.   Summarize, draw conclusions and give instructions for deep learning exercise.

4.   **Deep Learning Exercise:** Assign homework exercise asking students to answer in detail and with examples the following question: "Has Title IX met its promise?"

Title IX Lesson Discussion

The Title IX lesson begins with the question, "What are the benefits that flow from having an athletic scholarship?" The responses flow quickly from the students…education, athletic training, higher level coaching, academic tutoring support, employment opportunities from alumni and boosters, and potential opportunities as a professional athlete, coach or athletic administrator (see Figure 1).

The next question posed to the students is, "How long have men enjoyed athletic scholarships and their attendant benefits?" Most students do not know the answer to this question but, are not surprised to learn that men, specifically White men, have enjoyed athletic scholarships in the United States since the late 1800s when Amos Alonzo Stagg created "student service" scholarships for the football players at the University of Chicago (Lester, 1999). I ask the students to contemplate the volume of networks and benefits that have developed for men more than 130 years as a result of athletic scholarships opportunities.

Next, I ask students, "When were women awarded athletic scholarships?" Most associate the awarding of athletic scholarships to women with the passage of Title IX, but do not know that the Title IX statute was not passed into law until 1972 or that Congress did not pass Title IX Regulations until 1975, giving colleges and universities 3 years to come into compliance. I advise them that it was 1973, when the University of Miami (Florida) awarded the first athletic scholarships for women, fifteen in total. Even two years after the passage of Title IX, 50,000 men were attending colleges and universities in the United States on athletic scholarships compared to the less than 50 women who had by then been awarded one (U.S. Dept. of Education, 1997). Students are asked to compare the 43 years that women have benefited from similar professional networks as the 130+ years that men have had to do the same (see Figure 2). This activity gives students a clear understanding of how "Ol' Boy Networks" were established and how they are actively maintained. When opportunities arise, men call those in their network and for a variety of reasons, but most important one of time, members of those networks are most likely to be other men, and to be white.

I end the guided discussion by providing a historical context of the women's liberation movement and Title IX's place within it. The goal here to correct the widespread misunderstanding that Title IX's

Figure 1.

Figure 2. Years of benefits and network development

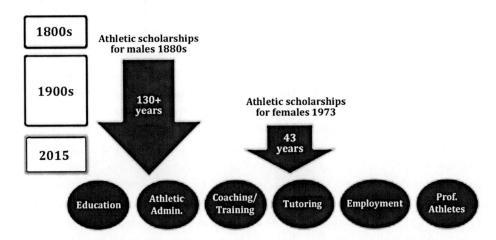

purpose was to provide opportunities for women in sport. To the contrary, Title IX has two stated purposes: 1."to avoid the use of federal resources to support discriminatory practices in education programs" and 2. "to provide individual citizens effective protection against those practices" (U.S. Department of Justice). At its passage it was initially unclear if college athletics was to be included. A 1974 amendment to Title IX directed the Department of Health Education and Welfare to publish regulations that specifically included intercollegiate athletic activities (U.S. Department of Justice.)

We begin the next class by discussing their responses to the deep learning exercise, the assignment to respond to the question: "Has Title IX met its promise?" With great confidence and little variation, students overwhelmingly believe that Title IX met its promise and cite as evidence the astronomical growth rate in women's sport participation. Looking solely at women's participation rates as a benchmark for success, their emphatic belief on Title IX's absolute success seems reasonable and so I ask them to look at all they have not considered: allocation of resources, opportunities in coaching and athletic administration for women, compensation. I push further by asking students to what degree they have considered participation rates for women of color. Most students believe that Title IX benefits women of color more than majority women and thus are surprised to learn that the converse was true. While the opportunities for women of color increased after the passage of Title IX, the opportunities were greater for majority females. This forces us to examine the unique circumstance that occurs at the intersection of race and gender…intersectionality.

After outlining intersectionality, it is necessary to provide additional historical context for the differing ways White and Black American women have entered sport. During the mid-19th century, middle to upper class White women were driven away from participation in sport because such behavior did not conform to Victorian notions of femininity. Conversely, Black women were viewed as neither frail nor feminine in part, because they were forced to engage in the physical labor demands of plantation work. While there was little free time for Black women, they still managed to be participants and spectators of sport (Tryce & Brooks, 2010). Not until the feminist movement of the late 19th century did White women emerge as sport participants albeit limited specifically to the type of socially acceptable sport typically offered at private colleges like tennis, archery, croquet and figure skating (Tryce & Brooks, 2010, citing Woman's Sports Foundation, 2001). Black women, however did not have access to the same colleges as White women. Aside from resource barriers, there were cultural barriers for Black women's participation in sport. Because sport was used for developing masculinity, Black women who chose to participate in sport had to combat the perception of being gender transgressors (Tryce & Brooks, 2010). This is still true today as demonstrated by Shamil Tarpischey, the Russian Tennis Federation President who referred to Venus and Serena Williams as the "Williams brothers" on a Russian late night show. He was subsequently fined $25,000.00 by the World Tennis Association (WTA) tour and suspended from tour involvement for a year (ESPN.com, 2014). Serena Williams has faced body shaming tactics her entire career and her recent 4th straight Wimbledon win on July 11, 2015, arguably took a back seat to the unrelenting scrutiny of her muscular, athletic build detailed in a New York Times article published the day before her win.

It is also critical for students to understand the impact of historically racist practices and exclusionary laws have regarding access to sport. My students did not know what Black Codes were and how these southern laws served to limit the liberties of newly freed enslaved peoples. These laws forced Black Americans, particularly in the South, into disadvantageous labor arrangements. The effect this had on their ability to improve their economic circumstance cannot be underscored enough. Jim Crow and neighborhood land covenants that forbid the sale of property to Blacks also forced Black Americans to settle in what we commonly refer to as inner cities and ghettos. These densely populated areas where poor minorities are forced to live do not often have the type of large, open, green spaces required for soccer, lacrosse, and tennis, which have been used to increase female participation rates in sport and thus maintain Title IX compliance. By utilizing an intersectional lens students are able to observe that gender falls within a matrix of sexism, racism, and classism that are interacting forces which "impact people's experiences within and beyond sport in divergent ways" (Knoppers & McDonald, 2010). Marketing students who are exposed to this type of critical thinking around diversity and inclusion are better equipped to make informed, respectful decisions about how to bring value to diverse consumers, particularly when it comes time to consider which products to develop, where they should be sold, how they should be promoted and at what price.

Chinatown Stadium Development Lesson Plan

1. **Learning Objective:**
   a. To understand who the stakeholders are in stadium development and to be able to explain their respective interests.
   b. Critically analyze the special reciprocity that exists between sports teams and their host cities and fan. Furthermore to explain how this reciprocity shapes the relationship that teams have with their publics (public relations), and the special considerations needed when impacting historically marginalized communities with little political clout.
2. **Materials:** Five block street map of Philadelphia's Chinatown with the following highlighted: public transportation stops, the interstate highway, The Pennsylvania Convention Center, a Federal Detention Center, a hospital, the Holy Redeemer Church.
3. **Procedures or Lecture Format:**
   a. Initiate a 40-minute discussion to determine the student's knowledge about stadium development.
   b. To test student synthetization of information discussed ask three key questions:
      i. Why is it important for sport's teams to have a good relationship with the local politicians and their fans?

  ii.   Why have cities allowed themselves to be held hostage by teams threating to leave unless a new stadium is financed?

  iii. What is it like to have a Stadium as a neighbor?

  c.   Summarize, draw conclusions and give instructions for deep learning exercise.

4. **Deep Learning Exercise:** During this in-class activity students are divided into three groups and given specific perspectives. Students will perform demographic and psychographic research on the Chinatown neighborhood to understand the make-up and needs of the community. Two groups will develop arguments informed by their research and each group will present their arguments to a third group, who is charge with making a determination.

One group represents the Philadelphia Phillies who threaten to leave Philadelphia if they are not given a new stadium in Chinatown. Another group represents a community group called "Stadium Out of Chinatown Coalition" (Coalition) who resists the relocation of the baseball stadium. The last group represents the City Council and will ultimately vote on whether or not the stadium can be relocated to Chinatown. Each group has about 15 minutes to perform market research on the Chinatown neighborhood and develop their arguments in support of their positions. During this time I meet with the students who represent the City Council and give them one charge- to be servant-leaders as articulated by Robert Greenleaf, founder of the modern Servant Leadership movement. They must understand their roles collectively and individually as a "servant first… [who] does what he can to have a positive effect on the least privileged in society." Throughout the presentations, I serve as a *consigliere* to the City Council.

Chinatown Stadium Development Discussion

In preparation of the in-class deep learning exercise I will have previously conducted a lecture/discussion centered on stadium development. Through it we gained an understanding of some of the factors that fuel the stadium development boom, past and present funding schemes, the use of eminent domain powers and issuance of utility easements, economic resource generators, and the value of corporate naming rights in advertising. We also examined the reasons cities are so willing to placate sport team's demands for new stadiums particularly when there may be no resulting loss of tax dollars, but perhaps only a shift how citizens' entertainment dollars are spent. We next turn our focus to stadium building in a residential neighborhood using Brooklyn's Barclay's Center as a case study. Examining the litigation around the attempted prevention of the Barclay's Center offered great insights to the concerns of the varying segments of the neighboring communities. We end the discussion by determining to what extent a stadium developer could and/or should meet a community's needs. The Barclay's discussion provides the framework for the Chinatown Stadium in class activity.

On the day of the activity, I take the class back to the hotly debate time in 2000 when a proposal was on the table to relocate the Phillies' baseball stadium from its current location in South Philadelphia to Chinatown. Making such a move meant that the baseball stadium would be relocated from South Philadelphia where it sits with other stadia in wide open spaces, to a congested area in downtown Philadelphia in a diverse neighbor with no room for growth. Students representing the Philadelphia Phillies often attempt to couch their argument for the move to Chinatown in very predictable ways. They indicate that there would be more patrons to Chinatown restaurants. They also promise to give Chinatown's residents jobs at the arena. I challenge their arguments, reminding them of all of the amenities/restaurants that are now housed within ballparks and referring them to their maps ask if they think people would realistically venture into Chinatown, across an expressway, on foot, to get food, when there are many food options in the ballpark. Additionally, I question the presumptions they make about the residents of Chinatown. Do they believe that the typical part-time job in a stadium, with no benefits would entice a Chinatown resident to happily accept so noisy a new neighbor? This offer presumes that there are unemployment issues among the residents of Chinatown and also presupposes that the residents are uneducated and/ or unskilled.

The students representing the Coalition tend to suggest predictable arguments as well and it in the further discussion around the topics that each group begins to think more deeply about the subject. They often state concerns over increased traffic, noise, trash and disruptions from construction. Few recognize and/or mention the diverse population of the location or seem to know that Chinatown is the only Asian American enclave in Philadelphia. The Philadelphia Convention and Visitors Bureau and Asian Americans/Pacific Islanders in Philanthropy (AAPIP) report that Chinatown has over 4,000 residents, many of whom retain their country of origin languages. Chinatown serves China and Southeast Asia immigrants living in Philadelphia as well as the tri-state area. It is one of the few places they can dependably obtain social services in their native language. (Guan & Knottnerus, 2006). Chinatown has been the target of "spatial threats" because of its desirable downtown Philadelphia location, and the lack of political influence of its residence and their low socioeconomic status (Guan & Knottnerus, 2006). The city's use of eminent domain throughout Chinatown has greatly inhibited growth. The proposed ballpark would be just another block to Chinatown's only ability to grow. This exercise highlights the need for cultural competence when making business decisions. It also highlights the possibility that the needs of a small, politically weak but culturally viable community, without a public school, library, recreation center and park should outweigh the business desires of a sport organization and the convenience of the downtown business community. I am happy to report that with each iteration of this in-class activity, the students representing City Council have voted in favor of the Chinatown community and against the Philadelphia Phillies.

Mandela's Post-Apartheid Rugby Rebrand Lesson Plan

1. **Learning Objectives:**
    a.   To be able to explain how the racially constructed system of apartheid operated in South Africa.
    b.   To understand the impact of apartheid on Rugby.
    c.   To know the history of the pre and post-apartheid South African Springbok Rugby Team specifically.
    d.   To become familiar with Nelson Mandela's detailed biography.
2. **Materials:** *The 16th Man* a 2010 ESPN 30 for 30 film (to viewed at home). Students are prompted to consider the following questions while watching the documentary:
    a.   Mandela, was challenged with the unfathomable task of rebuilding South Africa as a racially unified South Africa after fifty years of apartheid. Why did Mandela choose sport as his tool?
    b.   Specifically, why did he choose the White South African Rugby Team, the Springbok, the inimitable source of Afrikaner pride, as the vehicle to unite the majority Black South Africans and minority White South Africans?
    c.   How do you see this country's socio-political shift as a case study for rebranding a sport organization and a country?

3. **Procedures or Lecture Format:**
   a. Initiate a 10-15 minute discussion based on *The 16ᵗʰ Man* and the previously disbursed viewing questions
   b. To test student synthetization of information discussed ask three key questions:
      i. What are your understandings of the role of the Springbok Rugby Teams during apartheid in South Africa?
      ii. Why did Nelson Mandela reject changing the name of the Springbok Rugby Team in the post-apartheid period?
      iii. What is the political influence of sport?
   c. Summarize, draw conclusions and give instructions for deep learning exercise.
4. **Deep Learning Exercise:** Students are to prepare a research essay deconstructing Mandela's re-branding of South Africa's Springbok Rugby team and South Africa itself, using the knowledge they acquire about apartheid, biographical details of Nelson Mandela's life, and the power and influence of sports.

Mandela's Post-Apartheid Rugby Rebrand Lesson Plan Discussion

Students are to perform deep, historical research in preparation for class activities and projects. Despite this I do provide some resources to ensure that there is a minimum level of collective student understanding on the subject. These materials are typically some combination of a short lecture, readings, and the film *The 16ᵗʰ Man*. South African's apartheid history was violent by its very nature and thus some material in the documentary may be difficult for students to see. In part, this is why I require students to view this film on their own in advance of class. It allows them to control when and in what way they watch the film. I am mindful to inform students about the violent moments in the documentary before giving the assignment. I also ask students to view the film on their own to protect students of color in my class. Teaching at a predominately White institution, I am mindful that this minority population may feel a heightened sense of isolation or conspicuousness while watching such a film in a majority classroom. Finally individual viewing, gives all students the opportunity to reflect on their feelings without the possibility of peer pressure arising in a group setting.

This is not an exercise whereby students contemplate the decision to rebrand a team in isolation. Rather they are asked to do so within the context of post-apartheid South Africa under the leadership of the first democratically elected President, a lifelong activist, and former political prisoner who was once branded a terrorist. Students are required to be able to articulate the brutal legalized system of apartheid in South Africa. They must also demonstrate an understanding that during apartheid soccer was the most popular sport of the majority population: Black South Africans. Rugby was considered both a white sport and enjoyed its position as the most iconic sport in South Africa. The Springbok Rugby Team was the "personification of apartheid" (Korr, 2013). Furthermore, Rugby was so closely seen as a "metaphor for apartheid's brutality" (Minzesheimer, 2008) that Black South Africans cheered for visiting teams.

Given South Africa's merciless history of institutionalized discrimination, it is difficult to imagine a time in South Africa when Black South Africans would join in a collective rally for the Springbok Rugby Team? When Mandela was released from prison, he quickly played a primary role in dismantling apartheid and creating the pathway for a united South Africa. It was clear to Mandela that there could be neither a unified South Africa, nor peace without reconciliation. Mandela understood that sport has unifying and transformative powers and thus saw sport as the opportunity and rugby, a one-time symbol of hate, as the tool to achieve a united South Africa.

In 1995, post-apartheid South Africa hosted the international Rugby World Cup. Many anti-apartheid leaders plead with their newly president, Nelson Mandela, to change the name of the Springbok Rugby Team. Mandela understood that Springbok was the source of great Afrikaner pride. Mandela, the master conciliator, further understood that White South Africans "believed more in the Springbok than in guns" (Bestall, 2010). Mandela did not acquiesce to the pleas to change the name of its rugby team but, instead retained the Springbok name as a tool to achieve his greater goal of unifying South Africa. Mandela's motto was, "One Team, One Country" (Bestall, 2010). Perhaps retaining the Springbok name allowed White South Africans to retain some part of their heritage in the post-apartheid period. This coupled with the strength of Mandela's brand with Black South Africans, Mandela was confident that with South Africa as the host of the Rugby World Cup and his presence at the championship game dressed in the Springbok uniform, South Africa would make a monumental step toward a unified South Africa. Upon presenting the World Cup championship trophy to the Springbok captain, Mandela said, "...thank you very much for what you have done for our country" (Minzesheimer, 2008). The captain replied, "No, Mr. President. Thank you for what you have done for our country (Minzesheimer, 2008). P.W. Botha, former President of South Africa under apartheid, reflecting on Mandela's World Cup championship trophy presentation and stated, "That day he set us free (Bestall, 2010).

The unifying of South Africa serves as a case study in rebranding a team and a country with a historical past of grave racially motivated violence. Typically, decisions to rebrand can fall into three broad categories, 1. Corporate design (logos, uniforms, colors), 2. Corporate communications (i.e. advertising and Public Relations) or 3. Corporate behavior (i.e. internal values, or socio-cultural factors) (Dugar, 2012). Students research, analyze and explain Mandela's intentions through the lens of one or more of these rebranding strategies of a rugby team as a tool for reconciliation, peace and nation building.

SOLUTIONS AND RECOMMENDATIONS

Very often I have to teach history and context before I can embark upon marketing concepts, most particularly when the lesson plan centers on culture, ethnicity or race. Educators, educational institutions and textbook authors often treat multicultural topics as ancillary, and if covered at all, do so as the last lecture of a semester or the last chapter of a book. This stands incongruous with the carefully crafted mission statements that most institutions of higher education and their accrediting bodies create. With diversity forming such a significant aspect of those statements, it seems disingenuous to treat diversity education as an accouterment rather than as a meaningful part of a course that is strategically, thoughtfully and respectfully interwoven throughout it. There is a need for marketing educators to be culturally competent and institutions of higher education should provide and support on-going professional development in this area. Cultural diversity like marketing, is not static. It changes over time. As people move about the globe there is a need for more culturally diverse, real world marketing lesson plans. It is essential for the future benefit of both educators and marketing students.

The short-term solution is for marketing educators to take responsibility for ensuring their lesson plans include a wide range of diversity in substantive ways (see Table 1). Borrowing from the best practices of ensuring compliance with antidiscrimination laws, educators should be evaluated, in part, by the

Table 1. Tips for teaching cultural diversity

Assess and reflect on your cultural competence as an educator in your field of study. Constantly seek opportunities for professional development.
Create a safe learning environment. • Be responsive to the needs of students who feel isolated culturally. • Students should feel free to ask any question without judgement.
Embed cultural diversity into the entire curriculum, so as to avoid marginalizing cultural differences.
Provide students opportunities to assess their cultural competence and reflect on their biases.
Seek out like minded colleagues across academic fields for support and as collaborators for developing "jumanizing pedagogy" that will "inspire self and social transformation." (Camangian, 2015).

level of meaningful diversity and inclusion their marketing lesson plans articulate. The next generation of marketers will have to perform consumer behavior research, develop new products and services, and determine how those products and services should be delivered, advertised and priced in a profoundly more diverse world. Failing to prepare them to do so with cultural competence will minimize their ability to do so on a global scale.

Managing Diverse Human Capital

This chapter's focus is on developing culturally competent marketers. As marketing is a key component of business, so it managing human capital. As global nations become more, and more diverse, marketers will not only need to master the art of respectful multicultural marketing, but also master learning to effective manage diverse staff at all levels. It is important to understand having a diverse staff can positively affect the bottom line. It is also important to understand the potential challenges to group cohesion that may arise. Studying sport can be instructive in this area as well. According to Stura and Lepadatu (2014), there are two outcomes of diversity within an athletic team: 1). it "broadens the range of expertise, knowledge, insights, and ideas and 2). It can have negative effects. In these situations the negative effects are usually ameliorated when players focus on being athletes first and members of a particular race or ethnic group second. With the passage of time, teammates are able to engage athlete-to-athlete and athlete to leadership. The cultivation of these relationships ultimately reveals some of the long-term positive benefits of having a diverse team. Can this be true for non-sport businesses (Stura & Lepadtu, 2014)?

There are three schools of thought when it comes to whether or not a diverse workforce has a positive impact on business outcomes (i.e. increase in sales revenue, profits, market share, and customers). The first is that there is a positive impact of having a diverse workforce. The second is that having a diverse workforce increases conflict, reduces group cohesiveness, the result of which is an increase in employee absenteeism and turnover. Lastly, a diverse workforce causes both increased conflict and increased business performance. (Herring, 2009). Herring (2009) used a one-year national data sample of for-profit businesses to test eight hypotheses of the value-in-diversity thesis.

Herring's research concluded that notwithstanding the possibility for intergroup conflict that a diverse workforce may create, the net effect is positive in seven of the eight hypotheses tested. The explanation offered for the net positive result is the growth and innovation that results in superior problem solving; this is possible because of the diversity of bodies and the contesting ideas they bring to the fore. Herring further concludes that "homogeneity may lead to greater group cohesion but less adaptability and innovation." Group conflict caused by alleged discrimination can be overcome by an organization's procedural justice, that is, an organization commitment to support diversity (Triana & García, 2009). Triana and García remind us that "racial diversity is both a fact of life and a resource that must be managed." This thought extends to other types of diversity as well. Consider the changing demographics discussed previously and the fact that in 2013 there were over 93,000 discrimination charges filed with the Equal Employment Opportunity Commission (EEOC) in the United States. These claims crossed the gamut including discrimination and retaliation regarding race, sex, national origin, religion, color, age, disability, and equal pay. Despite whatever outcome these cases may have had, the fact of the charges result in a great expenditure of financial and intellectual resources.

As demonstrated here there are many facets to be managed in the context of diversity for the next generation of business leaders and they must manage it successfully; the bottom line depends on it. This chapter uses examples from the sport industry to demonstrate both a need and an avenue for developing cultural competence in our next business leaders.

CONCLUSION

The goal of this chapter was to provide some examples of how sport can be an effective way to examine cultural diversity and inclusion in developing cultural competence in the next generation of marketing leaders. This thrust of the chapter focused on gender and racial discrimination, but there are many more ways to explore cultural diversity and develop cultural competence using sport as the framework. Aside from gender discrimination, the modern workplace will have to grapple with gender identity issues, from the gender verification testing of India's Shanti Sounderajan and South Africa's Caster Semenya, to self-identified transsexual athletes like Dr. Renée Richards. Gender expression can be explored in the endorsement contract between Britney Griner and Nike, which allows her to wear clothes branded as menswear (Hing, 2013). It is no surprise that Nike would ink this type of contract with Griner. It was Nike who according to Bloomberg News, asked the president of the Golden State Warriors, who himself is openly gay to make it know that "anyone thinking about becoming the first openly gay athlete in major U.S. team sports – [should know] the company wants him as an endorser" (Stock, 2013).

Royce White, the basketball player recruited out of Iowa State, who was the 16th pick in the NBA draft wanted to address publicly his anxiety disorder in an effort to raise awareness of those who have mental health challenges. Additionally, Oscar Pistorius represents an intriguing issue in sport. Both able-bodied athletes and single amputee athletes, neither of whom wanted to race against him, accused Oscar of being advantaged in racing because he possessed two prosthetic legs.

There are many global cultures to examine through the framework of sport. Because sport is also a social practice, one in which most people connect as participant, fan and/or spectator, addressing issues of diversity and inclusion and thus creating cultural competence can begin with how these issues are addressed in the sport context. Sport is seen as a microcosm for life. While it may be up for debate whether it is the greater society outside of sport that pushes sport to change or if it is sport that pushes the greater society to change, it is clear that because there is a magnitude and variety of readily available and easily accessible data, sport centered lesson plans are an excellent tool to develop and strengthen cultural competence in marketing students.

REFERENCES

Adams, J. Q., & Welsch, J. R. (2009). Multiculturalism: The Manifest Destiny of the U.S.A.: An Interview with Ronald Takaki. *Multicultural Perspectives*, *11*(4), 227–231. doi:10.1080/15210960903475522

Bell, M. P. (2007). *Diversity in organizations*. Mason, OH: Thomason South-Western.

Bestall, C. (Producer and Director) & Mandela, N. (Performer). (2010). *The 16ᵗʰ man*. [Motion picture]. United States; 30 for 30 ESPN Films.

Bonilla-Silva, E. (2006). *Racism without racists: color-blind racism and the persistence of racial inequality in the United States*. Lanham, MD: Rowman & Littlefield.

Brooks, D. D., & Althouse, R. C. (Eds.). (2007). *Diversity and social justice in college sports: Sport management and the student athlete*. Morgantown, WV: Fitness Information Technology.

Camangian, P. R. (2015). Teach Like Lives Depend on It: Agitate, Arouse, and Inspire. *Urban Education*, *50*(4), 424–453. doi:10.1177/0042085913514591

Crenshaw, K. W. (1989). *Demarginalizing the Intersection of Race and Sex: A Black Feminist Theory and Antiracist Politics*. University Chicago Law Forum 139.

Cunningham, G. B. (2011). *Diversity in sport organizations*. Scottsdale, AZ: Holcomb Hathaway.

Deshpande, R., & Webster, F. E. Jr. (1989). Organization Culture and Marketing: Defining the Research Agenda. *Journal of Marketing*, *53*(1), 3–15. doi:10.2307/1251521

Dugar, A. (2012, Summer). Case study Rebranding: Yes or no? *Journal of Brand Strategy*, *1*(2), 149–163.

Equal Employment Opportunity Commission. (2014). *Charge Statistics FY 1997-FY 2013*. Retrieved from www.eeoc.gov/stats/charges.html

ESPN.com. (2014, October 18). *Shamil Tarpischev fined, banned year*. Retrieved from: espn.go.com/tennis/story/_/id/11718876/Russian-tennis-federation-president-shamil-tarpischev-sanctioned-serena-venus-williams-gender-comments

Gopaldas, A. (2013). Intersectionality 101. *Journal of Public Policy & Marketing*, *32*(Special Issue), 90–94. doi:10.1509/jppm.12.044

Guan, J., & Knottnerus, J. D. (2006). Chinatown Under Siege: Community Protest and Structural Ritualization Theory. *Humboldt Journal of Social Relations*, *30*(1), 5–52.

Herring, C. (2009). Does Diversity Pay? Race, Gender, and the Business Case for Diversity. *American Sociological Review*, *74*(2), 208–224. doi:10.1177/000312240907400203

Hing, J. (2013). *Brittney Griner's Nike contract is just the latest of her barrier-breaking moves*. Retrieved from http://colorlines.com/archives/2013/06/brittney_griners_gender-bending_nike_contract_just_the_latest_of_her_barrier-breaking_moves.html

Hughey, M. W. (2014). White backlash in the 'post-racial' United States. *Ethnic and Racial Studies*, *37*(5), 721–730. doi:10.1080/01419870.2014.886710

IEG LLC. (2015). *Sponsorship Spending Report: Where the Dollars are going and Trends for 2015.* Retrieved from www.sponsorship.com/Resources/Sponsorship-SpendingReport--Where-The-Dollars-Are.aspx

Keesing, R. M. (1974). Theories of Culture. *Annual Review of Anthropology, 3*(1), 73–97. doi:10.1146/annurev.an.03.100174.000445

Knoppers, A., & McDonald, M. (10, August 2010). Scholarship on Gender and Sport. *Sex Roles and Beyond, 63*(5-6), 311-323. Retrieved from www.ncbi.nlm.nih.gov/pmc/articles/PMC2928920/

Korr, C. P. (2013, December 6). Mandela used sport's power. *USA Today.*

Kroeber, A.L. & Kluckhohn, C. (1952). Culture: A critical review of concepts and definitions. *Papers of the Peabody Museum, 47*(1a).

Lester, R. (1999). *Stagg's University: The rise, decline, and fall of big time football at Chicago.* Chicago, IL: University of Illinois Press.

Maske, M. (2009). *NFL Extends Rooney Rule to Encourage Hiring of Minorities in Front Offices.* Retrieved from http://www.washingtonpost.com/wp-dyn/content/article/2009/06/15/AR2009061502806.html

Meyers, E. J. (2010). *Gender and sexual diversity in schools.* Springer. doi:10.1007/978-90-481-8559-7

Minzesheimer, B. (2008, August 14). How Mandela won over a nation. *USA Today.*

Pew Research Center. (2008). *U.S. Population Projections: 2005-2050.* Washington, DC: Author.

Rimer, E. (1996). Discrimination in Major League Baseball: Hiring Standards for Major League Managers, 1975-1994. *Journal of Sport and Social Issues, 20*(2), 118–133. doi:10.1177/019372396020002002

Smith, E., & Hattery, A. (2011). Race Relations Theories: Implications for Sport Management. *Journal of Sport Management, 25,* 107–117.

Stock, K. (2013). *Nike's Big Gay-Marketing Coup.* Retrieved from https://www.google.com/webhp?sourceid=chrome-instant&ion=1&espv=2&ie=UTF-8#q=nike%27s%20big%20gay-marketing%20coup

Stura, C., & Lepadatu, D. (2014). The Black Box of Diversity in Sports Teams: Converging Factors and Theoretical Explorations. *International Journal of Sport and Society, 4*(2), 47–56.

Title IX of the Education Amendments Act of 1972, 20 U.S.C.A. § 1681, et seq., on June 23, 1972.

Triana, M. D. C., & García, M. F. (2009). Valuing Diversity: A Group-value Approach to Understanding the Importance of Organizational Efforts to Support Diversity. *Journal of Organizational Behavior, 30*(7), 941–962. doi:10.1002/job.598

Tryce, S. A., & Brooks, S. N. (2010). "Ain't I a Woman?": Black Women and Title IX. *Journal for the Study of Sports and Athletes in Education, 4*(3), 243–255. doi:10.1179/ssa.2010.4.3.243

Tryce, S.A. & Smith, B. (2015). A Mock Debate on the Washington Redskins Brand: Fostering Critical Thinking and Cultural Sensitivity Among Sport Business Students. *Sport Management Education Journal, 9,* 1-10. 10.1123/SMEJ.2013-0016

United States Department of Education. (1997). *Title IX: 25 Years of Progress*. Retrieved from: www2.ed.gov/pubs/Title IX/index.html

United States Department of Justice. (n.d.). *Title IX Legal Manual*. Retrieved from www.justice.gov/crt/about/cor/coord/ixlegal.php

KEY TERMS AND DEFINITIONS

Business Case for Diversity: Differences in a company's workforce offers a direct return on investment in the form of profits and earning.

Cross Cultural Competence: The ability to engage productively with people from diverse communities, which is a process rooted in self-reflecting on ongoing learning.

Gender Transgressor: Appearance that defies the accepted attributes tied to one's sex.

Institutional Racism: Any intentional or unintentional act that results in the denial of access goods, services, housing or fair treatment to a person or group on the bases of race or skin color.

Racial/Ethnic Triangulation: Occurs when a dominant group (i.e. Whites) values a subordinate group (the triangulated group, i.e. Native Americans or Asian Americans), in relation to another subordinate group (i.e. African Americans), in order to dominate both subordinate groups and to exclude the triangulated group from political and civic membership.

Value-in-Diversity: A diverse workforce is generally good for business.

Chapter 8
Marketing Education in Sarawak:
Looking at It from the Employers' Viewpoint

Balakrishnan Muniapan
Wawasan Open University, Malaysia

Margaret Lucy Gregory
Universiti Teknologi MARA, Malaysia

Lim Ai Ling
Swinburne University of Technology – Sarawak, Malaysia

ABSTRACT

The state of Sarawak is the biggest among the 13 states in Malaysia. It is strategically located in South East Asia in the island of Borneo. In the state of Sarawak, Marketing education has seen a tremendous growth over the years. Marketing is one of the most sought-after business courses by many school leavers. In Sarawak, Marketing education is provided by public and private universities and institutions of higher education in the form of degree and diploma courses. Marketing education views marketing as a discipline that can be learned through the classroom (off the job). However the employers' perspectives differ as they prefer hands on (on the job). The main challenge confronting the Sarawak institutions of higher learning is to produce marketing graduates capable of being competent marketing practitioners serving in public and private sectors. The question that remains unanswered is whether the marketing education curriculum content matches the trends and major forces in our external environment as proper attention to these dimensions will enable the institutions to produce graduates equipped with the relevant skills in the workforce or whether the curriculum content has been designed in recognition of the fact that students will need to cope with the complex nature of today's business planning and decision-making. The literature on marketing education in Sarawak, is limited and very few research articles are found exploring the effectiveness. The authors have contributed to the field of Marketing education in Sarawak in one of their previous article published five years ago. Therefore this chapter is an attempt by the authors to explore the effectiveness of marketing education in meeting the organizational needs in Sarawak from

DOI: 10.4018/978-1-4666-9784-3.ch008

the perspectives of employers. This study uses qualitative methods which includes interview (face-to-face and telephone), informal discussions, email communications with managers, personal observations by the authors, and a review of literatures in the area of Marketing education. Marketing education, like marketing practice, is dynamic. Marketing education should continually evolve in such a manner to accommodate and satisfy various stakeholders such as government, business and industry, academics as well as students. The findings reveal several issues and challenges of Marketing education from the employers' perspectives in Sarawak. These findings will be useful for curriculum design of marketing courses. It will also assist marketing educators in understanding the organizational needs of marketing knowledge, skills and abilities required of a graduate. Future marketing students will also be able to know the industrial and organizational expectations required of them as a marketing graduate. This chapter clearly identifies some of the deficiencies in the area of practical skills required by marketing graduates in the context of Sarawak. This chapter is expected to provide the framework and prospect for conducting an in-depth quantitative research in Marketing education in future in Sarawak (Borneo).

1. INTRODUCTION[1]

Malaysia is a well known country located in Southeast-Asia with Singapore, Thailand, Brunei and Indonesia as neighboring countries. The state of Sarawak is the biggest among the 13 states in Malaysia. It is strategically located in South East Asia in the island of Borneo. It covers an area of 125,000 sq. km and has a population of 2.619 million and has 27 ethnic groups from diverse backgrounds living together (Yearbook of Statistics Sarawak, 2013). With its strategic location, Sarawak is emerging as a profitable investment hub offering cost-competitive advantages with good air transportation linkages.

Recently, the Sarawak Corridor of Renewable Energy or simply known as SCORE was launched by the Federal Government of Malaysia. It is one of the five regional development corridors being developed throughout the country. SCORE is a major initiative undertaken to develop the Central Region and transform Sarawak into a developed State by the year 2020. It aims to achieve the goals of accelerating the State's economic growth and development, as well as improving the quality of life for the people of Sarawak (http://www.sarawakscore.com.my/).

In this context, recently the Sarawak state government indicated that it will help some 4,000 graduates with diplomas and degrees (Marketing included) by giving them on the job training under a special program called " Capacity building for graduates in Sarawak" over the next two years (The Borneo Post, 2009). With this program, graduates could gain practical skills such as in manufacturing, IT, utilities, tourism, social and government, financial and professional services. The former Chief Minister Pehin Tan Sri Abdul Taib Mahmud said "in the coming years, there would be manpower requirement in industries like the agro-based ones with the development of the halal hub, aluminium and poly-silicon, construction and education and training in the SCORE". He also hopes that the jobs created in SCORE would go to the local people in Sarawak (The Borneo Post, 2009).

With all these developments taking place, the organizations in Sarawak in this millennium are becoming very competitive and demanding. This has a great implication for the state human capital development especially in the area of education and training of the workforce. The employees are expected to be multi-skilled and capable of taking greater responsibility and creative in solving problems and making decisions. Thus, the graduate students are expected to enter the workplace equipped not only with theoretical knowledge but also practical skills in several areas to satisfy employer expectations to a greater degree.

Marketing is one of the most sought-after business courses by many school leavers. In Sarawak, Marketing education is provided by public and private universities and institutions of higher education in the form of degree and diploma courses. In these institutions, students will usually undertake the units specified as 'prerequisites' such as language, communication, management, accounting, finance, information systems, economics, business law, business statistics before proceeding to the marketing specific units.

Hence the main challenge confronting the Sarawak institutions of higher learning is to produce marketing graduates capable of being competent marketing practitioners serving in the workforce in public and private sectors. The question that remains unanswered is whether the marketing education curriculum content matches the trends and major forces in our external environment as proper attention to these dimensions will enable the institutions to produce graduates equipped with the relevant skills in the workforce or whether the curriculum content has been designed in recognition of the fact that students will need to cope with the complex nature of today's business planning and decision-making.

2. LITERATURE REVIEW

There is abundance of literature in the field of Marketing. Marketing is an organizational activity that creates business. The current definitions of marketing are focused upon customer orientation and satisfaction of customer needs. The Chartered Institute of Marketing (CIM), which is the world's largest marketing body, defines marketing as the management process responsible for identifying, anticipating and satisfying customer requirements profitably (CIM, 2009). The American Marketing Association (AMA) defines marketing as the activity, set of institutions, and processes for creating, communicating, delivering, and exchanging offerings that have value for customers, clients, partners, and society at large (AMA, 2009). Renowned marketing experts and authors Kotler and Amstrong (2008), define marketing as a social and managerial process by which individuals and groups obtain what they need and want through creating, offering, and exchanging products of value with others.

Over the years, marketing has become an integral part of organizational strategy and strategic marketing planning has always been a part of organizational strategic management. The roles and the expectations of marketers in organizations are also changing and will continue to change as the business environment changes. Marketing is also a broad area that covers a range of aspects and functions such as market research, product planning, pricing, distribution and promotion which includes advertising, public relation, sales promotion and selling. In the past, marketing was equated with selling and people often confuse selling with marketing, when in fact the two are very different. Marketing is more than just selling; it involves identifying the needs and wants of the target market, translating it into product and services and selling it (Kotler & Amstrong, 2008). Selling is the actual transaction of getting a product or service into the hands of the final customers. The objective of marketing is to create transactions between two or more parties who provide something of value to each other. It is a well established fact that organizations without a marketing mindset are at a disadvantage in today's competitive business environment. It is imperative for organizations to train and develop their marketing personnel to meet the requirements of the marketplace. Therefore, the role of Marketing education is crucial in meeting the demands, expectations and the requirements of organizations.

Marketing education is the study of that business activity that occurs between the creation of products and services and the consumption of those products and services by the customers and ultimate consumer by businesses or institutions of higher learning. The aim of a marketing education is to achieve the ultimate objective of marketing. The objective of marketing is to create voluntary exchanges between two or more parties who provide something of value to each other. In line with the objective, marketing consists of nine basic functions: buying, pricing, selling, distribution, promotion, product or service planning, financing, risk management, and securing marketing information. These functions represent the major content of the Marketing education curriculum.

Academically, Marketing education involves and requires the application of mathematics, communications, psychology, economics, technology, and specific product and service knowledge in conjunction with human resource skills in problem-solving, decision-making, conflict resolution, group work, and goal-setting within the context of a marketing activity. Organizations need marketing professionals who are responsive to economic, social, cultural, technical and environmental change and can work flexibly and intelligently across business contexts. They also require marketing graduates who understand the part they play in building their organizations, and have the practical skills to work effectively in their roles. Even in the staff development of marketers which is handled by the continuing education (CE) marketing department, find it very challenging to keep pace with competition in a changing market place that requires the adult learners to adapt to new development, technologies and marketing strategies to become relevant in order to survive and advance (Fong, 2013).

In fact all business and management students need to understand the processes and procedures involved in marketing, while students planning to enter a career in marketing need in-depth instruction on the foundations and functions of marketing. The graduate workforce is a key part of the talent pool organizations looking to enhance their competitiveness. It is the goal of universities, institutions of higher learning and business schools to produce marketing graduates with the skills that are highly regarded by employers and are seen to contribute to the country's prosperity and social capital. However, today's employers are expressing their frustration about how practitioners' and organizations are providing training to university graduates rather than universities and institutions of higher learning in order for the graduates to be effective and efficient in their performance (Harrigan & Hulbert, 2011).

In the context of Malaysia, since the restructuring of the private higher education sector in 1996, the sector has been transformed into a full-fledge industry (Tan, 2002). In most universities and institutions of higher learning, marketing is offered as a subject or a major is part of many business and management programs; it comes within the scope of business education or management education. Therefore throughout this paper, unless otherwise stated, business and management education also includes marketing education. Business education in Malaysia has come under criticism in recent times from the industries due to the inability of graduates to put what they have learned into practice. The blame has been largely placed on the universities and institutions of higher learning for not producing the required quality graduates who can meet the needs of the employers (Muniapan, 2008).

Despite this increased attention on marketing education, unlike business education and management education, there has been limited empirical research on marketing education in Malaysia (Linget al, 2010). Most of the studies done explored business education and management education in which marketing is also included. Muniapan (2008) cited some of the studies done in the Malaysian context of business and management education, among which includes studies on the issue of quality and quality practices in Malaysian higher education was done by Sohail, Rajadurai and Abdul Rahman (2003). Their studies involved investigation of management systems prior to and after implementation of quality system for a private college in Malaysia. Their studies focused more on quality implementation system and were less related to Marketing education. Related studies on Human Resource Management (HRM) education in Malaysia was written by Muniapan (2010) and on business ethics (marketing) by Muniapan and Rajantheran (2011). An earlier study was conducted by Tay (2001), which was indirectly related to marketing education on management perception of MBA graduates. However the coverage of these studies was focused on business and management education in West Malaysia. Except for Ling et al (2010) and Lee et al (2011), the East Malaysian states of Sarawak and Sabah were not highlighted and not found in any of these studies.

In the international context, with reference to the effectiveness of Marketing education, many studies have been done in the context of America, the United Kingdom and Australia. In one of the studies done by Stringfellow et al., (2006) on the relevance of Marketing education to marketing practice in the context of the UK, there seems to be some significant gaps between the teaching offered by the academy in marketing, and the knowledge and abilities required by practitioners in marketing. They addressed the question of whether marketing education should be narrowly designed to meet employers' perceived needs, or designed with a broader scope incorporating general, liberal educational aims as well as a narrow "employability" agenda. This debate was also presented previously in the USA from the studies done by Narayandas et al., (1998); Shuptrine and Willenborg, (1998); Wilson, (1998), in France by Kumar and Usunier, (2001), in the UK by Garneau and Brennan (1999), and across other countries and regions by Howard and Ryans, (1993); and Howard et al., (1991) cited in Stringfellow et al., (2006).

Earlier studies made by Garneau and Brennan (1999) in the context of the UK detected a relatively narrow perspective among employers, with an emphasis on generic skills (e.g. numeracy, literacy) and attitudes (e.g. punctuality) and less emphasis on scientific and general knowledge. Similar findings were reported by Shuptrine and Willenborg (1998) in the USA. It is also interesting to note that Howard and Ryans (1993) and Howard et al. (1991) found that marketing educators in Europe and the Pacific Rim emphasized the role of marketing theory in marketing education more than American marketing educators. It is therefore essential for marketing educators to question the values and benefits of their marketing education to the organizations.

3. BENEFITS OF MARKETING EDUCATION

Muniapan (2008) cited Longenecker and Ariss (2002) in describing the benefits of management (marketing) education to the organizations. An effective marketing education program can help organizations create competitive advantage through:

- Exposing students or marketers to new/better ideas and business practices which are needed in rapidly changing business environments;
- Motivating students or marketers to improve performance (both theirs and that of their operation) and actually helping them develop and improve their skills;
- Providing opportunities for reflection and self-appraisal and helping students or marketers identify specific performance problems and deficiencies;
- Increasing student or marketer confidence, reducing stress level and challenging them to think differently about their business situation and themselves; and
- Encouraging students as future marketers to think about their career development and improve themselves through participating in marketing education programs.

The benefits of marketing education however, depend entirely on the ability of students to put what they have learned into practice depending upon the clarity and consistency of the theories, models, principles, and practices presented to them throughout the curriculum. Muniapan (2008) also cited a study by Pfeffer and Fong (2002) in the American context which suggests that business school (marketing) education overall has not been very effective. The education was not found to correlate with career success, and business school research was found to have little influence on marketing practice. In the context of Australia, a report called "Karpin Report" released in 1995, provides detailed outcomes from a major government task force set up to identify effective management (marketing) practices. The findings include recommendations as to how the tertiary education sector could improve marketing education programs to better meet the needs of the industry. Among the suggestions include an increasing emphasis on soft skills, internationalization, and cross-functional integration, diversity and links to industry (Holian, 2004).

To improve the strategy decision making approach of future global marketing managers in today's dynamic and ever-changing marketplace, it is suggested that curriculum development to emphasize on the importance and development of soft skills such as the ability to be flexible and adaptable to change in the business environment (Griffith & Hoppner, 2013). This soft skill development will enable the marketing managers to adapt to the ever changing environment and tackle real global business problems from a global perspective. This could be achieved by exposing students to the real ever-changing global challenges through experiential education and Baker and Henson (2010) reflected the importance of combining experiential learning with reflective techniques to produce the required business skills and professional competencies within university graduates.

4. SKILLS FOR EFFECTIVE MARKETERS

Smith, W.L., Schallenkamp, K. and Eichholz, D.E. (2007) in a study on entrepreneurial skills cited a study by Lyons (2002) who described four sets of essentials skills for effective and enterprising marketers. The skills highlighted by Lyons are beyond the traditional marketing skills such as product development, pricing, distribution, promotional efficiency, marketing research and include skills such as technical, managerial, entrepreneurial and personal maturity skills. Tables 1–4 (cited in Muniapan, 2008) describes the above mentioned skills.

In general, a marketing professional requires a wide range of skills such as good written communication skills to write promotional materials, persuasion skills to persuade colleagues, customers, suppliers and top management, good analytical skills in analyzing the pricing and key features of a products or service, investigative skills to be able to research the market such as product research, pricing research, customer research, distribution research, promotional research and other related research (Muniapan & Raj, 2014).

In the UK, a study by Gibson-Sweet, Brennan, Foy, Lynch and Rudolph (2010) examined the nature of undergraduates marketing education presented in 2009 which was then compared to prior studies conducted in 1999-2000. For example, in 2009, key issues in marketing education that are considered of highest priorities to teach to students by marketing academics are incorporation of active learning techniques, learning technology and usage of research activities, however these issues were not considered to be important by marketing academics in 1999. There are multiple perspectives in the teaching and the knowledge of marketing education gained by undergraduates, but one thing is certain, marketing education continues to evolve in such a manner to accommodate and satisfy the variety of interests including business, industry and students.

Table 1. Technical skills

Number	Skill Set	Description
1	Operational	The skills necessary to produce the product or service
2	Supplies/Raw materials	The skills to obtain them, as necessary
3	Office or production space	The skills to match needs and availability
4	Equipment/ Plant/ Technology	The skills to identify and obtain them

Table 2. Managerial skills

Number	Skill Set	Description
1	Management	Planning, organizing, supervising, directing, networking
2	Sales	Identifying customers, distribution channels, supply chain
3	Financial	Managing financial resources, accounting, budgeting
4	Legal	Organization form, risk management, privacy and security
5	Administrative	People relations, advisory board relations
6	Higher-order	Learning, problem-solving

Table 3. Entrepreneurial skills

Number	Skill Set	Description
1	Business concept	Business plan, presentation skills
2	Environmental scanning	Recognize market gap, exploit market opportunity
3	Advisory board and networking	Balance independence with seeking assistance

Table 4. Personal maturity skills

Number	Skill Set	Description
1	Self-awareness	Ability to reflect and be introspective
2	Accountability	Ability to take responsibility for resolving a problem
3	Emotional coping	Emotional ability to cope with a problem
4	Creativity	Ability to produce a creative solution to a problem

One of the private universities of Australian origin based in Kuching has addressed the importance of employability skills through their graduate attributes. These graduate attributes are incorporated into course outlines, learning objectives and content for each subject. Generic employability skills such as teamwork skills, analytical skills, problem-solving skills, communication skills, ability to tackle unfamiliar problems, and ability to work independently are being cultivated in undergraduates across all program areas.

The issues and challenges to prepare students with adequate knowledge and skills to solve complex problems in a day to day business decision making are believed by educators to be critically important to gainful employment and practice. Indeed universities are encouraged to embed critics actively in marketing education to provide students with critical thinking, reasoning and moral skills requisite to enter today's complex and dynamic marketplace (Lim & Svensson, 2013). A problem for critical approaches is that they are commonly adopted at the final year level.It is suggested by Tregear, Dobson, Brennan, and Kuznesof (2010) that future marketing curriculum should view critical perspectives and thinking from an early stage to allow students to fully benefit from the teaching and learning approaches. It seems then, if business schools are to prepare undergraduates for professions, a marketing curriculum that contains critical perspectives throughout the course is the key. Despite the continued interest in developing and reviewing the curriculum design for marketing education, resourcing appears to be a problem as there are insufficient time allocation and insufficient information provided by the management to support decision making when carrying out the reviews (Dennis, 2014).

While information on skills may be useful to marketing educators and students, it is also important to identify which skills are most critical that business organizations expect marketing graduates to possess. Thus, it is highly recommended that universities and marketing educators enhance the students' skills by inviting small to medium sized enterprises (SMEs), not-for-profits or public sector organizations to provide students with real life facilities and real time problems with the aim to provide students with good opportunities to see the relevance of the teaching and learning to practical work environment in order to adapt to workplace environments and solve real problems (Barker, 2014). The incorporation of real-world learning in marketing curriculum is designed to enhance students' learning and to provide a strong linkage between theory and practice. Marketing educators regard experiential learning desirable, however, some employers are of the opinion that experiential learning methods may not always be successful by mainly providing students with real-life or simulated experiences of marketing activities, which they think do not always prove to be sufficient to produce experiential learning (Brennan, 2014).

This approach that is taken by the university is to ensure that its graduates are well prepared in today's competitive marketplace that is facing increasing levels of competition among graduates for available jobs and the changing nature of skills needed.

5. METHODOLOGY

This paper uses qualitative methods to gather data. These methods include interview (face-to-face and telephone), informal discussion, email communication with managers and employers' representatives particularly in Kuching, personal observations by the authors, and literature review in marketing education (Muniapan, 2015).

Interviews and discussions were mainly used in gathering data (Patton, 2002; Muniapan, 2014). The interview process allows for a wide variety of information on the subject of marketing education. For the purpose of this paper we used convenience sampling methods. Convenience sampling involves choosing the nearest and most convenient persons to act as respondents (Parasuraman et al, 2009).

A total of 11 respondents holding managerial positions from various industries in Kuching responded. The small number of respondents was due to the small number of industries located in Kuching (East Malaysia). Besides face-face interview, email responses were also received from the employers and these included their general feedback on marketing education.

Information was also gathered through informal discussion with several marketing educators, consultants and marketing students, during meetings, seminars and conferences over the last five years. All their input, combined with the authors' own observations and experiences in marketing education were helpful in the preparation of this paper.

The data gathered were sorted based on the themes, issues and problems identified. Parasuraman et al (2009) cited in a study by Maxwell (1996) argues that the best way to deal with qualitative data is to start analyzing as soon as the first data collection process ends. He suggested (1996, p. 77), "....the experienced qualitative researcher begins data analysis immediately after finishing the first interview or observation and continues to analyze the date as long as he or she is working on the research, stopping briefly to write reports and papers." The themes, issues and problems identified by the respondents are highlighted and discussed to draw conclusions and to provide the recommendations.

6. FINDINGS AND DISCUSSION

The findings revealed that in the context of Sarawak, most marketing related jobs such as sales, advertising, public relations and others do not require a high level formal education. However, it also depends upon the type of position which graduates are seeking and the business nature, culture and the recruitment policy of the organization. Although a bachelor degree is not essential for all entry-level jobs, most of the employers agreed that a university degree is often a requirement for higher level positions such as executives and above. In this context, one of the respondents made the following comment:

... It depends on the position offered for recruitment. Generally, we would give priority to degree holders if the position requires more in-depth thinking, communication and strategizing elements......for executive positions, priority will be given to the degree holders...

An employer from an automobile industry however, was of the opinion that at entry-level for certain jobs, employers of small organizations tend to value specific experience and skills over a university degree. One of the employers was also willing to pay more for these abilities in new employees. This was his response:

... as for small and medium scale enterprises, I would prefer our employees to have positive mental attitude and experience ...I would go for someone who could fulfill these requirements even though the person may not have a good education background and pay them good salaries.

Some employers appear to be more eager to hire graduates who not only have strong academic preparation but also have developed their skills in real world situations and on real world problems and projects. Some of the common comments with regards to the above are:

... In most cases we did not even ask for the result scripts...as long as we can verify the academic certification they submitted....the specific knowledge which they gained previously as interns or part-timers will be crucial ...

... academic performance and reputation of the university are secondary...graduates with some level of experience in the real world are preferred as real life working experience is the major issue considered ...

Thus, a graduate who has some experience in the field and industrial placements and practical projects will have a better opportunity to secure a job. According to Kagaari (2007, p. 459), college-based practical training and industrial training are crucial in producing highly trained graduates that are effective and efficient in their job performance. Maguire (2005) cited in Kagaari (2007) added that 'university-industry linkages is key to good relationship between the individual, lifelong learning, the workplace and employability". Therefore, most employers would prefer somebody with quality industrial placements' and professional experiences. This was confirmed by two bank employers who made the following comments:

... Definitely prefer graduates with some experience unless the graduates had undergone a very structured and well-designed industrial placement at a reputable organization...

Experience is essential but less priority...both of real-time experience and internship are considered... however, graduates who completed industrial placement, especially with the company related to our core business operations are highly considered ...

Although industrial placement and experience are important in the workplace, this however is not very common in all circumstances. Unfortunately, there is a lack of quality industrial placement and professional work experience among university graduates as noted by another bank employer:

... at the moment, we have not found any graduates who have undergone a thorough industrial training and acquired the necessary skills and we gather the reason for that is the companies that they are attached to are not serious about imparting knowledge to the trainees and also the trainees are lacking in initiative to learn more about the job ...

It is also interesting to note that some employers looking for applicants to fill business or marketing jobs are especially drawn to the expertise graduates have built up in marketing degrees as they are likely to be more adept in marketing discipline areas than those with degrees in other disciplines as found in the following comments:

... if a candidate with a Bachelor of Marketing is taken, we would expect him/her to be more familiar with marketing proposal writing, strategic propositions and giving public presentations, etc compared with those with just a generic degree ...

... if the position is for Marketing then I would rather have someone with a Bachelor of Marketing degree as it is more specialized and suitable for the post ...

Meanwhile, there are also some employers who believe that university education can only focus on the general needs of the graduate in their line of discipline but not on the specific knowledge or skills of required for the job. In the real world, when these fresh graduates are hired, they will know very little of how to use the skills and knowledge learned at university. These graduates will soon realize they need a set of different skills to enable them to cope with the organizational culture and the demands of the job. Hence, it is vital for employers to provide in-house training or hands-on training based on the organizations' needs. The following comments from employers support the above arguments:

... I do not believe that there is a single university that can house all the industry-specific knowledge for all industries....we used to hire staff from local educational institutes to conduct a module of our training and the results were less than satisfactory....it turned out that the moderators from the university were incapable of answering the trainees' industry-specific queries ...

... although it is a general expectation that a graduate's specific knowledge should cover all, if not most areas of the job description, this may not prevail at all times as each company has its own specific working culture and organization...training sessions are usually carried out to ensure that the graduate fully comprehends the procedures and duties attached to his/her position, to prevent any shortfalls ...

Under such circumstances, it is thus not surprising to learn that these employers find it not necessary to just hire marketing graduates for marketing jobs. Since companies provide training, hiring graduates from other disciplines are also considered as long as they possess the correct and positive attitude. Booth (2005, p. 23) in citing a study by Hart, et al. (2007) suggested that "people with the right attitude can be trained but people with the wrong attitude cannot", meaning that skills and knowledge can be easily imparted to people with the right attitude, not just marketing graduates. In an earlier study made by Gray, B.J., et al. (2007) in looking at the essential skills of marketing graduates in the context of New Zealand, they found that willingness to learn was the most important attribute for new graduates to have if they want to be employed. This implies that the willingness to learn is an important attribute for all marketing positions. The following are some of those responses from employers from banking industries:

... majoring in a specific field may not be the main issue...the most essential factors are candidates' attitude and aptitude for the job, and also the nature of the job ...

... generally, it doesn't matter...as long as the candidate meet the basic requirement of degree level... the vital elements are the graduate's personality, drive and open-mindedness ...

Increasingly, employers want graduates to possess creative, decision-making and problem solving skills. Based on these expectations, most employers highlighted the importance of the university to tackle the practical issues in the industry by providing students with the competencies and skills required in the job market as follows:

... successful graduates must have the motivation to know more and be proactive in decision-making... it indicates that there is always a learning culture which is pertinent to a successful person and to the organization as a whole...the university must make it a point to have industrial training at relevant organizations so as to equip graduates with the required skills on day-to-day aspects of the job...the university must tie up with some major corporations or big companies where each semester a number of undergraduates would undergo a structured industrial training at the said company ...

... being an employee especially at the executive level requires constant decision-making that would be in favor of the company and guided by specific guidelines and procedures....creative conflict-handling would set the graduate apart from the rest...this is a special skill which is really lacking ...

However, there are employers who criticized the universities and institutions of higher learning in Sarawak for failing to equip students with these practical skills required by their employers which enable students to better understand the current challenges in the industry and become competent workers. The following comments were made by employers from a banking industry and a telecommunication industry:

... university has yet to develop the required practical skills as the focus is so much on paper chase and grades....these skills are very subjective and difficult to evaluate and have yet to appear in degree certificate or transcript ...

... developing and handling strategies is one of the expectations of most organizations...honestly, the university has not done much on this ...

The above findings pose several issues and challenges to marketing education in the context of Sarawak. We shall explore some of these issues and challenges.

7. ISSUES AND CHALLENGES RELATED TO MARKETING EDUCATION

In general, one of the most important factors that employers' in Sarawak (regardless of the industry they belong to) weigh heavily before recruiting and selecting an employee in the area of marketing is the individual's maturity and confidence to cope with the demands of the organization. It is probably impossible to find a perfect marketing education program and it is also probably impossible to find the best formula for efficient and effective marketing practice. In this context, most of the employers also agreed that it is impossible to expect graduates to have all the required knowledge, skills, and abilities in marketing upon graduation from institutions of higher learning.

Many respondents were of the view that graduates lack the required skills to perform marketing functions effectively. One of the marketing managers commented that many young graduates simply do not come across as being mature and confident enough for the professional world. The graduates tend to follow theories and approaches in the textbook which might not be applicable in the workplace. When the employers prove them wrong, they tend to withdraw and immediately lose their confidence in handling the issue and solving the problems. Muniapan (2008) also highlighted similar concerns as the teaching in the institutions of higher learning is based on and place greater emphasis on western marketing theories and concepts. These are also due to lack of research studies done in the area of marketing in Sarawak (and the rest of Malaysia), and teaching the Business or Marketing Program in institutions of higher learning is heavily dependent on American-based theories and case studies which have little or no relevance to the local context.

Employers in Sarawak also seem to favour graduates who are flexible, adaptable and receptive to change in the working environment. This is also due to the current business environment with rapid changes seen mainly in competition, customer taste, the economy, technology and also societal values. In this context, employers expect graduates to exhibit a range of intellectual abilities and skills as well as the ability to conceptualise issues rapidly and deal with large amounts of information. They want graduates who are inquisitive, innovative, logical, analytic, critical, creative, able to think laterally and conceptualise issues rapidly. Besides, good interpersonal skills and emotional intelligence will also provide the graduate with an edge at the workplace as today, the rules of the workplace are changing and emotional intelligence or EQ instead of traditional IQ is being used as the yardstick to judge people competency. EQ is especially essential as marketers deal with people, mainly customers, suppliers and fellow colleagues. The implication for institutions of higher learning is to improve and increase training for students in the area of interpersonal skills, human relations skills, teamwork and skills in handling conflict.

This is also related to another issue highlighted by an employer who asserted that a modern organisation requires employees with an ability to cope with pressure, manage stress, meet deadlines, and prioritise work and, most of all be independent. Teamwork is identified as the single most important skill employers look for. Fresh graduates working in the modern organisation have a poor understanding of the culture of a modern organisation, industrial relations issues and organisational politics such as how to deal with different levels of people in the organisation.

In this regard, the interpersonal skills and communication skills as highlighted earlier are very important to employers, but there is a gap between employers' expectations and employees' performances. Employers often perceive fresh graduates as full of arrogance, refusing to communicate with people who are not on the same intellectual level.

It is clearly evident that employers place a great deal of importance on graduates' communication skills and listening skills. These skills are important to employers because it is necessary for graduates in industry to communicate ideas, concepts and get feedback from colleagues and customers. Employers are often critical of graduates' grasp of fundamentals of written communication, especially basic grammar, sentence structure and punctuation. Employers are also concerned about the range of writing abilities of graduates. They may be good at producing essays, academic projects and dissertations but are relatively poor at producing other forms of written communication like business reports in the workplace. Reports are much more prescriptive than essays and graduates lack the skills and versatility to write in a variety of styles to suit particular genres such as a business report.

However on a positive note, in terms of information technology, most employers commented that they are very satisfied with the graduates' 'computer literacy.' The graduates also seem to show more enthusiasm when they use technology. This is not surprising as teaching-learning in universities takes place in a "hi-tech" environment which provides students with ample facilities to use technology in the form of online materials, online journals, etc to further their academic pursuits.

8. CONCLUSION

Marketing education, like marketing practice, is dynamic. Marketing education should continually evolve in such a manner to accommodate and satisfy various stakeholders such as government, business and industry, academics as well as students. This paper clearly identifies some of the deficiencies in the area of practical skills required by marketing graduates in the context of Sarawak. Most graduates enter the workplace with a reasonably strong theoretical knowledge of marketing principles and frameworks but do not seem to fully comprehend business and the organizational perspectives of marketing. Several employers are of the opinion that universities and institutions of higher learning in Sarawak fail to provide students with practical marketing skills required to better understand the current challenges in the industry and become competent workers. This calls for several recommendations and strategies to be implemented mainly by the universities and institutions of higher learning offering marketing programs.

9. RECOMMENDATIONS

Marketing education views marketing as a discipline that can be learned through the classroom (off the job). However the employers' perspectives differ as they prefer hands on (on the job). It is imperative that universities and institutions of higher learning in Sarawak incorporate practical training or industrial placement for Marketing students in their final year of studies. However, this may also be a problem for institutions with foreign affiliations as their co-curriculum and academic program are rather fixed or leave little room for flexibility.

The emphasis on western marketing theories and concepts used in teaching marketing education as highlighted by one of the respondents, calls for an increase in Sarawak-based marketing research and textbook publications, Sarawak (and Malaysian) based case studies and even developing Sarawak marketing management models or theories as in the case of American, Swedish, Japanese, Chinese and Indian marketing management theories. This can also help "glocalization" of marketing education.

Foreign marketing models can be taught in comparative marketing programs. This can be supported by the government through the Ministry of Higher Education and also the State Government in Sarawak which needs to provide incentives to local marketing authors, academics and researchers to conduct and publish research and marketing case studies in the Sarawak context, something yet to be found.

Furthermore, an urgent need is required for marketing education offered by the universities and institutions of higher learning to provide the required skills to meet the current and future challenges and the requirements of the marketplace. The current perception in Sarawak is that the universities and institutions of higher learning are not motivated to cooperate with the industries and vice versa. There is a strong need for the universities and institutions of higher learning to link with industries in terms of marketing research and development. This can be a win-win situation for the universities and institutions of higher learning and industries (Muniapan, 2008).

Also, there is a perception by some of the respondents that employability skills like initiative, leadership and problem solving are under-developed by the university. In addition to technical or discipline-specific skills and knowledge, these skills are very important for graduates to be employable. To address to this issue, it is very crucial that universities throughout Malaysia integrate these skills into the curriculum and course design and provide students with the opportunity to intelligently apply that knowledge in the work setting through work placements and increased exposure to professional settings. "Employability skills are defined as skills required not only to gain employment, but also to progress within an enterprise so as to achieve one's potential and contribute successfully to enterprise strategic directions" (DEST, 2002).

Business schools or the universities and institutions of higher learning should also invite marketing practitioners into classrooms as adjunct lecturers to share real life marketing experiences with the learners. The inputs from practitioners would enhance and add value to the learners on marketing skills at the workplace. Besides, a good, strong, motivated and committed leadership is also required in universities and institutions of higher learning to attract, develop and retain good academic staff in marketing, which eventually can contribute positively to the growth and the effectiveness of the universities and institutions of higher learning itself.

Besides, in the universities and institutions of higher learning, a paradigm shift from traditional teacher or lecturer-centered to student-centered learning of marketing is required. This is because excellence in teaching begins with the realization that it is not the teaching but the learning that is important. The responsibilities of the universities and institutions of higher learning goes beyond the teaching of marketing; it is to help students to develop and master various work skills such as interpersonal communication, decision-making and problem-solving skills (Muniapan, 2008).

In reality, the industry prefers students with employability skills that are relevant to the conditions of the job market. Therefore universities should focus on the critical and relevant skills to equip marketing graduates for filling marketing positions. The classroom experience should not merely focus on theory and memorizing information in the textbooks. It seems then, business schools have to reinvent themselves and review the marketing curriculum on a periodic basis to react to the current and future demands of the industry in order to improve students' employability. Although marketing education will have to face many challenges in the future, it is critical for the business schools to maintain a up-to-date curriculum by incorporating the marketing academics, marketing practitioners and business organizations perspectives.

Universities need to prepare undergraduates to adapt to an environment that is changing in significant ways as well as the challenges that await. The delivery of courses in the traditional campus classroom model has become far less relevant due to fast advancement in technologies that require the marketing faculty to adapt themselves to these changes. In addition, the faculty has to place a greater emphasis on the changing priorities in regard to the skills students need today to be successful in their business and marketing professions. A study by Delong and McDermott (2013) also emphasizes the importance of integrating sustainability in the marketing and business curriculum in the future to prepare undergraduates for the urgent challenges that require them to remain competitive in the ever-changing global marketplace. There is obvious concern for being able to focus on the skills and attributes considered necessary or perceived by the industry to be vital.

10. LIMITATION AND DIRECTION FOR FUTURE RESEARCH

The authors recognize that the number of interviews for this the study is limited, however they hope this paper will provide a framework for further research on marketing education and related topics in the context of Sarawak. Future research should be able to explore all the stakeholders' interests and expectations in marketing education in Sarawak which also includes perspectives of marketing learners, marketing graduates, marketing academics and also business schools, universities and institutions of higher learning. This approach will be able to present a balanced view of marketing education in the context of Sarawak. In addition, the study is only qualitative in nature. Therefore, the results of this study may lack generalisability. Instead, the results should be however taken as an initial starting point for future studies. Thus, future research obtained from quantitative data is required to enable a more in-depth treatment of the results in order to strengthen the authors' conclusion.

ACKNOWLEDGMENT

The authors would like to thank the reviewers for their comments and constructive feedback provided to the original version of this paper. Special thanks to Ms Helen who teaches English at Swinburne Sarawak for proof-reading and editing this paper.

REFERENCES

AMA. (2009). Available at http://www.marketingpower.com/Pages/default.aspx

Ayob, M. A., & Yaakub, F. N. (2000), *Development of Graduate Education in Malaysia: Prospect for Internationalization*. Paper presented at the 2000 ASAIHL Seminar on University and Society: New Dimensions for the Next Century held at Naresuan University, Phitsanulok, Thailand. Available at: http://mahdzan.com/papers/thaipaper00/

Baker, G. & Henson, D. (2010). Promoting employability skills development in a research-intensive university. *Education + Training, 52*(1), 62-75. doi: 10.1108/00400911011017681

Barker, B. (2014). Employability skills: Maintaining relevance in marketing education. *The Marketing Review, 134*(1), 29–48. doi:10.1362/146934714X13948909473149

Booth, J. (2005). Prospering with juggernauts: Implementing excellent customer service. *Control, 31*(1), 23.

Borneo Post. (2009, May 21). Govt. to help 4,000 graduates land jobs. *Borneo Post,* pp. 1-2.

Brennan, R. (2014). Reflecting on experiential learning in marketing education. *The Marketing Review, 14*(1), 97–108. doi:10.1362/146934714X13948909473266

CIM. (2009). Available at http://www.cim.co.uk/resources/understandingmarket/definitionmkting.aspx

Delong, D., & McDermott, M. (2013). Current perceptions, prominence and prevalence of sustainability in the marketing curriculum. *The Marketing Management Journal, 23*(3), 101–116.

Dennis, J. (2014). Designing relevant marketing curriculum: The state of the nation. *The Marketing Review, 14*(1), 49–66. doi:10.1362/146934714X13948909473185

DEST. (2002). Employability skills for the future. A report by the Australian Chamber of Commerce and Industry and the Business Council of Australia for the Department of Education, Science and Training, Canberra.

Fong, J. (2013). Preparing Marketing for the Future: Strategic Marketing Challenges for Continuing Education. *New Directions for Adult and Continuing Education*, (140). doi:10.1002/ace.20077

Garneau, J. P., & Brennan, R. (1999). *New relevance in the marketing curriculum: stakeholder perceptions of the effectiveness of marketing education*. Paper presented at the Academy of Marketing Annual Conference, Stirling.

Gibson-Sweet, M., Brennan, R., Foy, A., Lynch, J., & Rudolph, P. (2010). 'Key issues in marketing education: The marketing educators' view'. *Marketing Intelligence & Planning, 28*(7), 931–943. doi:10.1108/02634501011086508

Gray, B. J., Ottesen, G. G., Bell, J., Chapman, C., & Whiten, J. (2007). What are the essential capabilities of marketers? A comparative study of managers', academics' and students' perceptions. *Journal of Marketing Intelligence and Planning, 25*(3), 271–295. doi:10.1108/02634500710747789

Griffith, D. A., & Hoppner, J. J. (2013). Global marketing managers. *International Marketing Review, 30*(1), 21–41. doi:10.1108/02651331311298555

Harrigan, P., & Hulbert, B. (2011). How can marketing academics serve marketing practice? The new marketing DNA as a model for marketing education. *Journal of Marketing Education, 33*(3), 253–272. doi:10.1177/0273475311420234

Hart, C., Stachow, G. B., Farrell, A. M., & Reed, G. (2007). Employer perceptions of skills gaps in retail: Issues and implications for UK retailers. *International Journal of Retail & Distribution Management, 35*(4), 271–288. doi:10.1108/09590550710736201

Holian, R. (2004). The practice of management education in Australian universities. *Management Decision, 42*(3/4), 396-405. Retrieved on January 6, 2006 from: www.emeraldinsight.com/0025-1747.htm

Howard, D. G., & Ryans, J. K. J. Jr. (1993). What role should marketing theory play in marketing education: A cross-national comparison of marketing educators. *Asia Pacific Journal of Marketing and Logistics, 5*(2), 29–43. doi:10.1108/eb010249

Howard, D. G., Savins, D. M., Howell, W., & Ryans, J. K. J. (1991). The evolution of marketing theory in the United States and Europe. *European Journal of Marketing, 25*(2), 7–16. doi:10.1108/03090569110145150

Kagaari, J. R. K. (2007). Evaluation of the effects of vocational choice and practical training on students' employability. *Journal of European Industrial Training, 31*(6), 449–471. doi:10.1108/03090590710772640

Kotler, P., & Armstrong, G. (2008). *Principles of Marketing* (12th ed.). Prentice Hall.

Kumar, R., & Usunier, J.-C. (2001). Management education in a globalizing world: Lessons from French experience. *Management Learning, 32*(3), 363–391. doi:10.1177/1350507601323005

Lee, M. H., Ling, L. A., Muniapan, B., & Gregory, M. L. (2011). General enterprising tendency (GET) and recommendations to boost entrepreneurship education in Sarawak. *International Journal of Asian Business and Information Management, 2*(1), 32–47. doi:10.4018/jabim.2011010103

Lim, M., & Svensson, P. (2013). Embedding critique in the university: A new role for critical marketing education? *Journal of Applied Research in Higher Education, 5*(1), 32–47. doi:10.1108/17581181311310252

Ling, L. A., Gregory, M. L., & Muniapan, B. (2010). Marketing education in Sarawak: Some issues and challenges from the employers' perspectives. *Int. J. Education Economics and Development, 1*(3), 227–242. doi:10.1504/IJEED.2010.032876

Longenecker, C. O., & Ariss, S. S. (2002). Creating competitive advantage through effective management education. *Journal of Management Development, 21*(9), 640–654. doi:10.1108/02621710210441649

Lyons, T. S. (2002). *The Entrepreneurial League System: Transforming Your Community's Economy through Enterprise Development*. The Appalachian Regional Commission Washington.

Maxwell, J. A. (1996). *Qualitative research design*. London: Sage Publication.

Muniapan, B. (2005). *HRM Education: The Role of Malaysian Universities and Institution of Higher Learning. In Invent and Innovate* (pp. 344–346). Kuala Lumpur: Genuine Circuit.

Muniapan, B. (2008). Perspectives and Reflections on Management Education in Malaysia. *International Journal of Management in Education, 2*(1), 77–87. doi:10.1504/IJMIE.2008.016232

Muniapan, B. (2014). *The Roots of Indian Corporate Social Responsibility (CSR) Practice from a Vedantic Perspective. In Corporate Social Responsibility in Asia* (pp. 19–34). Springer International Publishing.

Muniapan, B. (2015). The Bhagavad-Gita and Business Ethics: A Leadership Perspective. Asian Business and Management Practices: Trends and Global Considerations: Trends and Global Considerations.

Muniapan, B., & Raj, S. J. (2014). Corporate Social Responsibility Communication from the Vedantic, Dharmic and Karmic Perspectives. In *Communicating Corporate Social Responsibility: Perspectives and Practice. Emerald Group Publishing Limited*.

Muniapan, B., & Rajantheran, M. (2011). Ethics (business ethics) from Thirukurral and its Relevance for Contemporary Business Leadership in the Indian Context. *International Journal of Indian Culture and Business Management*, *4*(4), 453–471. doi:10.1504/IJICBM.2011.040961

Narayandas, N., Rangan, V. K., & Zaltman, G. (1998). The pedagogy of executive education in business markets. *Journal of Business-To-Business Marketing*, *5*(1/2), 41–64. doi:10.1300/J033v05n01_05

O'Donoghue, J., & Maguire, T. (2005). The individual learner, employability and the workplace: A reappraisal of relationships and prophecies. *Journal of European Industrial Training*, *29*(6), 436–446. doi:10.1108/03090590510610236

Parasuraman, B., Satrya, A., Abdullah, M. M., Hamid, F., Muniapan, B., & Rathakrishnan, B. (2009, July). Analyzing the Relationship Between Unions and Joint Consultation Committee: Case studies of Malaysian and Indonesian Postal Industries. *International Journal of Business and Society*, *10*(1), 41–58.

Parasuraman, B., Satrya, A., Abdullah, M. M., Hamid, F., Muniapan, B., & Rathakrishnan, B. (2009, July). Analyzing the Relationship Between Unions and Joint Consultation Committee: Case studies of Malaysian and Indonesian Postal Industries. *International Journal of Business and Society*, *10*(1), 41–58.

Patton, M. Q. (2002). *Qualitative research and evaluation methods* (3rd ed.). Thousand Oaks, CA: Sage Publications.

Pfeffer, J., & Fong, C. T. (2004). The Business School 'Business': Some Lessons from the US Experience. *Journal of Management Studies*, *41*(8), 1501–1520. doi:10.1111/j.1467-6486.2004.00484.x

Shuptrine, F. K., & Willenborg, J. F. (1998). Job experience for marketing graduates – implications for university education. *Marketing Education Review*, *8*(1), 1–11. doi:10.1080/10528008.1998.11488614

Smith, W. L., Schallenkamp, K., & Eichholz, D. E. (2007). Entrepreneurial skills assessment: An exploratory study. *International Journal of Management and Enterprise Development*, *4*(2), 179–201. doi:10.1504/IJMED.2007.011791

Stringfellow, L., Ennis, S., Brenan, R., & Harker, M. J. (2006). Mind the gap: The relevance of marketing education to marketing practice. *Marketing Intelligence & Planning*, *24*(3), 245–256. doi:10.1108/02634500610665718

Tan, A. M. (2002). *Malaysian Private Higher Education: Globalization, Privatization, Transformation and Marketplaces*. London: Asean Academic Press.

Tay, A. (1995). Management's perceptions on MBA graduates in Malaysia. *Journal of Management Development*, *20*(3), 258-274. Available at http://www.emerald-library.com/ft

Tregear, A., Dobson, S., Brennan, M., & Kuznesof, S. (2010). Critically divided? *European Journal of Marketing*, *44*(1/2), 66–86. doi:10.1108/03090561011008619

Wilson, E. (1998). Commentary on: 'The pedagogy of executive education in business markets'. *Journal of Business-to-Business Marketing*, *5*(1-2), 65-70.

ENDNOTE

[1] This chapter is an extended version of a research paper on Marketing Education in Sarawak which appeared in International Journal of Education Economics and Development, Volume 1, Number 3, pp. 227-242 in 2010.

Chapter 9
Integrating Big Data Analytics into Advertising Curriculum:
Opportunities and Challenges in an International Context

Kenneth C. C. Yang
The University of Texas – El Paso, USA

Yowei Kang
Kainan University, Taiwan

ABSTRACT

With the assistance of new computing technologies and consumer data collection methods, advertising professionals are capable of generating better targeted advertising campaigns. Big Data analytics are particularly worth noticing and have presented ample opportunities for advertising researchers and practitioners around the world. Although Big Data analytic courses have been offered at major universities, existing advertising curricula have yet to address the opportunities and challenges offered by Big Data. This chapter collects curricular data from major universities around the world to examine what Big Data has posed challenges and opportunities to existing advertising curricula in an international context. Curricula of 186 universities around the world are reviewed to describe the status of integrating these developments into better preparing advertising students for these changes. Findings show that only selected advertising programs in the U.S. have begun to explore the potential of the data analytics tools and techniques. Practical and educational implications are discussed.

INTRODUCTION

With the assistance of new technologies and consumer data collection methods, organizations now are able to improve their performance by making the best use of information flow (Andrew & Brynjolfsson, 2012). Andrew and Brynjolfsson (2012) predict that the tools and philosophies of Big Data are likely to challenge what people think of the value of experience, the practice of management, and the nature

DOI: 10.4018/978-1-4666-9784-3.ch009

of expertise. They also claim that the challenges and opportunism posed by Big Data can be viewed as "a management revolution" (Andrew & Brynjolfsson, 2012, para 4). Similarly, the advertising industry also has shown "a big crush" on Big Data (Marshall, 2013) that has generated a dedicated topic session ("Big Data") in *AdWeek.com* as well as professional conferences on Big Data, data-driven marketing and advertising, or data analytics (Kaye, 2014). Although Big Data have rapidly attracted the attention among business researchers and practitioners in recent years (Glass & Callahan, 2014; Ignatius, 2012; Minelli, Chambers, & Dhiraj, 2013), administrators in higher education institutions are slowly catching up with the potential impacts of Big Data in terms of leveraging student information for revenue generation and course planning, and improving pedagogical qualities by teaching relevant and essential skills (AACSB International, n.d.; Pearson, 2014; Soare, 2012). In an accreditation document published by AACSB International (n.d.), skills related to big data analytics have been listed as an essential area in General Business and Management Knowledge area: "Information technology and statistics/quantitative methods impacts on business practices to include data creation, data sharing, data analytics, data mining, data reporting, and storage between and across organizations including related ethical issues" (para 12). Another accreditation agency, ACBSP, widely discussed the impacts of big data analytics in its annual conference (Pearson, 2014). Therefore, companies such as PWC have claimed that data analytics can be viewed as a disruptive innovation for businesses and will have impacts on what constitute essential skills in business education (PWC, 2015). Therefore, Schmarzo (2014) summarizes that higher education institutions can improve students' performance, engagement, and institution's performance by integrating the following Big Data-powered applications into their management: student acquisition, student course major selection, student performance effectiveness, student workgroup, student retention, student advocacy, student lifetime value, etc.

Situated within a higher education institution context, international and national advertising programs are comparatively slow to react to the challenges and opportunities presented by Big Data and increasingly data-driven marketing and advertising practices in business. According to a recently published report commissioned by the Internet Advertising Bureau (IAB), among 50 top level business executives and thought leaders, predictive analytics and market segmentation tools are ranked as most commonly used information technologies (Kaye, 2015; Winterberry Group, 2015). Big Data is forecasted to create 4.4 million jobs by 2015 (Gartner, 2012; *ITBusinessEdge*, 2012). The gap between what existing advertising curricula teach and what the industry needs is likely to reduce students' competitiveness in the job market and to worsen the challenges that Big Data has posed on the missions of higher education institutions.

Although Big Data analytic courses have been offered at major universities around the world (such as UT-Austin, Michigan State University, University of Ottawa in Canada, York University in U.K., etc.), present advertising curricula in major universities have yet to address the opportunities and challenges offered by Big Data. Industry experts have noticed the lack of talents produced by higher education institutions to meet the demand of Big Data specialists (*ITBusinessEdge*, 2012; Orihuela, & Bass, 2015; Patrizio, 2015). Integrated marketing communications guru, Dr. Don Schultz (2014) has offered his analysis of why integrating Big Data into current advertising and marketing research and practice is difficult. These problems include the amount, structure, and length of data as well as the unfamiliarity among many advertising and marketing educators about these technological advancements. The lack of Big Data proficiency among college instructors is likely to affect whether advertising and marketing students are prepared for these challenges. Given the growing importance of Big Data on the advertising industry as well as education, this chapter discusses and examines how Big Data has posed challenges to existing advertising curricula around the world.

BACKGROUND

A massive amount of data from mobile, web-based, and sensor-generated devices has been produced at a terabyte, even Exabyte proportion (*The Economist*, 2010a, 2010b). About 2.5 exabytes of data are created everyday as of 2012 and in about every 40 months, the number doubles (McAfee & Brynjolfsson, 2012). For example, the retailing giant, Wal-Mart, collects more than 2.5 petabytes of data every hour from monitoring its customer transactions (Libert, 2013). These new technological developments in data collection, storage, and analysis have enabled scholars to better understand human behaviors (Boyd & Crawford, 2012).

The Emergence of Big Data in Advertising Strategic Planning

Carlton Associates, Inc. claims that Big Data is likely to transform how advertising professionals practice their trade. The latest developments in Big Data analytics are particularly worth noticing and have presented ample opportunities for advertising researchers and practitioners. The consulting firm also emphasizes that advertising professionals need to embrace the challenges of Big Data, and collaborate with data specialists to take advantage of these opportunities. Most noteworthy is the impacts of Big Data upon the digital advertising agencies. Philip (2014) offers the changes in the industry in terms of the agency's abilities to conduct real-time analysis to better understand consumer behaviors, to produce more personalized and targeted advertising campaigns, and to develop hyper-localized advertising messages. Other researchers and practitioners also noted agency's capabilities in generating better targeted and more effective campaigns (Ball, 2014; Cunningham, 2010; Glass & Callahan, 2014; Hallahan et al., 2007).

A recent diffusion of smart and mobile devices, which promises a seamless integration of multi-media and personalized services, has also led to the emergence of many location-based services that enable marketers to collect a large amount of consumer behavioral data (Dhar & Varshney, 2011; O'Leary, 2013; Tussyadiah, 2011). The technological convergence is a result of technology consumerization and the complementary capabilities among various technological platforms (Cloud Standards Customer Council, 2013). The convergence of mobile, social media, and cloud computing technologies has also posed challenges and opportunities to the advertising profession that demand rethinking of their business models and advertising strategies (Cloud Standards Customer Council, 2013; Dhar & Varshney, 2011; Tussyadiah, 2011). For example, many experts have argued that these developments have generated deeper insights into consumers, new channels to reach potential customers, new innovations, and collaborative efforts among businesses, customers, and other participants in the marketing communication process (Cloud Standards Customer Council, 2013; Nesamoney, 2015). Because advertising professionals require data and business intelligence to make rational strategic decisions, the growing popularity of Big Data analytics has been observed as one of the main catalysts to generate a large amount of data to facilitate advertising campaign planning (Glass & Callahan, 2014; Hendrick, 2014; Nesamoney, 2015).

Big Data: The Concept

Big Data has enhanced the business value of technological convergence trends in social and mobile media (Ballve, 2014; Cloud Standards Customer Council, 2013; Hoelzel, 2014). Generally speaking, the term often refers to "the collection, storage and analysis of data that is very large in size" (Cloud Standards Customer Council, 2013, p. 20). Big Data, a concept first proposed in 2001 by Doug Laney (2001), is often examined by exploring how rapid data growth will impact organizations, social movements, or the decision-making among managers (Brown, Chui, & Manyika, 2012; Watson & Marjanovic, 2013). The term inherently implies "bigger and bigger data sets over time" (Mahrt & Scharkow, 2012, p. 22). According to Doug Laney (2001), the challenges and opportunities posed by Big Data are likely to be three-dimensional in terms of extremely high volume ("amount of data"), variety ("range of data types and sources"), and velocity ("speed of data in and out") (Esteves & Cuto, 2013, p. 37). Its high variety often refers to "the heterogeneity of data types, representation, and semantic interpretation" while high velocity addresses "both the rate at which data arrive and the time in which it must be acted upon" (Cloud Standards Customer Council, 2013, p. 20). These characteristics are likely to demand new forms of data processing capabilities to allow enhanced business decision-making in the advertising industry (Esteves & Cuto, 2013).

To explain these three dimensions further, its massive size often implies the dataset has large, more varied, and complex structure, accompanied by difficulties of data storage, analysis, and visualization (Sagirouglu & Sinanc, 2013). Big Data, as "high-volume, -velocity and –variety information assets, demand cost-effective, innovative forms of information processing for enhanced insights and decision making" (Gartner, cited in Pavolotsky, 2013, p. 217). On the basis of the technical attributes of Big Data, Manyika et al. (2011) focus on whether the datasets can be easily captured, stored, managed and analyzed by typical database software tools. From a search utilization perspective, boyd and Crawford (2012) thus define Big Data as a set of data that have the 'capacity to search, aggregate, and cross-reference large data sets" (p. 663).

Impacts of Big Data on the Advertising Industry

The combination of mobile devices and social media helps produce a large amount of personal consumer information to design better targeted and more effective advertising campaigns. A survey of professionals in the advertising industry concluded that the convergence of mobile and social media marketing enables advertisers to create location-sensitive and personalized campaign materials (Aquino, 2012). Big Data has been said to help advertisers make better decisions in strategizing their campaigns (Fulgoni & Lipsman, 2014; Hendrick, 2014; Glass & Callahan, 2014). The relevance of Big Data to advertising professionals goes beyond its technical attributes that are discussed above. As a result, many advertising agencies like WPP have now claimed itself to be a data company, not an advertising agency as WPP chief executive Martin Sorrell has pointed out (Marshall, 2013). Citing Sorrel's words, Marshall (2013) concludes a change of thinking in advertising business: "It suggests the legacy approach of media and art, not science. We want to be as aggressive in the science part of the business as we can possibly be. We've moved on from the days of Mad Men" (para. 2).

A recent report by Rocket Fuel (2013) also shows that 92% of the marketers that relied on Big Data to plan their marketing activities said using Big Data has met or exceeded their goals. In a recent success story by AT&T's "It's not Complicated" campaign, Neff (2014) reports that this campaign was based on an extensive analysis of 370 AT&T's and its competitor's ads in the past to generate insights for the planning process. AT&T also used the data collected from consumer premise set-top boxes to predict which demographic segments will be watching TV in the future to better plan commercials (Simonite, 2014). Predictive intelligence from mining a large amount of data has been used in the planning of advertising campaigns. Companies like Simulmedia have emerged to help broadcasters to better spend their promotional budgets through Big Data to predict how many new viewers each campaign can recruit (Lafayette,

2013). Harvey, Herbig, Keylock, Aggarwal, and Lerner (2012) examine a large dataset collected from 60 million households across the U.S. and 2 million household viewing behaviors to study the relationship between household purchase behaviors and their second-by-second TV viewing behaviors. They envision that Big Data enable market researchers to have a more in-depth understanding of consumer purchase behaviors and multiple marketing efforts. Hazan and Banfi (2013) therefore conclude that "'Big data' offers companies unlimited possibilities to improve their marketing efficiency" (para. 12).

Given that the planning of a successful advertising campaign is contingent on consumer insights, McAfee and Brynjolfsson (2012) further claim that "data-driven decisions are better decisions—it's as simple as that. Using big data enables managers to decide on the basis of evidence rather than intuition" (p. 63). Nowadays, the planning and implementation of any advertising campaign relies on how consumer behavioral data are analyzed and applied. Big Data can help advertising professionals "to decide on the basis of evidence rather than intuition" (McAfee & Brynjolfsson, 2012, p. 63). For example, National Football League (NFL) has used social media and mobile applications to engage its fans for better campaign results. Mobile-optimized websites are set up to enable fans to easily retrieve team news on their mobile devices (Smith, 2012).

In conclusion, celebrated as the fourth data management generation to help businesses make their decisions (Watson & Marjanovic, 2013), these large-scale consumer data will help marketers and advertising agencies to make better decisions in strategizing their campaigns. However, the availability of Big Data does not necessarily mean better campaign outcomes for advertisers (Fulgoni, 2013). Therefore, scholars like Davenport (2013) argue that businesses should not stop at Big Data (Analytic 2.0), but should focus on data-enriched decisions (Analytic 3.0).

MAIN FOCUS OF THE CHAPTER

Issues, Controversies, Problems

Emerging best practices have demonstrated the opportunities and challenges of Big Data for the advertising industry (Krajicek, 2013). For example, Twitter is reported to sell its tweet archive to a company in the UK and over 1,000 companies are interested in these detailed consumer data (Greengard, 2012). Netflix's movie rating filtering algorithm caused concerns among its users about how users' viewing behaviors are recorded and used for commercial purposes (Chen, Chiang, & Storey, 2012). Ovum's Consumer Insights of 11,000 respondents from 11 countries confirmed that global consumers are concerned about privacy issues in the era of Big Data. According to this survey, sixty-eight percent of these respondents indicate that they prefer a "do-not-track" (DNT) feature if it is made available (*Network World Asia*, 2013).

Combining social media with mobile devices has provided advertisers with groundbreaking opportunities, but has also created more severe infringement on consumer privacy (Kaye, 2013). Sunoco, Marathon, Phillips 66 were reported to use mobile tracking technologies to monitor the number of people who drive by their stores and their mileage to offer timely discount offerings (Kaye, 2013). However, there are concerns about the collection and commercial application of these consumer-generated geospatial footprints (Li, 2013; Smith et al., 2012).

The impacts of Big Data on the advertising industry are not only on how consumer data is collected, but also on how these data are analyzed and interpreted to produce marketing insights in advertising strategic planning (Marshall, 2013). Data analytics have enabled advertising professionals to better predict an array of consumer behaviors and create more effective advertising campaigns. However, the increasing dependence on Big Data for business decision-making has led to a talent gap as to whether present advertising curricula are able to train future advertising professionals to address the demand. In order to equip students with the most up-to-date professional knowledge and skills, higher educational institutes are required to adapt their curricula. Some universities have begun the curricular revision processes. For example, many business schools are pondering over the integration of Big Data into existing business courses to better understand consumer behaviors (Chaturvedi, 2015). Recently, Columbia Business School has begun to revamp its Decision Models core courses to recognize the importance of Big Data in the business ecosystem (Autheres, 2013; Columbia Business School, 2013).

This book chapter intends to explore the challenges and opportunities facing advertising programs around the world in the age of Big Data. The book chapter aims to provide discussions about and answers to the following research questions pertinent to advertising education:

Research Question 1: How will the advent of Big Data impact advertising education?
Research Question 2: What should advertising programs around the world do in response to the opportunities and challenges of Big Data analytics?
Research Question 3: What should advertising educators do to develop a more up-to-date program to address the opportunities and challenges of Big Data analytics and other new media developments?

Theoretical Foundation to Understand the Integration of Big Data into Advertising Curricula

Researchers in various fields have begun to explore the adoption of Big Data (Esteves & Curto, 2013; Fan, Lau, & Zhou, 2015; Vogel, Zhou, & Hu, 2015). For example, Esteves and Curto (2013) derived from information system research (such as Venkatesh, 2006) and theory of planned action to examine why businesses decide to adopt Big Data technologies and methodologies. Esteves and Curto (2013) focused on the importance of perceived risks and values in affecting businesses' adoption of Big Data. In the following table (Esteves & Curto, 2013, p. 38), both benefits and risks of adopting Big Data among business organizations are considered before making adoption decisions. On the other hand, Vogel, Zhou, and Hu (2015) discussed the application of Big Data on business, computation, and health care in a special issue of a brand new journal, *Big Data Research*.

However, business organizations are more responsive when making decisions about considering the innovations provided by Big Data, if compared with higher education institutions (Mortimer & Sathre,

Table 1. Benefit and risk perceptions related to Big Data adoption among business organizations

Benefits	Risks
• Creating transparency by making data accessible to relevant stakeholders in a time manner. • Improve operational efficiency (cost, revenue and risk) • Use data and experiments to expose variability and raise performance • Segmentation populations to customize the way your systems treat people • Use automated algorithms to replace and support human decision making • Innovate with new business models, products, and services • Sector-specific business value creation	• Data quality • Talent scarcity (lack of data scientists) • Privacy and security concerns • Big data integration capabilities • Decision-making • Organizational maturity level

Source: Esteves & Curto, 2013, p. 38.

2007). Business programs, among many disciplines, are the most proactive to address the challenges and opportunities by Big Data (Authers, 2013; Columbia Business School, 2013). The process of curriculum revisions in higher education institutions are often hindered by external, organizational, and internal influences (Stark & Lattuca, 1997). Examples of external influences include alumni, government, society, and accreditation organizations (Stark & Lattuca, 1997). Organizational influences include the disciplinary boundaries among various units inside a higher education institution (Innes, 2004). Internal influences include change agents, faculty members, and campus community (Oliver & Hyun, 2011). In his interview about recent changes in marketing curricula, Dr. Dawar has discussed both current business practices (i.e., external influences) and change agents among the faculty members (i.e., internal influences) lead to the integration of Big Data into the business curriculum in University of Western Ontario. Similarly, these factors are likely to influence how Big Data will be integrated into existing advertising curricula around the world.

Big Data and Impacts on the Advertising Education

The first research question in this book chapter asks, "How will the advent of Big Data impact advertising education?" In spite of the buzz about how Big Data will impactthe advertising industry, comments from advertising professionals seem to suggest the essential skills for advertising professionals depend on whether they are able to analyze and integrate these insights (Pollack, 2014). The comment from Mr. Tham Khai Meng, worldwide chief creative officer and chairman of Ogilvy, best describe what essential skills are needed to train advertising professionals in the age of Big Data: "At its heart, data are insights best used as an inspiration to reach and identify an audience" and "Human beings are not a collection of algorithms," (Pollack, 2014, para. 4). Campaign examples with great success (such as Dove's *Real Beauty* campaign, or Johnny Walker' *Keep Walking* campaign) often rely on a few consumer insights to develop these highly acclaimed and memorable campaigns (Pollack, 2014).

A review and analysis of publications in the *Journal of Advertising Education* have found that technology often affects what will be taught (Barnes, 1996; Martin, 2001). For example, Barnes' (1996) article in the introductory issue of the journal records the influence of nascent World Wide Web on what needs to be taught in the advertising curriculum. Martin (2001) examines other computer-mediated technologies on teaching media planning. The popularity of social media, Web 2.0, and Web 3.0 has prompted advertising educators to revisit existing advertising curricula as seen in several Journal of Advertising Education (JAE) articles. (Caravella, Ekachai, Jaeger, & Zahay, 2009; Kalamas, Mitchell, & Lester, 2009; Scovotti & Jones, 2011). Kalamas et al. (2009) examine the rise of social media and its impact in higher education. Similarly, Caravella et al. (2009) further study the opportunities and challenges proposed by Web 2.0, while Scovott and Jones (2011) study how Web 3.0 will impact advertising courses when social media and users-generated contents become popular as emerging advertising practices. Given the close relationship between advertising practices and technological development, advertising educators are relatively responsive when dealing with these changes to better train future advertising professionals (Robbs, 2010).

New technologies are also found to change pedagogical approaches in advertising education (Beard & Tarpening, 2001; Eckman, 2010; Kim & Patel, 2012; Quesenberry, Saewitz, & Kantrowitz, 2014). For example, digital video on the desktop was examined to explore its potential to teaching TV advertising creative courses (Beard & Tarpening, 2001). Kim and Patel (2012) reflect upon how to teach advertising media planning in an age of ever-changing multiplatform advertising landscape. Eckman (2010) reports the integration of ning.com in the advertising classroom to enhance students' engagement when teaching social web marketing. Similarly, the integration of blogging in the classroom has been explored for how Wordpress blog and buddy press plugin can be used as a learning tool. Recently, the advent of Big Data and other consumer analytics has attracted educators' attention to examining what opportunities and challenges these developments have generated for advertising and integrated marketing communication courses (Chennamaneni, Lala, Srivastava, Goutam, & Chakraborty, 2011).

Big Data and Talent Gaps in the Advertising Industry

New advances in technologies and advertising thinking have often caused advertising educators to ponder over how to better meet the industry's demand on much-needed new talents (Kalamas et al., 2009; Stanaland, Helm, & Kinney, 2009). For example, Stanaland et al. (2009) discuss the demand of an IMC talent gap in high education institution to meet the demand in the industry. Following McMillan, Sheehan, and Frazier's (2001) approach to analyze advertising employment ads to understand the demand of the advertising industry, the book chapter uses a similar approach by searching job postings in the AdAge.com Talent Works section using the following keywords: "Big Data" (360 hits), "data analytics" (180 hits), or "data-driven marketing" (294 hits). The following table reports search results using these keywords (refer to Table 2).

This book chapter is not designed to analyze these employment ads in the advertising industry. However, a cursory analysis of these ads has identified the following skill requirements. For example, in an employment ad for a Senior Director, High Tech Customer Analytics on the GDIA at Dun & Bradstreet shows the following skills: "Strong analytic skills and experience in developing analytic and score-oriented solutions" and "Current knowledge of D&B's Analytics capabilities is recommended." Similarly, an employment ad for a Senior Manager, Marketing Analytics, Charles Schwab demonstrates the following technical and function skills requirements: "Work independently or collaboratively throughout the complete analytics project lifecycle including data extraction/preparation, analysis and documentation of results", "Pro-actively analyze data to uncover insights that increase business value and impact", and "Strong understanding of how analytics supports a large organization including being able to successfully articulate the linkage between business decisions, business objectives, and analytical approaches & findings." On the basis of these two sample job ads, it is clear that the abilities to use analytics software packages to interpret data and to generate marketing insights are essential for future advertising professionals.

Table 2. Advertising employment ads in AdAge.com TalentWorks

Keywords	Search Results	Date Range of the Results
Big Data	360	May 26, 2014-Feburary 9, 2015
Data Analytics	180	December 31, 2013-February 9, 2015
Data-Drive Marketing	294	June 2, 2014-February 9, 2015

SOLUTIONS AND RECOMMENDATIONS

Sampling and Sampling Characteristics

To better understand how advertising programs around the world have done in response to the opportunities and challenges of Big Data analytics, the chapter collects curriculum information from some of the major advertising programs around the world. The researchers used the list of advertising programs complied in *FindtheBest* site (http://colleges.findthebest.com/d/o/Advertising). A total of 161 programs is identified in the list, ranging from the prestigious global University of Florida (95% smart rating on the basis of admission selectivity, academic excellence, expert opinion, and financial affordability), The University of Texas at Austin (94% smart rating), to a less known local university, Miami Ad School (at San Francisco) (24% smart rating). Refer to Table 3 for a complete list of U.S. schools in the sample.

Table 3. U.S. advertising programs in the sample (N=161)

School/Program Name	State	Smart Rating	Acceptance Rate	Student Enrollment
University of Florida (UF)	Gainesville, Florida	95	46.5%	49,589
New York University (NYU)	New York, New York	95	26.0%	43,911
University of Miami (UM)	Coral Gables, Florida	95	40.4%	16,068
University of Illinois at Urbana-Champaign (UI)	Champaign, Illinois	94	62.4%	44,407
The University of Texas at Austin (UT)	Austin, Texas	94	40.2%	51,112
University of Georgia (UGA)	Athens, Georgia	94	56.1%	34,816
Pennsylvania State University (PSU)	University Park, Pennsylvania	94	54.2%	45,628
Boston University (BU)	Boston, Massachusetts	94	45.6%	32,439
Marquette University	Milwaukee, Wisconsin	93	57.5%	12,002
Southern Methodist University (SMU)	Dallas, Texas	93	50.7%	10,982
Drake University	Des Moines, Iowa	93	66.0%	5,384
Xavier University (XU)	Cincinnati, Ohio	93	70.0%	6,945
Union University	Jackson, Tennessee	93	74.1%	4,007
Brigham Young University-Provo (BYU)	Provo, Utah	93	49.4%	34,101
Bradley University (BU)	Peoria, Illinois	93	66.9%	5,639
University of Denver (UD)	Denver, Colorado	93	76.7%	11,797
Syracuse University (SU)	Syracuse, New York	93	49.5%	20,829
Quinnipiac University (QU)	Hamden, Connecticut	92	67.2%	8,352
The College of Saint Scholastica	Duluth, Minnesota	92	72.7%	4,014
Michigan State University (MSU)	East Lansing, Michigan	92	68.6%	47,825
Harding University	Searcy, Arkansas	92	76.3%	7,056
Spring Arbor University	Spring Arbor, Michigan	92	65.0%	4,271
Campbell University	Buies Creek, North Carolina	92	69.8%	6,182
University of South Carolina-Columbia (SC)	Columbia, South Carolina	92	60.6%	30,721

continued on following page

Table 3. Continued

School/Program Name	State	Smart Rating	Acceptance Rate	Student Enrollment
Webster University	Saint Louis, Missouri	92	58.1%	19,224
Oklahoma Christian University (OC)	Edmond, Oklahoma	92	63.2%	2,172
The University of Tennessee (UT)	Knoxville, Tennessee	92	72.5%	30,194
North Park University	Chicago, Illinois	92	52.3%	3,220
Pepperdine University	Malibu, California	92	37.3%	7,539
University of Alabama (UA)	Tuscaloosa, Alabama	92	56.5%	31,647
School of Visual Arts	New York, New York	92	74.9%	4,195
Hastings College	Hastings, Nebraska	91	73.6%	1,240
Iowa State University (ISU)	Ames, Iowa	91	82.5%	29,611
Florida Southern College	Lakeland, Florida	91	49.9%	2,442
Oklahoma City University (OCU)	Oklahoma City, Oklahoma	91	72.0%	3,575
University of Central Florida (UCF)	Orlando, Florida	91	48.9%	58,465
University of Nebraska-Lincoln (UNL)	Lincoln, Nebraska	91	64.0%	24,593
Appalachian State University (ASU)	Boone, North Carolina	91	63.2%	17,344
Waynesburg University	Waynesburg, Pennsylvania	91	75.2%	2,458
Northwood University-Michigan	Midland, Michigan	91	65.4%	3,538
University of Oklahoma (OU)	Norman, Oklahoma	91	80.4%	27,138
University of San Francisco (USF)	San Francisco, California	91	61.3%	9,799
Saint Mary-of-the-Woods College	Saint Mary Of The Woods, Indiana	91	97.5%	1,441
St John's University-New York (SJU)	Queens, New York	91	53.2%	21,067
University of Oregon (UO)	Eugene, Oregon	91	74.2%	24,396
Gannon University	Erie, Pennsylvania	91	80.4%	4,076
Lindenwood University	Saint Charles, Missouri	91	66.3%	11,483
Carson-Newman University	Jefferson City, Tennessee	91	66.6%	1,970
Point Park University	Pittsburg, Pennsylvania	91	73.9%	3,861
Lee University	Cleveland, Tennessee	91	91.7%	4,411
Temple University (TU)	Philadelphia, Pennsylvania	91	63.9%	36,855
Northwest Missouri State University	Maryville, Missouri	91	72.4%	7,225
Rider University	Lawrenceville, New Jersey	91	71.9%	5,598
Southern Adventist University	Collegedale, Tennessee	90	38.3%	3,200
Grand Valley State University (GVSU)	Allendale, Michigan	90	82.6%	24,662
Drury University	Springfield, Missouri	90	80.9%	5,324
Fontbonne University	Saint Louis, Missouri	90	65.2%	2,293
Texas State University-San Marcos (TxSt)	San Marcos, Texas	90	75.1%	34,087
Murray State University (MSU)	Murray, Kentucky	90	82.2%	10,623

continued on following page

Table 3. Continued

School/Program Name	State	Smart Rating	Acceptance Rate	Student Enrollment
New York Institute of Technology (NYIT)	Old Westbury, New York	90	74.1%	8,306
Northwood University-Florida	West Palm Beach, Florida	90	51.0%	663
Texas A & M University-Commerce (TAMU)	Commerce, Texas	90	68.2%	11,417
University of Southern Mississippi (USM)	Hattiesburg, Mississippi	90	66.3%	16,604
Northern Arizona University (NAU)	Flagstaff, Arizona	90	91.4%	25,359
Texas Wesleyan University	Fort Worth, Texas	90	29.9%	3,180
Texas Tech University (TTU)	Lubbock, Texas	90	66.3%	32,327
Suffolk University	Boston, Massachusetts	90	82.5%	9,101
University of Houston (UH)	Houston, Texas	90	58.4%	39,820
University of Southern Indiana (USI)	Evansville, Indiana	90	69.3%	10,820
The University of Texas at Arlington (UTA)	Arlington, Texas	90	60.0%	33,439
Western Kentucky University (WKU)	Bowling Green, Kentucky	90	92.3%	21,036
University of Idaho (UI)	Moscow, Idaho	89	65.6%	12,312
West Texas A & M University (WTAMU)	Canyon, Texas	89	74%	7,886
Wesleyan College	Macon, Georgia	89	43.4%	681
San Jose State University (SJSU)	San Jose, California	89	63.5%	30,236
University of Nevada-Reno (UNR)	Reno, Nevada	89	84.0%	18,004
Northwood University-Texas	Cedar Hill, Texas	89	25.8%	773
Central Michigan University (CMU)	Mount Pleasant, Michigan	89	63.0%	28,194
Hawaii Pacific University	Honolulu, Hawaii	89	64.1%	8,071
Rowan University	Glassboro, New Jersey	89	59.2%	11,786
University of Texas at El Paso	El Paso, Texas	89	99.8%	22,640
University of Puerto Rico-Carolina	Carolina, Puerto Rico	89	80.6%	3,530
Kent State University at Kent (KSU)	Kent, Ohio	88	83.0%	27,855
Southern New Hampshire University	Manchester, New Hampshire	88	78.7%	11,851
Saint Joseph's College of Maine	Standish, Maine	88	77.8%	3,129
Lamar University	Beaumont, Texas	88	76.8%	14,020
University of Arkansas at Little Rock (UALR)	Little Rock, Arkansas	88	52.7%	13,068
Pace University-New York	New York, New York	88	76.8%	12,593
Salem State University	Salem, Massachusetts	87	69.3%	9,646
Saint Ambrose University	Davenport, Iowa	87	96.2%	3,567
Morningside College	Sioux City, Iowa	86	53.4%	2,047
Ferris State University (FSU)	Big Rapids, Michigan	85	75.9%	14,560
Marist College	Poughkeepsie, New York	85	37.4%	6,303
Western Michigan University (WMU)	Kalamazoo, Michigan	84	82.8%	25,086
University of Central Oklahoma (UCO)	Edmond, Oklahoma	84	84.0%	17,239

continued on following page

Table 3. Continued

School/Program Name	State	Smart Rating	Acceptance Rate	Student Enrollment
Moore Norman Technology Center	Norman, Oklahoma	83	69.9%	242
The New England Institute of Art	Brookline, Massachusetts	78	N/A	1,290
The Art Institute of Fort Lauderdale	Fort Lauderdale, Florida	77	N/A	2,543
The Art Institute of California-San Diego	San Diego, California	77	N/A	2,101
Johnson & Wales University-Denver (JWU)	Denver, Colorado	77	78.5%	1,672
AI Miami International University of Art and Design	Miami, Florida	76	N/A	4,068
The Art Institute of Pittsburgh	Pittsburgh, Pennsylvania	76	N/A	2,245
The Illinois Institute of Art-Chicago	Chicago, Illinois	75	N/A	3,039
Art Center College of Design	Pasadena, California	75	81.7%	1,842
The Art Institute of Atlanta	Atlanta, Georgia	74	N/A	3,662
Johnson & Wales University-Providence (JWU)	Providence, Rhode Island	74	76.0%	10,849
University of Sacred Heart	Santurce, Puerto Rico	72	31.9%	6,518
The Art Institutes International-Minnesota	Minneapolis, Minnesota	72	N/A	1,804
Autry Technology Center	Enid, Oklahoma	71	89.4%	618
South University-The Art Institute of Dallas	Dallas, Texas	71	N/A	1,893
The Illinois Institute of Art-Schaumburg	Schaumburg, Illinois	71	N/A	1,351
The Art Institute of Pittsburgh-Online Division	Pittsburgh, Pennsylvania	69	N/A	9,820
Pontifical Catholic University of Puerto Rico	Ponce, Puerto Rico	69	65.0%	8,782
The Art Institute of California- San Francisco	San Francisco, California	68	N/A	1,617
The Art Institute of Washington	Arlington, Virginia	66	N/A	2,094
Canadian Valley Technology Center	El Reno, Oklahoma	64	N/A	1,439
Art Institute of Wisconsin (The)	Milwaukee, Wisconsin	63	N/A	273
The Art Institute of Phoenix	Phoenix, Arizona	63	N/A	1,190
Fashion Institute of Technology	New York, New York	63	44.8%	10,225
Barry University	Miami, Florida	61	46.8%	8,905
The Art Institutes International-Kansas City	Lenexa, Kansas	61	N/A	560
Youngstown State University (YSU)	Youngstown, Ohio	60	N/A	14,483
St Cloud Technical and Community College	Saint Cloud, Minnesota	60	N/A	4,708
The Art Institute of Portland	Portland, Oregon	60	N/A	1,676
The Art Institute of Ohio-Cincinnati	Cincinnati, Ohio	59	N/A	726
The Art Institute of California-Orange County	Santa Ana, California	59	N/A	2,227
Southwest University of Visual Arts-Tucson	Tucson, Arizona	58	N/A	258
International Academy of Design and Technology-Tampa	Tampa, Florida	57	N/A	971
The Art Institute of Virginia Beach	Virginia Beach, Virginia	56	N/A	427
The Art Institute of Tennessee-Nashville	Nashville, Tennessee	56	N/A	1,068
South University-The Art Institute of Fort Worth	Fort Worth, Texas	55	N/A	393

continued on following page

Table 3. Continued

School/Program Name	State	Smart Rating	Acceptance Rate	Student Enrollment
The Art Institute of Washington-Northern Virginia	Sterling, Virginia	55	N/A	245
The Art Institute of Tucson	Tucson, Arizona	54	N/A	491
Metropolitan State University	Saint Paul, Minnesota	53	100.0%	8,170
Mohawk Valley Community College-Utica Branch	Utica, New York	53	N/A	7,643
The Art Institute of Michigan	Novi, Michigan	52	N/A	963
The Art Institute of Austin	Austin, Texas	49	N/A	1,694
International Academy of Design and Technology-Orlando	Orlando, Florida	47	N/A	771
Globe University-Madison East	Madison, Wisconsin	47	N/A	348
Orange Coast College (OCC)	Costa Mesa, California	46	N/A	22,654
Globe University-Wausau	Rothschild, Wisconsin	44	N/A	394
Luzerne County Community College	Nanticoke, Pennsylvania	44	N/A	6,779
Southwest University of Visual Arts-Albuquerque	Albuquerque, New Mexico	43	N/A	261
Fresno City College	Fresno, California	43	N/A	20,135
Los Angeles City College	Los Angeles, California	42	N/A	21,028
North Hennepin Community College	Brooklyn Park, Minnesota	42	N/A	7,432
North Central Michigan College	Petoskey, Michigan	42	N/A	2,959
Santiago Canyon College	Orange, California	40	N/A	12,372
Kanawha Valley Community and Technical College	South Charleston, West Virginia	39	N/A	1,683
Portfolio Center	Atlanta, Georgia	38	86.7%	93
Three Rivers Community College (Norwich)	Norwich, Connecticut	38	N/A	5,154
Del Mar College	Corpus Christi, Texas	38	N/A	12,071
Santa Ana College	Santa Ana, California	37	N/A	30,289
Amarillo College	Amarillo, Texas	37	N/A	11,616
Union County College	Cranford, New Jersey	36	N/A	12,416
Palomar College	San Marcos, California	36	N/A	25,427
International Academy of Design and Technology-Online	Tampa, Florida	35	N/A	1,896
Globe University-Green Bay	Green Bay, Wisconsin	34	N/A	285
Miami Ad School-Minneapolis	Minneapolis, Minnesota	28	N/A	43
Miami Ad School-Miami Beach	Miami Beach, Florida	28	N/A	181
Miami Ad School-San Francisco	San Francisco, California	27	N/A	124

Source: http://colleges.findthebest.com/d/o/Advertising. The researchers used *BachelorStudies.com* (http://www.bachelorstudies.com/ Bachelor/Advertising/Europe/) to locate "Bachelor Programs Advertising in Europe 2015." Eleven programs are identified in Table 4.

Table 4. European advertising programs in the sample (N=10)

School/Program Name	Country
Bachelor in Media and Communication Design, Macromedia University for Media and Communication	Germany
Bachelor in Advertising Communication IED- Istituto Europeo Di Design	Turin, Turkey
Bachelor in Advertising Communication, Rome IED- Istituto Europeo Di Design	Italy
B.A. Marketing, Advertising and Branding (Hons), University of Gloucestershire	U.K.
Bachelor in Advertising Communication, Milan Istituto Europeo Di Design	Italy
Bachelor in Advertising, Marketing and Public Relations, Mallorca, ESERP Business School	Spain
Bachelor in Advertising, Marketing and Public Relations, Barcelona, ESERP Business School	Spain
Public Relations and Advertising, Latvia Business College	Latvia
Bachelor in Cross-Media Communication Manager, Mod'SPe, Paris	France
Undergraduate: Advertising and Public Relations, Irkutsk State Linguistic University	

Source: http://www.bachelorstudies.com/Bachelor/Advertising/Europe/. Advertising programs in the Greater China Region (which include Taiwan, Hong-Kong, SAR, Macao, SAR, and Republic of Singapore) are included in the sample after conducting Google searches (Table 5).

Table 5. Advertising programs in the greater China region in the sample (N=10)

School/Program Name	Country
Department of Advertising and Public Relation, Fu Jen University	Taiwan
Department of Advertising, Ming-Chuan University	Taiwan
Department of Advertising, Cheng-Chi University	Taiwan
Department of Public Relations and Advertising, Shih Hsin University	Taiwan
Department of Advertising, Chinese Cultural University	Taiwan
Department of Public Relations and Advertising, Kun Shan University	Taiwan
Public Relations and Advertising Division, Department of Communication Studies, Hong-Kong Baptist University	Hong-Kong, SAR, China
Integrated Strategic Communication (BAISC), Department of Media and Communication, City University of Hong-Kong	Hong-Kong, SAR, China
Journalism and Public Communication, The Department of Communication, University of Macau	Macau, SAR, China
Division of Public and Promotional Communication, Nanyang Technological University	Singapore

Analysis of Results

After downloading and analyzing curricula information from the advertising programs of the U.S., Europe, and Asia (the Greater China Region), the book chapter has attempted to identify course titles containing keywords such as "Big Data", "Data-Driven Marketing and Advertising", "Consumer Analytics", "Predictive Analytics", and "Metrics." It has been found that only a few advertising programs mainly in the U.S. have used these keywords in the course title (description). The Department of Advertising at the University of Texas-Austin has shown its innovativeness in its program. In upper level courses such as, *Advertising 337M (Media Studies)*, contents related to Big Data and analytics tools have been incorporated into the course. For example, the course description shows that one of the course topics will deal with "development of data analysis skills using various analytical techniques" and "digital metrics...... examines the evolving scope of digital metrics and analytics by looking at three dimensions of digital media: business, communications, and technology" (Table 6).

FUTURE RESEARCH DIRECTIONS

Curriculum in a higher education institution can be viewed as an educational project that forms its identities through three main domains: action, knowledge, and self (Barnett, Parry, & Coate, 2010). Advances in media technologies have greatly impacted media education and curricula around the world (Berkeley, 2009). Berkeley (2009) uses a case study approach to record the curriculum changes at RMIT University to explore the impacts of media technologies on media education to create a more student-centered learning environment. Changes in advertising, communication, and media curricula not only create educational contents more in line with the industry demands, but also enable students to become independent learners in a fast-changing environment (Berkeley, 2009; Lester, 2012). Many communication programs at major universities in the U.S. have added new courses to their existing curricula. Advertising instructors also adapt existing courses by integrating emerging media platforms such as social media into students' campaign projects (Lester, 2012). For example, data visualization courses in their journalism programs (e.g., the University of Nebraska-Lincoln, University of California at Berkeley, University of Missouri, and The University of Maryland) (Wordsman, 2014). The new course, *Interactive Data Visualization*, is designed for "journalists who are in high demand – with a wide breadth of skills to help news organizations do good journalism and present it in interactive and meaningful ways" (Wordsman, 2014, para. 36). Another new course, *Connecting the Dots: Data Driven Storytelling for Converged Communication*, at The University of Southern California will be taught in Spring 2015 to explore the impacts of audience analytics and digital strategies (Wordsman, 2014, para. 38). Other less known universities in the U.S., such as Elon University, have also ventured to revamp its journalism curriculum to help students to "confront the realities of analyzing and interpreting metrics to guide decision-making in competitive media environments" to develop better targeted messages and campaigns (Wordsman, 2014, para. 40).

Table 6. Analysis of Big Data-related courses in advertising curricula of different geographical areas

Course Title (Description) Containing the Following Keywords	U.S. Programs (N=116)	European Programs (N=10)	Asian Programs in the Greater China Region (N=10)
"Big Data"	0	0	0
"Data-Driven Marketing or Advertising"	0	0	0
"Consumer Analytics"	0	0	0
"Predictive Analytics"	0	0	0
"Analytics"	1	0	0
"Metrics"	1	0	0

Research findings from this book chapter suggest that when compared with other departments in the communication discipline, a relatively slow response among national and international advertising programs is necessary to better address the challenges and opportunities of Big Data and predictive analytics. There are several potential research directions that can be derived from this book chapter to further explore curricula revamping initiatives among national and international advertising programs. First, a more comprehensive analysis of employment ads in advertising, marketing, and marketing communication areas will ensure the identification of essential skill requirements for entry-level, mid-career, and senior positions to allow higher education institutions to develop advertising programs suitable for students at various stages of their careers. Secondly, research should also be conducted to examine instructors' perceptions of, attitudes toward, and possible resistance to these opportunities and challenges brought up by Big Data and an array of analytic tools. Thirdly, students' needs should also be studied in a more systematic manner to understand their needs once the revamping of existing advertising program is undertaken.

CONCLUSION

In conclusion, what should advertising educators do to develop a more up-to-date program to address the opportunities and challenges of Big Data analytics and other new media developments? The abilities to collect, analyze, and interpret consumer behavior data are found to be essential to the success of future advertising professionals. These skills are expected to be beneficial to students' success in the growing data-driven marketing and advertising industry. The pressure for the advertising industry to justify a return on investment has also increased with the presence of multi-platform advertising channels, ranging from digital TV, social media, websites, and mobile devices (Price, 2014). Emerging practices such as data-driven marketing or behavioral targeting are now made possible and easier through an array of Big Data and consumer analytics tools. To succeed in this competitive environment, future advertising professionals need to excel in integrating insights from these analytics tools into planning more effective campaigns.

REFERENCES

AACSB International. (n.d.). *Standard 9: Curriculum content is appropriate to general expectations for the degree program type and learning goals.* Retrieved June 26, 2015 from http://www.aacsb.edu/en/accreditation/standards/2013-business/learning-and-teaching/standard9/

AdAge. (2014, January 13). *How the Marine Corps enlists Big Data for recruitment efforts: The USMC has worked closely with JWT Atlanta for around 65 years.* Retrieved January 3, 2015 from http://adage.com/article/datadriven-marketing/marine-corps-enlists-big-data-recruitment/291009/

Andrew, M., & Erik, B. (2012, October). The management revolution. *Harvard Business Review*, *90*(10), 60–68. PMID:23074865

Aquino, J. (2012, January). 5 hot marketing trends: Customer strategists must step up their engagement efforts as mobile's mercury rises. *CRM Magazine*, *16*, 20.

Authers, J. (2013, December 8). The changing face of the MBA curriculum. *FT.Com.* Retrieved March 1, 2015 from http://www.ft.com/cms/s/2/b52b57d8-5d07-11e3-81bd-00144feabdc0.html#axzz3RGW3FcND

Ballve, M. (2014, October 22). Mobile, social, and big data: The convergence of the internet's three defining trends. *Business Insider.* Retrieved June 26, 2015 from http://www.businessinsider.com/mobile-and-social-drive-big-data-industry-2014-2019

Barnes, B. E. (1996). Introducing introductory advertising student to the World Wide Web. *Journal of Advertising Education, 1*(1), 5–12.

Barnett, R., Parry, G., & Coate, K. (2010, August 25). *Conceptualising curriculum change.* San Diego, CA: Academic Press.

Beard, F. K., & Tarpening, D. (2001, Spring). Teaching TV advertising creative using digital video on the desktop. *Journal of Advertising Education, 5*(1), 24–33.

Berkeley, L. (2009). Media education and new technology: A case study of major curriculum change within a university media degree. *Journal of Media Practice, 10*(2-3), 185–197. doi:10.1386/jmpr.10.2-3.185_1

boyd, D., & Crawford, K. (2012). Critical questions for big data. *Information, Communication & Society, 15*(5), 662-679.

Brown, B., Chui, M., & Manyika, J. (2012, May). Are you ready for the era of big data? *Intermedia, 40*, 28–33.

Caravella, M., Ekachai, D., Jaeger, C., & Zahay, D. (2009, Spring). Web 2.0 opportunities and challenges for advertising educators. *Journal of Advertising Education, 13*(1), 58–63.

Carlton Associates, Inc. (n.d.). *Is your agency ready for big data?* Chagrin Falls, OH: Carlton Associated Incorporated.

Chaturvedi, A. (2015, February 5). Big data embedded into marketing curriculum at B-schools: Niraj dawar, ivey business school. *The Economic Times of India.* Retrieved January 10, 2015 from http://articles.economictimes.indiatimes.com/2015-02-03/news/58751790_1_big-data-customers- tilt.

Chen, H., Chiang, R. H. L., & Storey, V. C. (2012, December). Business intelligence and analytics: From big data to big impact. *Management Information Systems Quarterly, 36*(4), 1165–1188.

Chennamaneni, P. R., Lala, V., & Srivastava, P., Goutam, & Chakraborty. (2011, Spring). Teaching consumer analytics in advertising and IMC courses: Opportunities and challenges. *Journal of Advertising Education, 15*(1), 52–58.

Cloud Standards Customer Council. (2013, June). *Convergence of social, mobile and cloud: 7 steps to ensure success.* Retrieved March 1, 2015 from http://www.cloud-council.org/ Convergence_of_Cloud_Social_Mobile_Final.pdf

Columbia Business School. (2013, August 28). *Press release, Columbia Business School unveils redesigned core curriculum for first-year MBA students.* Retrieved January 10, 2015 from http://www8.gsb.columbia.edu/newsroom/newsn/2450/columbia-business-school-unveils-redesigned-core-curriculum-for-first-year-mba-students

Dai, J., Huang, J., Huang, S., Liu, Y., & Sun, Y. (2012). The hadoop stack: New paradigm for big data storage and processing. *Intel Technology Journal, 16*(4), 92–110.

Davenport, T. H. (2013). *Enterprise analytics: Optimize performance, process, and decisions through big data*. Upper Saddle River, NJ: FT Press.

Davenport, T. H. (2013, December). Analytics 3.0. *Harvard Business Review*, 64–72.

Eckman, A. (2010, Spring). It's not new to them: Using ning.Com to enhance student engagement in the study of social web marketing and web 2.0 direct response methods. *Journal of Advertising Education, 14*(1), 15–19.

Esteves, J., & Curto, J. (2013). A risk and benefits behavioral model to assess intention to adopt big data. *Journal of Intelligence Studies in Business, 3*(3), 37–46.

Fan, S., Lau, R. Y. K., & Zhao, J. L. (2015, March). Demystifying big data analytics for business intelligence through the lens of marketing mix. *Big Data Research, 2*(1), 28–31. doi:10.1016/j.bdr.2015.02.006

Fulgoni, G. (2013, December). Big data: Friend or foe of digital advertising? Five ways marketers should use digital big data to their advantage. *Journal of Advertising Research, 53*(4), 372–376. doi:10.2501/JAR-53-4-372-376

Gartner. (2012, October 22). *Gartner says Big Data creates big jobs: 4.4 million IT jobs globally to support Big Data by 2015*. Retrieved January 15, 2015 from http://www.gartner.com/newsroom/id/2207915

Glass, R., & Callahan, S. (2014). *The big data-driven business: How to use big data to win customers, beat competitors, and boost profits*. Hoboken, NJ: Wiley.

Greengard, S. (2012, August). Advertising gets personal. *Communications of the ACM, 55*(8), 18–20.

Gross, S. T. (2012, July 5). The new millennial values. *Forbes*. Retrieved January 1, 2015 from http://www.forbes.com/sites/prospernow/2012/07/05/the-new-millennial-values/

Hazan, E., & Banfi, F. (2013, August). *Leveraging big data to optimize digital Marketing*. McKinsey & Company. Retrieved January 13, 2015 from http://www.mckinsey.com/client_service/marketing_and_sales/latest_thinking/leveraging_big_data_to_optimize_digital_marketing

Hendrick, D. (2014, December 11). 6 ways big data will shape online marketing in 2015. *Forbes.com*. Retrieved June 26, 2015 from http://www.forbes.com/sites/drewhendricks/2014/2012/2011/2016-ways-big-data-will-shape-online-marketing-in-2015/

Hoelzel, M. (2014, September 25). The social media advertising report: Growth forecasts, market trends, and the rise of mobile. *Business Insider*. Retrieved January 5, 2015 from http://www.businessinsider.com/social-media-advertising-spending-growth-2014-2019

Ignatius, A. (2012, October). Big Data for Skeptics. *Harvard Business Review*. Retrieved January 5, 2015 from https://hbr.org/2012/10/big-data-for-skeptics

Innes, R. (2004). *Reconstructing undergraduate education: Using learning science to design effective courses*. Mahwah, NJ: Lawrence Erlbaum Associates.

ITBusinessEdge. (n.d.). Big Data is creating big jobs: 4.4 million bBy 2015. *ITBusinessEdge.* Retrieved January 5, 2015 from http://www.itbusinessedge.com/slideshows/big-data-is-creating-big-jobs-4.4-million-by-2015.html

Kalamas, M., Mitchell, T., & Lester, D. (2009, Spring). Modeling social media use: Bridging the gap in higher education. *Journal of Advertising Education, 13*(1), 44–57.

Kaye, K. (2013, August 19). Big data. *Advertising Age, 84*, 14. PMID:24229463

Kaye, K. (2014, August 20). Get a hands on education at Ad Age Data Conference 2014: Two days of practical and entertaining insights in New York this October. *AdAge.com.* Retrieved January 3, 2015 from http://adage.com/article/datadriven-marketing/hands-education-ad-age-data-conference-2014/294635/

Kaye, K. (2015, January 20). IAB survey: Marketers using a hodge-podge of data-tech tools trade group's study showed marketers use upwards of 12 systems. *AdAge.com.* Retrieved January 4, 2015 from http://adage.com/article/datadriven-marketing/iab-surveys-marketing-execs-data-tech/296653/

Kim, H. J., Pelaez, A., & Winston, E. R. (2013, April). *Experiencing big data analytics: Analyzing social media data in financial sector as a case study.* Paper presented at the 2013 Northeast Decision Sciences Institute Annual Meeting Proceedings, New York, NY.

Kim, Y., & Patel, S. (2012, Fall). Teaching advertising media planning in a changing media landscape. *Journal of Advertising Education, 16*(2), 15–26.

Laney, D. (2001). *3d data management: Controlling data volume, velocity and variety.* Retrieved January 4, 2015 from http://blogs.gartner.com/doug-laney/files/2012/01/ad949-3D-Data-Management-Controlling-Data-Volume-Velocity-and-Variety.pdf

Lester, D. H. (2012, January). Social media: Changing advertising education. *Online Journal of Communication and Media Technologies, 2*(1), 116–125.

Mahrt, M., & Scharkow, M. (2012). The value of big data in digital media research. *Journal of Broadcasting & Electronic Media, 57*(1), 20–33. doi:10.1080/08838151.2012.761700

Manyika, J., Chui, M., Brown, B., Bughin, J., Dobbs, R., Roxburgh, C., & Byers, A. H. (2011, May). *Big data: The next frontier for innovation, competition, and productivity.* McKinsey Global Institute (MGI). Retrieved January 1, 2015 from http://www.mckinsey.com/insights/business_technology/big_data_the_next_frontier_for_innovation

Marshall, J. (2013, September 25). The advertising industry has a big crush on Big Data. *DigiDay.* Retrieved March 1, 2015 from http://digiday.com/platforms/dstillery-advertising-data-crush/

Martin, D. G. (2002, Spring). In search of the golden mean: Impact of computer mediated technologies on the media planning course. *Journal of Advertising Education, 6*(1), 25–35.

McAfee, A., & Brynjolfsson, E. (2012, October). Big data: The management revolution. *Harvard Business Review,* 59–68. PMID:23074865

McMillan, S. J., Sheehan, K. B., & Frazier, C. (2001, Fall). What the real world really wants: An analysis of advertising employment ads. *Journal of Advertising Education, 5*(2), 9–21.

Minelli, M., Chambers, M., & Dhiraj, A. (2013, January). *Big data, big analytics: Emerging business intelligence and analytic trends for today's businesses*. Hoboken, NJ: John Wiley & Sons.

Mortimer, K. P., & Sathre, C. O. (2007). The art and politics of academic governance: Relations among boards, presidents, and faculty. Westport, CT: Praeger Publishers.

Nesamoney, D. (2015). *Personalized digital advertising: How data and technology are transforming how we market*. Old Tappan, NJ: Pearson Education, Inc.

O'Leary, D. E. (2013, December). Exploiting big data from mobile device sensor-based apps: Challenges and benefits. *MIS Quarterly Executive, 12*(4), 179–187.

Oliver, S. L., & Hyun, E. (2011). Comprehensive curriculum reform in higher education: Collaborative engagement of faculty and administrators. *Journal of Case Studies in Education*, 1-20.

Orihuela, R., & Bass, D. (2015, June 4). Help wanted: Black belts in data. *Bloomberg Businessweek*. Retrieved June 26, 2015 from http://www.bloomberg.com/news/articles/2015-2006-2004/help-wanted-black-belts-in-data

Patrizio, A. (2015, March 23). 4 ways to beat the big data talent shortage. *Network World*. Retrieved June 26, 2015 from http://www.networkworld.com/article/2897617/big-data-business-intelligence/2897614-ways-to-beat-the-big-data-talent-shortage.html

Pearson, P. G. (2014, June 27-30). *Putting the learner at the center: Just saying 'digital' is not enough*. Paper presented at the ACBSP 2014 Annual Conference: Teaching Excellence and Teaching Excellence Global Business Education Concurrent Sessions, Chicago, IL.

Philip, N. (March 14, 2014). *The impact of big data on the digital advertising industry*. Mountain View, CA: Qubole Data Service. Retrieved January 3, 2015 from http://www.qubole.com/blog/big-data/big-data-advertising-case-study/

Pollack, C. (2014, September 29). It's not big data, it's the big idea, stupid. *AdAge*. Retrieved January 2, 105 from http://adage.com/article/advertising-week-2014/big-data-big-idea-stupid/295199/

Price, C. (2014, September 2). Attracting the right audience with big data insights. *The Telegraph*. Retrieved January 2, 2015 from http://www.telegraph.co.uk/sponsored/technology/4g- mobile/engaging-customers/11070094/attract-right-audience-big-data.html

PWC. (2015, February). *Data driven: What students need to succeed in a rapidly changing business world*. Retrieved June 26, 2015 from http://www.pwc.com/us/en/faculty-resource/assets/pwc-data-driven-paper-feb2015.pdf

Quesenberry, K. A., Saewitz, D., & Kantrowitz, S. (2014, Spring). Blogging in the classroom: Using wordpress blogs with buddy press plugin as a learning tool by. *Journal of Advertising Education, 18*(2), 5–17.

Robbs, B. (2010, Fall). Preparing young creatives for an interactive world: How possible is it? *Journal of Advertising Education, 14*(2), 7–14.

Schultz, D. E. (2014, May). *Why Big Data is so difficult. Marketing News.* American Marketing Association. Retrieved January 2, 2015 from https://www.ama.org/publications/MarketingNews/Pages/why-big-data-so-difficult.aspx

Scovotti, C., & Jones, S. K. (2011, Spring). From Web 2.0 to Web 3.0: Implications for advertising courses. *Journal of Advertising Education, 15*(1), 6–15.

Simonite, T. (2013, February 5). AT&T brings online ad targeting tactics to TV commercials. *MIT Technology Review.* Retrieved June 26, 2015 from http://www.technologyreview.com/news/510186/att-brings-online-ad-targeting-tactics-to-tv-commercials/

Soare, L. (2012, March 22). The rise of Big Data in higher education. *EDUCAUSE BRIEF: Spotlight on Analytics Series.* Retrieved January 4, 2015 from https://net.educause.edu/ir/library/pdf/LIVE1208s.pdf

Stanaland, A. J. S., Helm, A. E., & Kinney, L. (2009, Spring). Bridging the gap in IMC education: Where the academy is falling short? *Journal of Advertising Education, 13*(1), 38–43.

Stark, J. S., & Lattuca, L. R. (1997). *Shaping the college curriculum: Academic plans in action.* Needham Heights, MA: Allyn and Bacon.

Vogel, D., Zhou, H., & Hu, D. (2015, March). Special issue on computation, business, and health science. *Big Data Research, 2*(1), 1. doi:10.1016/j.bdr.2015.03.002

Watson, H. J., & Marjanovic, O. (2013). Big data: The fourth data management generation. *Business Intelligence Journal, 18*(3), 4–8.

Wordsman, E. (2014, December 14). Journalism schools add courses in sports, emerging technology. *American Journalism Review.* Retrieved January 4, 2015 from http://ajr.org/2014/12/18/journalism-schools-add-courses-sports-emerging-technology/

ADDITIONAL READING

Church, A. H., & Dutta, S. (2013). The promise of big data for OD: Old wine in new bottles or the next generation of data driven methods for change? *OD Practitioner, 45*(4), 23–31.

Kudyba, S., & Davenport, T. H. (2014). *Big data, mining, and analytics: Components of strategic decision making. Boca Rotan.* CRC Press. doi:10.1201/b16666

Lenhart, A., Purcell, K., Smith, A., & Zichuhr, K. (February 3, 2010). *Social media & mobile internet use among teens and young adults* (No. http://files.eric.ed.gov/fulltext/ED525056.pdf). Washington, D.C.: Pew Research Center.

Maimon, O. Z., & Rokach, L. (2005). *Data mining and knowledge discovery handbook.* New York: Springer. doi:10.1007/b107408

NetworkWorld Asia. (2013, March/April). Big data - big hype or big worry? pp. 6-7.

Nunan, D., & Domenico, M. D. (2013). Market research and the ethics of big data. *International Journal of Market Research, 55*(3), 2–13.

Sagirouglu, S., & Sinanc, D. (2013, May 20-24). *Big data: A review.* Paper presented at the 2013 International Conference on Collaborative Technologies and Systems, San Diego, CA.

KEY TERMS AND DEFINITIONS

Behavioral Targeting: A term used to describe a wide variety of technologies and techniques among online publishers and advertisers through the analysis of Internet navigation behavioral data.

Big Data: The term refers to the dataset that has large, more varied, and complex structure, accompanies by difficulties of data storage, analysis, and visualization. Big Data are characterized with their high-volume, -velocity and –variety information assets.

Data Analytics: Sometimes, abbreviated as DA. The term is often defined as the science of investigation raw data to draw conclusions about consumers. A technique used in many business areas to enable organizations and companies to make more informed business discussions by making inference from analyzing patterns and relationships in consumer behavior data.

Data Mining: Also known as data or knowledge discovery. It is a term to refer to an interdisciplinary sub-field of computer science to describe the computational process of pattern discovery in large datasets.

Data-Driven Marketing: The term refers to using data-based consumer insights to make business decisions. It refers to the analysis of secondary data (such as online social interactions, web navigation and search behaviors) or primary data to help marketers to collect, integrate, and analyze consumer data from both internal and external sources.

Metrics: The term refers to measures to assess success or effectiveness of advertising and marketing campaign. Depending on the platforms, different metrics are developed by practitioners. For example, for content marketers, unique visitors, page views, search engine traffic, bounce rate, conversion rate are some of the popular metrics to measure if a content marketing campaign is successful.

Predictive Analytics: A term that is used to refer to the procedure and technique to extra information from existing datasets to determine and identify patterns and insights to predict future trends and outcomes. The practice of predictive analytics helps forecast what might happen in the future with an acceptable level of reliability, what-if scenarios, and risk assessment.

Variety: A term that is used to refer to the range of data sources and types of Big Data. This term often refers to the heterogeneity of data representation, types, and semantic interpretation.

Velocity: A term that is used to refer to the speed of data input and output of Big Data. In general, the term addresses the rate at which data are input and the time upon which data are analyzed.

Volume: A term that refers to the amount of data that can be collected, stored, and analyzed in Big Data.

Chapter 10
Two Different Aspects of Technology Regarding Marketing Education

Amiram Porath
AmiPorCon Ltd, Israel

ABSTRACT

The role of technology in marketing education can be described from two different points of view, the role of the technology as a tool for marketing education and the role of technology in marketing as part of the curriculum of marketing education. We begin with a description of the role of technology in education in general. That has been a focal point for research for the last two decades and in that aspect marketing education is no exception, in fact it is even more relevant for marketing education as marketing uses communication as a major tool. Alternatively, the changing world of communication changes how marketing is viewed, opening new venues for opportunities but also exposing new threats, one cannot be called a marketing expert without understanding the new rules of communication. The chapter will than present two cases one of a threat and another of an opportunity to demonstrate that point while also discussing the role of technology in education in an effective way for marketing education. It ends with a suggestion for electives for marketing education curriculum.

THE ROLE OF TECHNOLOGY IN EDUCATION

Current Status of Education Technology

The models dealing with the use of new technologies cannot be separated from general models of learning. The models of technology use in learning those as Siemens has shown (2004), require us to adapt the learning process to the technology as it changes the learning process as it has changed our daily lives. These models (Siemens, 2005) are ever changing and require constant monitoring to better understand the way they change.

DOI: 10.4018/978-1-4666-9784-3.ch010

The use of social networks has created communities of learning and their impact on the learning process nor their importance for the learning experience can be ignored (Arbaugh, 2008), moreover, it requires constant watching for developments and new emerging models (Garrison, 2009).

To order the analysis of the status of technology in education we shall make use of their impact on three types of interactions involved in the learning process, as described by Anderson (2003):

Student - Teacher Interaction

When entering the classroom 20 years ago, it seemed to be like any other daily activity. There was a person in the front talk, writing by hand information on the black board, or in some special cases presenting a power point presentation. The pace and the intensity of the activity were very much like that required in other places.

Today of course, such activities would seem to be boring and slow, compared to everyday activities, not because they have changed, but rather because the rate of information retrieval has changed drastically. A single person talking to a group for about forty-five minutes, with few interruptions would seem exhaustive, compared to the rate of information retrieval that can be accomplished outside the class. In addition the availability of knowledge has increased that the role of the teacher has changed from that of information provider, to that of interpreting the information and demonstrating its use.

True, in higher education, the role of the teacher has always been at least partly that of interpreter and demonstrator rather than that of an information provider, however, that has changed in magnitude, as most of the information can be retrieved easily enough using on-line technologies. Therefore while the information can be retrieved its use and its meaning need to be explained and demonstrated, and quite a lot of the role of gathering the information and organizing it has moved to the students – to be done at their own discretion, off line. This again was done to certain extent already in the past in higher education, but while in the past the sources were controlled to a large extent by the teacher, that again is no longer the case. The books introduced into the library are no longer the single sources available to the students and in some cases due to the slow rate of supply not the preferred choice in any case.

The teacher was available mostly during the class time, and perhaps also during certain hours in which they were made available to the students for questions, clarifications. The scene at the end of the lesson when the students crowed the teacher in order to get one last question in, and to interact at least seemingly on a one-on-one basis, is well familiar.

Today of course that is no longer the situation. The teachers are available on line and off-line seemingly 24/7, and their material certainly is available on such levels. The students can post questions to a course website or in a more discrete manner email their teacher or even make use of social networks to interact.

That change in the availability has changed the nature of the interaction between the student and the teacher, removing some of social distance between them (members of the same network), and making it much more intensive.

In fact, one side effect is evident when the fast moving visual aids, so similar to their hobbies and games, help the student, even for those that are "concentration challenged", to keep their focus on the topics learnt during the 45 minutes lessons. Less "daydreaming" seen in the classroom. For the current generation used to rapid updating and constant stimulation the remote learning applications and the new way the material is provided, help maintain concentration that otherwise, in the classic classroom would be difficult to maintain, as it would be more difficult to keep concentration than for former generations less excitement craving as they were.

So both the role of the teacher and the nature of the interaction has changed (Anderson, 2003).

Student - Material Interaction

In education in the past the material was provided by the teacher, the list of reading material was to a large extend controlled by the teacher in two ways. First by providing the list itself an thus defining the topics discussed in the classroom, and secondly by the availability of the literature in the relevant library. Due to the cost of books, normally books that were not available in the library were not available for most students and certainly not widely so. That has changed dramatically with the open access today to information sources, e.g. Google Scholar (http://scholar.google.com/) where books and articles can be accessed freely and quickly and alternative information is easily and freely available. The teachers have lost to some extent the controlled over the information discussed in their courses. The interaction between the student and the material is more direct one. It is an interaction of search, identify and retrieve, with the understanding and accumulation done by the students, with the ability to approach the teacher for interpretation and explanations required – as mentioned above with a 24/7 availability. The interaction with the material has also become more intensified as the information high-way is providing much more information than was previously available. This poses two major problems:

1. In most cases there is more information available than the students can process and therefore the information needs to be prioritized, and only the most relevant or the higher quality needs to be accessed – identified and retrieved.
2. The information in most cases is not filtered and errors and misleading information are mixed with the relevant and correct information. The students in most cases lack the ability to discern the two types and are likely to treat all information retrieved as similarly reliable.

Therefore the students interaction with the material can become more superficial, preferring short and informative resources over resources discussing certain single points in depth, as the transaction cost of dealing with extensive sources dealing with in depth analysis of certain points only to discover that the discussion is less reliable than other sources is too high. In addition the patience and focus time span of students in their daily activities has shortened and therefore their willingness to deal with lengthy information sources is reduced.

However, it is important to bear in mind that the material and the delivery have to be constantly updated in order to maintain interest, which burdens the teacher with the additional updating of the material and delivery. It is no longer possible to re-use old classes every year.

So the role of technology regarding that specific interaction has been to increase the intensity while raising new questions regarding the reliability of sources and efficient ways of dealing with multiple sources and an overflow of information. On the other hand the preference for short, informative sources over in depth analysis has increased and has changed the interaction as well.

Student - Student Interaction

While most of the student – Student interaction in the past occurred face to face and in the education organization premises (classroom or outside), quite a lot of it has moved into the cyberspace and is done remotely, on-line and through social networks.

The use of social network for student interaction has led to its use in the learning process (Anderson & Dron, 2011), allowing for groups to come together, making it easier to work together on joint papers, share study materials, prepare for exams, and other similar joint activities. Information sharing, including or excluding the teacher is made easier through technology and if combined with the Teach interaction and the enhanced material interaction has changed the process of learning completely – outside the classroom. The ease of Student-Student interaction and its increased speed, and especially the fact that it uses everyday tools that the students are familiar with and have no problems using, has made this an effective learning process. The increased collaboration in the learning environment to address both issues of quality and efficiency can be viewed via the increased usage of Wiki's and What's-Up for group study. While this, as a model was not shared by all (Annand, 2007), it clear benefits in quality and efficiency (Garrison & Vughan, 2007; Twigg, 2003) are making it undisputedly legitimate. We are yet to see if Annand's (2007) prediction regarding the university structure is yet to come true.

It may seem that there are only up-sides to remote learning; however that is not the case. Unmediated interaction between students allows them to develop "people skills", to learn to tolerate the others, as you cannot disengage quickly and re-engage just as fast, you have to stay in the group. The unmediated interaction which is lacking in that aspect in remote leaning is especially important is marketing education, as this requires the developed "people skills" (e.g. no idea how to interpret or react to body language – can hamper the future marketing expert).

The Classroom

When discussing technology in education one need to recall that technology is a means to an end and only rarely the end goal of the education. There has been much discussion regarding the potential of introducing modern technology and technology advances into the classroom and the curriculum.

It is regarding the introduction of new technologies into the learning experience both in the classroom and outside it that one needs to remember that for the students of today, the classroom is more boring than their daily activities. It must feel like going back in time for students when they enter the classroom with the blackboard and chalk. Even using presentations and other fixed visual aids may seem outdated. Compared to the fast changing short (verbally) messages that the students are used to in their daily life the lecture or the lesson are both long and tedious. The introduction of the new technologies allows the classroom to become more compatible with the daily life of the students. It allows them to interact in a familiar way, and it allows them to approach the lesson material in a more common way for them and therefore to better interact with it.

The use of social networks helps in increasing the student-student interaction and student-teacher interaction. However, that increase in the experience results from the usage of the social networks, as the student do in their "private" lives. The increase usage of the social networks in the education environment allows the student to learn from each other and exchange ideas in a more efficient way than during frontal teaching in the classroom.

That the student-teacher interaction similarly increases the learning experience allowing the teacher to mass interact in a private way. The teacher can connect directly and privately to each of the students or approach them in a group. This connection can be done 24/7 if the teacher allows it, and increases the availability of the interaction for the students. It can make use of synchronous tools for teaching or a-synchronous tools for additional information.

The teachers in the classroom face a new challenge in their roles of interpreters and demonstrators, they need to show stronger control of the material, not only presented int eh classroom or included in the curriculum but related material available on the net. While at the same time they need to make the classroom experience as fast and as adapted to the attention span of their students as possible. But most important they need to be able to use the technological tools available to continue the learning process outside the classroom and to recognize that it is an inseparable part of the learning process and should be treated as such. The social networks tools should be incorporated into the learning process making it more compatible with the students' everyday life and thus integrating the learning process easier into the students' lives. These are tough challenges as they require the teachers to keep up with the new technologies and the opportunities they present, as well as for the system in the education organization to make the relevant platforms available for teachers and students. These challenges, the familiarity with the new technologies and their opportunities and the availabilities of relevant infrastructures are going to be the challenges of future education.

The Other Aspects of Technology in Marketing Education

Marketing deals with introduction of ideas and products to people and therefore combines psychology and communication. While the psychology of people is of a more permanent nature, the communication is based on technology, and therefore changes with time, and the introduction of new technologies.

In the 1980's and until recently both academic marketing and management experts and popular marketing and management authors have focused on the psychology basis for marketing and analyzed its implications (Porter, 1980, 1985; Brown & Eisenhardt 1998; Hill, 1967 ; Peters, 1982, 1993,1994 ; Mackay, 1988, 1990; Rapp & Colins, 1987). These concepts and their validity have been research and probed for a long time and the resulting validity is well founded. Once again like the classroom they could focus on the aspects of strategy and psychology since the marketing interactions were the same as everyday interactions and just had to be put to the right psychological use.

Both the opportunities that, and the dangers, that the new technologies and the way that people interact, present themselves and need better understanding for optimal utilization.

The usage of the opportunities presented by the new technologies, as presented by the case study below, allow the usage of the technologies in better fit to general unchanging marketing principals.

The optimal usage of the new technologies in marketing requires both creativity as well as familiarity with the technologies and the opportunities it offers.

CASE STUDIES PROS AND CONS

In order to illustrate the increased relevance of understanding the new technologies, the opportunities as well as the threats they present two very short case studies are presented below. One to demonstrate the opportunities and the other potential threats. They also come to present the rate in which the world marketing operates is changing and that marketing education needs to keep up with times. Technology can no longer be second place.

The Positive Aspect: The Korean Advertising for the Bank

New technologies can open new opportunities for advertising and for segmentation of the markets. In the case of the bank. It identified that the customers' visits were reduced during the lunch time. In order to increase the attractiveness of the bank during that specific period time, use was made of a QR code offering special conditions to bank customers at that time. The QR Code was revealed to the potential customers by using 3D structures that formed the code by sun light and shade only at noon – a modern sundial of sorts. That QR Code led to a specific site where the special offers were made available.

The gimmick attracted people at first, which allowed the special offers to be made to the right target market segment, which than responded and results were better than expected. This use of new technologies coincided with the old marketing tools of market segmentation and offering specific offers to each segment, but such am activity could not take place without the new technology that can allow for updated information – the special offer to be made real time, and bring clients at the specific time required.

EMART Sunny Sale Case

EMART the Walmart of Korea has 141 stores all over the country. They found out that during lunchtime sales went down, and decided to try and change that situation. The classical marketing solution is to use publicity and special offers to target customers segmenting the market and approaching the right segment to attract them at the right time to the stores.

The way the above classical marketing solution is executed is by using new technologies. The idea was to introduce a noel purchasing experience that would enhance the shopping experience at this specific time and thus attract the target segment – using new technologies allowed the segmentation to focus on users of these technologies – normally younger people with a strong purchasing power. The technology utilized was by creating a QR code that could be read using smart phones and which directed the user to a specific site with special offers for that time only. The uniqueness of the timeframe was achieved by using shadow technique to create the QR code so it could be created only by the noon sun. The website offered such long tried and proved tools as coupons and free special delivery to on-line shoppers through the website. The direction to the website with the special offers became available during that time frame to owners of smart phones in the city of Seoul. The success of the marketing effort proved in increase of over 25% in the EMART membership compared to previous month, and an increase in sales as well as media coverage and free advertising for the firm due to the new and bold move.

This case study comes to show that the new technologies offer us new ways to better employ old known theories and practices of marketing, segmentation, coupons, move to purchase, reduce the transaction costs etc. all these are enhanced by the use of the technology, and come to show that that smart use of new technologies has its rewards, while keeping the principals of marketing in place. However, to create such promotion activities one has to be familiar with the potential of the new technologies, and be in touch with the market to know not only what would work, but also how to best employ it. Therefore, it would seem smart to include in the marketing education some aspects of technology utilization that would create the basic familiarity with the technologies and what they have to offer.

It would be expected that while the basics of marketing stay valid permanently. Based as they are on human nature and psychology, the technology and methods of achieving them are constantly changing. It is important to include the technological element in the marketing studies otherwise the effective use of technology will always leg behind. The technology included education will allow future marketing experts also to direct technological developments that will be used in marketing activities more effectively and not just "hitch-hike" on existing technology.

The Negative Side: The Lesson of the Palm Oil Company

While knowing the technology has its positive side by the ability to utilize such advantages for enhancing the marketing principals there are other advantages in familiarity with the new technology and that is avoiding pitfalls the new technology place in front of us, which due to our lack of experience with these technologies were are prone to fall into. One such issue which cannot be disconnected from marketing is public relations and the usage of new technologies for that purpose. Here the technological aspects that need to be explored by the marketing experts include the impact of the type of interaction with the public, the new tools afford, and how to utilize it. Misunderstanding the new rules of public communication can result in a fast and devastating response from the public.

To demonstrate this point let us consider the case of the Palm oil incident regarding Unilever and Nestle.

Unilever and the Palm Oil Case

As the Economist reported (Economist 2010):

EARLY on April 21st 2008, Greenpeace activists dressed as orang-utans stormed Unilever's headquarters in London. Similar raids took place at the multinational's facilities on Merseyside, in Rome and in Rotterdam. Furry protesters scaled buildings, occupied production lines and unfurled banners. Many read: "Unilever: Don't Destroy the Forests". Dove, one of the company's best-known brands, was singled out by name.

The protest against Unilever headed by environmentalist was a case study for media students. The actions of the firm in trying to secure the raw material for its production seemed to have heavy consequences for the environment and the environmentalist groups decided to move ahead with a media campaign against the firm. In another attempt to single out the firms, a video was published on the net deriding the Nestle favored product Kit-Kat, which the firm originally trued to bury but after 1/5 million viewing and over 200,000 angry emails had to change track (Economist, 2010).

It would seem that while its college Nestle which buckled under the public pressure and instituted measures to present a firm policy to be more environmental friendly, Unilever managed to avoid the scandal at first, but did not manage to avoid it all together (EJOLT, 2012). While it originally promised to purchase sustainable palm oil, it did not do so exclusively and that was the main goal of the public attack and the close scrutiny the firm has been facing since. It would seem that the environmental groups have learnt to use the social networks to create public opinion against the firms violating the environment and to help them recruit also government aid. As in the above case Facebook and other social networks helped bring the companies to their knees (Economist, 2010). After two years of discussion without results with Nestle it has taken two months of public campaign to make the company take strong measures to assure the green environmentalists that it is taking the issue seriously, and reorganizing its supplier list accordingly.

The main lesson to be learnt, is that today firms can no longer bury issues and that understanding the new technologies and their potential to raise issues and reach vast public segments require firms to be ready to respond in another manner than the old one, things can no longer be easily discarded or issues hidden. The public may forget, but special groups can recall the information, and once it is out there it cannot be un-published.

CONCLUSION

In the current rapidly changing world, technologies are shaping our lives and having an ever increasing impact on the way we do things, and the way we view things. While classical marketing education can continue based on the classical human characteristics, it requires a technological supplementary that includes introduction to the potential and pitfalls of technology usage.

Technology cannot be left out side as it has become a major tool in the marketing expert tool box, and therefore needs to be included in the basic training. It can help the creativity of the marketing person, but it also needs to be there for the average student to understand and be ready to employ.

On the other hand, technology usage in the teaching process is a requirement that will increase in importance as the younger generations become more and more digitally enabled. These newer generations will not be ready to accept that education, the tool for their future is backwards compared to their daily life. How such backwards activities prepare them for the future? How can they lead if they are already behind? Teachers will need to become adept at using these technologies, and configuring their courses to fit these technologies in order to keep up, as well as the education organizations which will need to invest more and more in the relevant infrastructure, and first of all, understand how to design it, and how to design for future developments.

REFERENCES

Anderson, T. (2003). Getting the mix right again: An updated and theoretical rationale for interaction. *The International Review of Research in Open and Distributed Learning*, 4(2).

Anderson, T. & Dron, J (2011). Three generations of distance learning education pedagogy. *The International Review of Research in Open and Distributed Learning*.

Annand, D. (2007). Re-organizing universities for the information age. *International Review of Research in Open and Distance Learning*, 8(3). Retrieved from http://www.irrodl.org/index.php/irrodl/article/view/372/952

Arbaugh, J. B. (2008). Does the community of inquiry framework predict outcomes in online MBA courses? *The International Review of Research in Open and Distributed Learning*, 9(2).

Brown, S. L., & Eisenhardt, K. M. (1998). *Competing on the edge*. Harvard College.

Economist. (2010). *The other oil spill*. Retrieved 10 April 2015 from http://www.economist.com/node/16423833

Ejolt. (2012). *Unilever and how to greenwash tropical devastations*. Retrieved 10 April 2015 from: http://www.ejolt.org/2012/09/unilever-and-how-to-greenwash-tropical-devastations/

Garrison, D. R., & Vaughan, N. (2007). *Blended learning in higher education*. Jossey-Bass. doi:10.1002/9781118269558

Garrison, R. D. (2009). Implications of online learning for the conceptual development and practice of distance education. *International Journal of E-Learning & Distance Education, 23*(2), 93–104.

Hill, N. (1967). *Think and Grow Rich*. Dutton, Penguin Books.

Mackay, H. (1988). *Swim with the sharks without being eaten alive*. Mackay, USA: Harvey B.

Mackay, H. (1990). *Beware the naked man who offers you hi shirt*. Mackay, USA: Harvey B.

Peters, T. J. (1993). Liberation management. Pan books Ltd.

Peters, T. J. (1994). *The Tom Peters Seminar*. Excel.

Peters, T. J., & Waterman, R. H. (1982). *In search of excellence: Lessons from America's best-run companies*. New York: Harper & Row.

Porter, M. E. (1980). *Competitive Strategy*. The Free Press.

Porter, M. E. (1985). *Competitive Advantage*. The Free Press.

Rapp, S., & Collins, T. L. (1987). Maximarketing. McGraw-Hill USA.

Siemens, G. (2004). *A learning theory for the digital age*. Elearnspace: everything learning. Downloaded April 10 2015.

Siemens, G. (2004). *Connectivism: Learning as network-creation*. Retrieved 9 April 2015 from https://www.youtube.com/watch?v=EvIJfUySmY0

Twigg, C. A. (2003). Improving learning and reducing costs: New models for online learning. *EDUCAUSE Review, 38*(5), 29–38.

Chapter 11
Preparing Students to Use Marketing Technology for Decision–Making

Camille P. Schuster
California State University – San Marcos, USA

ABSTRACT

Organizations have increased expectations for expertise in data analytics by marketing students. The chapter describes the change taking place in business in general and in marketing specifically and the disconnect between demand and supply. While tools have been available to teach marketing research using survey, experimental, and qualitative methodologies. However, a lack of materials and a huge learning curve are major reasons for methodologies for analyzing digital data, big data, or social media data not being used. Teradata, Inc., worked with Marketing Information Systems academics to create TeradataUniversityNetwork.com (TUN) as a place for sharing tools, software, articles, and data so analytics can be taught in the classroom. As of August 2014, (TUN) is a resource for sharing tools, software, articles, and videos that focus on marketing analytics. This chapter describes the range of materials available and how they can be used in the classroom.

INTRODUCTION

The future of marketing lies in companies' abilities to collect and connect large amounts of data and rapidly analyze it in order to make their marketing interactions relevant for each individual customer. Marketing students today need to enter the workforce with a solid foundational understanding of the technology, tools, and processes required to make this happen. (Darryl McDonald, President, Teradata Applications "Global Skills Shortage," 2014)

Understanding where consumers go, how they use their time, the kind of messages they send, the searches they conduct before purchasing products, and what devices they prefer using when searching or making purchases are all important issues to understand when creating and evaluating marketing strategies and

DOI: 10.4018/978-1-4666-9784-3.ch011

tactics used to draw consumers to retail outlets, services, or products. To gather this information, aggregate it, analyze it, and create a format that conveys relevant insights to decision makers, marketers need to interface with technology and software. The movement to use marketing automation and marketing analytical tools by companies is gaining momentum, thereby changing the requirements for the skills of students graduating from marketing programs.

Organizations such as Accenture, Deloitte, and IBM are opening new analytics centers (Chen, Chiang & Storey, 2010; IBM, 2009; Luftman & Ben-Zvi, 2010; Pettey & Goasduff, 2011; Turban, Sharda, Dursun & King, 2011). Research by McKinsey Global Institute forecasts a 50 to 60 percent shortfall of qualified people for analytics positions, which is about 140,000 to 190,000 unfilled positions by 2018 (Manyika et al., 2011). In addition, about 1.5 million current managers and analysts do not have the necessary skills to understand and make decisions based on the analysis of large amounts of data (Manyika, et al., 2011). Business schools need to prepare graduates in business intelligence (BI) (Connolly, 2012; Conway & Vasseur, 2009; "Global Skills Shortage," 2014; Sircar, 2009; Watson, 2008; Wixom et al., 2011).

Business professionals now expect that marketing students will have experience with BI tools (Connolly, 2012; Conway and Vasseur, 2009; "Global Skills Shortage," 2014; Sicar, 2009; Watson, 2008; Wixom et al., 2011). Interfacing with technology and software beyond Excel, SPSS or SAS has not been a significant part of marketing classes for a number of reasons. One major reason for not incorporating automation and analytics tools is the lack of materials for demonstration and class assignments ("Intelligence in Harmony, "2012; Wixom et al., 2011; "State of the Industry," 2012). Without materials faculty can only talk about the role of marketing analytics. However, a faculty member talking about the process does not allow students to achieve higher levels of learning, i.e., analysis and synthesis. Students develop analysis and synthesis skills through practice. Access to data, case materials, and marketing-related software is necessary for creating student assignments that provide students the opportunity to practice with the tools.

The purpose of this chapter is to describe activities and materials that can be used with students to develop marketing analytics skills and Teradata University Network (TUN) which is a repository for such material. The first section of the paper provides a rationale for why analytics needs to be taught in marketing classes. The second section provides an example of the resources available on www.teradatauniversitynetwork.com (TUN). The third section presents results when using this material in the classroom.

BACKGROUND

Procter and Gamble describes the old IT model within companies as the process of figuring out which reports people wanted, capturing the data and delivering it to the key people weeks or days later (Murphy, 2012). That model is now obsolete. Marketing students are entering a marketplace with an increased demand for skills to analyze data, interpret data, and use the results to inform decision making in near real time. The new model being envisioned is a virtual, instant-on war room, where people huddle, in person or by video, around the needed data to determine how it can inform decision making. This approach requires better collaboration using video, more real time data, and business analytics expertise according to Filippo Passerini, P&G CIO (Murphy 2012). In 2012, Gartner predicted that by 2017 the Chief Marketing Officer will spend more money on information technology than the Chief Information Officer (McLellan, 2012).

Business professionals expect that marketing students have experience with BI tools (Connolly, 2012; Conway & Vasseur, 2009; "Global Skills Shortage," 2014; Sircar, 2009; Watson, 2008; Wixom et al., 2011). Discussing or analyzing data for data's sake is not a good investment. Data needs to drive actions that generate conversions and revenue (DeMera, 2014). Therefore, the focus for preparing marketing students should be on analyzing data, articulating the implications for business, and working with colleagues through the implementation process. Analysis needs to focus on what the data mean and how they relate to key performance indicators (KPIs) that impact sales and profits (DeMera, 2014). Spreadsheets, a commonly used tool for analysis, have been described as the "fast food" of strategic decision making (Christensen & van Bever, 2014). They are not sufficient for the type of analysis demanded in today's marketplace (see Table 1). According to The Economist, "The new marketer combines operational and data skills with a grasp of the big picture" ("The Rise," 2015).

Traditional marketing research allows marketers to identify consumers' intentions, attitudes, and plans. However, often these metrics are not connected to behavior and do not directly inform business decisions. For example, in an attempt to connect consumer data with KPIs, spreadsheets focusing on invested capital or an internal rate of return are often used for marketing analysis (Christensen & van Bever, 2014). This perspective does not create a better understanding of how consumers make decisions or how consumers respond to specific marketing tactics.

The lack of data, cases, and materials for marketing faculty to use is the biggest hurdle in teaching new tools and skills or in integrating this knowledge and skill-building into the marketing curriculum ("Intelligence in Harmony," 2012; Wixom et al., 2011; "State of the Industry," 2012.) One recent survey of Fortune 500 executives stated that the biggest talent and hiring gap in online marketing is in the

Table 1. Additional capabilities of a marketing automation system*

Criteria for Comparison	Email Service Provider	Marketing Automation
Sends mass emails	x	x
Tracks open rates and clicks	x	x
Easy to build landing pages and forms		x
Website behavior tracking		x
Easy to create dynamic segments based on cross-channel behaviors		x
Powered by a smart marketing database		x
Easy to create multi-step campaigns with conditional logic		x
Coordinate cross-channel interactions (e.g., direct mail, SMS, CRM systems)		x
Connect and track social media interaction		x
Social sweepstakes and referral applications		x
Ability to define and measure a data-driven view of the buying cycle		x
Customizable reporting on marketing performance		x
Behavioral and demographic scoring		x
Manage marketing budgets and forecasts across teams		x
Measures impact of marketing programs on revenue		x
Ability to design and measure a data-driven view of consumers, behaviors, and buying cycle		x

*Based upon "Enter Marketing Automation" Table in Marketo Whitepaper ("Graduating From," 2013)

analytics space (37%). Companies surveyed said that they "desperately needed staff with serious data chops" (Singer, 2013).

Discovery is a new core process in this new era of data and analytics (Davenport, 2013). According to this article, in Analytics 1.0 discovery was less essential in traditional analytics environments, when data exploration was slow, and analytics were not heavily relied upon for decisions at scale. Firms analyzing big data in Analytics 2.0 had their own discovery processes, relying upon time consuming work by a few "data scientists" who had to do extensive programming. In the Analytics 3.0 era, as analytics on all types of data becomes mainstream, understanding relationships in the data is an essential process for strategic decision making and needs to be conducted with speed and efficiency at large volume (Davenport, 2013). A newer approach to marketing analytics is about finding the right data, collating data from different sources, conducting difficult analyses, and creating predictions (Friedman, 2013).

Marketing Information Systems (MIS) faces a similar challenge regarding Analytics 3.0, but this discipline has always been involved with teaching analytics. As a result, many of the software companies, such as Oracle, IBM, SAS, and Teradata, have worked with MIS and Computer Science (CS) academics to create resources that can be used when teaching courses related to the creation and execution of data warehouses, data analysis, and business intelligence. One example is the TUN website, hosted by Teradata, Inc. and initially administered by MIS faculty. On this website, materials for classes, e.g., homework assignments, videos, data and business articles, have been made available for MIS professors and students. By 2015, over 40,000 students, 4,900 faculty, and 2,200 universities in 106 countries have used TUN ("TUN KPI Summary," 2015).

The need for a similar resource for marketing academics has become a major issue as the use of software designed for marketing professionals and the demand for marketing analytics has increased dramatically. This type of resource, with analytics course material specifically designed for the marketing discipline, has not been available until the summer of 2014 when TUN announced a special section for marketing materials on TUN. The following section describes materials that can be used by faculty when teaching marketing analytics either as an introduction to specific concepts or a hands-on use of marketing software.

RESOURCES ON TUN

Recently "data scientist" has been described as a "sexy job" (Friedman, 2013). These "data scientists" need to triangulate data, make inferential insights, use passive listening, and track what people do during shopping trips in stores or online. Since analyzing this data encompasses a wide variety of data types, a broader range of analytical tools need to be employed in the marketing curriculum. In addition to mining data, interpreting third party reports, and conducting statistical analyses of survey or experimental data, students also need to learn how to use tools to evaluate social media data (e.g., Facebook, Instragram, Twitter, LinkedIn), the data embedded in Customer Relationship Management (CRM) tools, and the data available in software packages designed to manage marketing activities. These resources are being used in organizations, but the materials and tools for teaching the use of these resources are not typically addressed in most marketing classes because faculty are not familiar with using these tools, the learning curve for mastering these tools is high, and materials for assignments are not readily available. Some marketing classes are beginning to focus on social media analytical tools. However, marketing automation software is not normally included in marketing analytics presentations because faculty and students do not have access to this software in the classroom or for homework assignments.

After Teradata, Inc., purchased Aprimo, one of the leading marketing automation systems, the TUN Advisory Board decided to expand their work to include Marketing and Consumer Science. As of August 2014, the TUN website has a gateway page for marketing faculty, materials specifically designed for marketing faculty, and exercises using marketing automation software. After registration, access to TUN is free for faculty and students. Faculty need give the designated password to their students. This section of the paper focuses on the development of tools that can be used by marketing faculty to teach marketing analytics. Realizing that marketing faculty have different levels of expertise in this area, that marketing analytics can be presented in a variety of ways, and that the emphasis on marketing analytics will differ across courses, TUN materials include videos, Powerpoint presentations, articles, case studies, and software exercises. For advanced analytics courses, the wealth of MIS materials are also available on TUN for marketing faculty.

In some classes, examples of what kind of analytics are being used to facilitate business decision making would be a welcome addition to a lecture. While working for Teradata, Dr. Dave Schrader created materials to help the Teradata sales force demonstrate what could be done using Teradata tools alone and in conjunction with technology partners. These Business Scenario Investigation (BSI) videos (at least 13) are now on TUN. They follow the Crime Scene Investigation (CSI) format: what is the business problem, what evidence can be gathered, what does the analysis reveal, what kind of solutions can be presented and tested. In addition to the videos, the BSI cases also include Powerpoint presentations and discussion guides. Depending upon how much detail and/or how much discussion of the process is relevant for a particular course, a faculty member can choose to use the BSI videos, Powerpoint presentations, or both. Each video addresses a different topic (see Table 2) so it is possible to provide

Table 2. BSI videos available on TUN

Title	Topics
The Case of the Retail Tweeters	Using social media tweets to get insights on hot and cold products and to find the influencers.
The Case of the Fragrant Sleeper Hit	Analyzing social media data in conjunction with point of sale data to determine how many units of each of five fragrances to manufacture.
The Case of the Defecting Telco Customers	Analyzing product rollout, pricing, and installations to identify reasons for unusual drops in monthly revenue
The Case of the Retail Turnaround	Analyze web walks and bailouts to drive customers living near stores to become omnichannel shoppers using Teradata, Aster, Teradata Marketing Applications and Tableau.
The Sad Case of Stagno Bank #1	Create new ideas for better marketing, customer service and mobile apps using Teradata, Aprimo, Aster
The Sad Case of Stagno Bank #2	Creating a centralized customer contact center
The Sad Case of Stagno Bank #3	Create ideas for consumer apps and geospatially relevant messages to provide better customer service
The Shocking Case of Home Electronics Planet	Evaluating search keywords, refining customer segments, real-time web page personalizations, revising email
The Case of the Credit Card Breach	Using data analytics to find the culprit responsible for spurious credit card charges
The Case of the Tainted Lasagna	Create a better/faster track and trace system using Big Data analytics

examples in different classes on a variety of topics without using the same video. Teaching notes are also available for faculty use.

TUN also houses case studies and Powerpoint presentations on a variety of topics that can be used in class. By going to the Library section of TUN, faculty can either select Case Study or Presentations in the dropdown box or use the filters to sort through material to find cases for class homework/discussions or Powerpoint presentations for class presentation/discussion; materials include teaching notes. The topics specifically relevant to marketing management include CRM / Campaigns / Segmentation, Customer Insight / 360 degree view, Digital Marketing / Messaging / Marketing Operations / Social Media. These tools are also useful for presenting examples of how marketing analytics is and/or can be used in companies for marketing decisions. The filter section can be used to find articles on specific topics, tools, and types of analysis including all of the MIS materials.

The suite of software tools on TUN is Teradata Marketing Applications which can be accessed by clicking on Software and then on Teradata Marketing Applications. This suite currently includes demonstrations and exercises for three software programs: Marketing Operations (MO), Customer Interaction Manager (CIM), and Real-Time Interaction Manager (RTIM). Most marketing faculty do not have time to learn every tool that companies use, every new software that comes on the market, or every new analytical tool. The materials on TUN for these three software tools do not require any upfront learning time other than reading through the directions.

The purpose of the MO (Marketing Operations) software is to synchronize and optimize company resources for maximum efficiency. The Instructor Demo file provides step-by-step directions for accessing the software and going through a demonstration and trial activity. After registering on TUN, any faculty member can access the demonstration and go through it before using it in class. The same step-by-step directions are provided for the students so they can do the exercises on their own. After reading through the directions, doing the demonstration in class, and having the first exercise completed by either the faculty member or students, the results (see Table 3) can be displayed in class. The demonstration used a 10% off coupon and the in-class trial used a buy-one-get-one-free coupon. Obviously, one resulted in more units moved and one generated more profit. So the question for the marketing manager is which coupon optimizes resources for efficiency. Students often jump to the conclusion that, of course, it is the 10% off coupon. However, the instructor can ask if that is still true if the objective is to move merchandise off the shelf to make room for a newer model or new product? Choosing to use a coupon to move product is not a sufficient tactical choice; marketing managers need to know which type of coupon is most effective for achieving what goal. These discussion questions are included in the instructor's file. There are four more exercises that can be used in class or as homework activities. Each exercise includes discussion questions that can be answered by the students as homework activities or used for discussion in class.

The purpose of the CIM (Customer Interaction Manager) software is to target customer segments with timely and relevant messages for the best response. Again the instructor demonstration can be used to showcase the software in class. At this time, the software is configured so that the immediate result

Table 3. Results from MO demonstration and first trial

Activity	Units Sold	Profit
Demo	4,400	$149,000.00
First Trial	5,200	$36,200.00

is the number of people in the selected segment receiving a message. An assumption being made is that messages will be sent to those selected consumers and data will be collected over a four-week period. Table 4 provides the results available at the end of four weeks. This information is available in a Powerpoint file that is available to faculty. The demonstration provides limited information but it is a good example of having to be careful about reporting results, e.g., the people receiving an email cannot be assumed to have seen the email and the number of people downloading a coupon cannot be assumed to have used the coupon. The results emphasize that it is important to collect and analyze data at each step of the process. These results are also a good empirical demonstration of the marketing funnel.

The students have directions for doing the same activity for five separate consumer segments. Either five members of a group can each do a separate activity and bring their results back to class or five different groups of students could do the activity in class to generate results. Table 5 has the results of the demonstration and for the five additional segments. The marketing funnel is evident for all segments. There are discussion questions that the students can be asked to address for homework or in class. For example, not all segments respond the same way, e.g., the coupon redemption rate is lowest for men both in and out of the state of Washington. The discussion often starts with the claim that more information is needed. However, students can be pushed to generate hypotheses (as marketing managers crunched for time often are asked to do): e.g., men redeem fewer paper coupons than women. If more data supports this hypothesis what could be done? Maybe coupons could be delivered in another way, like on a mobile device. There are a number of directions this discussion could take and the faculty version provides discussion questions for some of those directions.

The purpose of RTIM (Real-Time Interaction Manager) is to build persuasive inbound marketing strategies to generate sales when customers contact a company. Automating this process requires disciplined

Table 4. Results of CIM demonstration

Output Segment Name	Output Segment NET	Email Open Rate	% Email Open Rate	Coupon Down-load Rate	% Coupon Down-load Rate	Coupon Redemption Rate	% Coupon Redemption Rate
Female/Open/ Not in WA	13108	12134	92.6%	11678	89.1%	11142	85%

Table 5. Results of CIM demonstration and five additional segments

Output Segment Name	Output Segment NET	Email Open Rate	% Email Open Rate	Coupon Down-load Rate	% Coupon Down-load Rate	Coupon Redemption Rate	% Coupon Redemption Rate
Female/Open/ Not in WA	13108	12134	92.6%	11678	89.1%	11142	85%
Male/Not in WA	18364	16488	89.7%	13865	75.57%	11884	64.7%
Male & Female/Not in WA	30065	27069	90%	24862	82.7%	22398	74.5%
Female / In WA	6033	5917	98.1%	5122	84.9%	4786	79.3%
Male / In WA	8279	8105	97.9%	6195	74.8%	4268	51.5%
Male & Female In WA	13605	13338	98%	10228	76.6%	9125	67.1%

thinking and decision making BEFORE working with the software. Most often students want to jump to do the doing part of an activity without taking the time to think through a situation and alternatives first. The current faculty demonstration and student exercise for RTIM focuses on the thinking that has to occur before manipulating the software. Again, the faculty demonstration and student exercises provide step-by-step directions for an example of customers interacting over the phone with a call center representative, over the Internet on the bank website, or in person at a bank. To have the software determine which offers are made to which customers, a series of decisions need to be made in the planning process: what are the objectives and who is responsible for achieving that objective (see Table 6); what content should be presented and who is eligible for the offer (Table 7); which Message Classes are relevant for which Objectives (Table 8); and what Interaction Points are relevant for the situation (Table 9). One inbound situation is used in class; all three inbound situations are used in the student exercises and can be done either as homework or in class. One of the discussion questions focuses on the value of this planning process which the students find tedious. After some discussion (sample discussion questions are included in the faculty file), the point of the exercise becomes clear. Without documenting what messages are being used with which offers to which groups of consumers in which situations to achieve which objectives, making decisions about what should be manipulated in the software would be very confusing. In addition, evaluating which offer worked in which situation would be impossible without documenting the specific offer made to which consumers in which situation. As the work of developing exercises continues, there will be exercises involving manipulation of the software.

Faculty members do not need to learn the software before using any of these activities in class. The step-by-step directions make it possible for any faculty member to demonstrate the software and for students to use the software. This resource is free for marketing faculty and students so department and

Table 6. Objectives and ownership

Objective	Owner of Objective	Description
Increase the Number of Bank Services for Each Consumer Calling Bank	Call Center	Each consumer will enroll in one more service.
Create Positive Consumer Experience	Marketing	Ensure consumer understands we value their business.

Table 7. Message name, message eligibility criteria

Message Name	Message Content	Eligibility Criteria
New checking $20 incentive offer	Get $20 when you open a checking account TODAY	Everyone
Silver to gold card upgrade offer	Upgrade to a gold card for free within NEXT 30 DAYS	Has a silver card
Gold to platinum upgrade offer	Upgrade to a platinum card for free within NEXT 30 DAYS	Has a gold card
Bundle savings - checking incentive offer	Earn $50 when you sign up for a BUNDLED savings and checking account	Everyone
Bundle card-checking limited incentive offer	Receive 10% APR for 12 months when you sign up for BUNDLED credit card and checking account	Everyone
Auto loan customer satisfaction offer	Sorry for your trouble - we'll credit your auto loan account $50. Your SATISFACTION is guaranteed at Moneybags.	Has current auto loan; complain about charge on auto loan account

Table 8. Message classes and objectives

	Objective 1	Objective 2
Message	Increase the Number of Bank Services for Each Consumer	Create Positive Consumer Experience
Checking Offers		
Credit Card Offers		
Bundle Offers		
Customer Satisfcation Offers		
Customer Assistance Offers		

Table 9. Interaction points by channel

Channels	Interaction Points
Branch	Enter the branch
	Conduct transaction with teller
	Get a question answered
	Leave branch

college budgets are not an issue. The TUN materials make it possible to include marketing analytics in the classroom in many ways, such as videos, case discussions, demonstration of software, or student use of software, to accomplish different learning objectives. The Teradata Marketing Applications (MO, CIM, and RTIM) materials provide experiential learning tools for students without faculty having to invest a lot of time learning the details of a software package beforehand. In addition to using tools in class, there is always the question of their effectiveness.

RESULTS

The BSI videos and presentation materials on the TUN site have been used by marketing faculty in many classes. The feedback from faculty has been extremely positive. Dr. Dave Schrader continues to be invited to make presentations at universities and the number of faculty accessing these videos continues to increase. More marketing faculty are joining TUN at about 5% a month and accessing presentations, cases, and software exercises. One online university now includes TUN materials in the marketing data analysis part of their curriculum.

Students in the first section of the author's Customer Lifecycle Marketing course were part of the pilot test when the Teradata Marketing Application exercises were being created. Students in subsequent offerings of the course continue to be assigned at least one homework assignment for each of the MO, CIM, and RTIM software tools. Students have responded positively. Here are two examples of their comments:

After taking your class this past semester on CLM, I became quite interested with the Teradata applications we used. I am truly interested in what I have learned so far about the world of data analytics and the growing demand for data scientists. I am curious to know if you have any suggestions/recommendations for moving forward with my interest in this field?. . . Thank you once more for sparking the lightbulb in my brain on the topic of analytics.

The customer lifecycle management course helped me understand how marketing is evolving in this modern day of technology. Being able to work with CRM tools and the analytics they offer taught me how businesses, big and small, can now better see and manage their customers as they move through the marketing hourglass and customer lifecycle. And learning about how to use and act upon this insight to increase the lifetime value was a very interesting experience.

In addition, students are getting internships and jobs after taking the Customer Lifecycle Marketing course in which these tools are used. One of the students accepted a position as an intern for a local CRM company and, after one month, was offered a paid position. After the second version of the course, in which students were more heavily involved in using a CRM tool and these exercises, two students were offered internships; they were offered paid positions after a month. More companies are requesting students with these skills for internships. In addition, marketing students are requesting more analytics content in their other marketing courses.

CONCLUSION

Having cases, videos, articles, Powerpoint presentations, and activities using software and data for making marketing decisions on TUN is a significant resource for marketing faculty. This is an outstanding step in addressing the lack of materials that has made it difficult to include marketing analytics demonstrations and homework in classes. The variety of material available on TUN makes it possible to provide quick examples of analytics in different classes, have case discussions regarding marketing analytics in other classes, and have students be involved in using software and conducting analyses in other classes. This is a major step in providing materials for teaching skills that students need in today's marketplace.

More marketers in 2014 (87%) than in 2013 (46%) consider data the most underutilized asset in organizations ("Teradata 2015 Global Data", 2015). Using the videos and cases to stimulate class discussion about how data is being used for decision-making by marketing managers is a good place to begin. Demonstrating the software and using the homework assignments provides hands-on experience for students so they can actually use the tools rather than talk about them. This is just the beginning. As more cases, presentations, and exercises continue to be added to TUN, the choices for use in the classroom continues to grow. TUN is enabling faculty and students to develop expertise in marketing analytics to meet current demand for skills in the marketplace

REFERENCES

Chen, H., Chiang, R. H. L., & Storey, V. C. (2010). Business intelligence research. *Management Information Systems Quarterly, 34*(1), 201–203.

Christensen, C. M., & van Bever, C. (2014). The capitalist's dilemma. *Harvard Business Review*, (June): 61–68.

Connolly, D. (2012). Why b-schools should teach business intelligence. *Bloomsberg Businessweek*. Retrieved from http://www.businessweek.com/articles/2012-04-23/why-b-schools-should-teach-business-intelligence

Conway, M., & Vasseur, G. (2009). The new imperative for business schools. *Business Intelligence Journal, 14*(3), 13–17.

Davenport, T. H. (2013). Analytics 3.0. *Harvard Business Review*. Retrieved from https://hbr.org/2013/12/analytics-30

DeMera, J. (2014). 2014 is the year of digital marketing analytics: What it means for your company. *Forbes, 5*(June). Retrieved from http://www.forbes.com/sites/jaysondemers/2014/02/10/2014-is-the-year-of-digital-marketing-analytics-what-it-means-for-your-company/

Ditch the silos: Data integration is key tech need in 2013. (2013, Spring). *Chief Marketer*, 17.

Friedman, L. (2013). *Big data little data new data*. Presentation at Consumer Intelligence Conference.

Global skills shortage in marketing analytics remedied by Teradata University Network. (2014). Retrieved from http://online.wsj.com/article/PR-CO-20140812-908039.html

Graduating from an email service provider to marketing automation. (2013). Marketo, Inc. Retrieved from http://www.marketo.com

IBM. (2009). *The new voice of the CIO: Insights from the global chief information officer study*. Retrieved from http://www-304.ibm.com/businesscenter/cpe/download0/183490/NM_CIO_Study.pdf

Intelligence in harmony: How an integrated analytics model is driving retail success. (2012, February). Oracle Whitepaper.

Luftman, J., & Ben-Zvi, T. (2010). Key issues for IT executives 2009: Difficult economy's impact on IT. *MIS Quarterly Executive, 9*(1), 49–59.

Manyika, J., Chui, M., Brown, B., Bughin, J., Dobbs, R., Roxburgh, C., & Hung Byers, A. (2011). *Big data: The next frontier for innovation, competition, and productivity*. McKinsey Global Institute. Retrieved from http://wwwmckinsey.com/Insights?MGI/Research?Technology_and_Innovation/Big-data_The_next_frontier_for_innovation

McLelland, L. (2012). *By 2017 the CMO will spend more on IT than the CIO*. Gartner Webinar. Retrieved from http://my.gartner.com/portal/server.pt?open=512&objID=202&mode=2&PageID=5553&resid=1871515

Murphy, C. (2012). Why P&G CIO is quadrupling analytics expertise. *Information Week, 16*(February). Retrieved from http://www.informationweek.com/news/global-cio-interviews/232601003

Pettey, C., & Goasduff, O. (2011). *Gartner executive programs worldwide survey of more than 2,000 CIOs identifies cloud computer as top technology priority for CIOs in 2011*. Stamford, CT: Gartner Research.

Singer, A. (2013). Analytics = Most Desirable Skill (And Largest Talent Gap) for 2014. *The Future Buzz*. Retrieved from http://thefuturebuzz.com/2013/12/04/analytics-most-desirable-skill-and-largest-talent-gap-for-2014/

Sircar, S. (2009). Business intelligence in the business curriculum. *Communications of the Association for Information Systems, 24*(17), 289–302.

State of the industry research series: Big data in consumer goods. (2012). Whitepaper, Edgell Knowledge Network. Retrieved from www.eknresearch.com

Teradata 2015 global data-driven marketing survey: Progressing toward true individualization. (2015). Teradata, Inc. Retrieved from http://www.teradatauniversitynetwork.com/assetmanagement/Downloa-dAsset.aspx?ID=204376de-2dfd-4201-9352-5c06a8c73a1f&version=c2fbe4de34304ae08b724028f5 dacec41.pdf

The rise of the marketer: Driving engagement, experience and revenue. (2015). The Economist Intelligence Unit. Retrieved from http://futureofmarketing.eiu.com/briefing/EIU_MARKETO_Marketer_WEB.pdf

TUN KPI Summary. (2015). Presentation at April TUN board meeting. Minutes from Board Meeting.

Turban, E., Sharda, R., Dursun, D., & King, D. (2010). *Busness intelligence: A managerial approach* (2nd ed.). Upper Saddle River, NJ: Pearson Prentice Hall.

Watson, H. J. (2008). Business schools need to change what they teach. *Business Intelligence Journal, 13*(4), 407.

Wixom, B., Ariyachandra, T., Goul, M., Gray, P., Kulkarni, U., & Phillips-Wren, G. (2011). The current state of business intelligence in academia. *Communications of the Association for Information Systems, 29*(16), 299–312.

Chapter 12
Ethical Marketing

Carlos Ballesteros
Universidad Pontificia Comillas, Spain

Dulce Eloisa Saldaña
Tecnologico de Monterrey, Mexico

ABSTRACT

This chapter addresses those fundamentals and ethical issues related to the profession of marketing, as well as indirectly to other decision makers in companies, to guide human action in a moral sense. The main objective will be to provide different insights to business and marketing professionals to identify and analyze ethical problems in the various elements of a marketing strategy to propose alternatives, so that they may adjust their behavior according to the set of life and judging human acts (own and externals) according to the accepted norms and values. The chapter leads readers to an open invitation to reflect about his/her professional field: how I can contribute from an ethical perspective? From the ethics of marketing, how I can make decisions based on principles such as confidentiality, truthfulness, loyalty, transparency, fairness and accountability?

INTRODUCTION

One of the reasons to explore into the issue of ethics Marketing is related to what we live daily in a globalized world, with inequality, complexity, individualism, violence, and strong environmental problems, any of all resulting from decisions taken by businessmen, heads of large and small corporations, university graduates of academic excellence and some with top honors, for whom the moral and business seems not be compatible. It is, however reasonable to ask those leaders if they knew the consequences of their acts and decisions. For many managers (and academics in Marketing) profit maximization within the law is the unique basis for evaluating marketing practice: as long as the activity is legal and serves a business purpose (and hence is profitable), it is ethical. But not everybody agree.

Adela Cortina (2002) paraphrasing Adam Smith, think that Economy is not just a talk about exchange, but also deals with the production and distribution, and ethics should be present every moment: implementing contracts, committing product quality, reliability of the institutions and other motivations to self-interest versus common one. Casares (2010) also highlighting the work of Smith thinks his hero

DOI: 10.4018/978-1-4666-9784-3.ch012

is ethics, not greed; and discusses the positive aspects resultant of self-control, kindness, prudence and justice.

It seems that those positive aspects, related with the last paragraph, are somehow absent from business arena and becomes increasingly urgent that each and every one of the people from their professional field must work towards a planet where justice, solidarity, sustainability, equity, and accountability will prevail. However the ethics concern becomes more and more urgent and many Business Schools demands ethical reflection in their MBAs programs (USAnews, 2011) as well as Deans and Academic directors of the most prestigious schools are now questioning their methods, asking themselves to which extent they are guilty of the current situation (moral depravation at business decisions as e.g. Leman Brothers bankruptcy). (El Pais, 2009). And it is also true that Corporate Social Responsibility (CSR) have become an asset for an increasing number of companies. Today, almost every handbook in Finance and Management include at least a chapter on ethics, while in the Marketing field is something that needs to go further (as for example had declared J.L. Retolaza, elected president of the Spanish Chapter of the European Business Ethics Network (EBEN), June 2015). Nevertheless, in a recent curation of the Journal of Consumer research paper "Morality and Markets" is reminded how in 1974, in JCR´s first issue, Jacoby, Speller, and Berning (1974) explored how marketers should balance the moral imperative of providing full product information against the psychological effects of information overload (Grayson, 2014)

For those reasons this chapter addresses those fundamentals and ethical issues related to the profession of marketing, as well as indirectly to other decision makers in companies, to guide human action in a moral sense. The main objective will be to provide different insights to business and marketing professionals to identify and analyze ethical problems in the various elements of a marketing strategy to propose alternatives, so that they may adjust their behavior according to the set of life and judging human acts (own and externals) according to the accepted norms and values.

This will be achieved by applying an accurate way of reasoning modes of duty ethics, virtue ethics, utilitarian ethics, and ethics of dialogue. It also seeks to identify and analyze various ethical problems in various marketing strategies proposing improvements beyond producing higher profitability or competitiveness. It is a must to include also the consumers' perspective and understand their motivations, identify their deepest beliefs, and help them to build universal and inclusive lifestyles (Torres 2007). According to Brown, "though it may seem strange, the purpose of ethics is not that people behave in ethical way, but that they are able to make better decisions" (Brown et al., 2005). Cortina (1994, 18) also offers two modes of rationally guide action: learning to make wise decisions and learn to make morally correct decisions. Argandoña (2004, 74) stablished that "talking of ethics not necessarily have to be a talk of negative issues (do not bribe, do not lie, do not create false expectations, etcetera) but also a conversation on how to avoid all those behaviors who degrades me as a person and teach me to continue doing the evil and, furthermore, how could I be a better person throughout my managerial decisions towards doing *all the good I can"*

The first part of the chapter includes then a theoretical framework of business ethics, which includes marketing ethics. This section seeks to make the reader reflect on how to apply the philosophy of business on the premise that each person is an end in itself (Cortina 1994; Torres 2007) and achieving the greatest benefit for the greatest number of people. The reason that this chapter focuses on the ethics of marketing rests on three elements: first, the functions of marketing transcend the overall strategy of the organization; second, it is an area that is directly related outbound the company: consumers, customers, suppliers, media, society in general, among other stakeholders; additionally to their actions different unethical problems may arise as misleading advertising, distorted arguments with customers to make a sale, handling information, exploitation of children, sexual content ads, cheating on prices, price discrimination, unfair competition, among a long list. These problems are present regardless of their origin. The first part also includes a discussion of the marketing as satisfier and/or creator of needs, including the issue of consumerism, where efforts are presented by consumers to protect themselves from the manufacturers. This part ends with issues of ethical principles and codes of conduct reflecting on their marketing presence and mandatory regulatory function and regulation to reduce or even stop the deception to different stakeholders.

The second part presents an analysis and various proposals on the ethical dimension of marketing strategy. A discussion of ethical issues in the field of market research, ethical dilemmas about the product, price, distribution, communication and sales is presented.

Given this, it is expected to achieve a deep reflection that allows the reader to clarify the decision-making processes in the company contributing to a critical look at the marketing mix without losing sight of the consumer, business and the consequences of these decisions in all stakeholders; this is complicated but required to follow under the implementation of ethical standards. Likewise, the intention of this chapter is to give some clues to create a new professional, business and marketing culture.

BACKGROUND

The construction of a theoretical framework of ethical issues in marketing forwards, necessarily, to questions of applied ethics and in particular to the business ethics, whose mission is to apply philosophical principles to the business, so then decision-making is improved. Ethic is understood in this chapter as a systematic reflection, a theoretical inquiry, about the most appropriate way of acting mainly at the business arena, to make this 'good' (achieved the most fulfilled life possible) without forgetting to let the rest of the humanity to do the same, as every person have the same right as me to live his/her fulfilling life.

There are some previous assumptions that we have to do in order to define what a good life is:

- Human behavior differs from the other beings because human beings are free and possesses self-awareness of being so. Therefore managers and people in general are not only free to choose between good or bad decisions (from an ethical point of view) but this implies they are conscious of what they are doing. And everybody have A) the right to give his own definition of what a good life is and B) the right of making this life true. This is not hence, relativism, as we are not defending all types of life, but those which permit the rest of the humanity to decide and prosecute happiness too.
- Ethics does not invent life (but life does) "Homo sum, humani nihil a me alienum puto"[1]: non-selfish trend vs altruistic norms and moral ideals trying to bring coherence and order relations. Everybody can choose his/her way of living their life, and everybody is free to be generous or egoist, individualistic or social focused.
- Culture is responsible for filling the vacuum, institutionalize life and to respond about person models. Culture norms, costumes, values and mores help people to answer questions about how to behave, which decision to take. Culture is, somehow, a collective prism through which people view the world they live in in and try to make sense of their own and other people's behavior
- Throughout history there have been different cannons of what is understood as "desirable to live fully the life": the Hero (Homer); the Free Citizen (Aristotle); the Wisdom (stoic); The Saint

(Christian) or the Gentleman. Whether the late XXth Century proposes the *yuppie* as the model of a self-made, wealthy, successful person, the 2000s are suggesting that a success and full life is not only a question of money.

- Circumstances are varied and changing, and environment and factual conditions can change decisions and even values. It was not the same doing business in the rich and affluent 1990s than in the current crisis. Many firms who highlighted the CSR flag during those years, nowadays have abandoned their good wishes to build a better world just to survive.
- Moral is vivid, ethic is thought: What kind of person I want to be? In which society I want to live and work? Which world I will leave to my descendants? A piece of thought on these questions might change behaviors.

Before going further on the different approaches it is interesting to make a briefly review over the principal philosophers realizations and thoughts, in order to have a complete, thus short, framework.

- Starting with the ancient Greeks, Plato was concerned about the search for justice (the governance of the *Polis* has to be in the hands of philosophers: people worried about the others.); Aristotle though that Ethics were above Economy, as ethics deal with the ultimate purposes of life while economy is a mean for achieving a fulfilling one. Governance, therefore, should be in the hands of honest people (not necessary wisdom, as Plato thought). It can be said that Aristotle is the father of the Distributive Justice. Furthermore, Greeks (and later on Christians) establishes that just citizens build fair societies. There is also worth mention here the discussion between Stoicism and Epicureanism, as they differs on wow the search for virtue is seen: seeking for frugality and scarcity (the first ones) rather than hedonic experiences and pleasure (the second).
- Thomas Aquinas determined that economy contributes to public happiness, as he thought that everything has a cause (and the Ultimate cause is God). A person is not equally responsible of all the effects his/her behaviour has. There is a fundamental difference if these effects are merely foreseen or pretended.
- Modern Age brings rationality and logics (Descartes, Pascal). Kant established that the Reason (nor the Faith neither the Experience) was the source of morality and tried to solve the dispute between empirical and rationalism: for the first ones knowledge comes through experience; the latter maintained that reason and innate ideas were prior. Kant argued that experience is purely subjective without first being processed by pure reason. He also said that using reason without applying it to experience only leads to theoretical illusions. He tries to look for a universal ethic, valid whatever the circumstances are, and therefore experience *per se* can not be used to articulate such general envision. Kant establishes a certain idea of apriorism in ethic imperatives: they must be categorical rather than hypothetical (If you want "B" as a result then do "A" as a behavior)
- Later on, Hegel with his dialectic introduced the concept of the collectivism that will be followed by Marx and Engels. Hegel proposed that dialogues (confrontation between an idea and its opposite) and consensus-building were the best way to pursue the truth and take good decisions. Adam Smith, the so called father of the modern economy make differences between wisdom and virtue when managing the economic forces. Marx and Engels developed a materialist interpretation of historical development, a dialectical view of social transformation, based in class conflict. Marxism defends that necessary economic activities are required to satisfy the material needs of human society and that market forces and industries have take advantage on that, alienating the

working class with consumption evils. Some of these ideas are also presented in the Veblen´s Theory of the Leisure Class where he establish that the working class emulates the leisure one through consumption.

- Yet in the beginning of the 20ᵗʰ century, Keynes considered that decisors have to be cultured, wise and have to search for the common good, that will necessary convey to the welfare. This, hovewer, opposites to some current ideas about modern governances (Bauckburn, 2001, 13) that establishes that a good governance system (e.g. democracy) is good independent of its leaders. Another interesting discussion is the difference between the *Homo Ecomnomicus*, as J. S. Mill named to those who rational and narrowly seeks their subjectively defined ends in their judgements and decisions; the *Homo Reciprocan,* that think that people interact each other with a propensity to cooperate. Some authors, following Durkheim, think that there is a *Homo Duplex* who is always moving back and forth between a lower (individual) and higher (collective) level (Kluver, Frazier & Haidt, 2014).

- We can finish this brief review paying attention to Amartya Sen's thoughts. He first establishes than modern democracies (and to extent modern organizations) are valid independent of private vices of whom which belong or are part of them. He elaborates the concept of "social choice", that criticizes utilitarianism in economic decisions and suggests to include "goods" as freedom or justice in the economy.

Definitively, many different schools of thought, that may be summarized as shown in figure 1, tried to define what is the best approach and path to pursue the ultimate purpose of ethics, that is to learn how to live a good life. It is important to highlight that, as said above, for some authors, there are not ethical (or non-ethical) decisions themselves but decision's dimensions: ethical, economic, environmental, socio-political, etcetera (Brown et al. 2005). Each decision we take lead us to be better persons.

Figure 1. Different ethical approaches (own elaboration based in Casares, 2010)

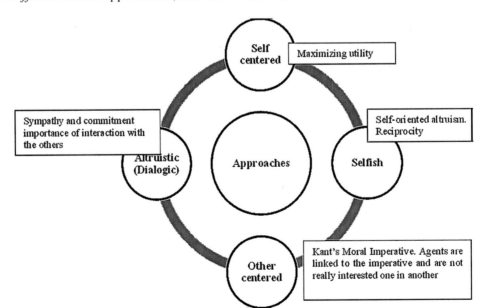

Somehow, if we accepted that marketing is a managerial function that tries to satisfy consumer needs in the best way possible and obtain a reward for this (in terms of price), marketing as a concept could be easily placed in the figure 1 somewhere between self-centered (maximizing the utility of the marketing efforts) and selfish (I give you a solution for your needs in exchange of your money).

Last (but not least) some brief remarks are needed to explain different (and somehow opposite) schools that can be found when talking about ethical approaches:

- *Fundamentalism* considers that human beings are able to make objective judgments about what is right and what is wrong versus *Relativism* that refers values to a certain situation: it is impossible to objectively determine what is right (Ortega: "I am I and my circumstance").
- *Ethics of Minimums* vs *Ethics of Maximuns*: the first one finds pillars that are non-negotiable pre-requisites, conditions of possibility while the maximum approach establishes optional proposals for action from a global perspective that can be shared or not but that means an ideal. Those which declare a "maximum" are convinced that that way of seeing things is better than their opponents.
- *Consequentialist Ethics*, which deals with consequences of behaviors and rules versus *Virtue Ethics* that tries to produce an ideal person build up around wellness and generosity. For the first one there are also many explanations: The point of *Utilitarianism* is to look for the best action, which is that one that produces the best consequences for many people; for the *Morale Altruism* the best action is the one that produces the best consequences for everyone; *Moral Selfish* (Kant) says that an agent best action is that one which produces the best consequences for himself.

The 20th century brought, to the developed world, the consumption society and later on the phenomena known as Globalization. When consumption became much less of a necessity (buying and eating) but rather a way of life, a behavior even a culture, the Marketing appears as a discipline and a function in the firms that contributes to build these lifestyles. Is then marketing guilty of consumerism, materialism and other evils? Or is it only a tool (one more) for making decisions that can be guided towards an inclusive, happy and fulfilled life for everyone? The next paragraph will go further on how ethics can guide marketing managers to take good choices.

MARKETING ETHICS

An Overview

Marketing is often considered, especially the one operating at the business area, as guilty of many of the evils lurking in the world: materialist culture, consumer waste, increasing gap between rich and poor and among other functional areas of business received considerable attention as the one most often charged with unethical practices (Akaah, 1990). The subsequent discussion is whether Marketing is, as it establishes the successive definitions made by the American Marketing Association, "a role of organizations aimed to creating value both in individuals and in organizations and society" (AMA, 2007) or the creator and accelerator of unnecessary needs that increase that materialistic culture as was talked about above (see introduction) and the Marxism somehow defends. Sirgy et al (2012) considers that marketing activity does contribute to social well-being while others (Torres, 2007; Martin & Johnson, 2007) think that this is something expected by stakeholders which not always is true: "in the case of ethical over conformity, firms exceed stakeholder expectations by adopting behaviors that go above and beyond what society has determined is acceptable. On the opposite end, firms choose under conformity or a conscious subversion of ethical norms through marketing programs, activities and behaviors" (Martin & Johnson, 2012, 103). Smith (1995) drew a Marketing Ethics Continuum as it is shown in figure 2.

This continuum presents, in some extent, all different situations where ethics has something to deal with. And it is not necessary true that the more to the right (of the continuum) the better. In every step of this scale, ethical dilemmas and decisions may arise and have to be answered in one or another sense depending the paradigm you choose. For instance, talking about what Smith called "Caveat Emptor" and from a utilitarian point of view, may the decisions taken by industries favor more people. Or from the ethics of minimum, codes of conduct are seen as sufficiently committed with ethics, while from the opposite (ethics of maximum) are considered insufficient as they envisage ways for not doing the evil but not necessarily do the good.

On the other hand Torres (2007) points out that the major ethical issues that Marketing managers facing are, among others, false and misleading advertising; the issue of gift-giving for commercial purposes; manipulation of data and results of market research; the exploitation of children for advertising; the use of discriminatory prices; different quantities into same packaging, etcetera. The figure 3 shows three levels of possible ethical conflicts in Marketing, from those which affects consumer (individuals) to those which affects the entire society.

May we propose a new sight (as shown in figure 4) in which (following what Argandoña 2004 and others said) not only the negative impacts but positive ones are envisaged.

And it is not also a matter that relates only to specialists in this area because as Grönroos (1996) points out marketing involves the entire organization and all of it should understand its clients and contribute to the value development. However, Robin and Reidenbach (1993) considered that given the relationships of unequal power in marketing, the direct application of moral philosophies, deontology or utilitarianism

Figure 2. Marketing ethic continuum (Smith, 1995)

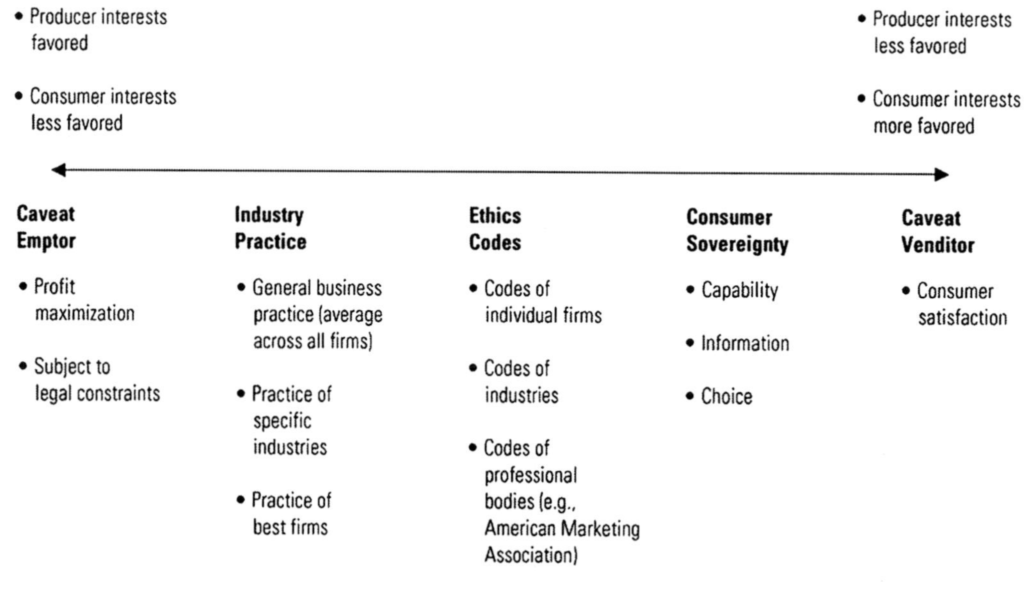

Figure 3. Pyramid of possible ethical impacts in/of marketing (Torres, 2007)

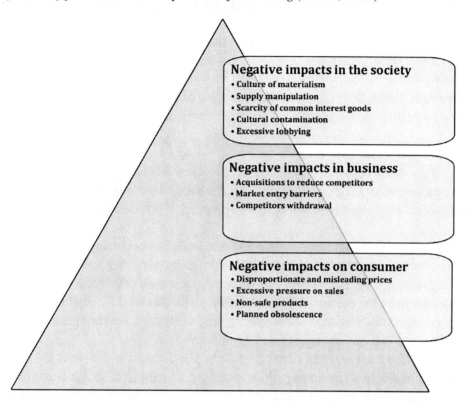

Figure 4. Redesigning Torres (2007) pyramid of possible ethical impacts in marketing (own elaboration)

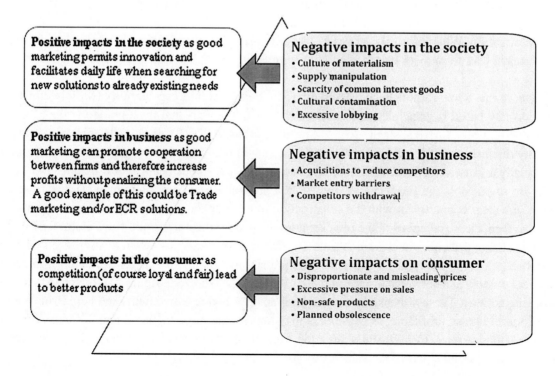

as a basic rule of behavior is insufficient and that they should develop specific criteria which constitute a theoretical frame of reference itself.

However, little attention has been paid by academics in the literature, during the last 25 years. It is true, following Smith (1995), that since 1990s tiny advances on this topic have been done, as some of the earliest marketing writing on the topic emerged in the 1960s and the 1970s and reach its peak in the 1980s.

Some of them, as Laczniak's *Framework for Analyzing Marketing Ethics* (1983) are, in some extent, basic as it only presents basic questions/rules to be answered in a standard way:

Do unto others as you would have them do unto you; Would I be embarrassed in front of colleagues/ family/friends if the media publicized my decision?; Are there any payments that could not be fully disclosed in company accounts?; Good ethics is in the firm's long-term best interests; Would an objective panel of professional colleagues view this action as proper?; When in doubt, don't.

Others, as Ferrell and Gresham (1985) contingent one present some contingent factors (as "significant others" or "organizational factors") that influences ethic decision making. Some other models of ethic decision making such as Hunt and Vitell's general theory have been developed, but they mainly follow those guidelines given by the pioneers so it is not worth go further on this chapter. Also "These frameworks make a valuable contribution to the marketing ethics literature, but they presuppose a familiarity with moral philosophy that few managers have" (Smith, 1995).

Maybe Smith 1995 test of consumer sovereignty should be the most useful check list for this purpose, although is not applicable to all marketing ethics issues but it is restricted to consumer issues. This test moves forward philosophy and presents three questions to be addressed before a marketing action should be took:

- Capability. What is the consumers' actual or potential vulnerability and its impact on their decision making?
- Information. What information does a consumer need to make a purchasing or related decision?
- Choice. Can consumers switch to another supplier?

Furthermore, some authors have worked on a Marketing Social Responsibility (MSR) definition as a "philosophy based in principles and values with ethical contents that must guideline the Marketing activity" (Schwalb &Arrizabalaga, 2013). Martin &Johnson (2012) discuss the chicken-or-the-egg causality dilemma whether marketing decisions are an automatic response to institutional environment and socially normative influences or does not, becoming a conscious beat for doing things in a certain mode. Be responsible (or good) can be, thus only a profitable response when markets reward this behavior, or a clear commitment with the construction of a better society when operating at the business arena (so then, clearly attached to the firm's mission and vision).Both visions, thus, claim for a code of conduct, a list of principles or criteria that a marketing manager must follow. In this sense. Schwalb and Arrizabalaga (2013) conducted a 141 items' Delphi survey among 40 experts (academics, managers, consumer unions) and delivered a scale of the six dimensions (shown in figure 5) which must guide the Marketing activity. These dimensions content both positive and negative items and help firms not only to be honest but also profitable, as consumers may remunerate more the good and fair behavior rather than the opposite ones. Consequently, an ethic framework for decisions becomes also a competitive advantage and essential part of the value chain for a firm.

Figure 5. The six dimensions of the MSR (Schwalb and Arrizabalaga, 2013, 447)

Dimension	Some possible contents
Quality of product and services	• Expected quality related to price payed • Durability • Sufficient variety offered that permits a free election • Green design • Services (e.g. financial) adapted to real consumer needs
Quality of Customer Service	• Sincere interest for understanding consumer needs and situation • Easy procedure for complaints • Good quality of post-purchase services: advising, repairs, maintenance • Good manners • Comfortable and convenient point of sale
Advertising and Promotion Practices	• Transparency and honesty • Nondiscriminatory advertising practices • Non aggressive techniques • Truthful ads
Information provided to Consumer	• Relevant, out to date, transparent and objective information • Adequate packaging and labelling • Transparency of pricing policies
Privacy	• The information collected about the consumer is only essential data • Confidentiality
Ethics and Social Responsibility	• Respect for Human dignity, cultures, values • Fair relationship • Fair financial conditions • Sight on long term consumer needs (not only immediate) • Fair competition • Reasonable profit margins

However, societal changes, technological advances and consumer education lead us to conclude that may be worth to further research towards a new ethic in marketing theory, which provides an up-to-date framework for analysis and decision making to current managers and help them to behave towards a fairer, cleaner world. The problems and situations that authors and firms faced in the second half of 20th century are far away to be the same as todays'. Globalization of consumer culture, internet and web 2.0 among other issues arise new dilemmas to be addressed.

Marketing Principles

The American Marketing Association establishes in 2004 that "As marketers we must do no harm, foster truth and embrace ethical values" (AMA, 2004). This is something that every person working in marketing (no matter if as manager, as academic or whatever role) has to sign if he/she wants to become part of the largest Marketing association in the world, with more than 30.000 associates (AM, 2015). Marketing is not a chartered neither a regulated-by-law profession (as Doctor, Lawyer or Engineer is) where strict rules establish which is good and not in their field. Obviously, consequences of a badly professional execution in the case of a doctor or an architect are apparently more dangerous than consequences derived from bad decisions taken by a marketing manager. Everybody can work in marketing without a complimentary signature of a code of conduct, but this is simply not a carte blanche for mismanagement. And some other professional associations, as the Spanish Marketing Association, have recently become to develop code of conducts and/or Ethical Committees. The market research (here considered as a subsector of Marketing) designed many years ago (1948 is the first edition of the ESOMAR "Market research code of conduct) an ethical framework for conducting surveys and research. Almost every market research agency follow these rules.

For the AMA, the ethical principles to be pursued by a marketing manager are:

- **Honesty:** To be forthright in dealings with customers and stakeholders.
- **Responsibility:** To accept the consequences of our marketing decisions and strategies.
- **Fairness:** To balance justly the needs of the buyer with the interests of the seller.
- **Respect:** To acknowledge the basic human dignity of all stakeholders.
- **Transparency:** To create a spirit of openness in marketing operations.
- **Citizenship:** To fulfill the economic, legal, philanthropic and societal responsibilities that serve stakeholders.

One or another or even whichever other code you follow, what is common sense and a universal demand is that, as said above, the important issue is to take decent decisions aligned with noble criteria. In this sense three main questions are to be made and answered:

The first one deals with the integrity of an action by itself, by its nature and essence (in Thomas Aquinas words). For some ethics, there are actions that, by their nature are "good" (e.g. to share) or "evil" (e.g. to kill, to steal,). This moral provide safety to individuals when exercising their freedom to act and consequently establishes prohibitions and permissions according to the essence of things. The Catholic Church had follow often this idea, especially for bad acts: The Pope Joan Paulus II, in his encyclical letter "Veritatis Splendor" (1993, 115) establishes "the universality and immutability of the Commandments specifically those who speak about inherently depraved acts". Speaking about Marketing and Business the question is however more complex to answer as you cannot give a unique, acceptable answer about the goodness of actions as "to sell" or "to advertise" just to cite two of many.

The second one refers then to the last reasons of the one who executes the action. If motives are positive, then the action should be good. Kant (1785, 3) thought that "There is nothing in the world, neither out of it, that it is possible to think that it is good (or evil) without restriction, unless the goodwill". Actions that had been made with the intention of causing good are good. The problem here resides, mostly, in the hidden motives of human behavior. So when a salesperson offers a good price for a product just thinking in his/her own benefit (better incentives) may not be acting ethically but if the same proposal is made thinking in the consumer advantage then it should be just.

The last question can be classified as utilitarian. An action is good or evil depending on its consequences. If the final result has better rather than negative results then the decision was correct. Hence a manager who wants to act ethically has to raise questions as How many people will benefit from this decision? For how many should be harmful? What is more costly (to do or not to do)? If the first question was the most restrictive, utilitarianism is the most tolerant but the less universal.

Marketing has to be redesign after the latest societal changes and challenges. The starting point at the beginning of the Market-oriented era was to advertise products referring their physical characteristics and features, trying to be the best solution to the consumer problems. The late 20th century and the first decade of the 21st brought the focus to the consumer, changing from what the product can do for the consumer to the feelings and emotions the consumer experiments when using the product: in the first case a car manufacturer may advertise his late model talking about low consumption, acceleration power, leather coated seats etcetera. The second case best example is BMW's ad where the car became secondary and you can only see a man's arm outside the driver's window, playing with the air and the suggestive slogan *Do you enjoy driving?*. Kotler, Kartajaya and Setiawan (2010), establish the concept of a Marketing 3.0 era where marketing efforts have to go towards what the product (service, idea) can do for humanizing the world. Thus, from the deliverance of satisfaction (marketing 1.0) and the aspirational realization (marketing 2.0), marketing has to move towards compassion (marketing 3.0). Some other authors go further and define ethical marketing as a "process of designing and development marketing activities that contributes specifically to a non-commercial effort that generates a positive effect in the exchange between a consumer and a brand" (Gicquel, 200, 61)

Marketing Mix Ethical Dilemmas

Once some key issues and principles have been established, it is now time to summarize some ethical controversies that can be addressed in concrete aspects of Marketing. For this purpose, we are organizing them following the classical McCarthy (1960) 4Ps scheme, plus a reference to Market Research.

Product

Speaking about product (service), the principal ethical dilemmas to be faced are:

- Does the product actually respond to a real need of the consumer? Many false-miracle products, useless stuff are constantly launched to the market, without a thought on the real necessity they may cover.
- Design: which are the basic and core benefits?; Does a new version actually make differential characteristics from competitors?; Conformity, quality standards and a cost/safety equation; have possible product missuses been taken into account?; Low cost equals bad quality?; The use of raw materials and the environment care (green design).
- Labelling and Packaging: does it provide sufficient information? Does it include avoiding danger recommendations? Have the package been made with reuse/recyclable materials?
- Lifecycle: at the RD stage: Spying competitors to be aware of new features, launch of new products; at the Maturity stage: copying/plagiarism. Planned Obsolescence at the final stage.
- Other dilemmas: Factory Defective items.

Price

The discussion about "fair prices" is very old. A Renaissance Spanish philosopher (Father Luis de Molina 1535-1600) established that a fair price should be "this which responds to the common people assessment". Later on, Monique Zollinger (1993) developed her Theory of Structured Prices, in which the "expected price" (just) plays a key role as there is an interval of prices considered just by consumers (average estimated price). Above this interval the classical economy rules work: the higher the price, a smaller amount of product should be required, as consumer would equal "expensive" to "unfair" (the firm is somehow taking advantage of him). Below the interval, on the contrary, it does not work conventional economic rules, as the lower the price also the lesser quantity, as consumer would equal "cheap" to "bad quality".

The second dilemma about prices conducts to market structure and forms of competition (as the regulatory mechanism of the market system). Among them Monopolistic competition, also called Competitive Market or the idyllic Perfect Competition where there is a large number of firms, each having a small proportion of the market share, there are no entry barriers and a perfectly elastic demand curve seems to be the most ethical structure. Oligopoly, in which a market is run by a small number of firms that together control the majority of the market share or Monopoly, where there is only one provider of a product or service faces many ethical questions.

A third group of questions regarding price refers to some practices:

- **Predatory Prices:** A situation in which a firm lows their prices (even below the costs line) substantially to avoid the entry of a competitor
- **Cross Selling:** When the price of the main product (e.g. a printer, a vacuum cleaner, a razor blade) is considerably low but the spare parts (ink cartridges, bags, blades) that are unique for this model are sold at very high price.
- **Use of a Hook-Pricing Policy:** A store deliberates set the price of certain products at very low ranges in order to make the consumer think the price policy of the total store supply is similar (hook). But prices of products that are not sensitive and consumer has not price references are, on the contrary, very high. For example a store set the price of milk, bread, coffee (first necessity goods, frequent purchasing, expected price) cheaper than expected by the consumer but charges very high margins for broom, salt, olives and other products which the consumer should not be aware of the real (normal) price.
- False selling out (sales).

Place

Some real situations: excessive and aggressive pressure to the customer in order to close a sale; the purchaser deliberate harms an item and ask for a deal; to sell something to someone that the seller absolutely knows it cannot be sold (e.g. alcohol to minors); to seize (or to sell) free samples which were destined to final consumer; to ignore a client because a potential better one enters the store; to sell the product that makes more margin to the store rather than the most appropriate to the customer needs; misuse of change money;

Other issues with this marketing mix element are not placed at the final link of the chain but in the intermediate process. Nothing to say (of course) about bribes and other gifts given in order to obtain a certain execution of a contract, but historically the relationship between producers and sellers (commercial distribution) is full of abuses: false stories about better competitors prices or offers; first opening fees; higher fees for less loyalty, etcetera.

Advertising and Promotion

Advertising is not only a commercial tool but a cultural expression, a sociological explanation of the values and beliefs of a culture and a psychological evasion. Ads are somehow promises of happiness, better and ideal world. And persuasion is a keen technique of going into someone more profound dreams and complexes promising a solution for every problem. If you are sad, feel ugly, stressed, etcetera, there is a perfect universe on your TV screen that helps you to escape your day to day problems and feel like a princess, a hero or merely happier. So advertising face again many ethical issues as:

- Authenticity. People have the right to defend from ads and their idyllic sight. People have the right to know when a media is delivering information and when is delivering persuasive messages. People need to and have the right to differentiate advertising and entertainment. So hidden advertising, bartering, product placement and other techniques used by advertisers are doubtfully ethical. In certain places there are also laws against advertising products like cigarettes or alcohol but surrogate advertising finds ways to remind consumers of these products without referencing them directly.
- Truthful. Ads have to tell the truth. Given the necessary creativity and what advertisers called exaggeration (those messages that nobody can think they are true because are extremely exaggerated) ads have to be verified. Dishonest, subliminal messages are not the best way to tell a story. Some advertisers use even false claims about a product's quality.
- Discriminating messages. The use of non-related images to attract certain targets, as for example the use of seducing women to sell products targeted to men or the use of tender, loving children to sell e.g. insurances using a message of nonexistent dangers for the children (in a some kind of an emotional blackmail).
- Attempt to dignity and human rights. Misuse of sex and human bodies (usually women). Women in advertising have often been portrayed as sex objects or domestic servants. This type of advertising traffics in negative stereotypes and contributes to a sexist culture. Children consume huge amounts of advertising without being able to evaluate it objectively. Exploiting this innocence is one of the most common unethical marketing practices.

In relation with sales and other promotion techniques the principal issue to discuss is whether the coupons, samples, gifts or discounts distract from the principal purpose of the purchase. Even more when affects vulnerable consumers as e.g. childhood. Sometimes it is more important for them to obtain the collectibles given beside the yogurt than the yogurt itself. Also when organizing a promotional campaign it is important to take into account:

- If the rules and participation mechanism is clear for everybody and there are not "small letters".
- You have to meet your promises. So you have to assess the possible over-success of a campaign.

Market Research

Although Market research is not an element of the marketing Mix, it is one of the most important functions of marketing and may confront many ethical issues. Similar to what was said above on advertising, market research is inquiring into deep, sometimes even non conscious, facets of the people. Asking questions is an *art* that have to be used in a proper way. So then some ethical principles have to be followed:

- Neutrality, thus not be unaffiliated with social problems or specific individual situations.
- Avoid subjectivity (that is the same to say be a professional).
- Confidentiality.
- Authenticity that is the people right to know they are being investigated).
- Privacy intromission, as for example with the use neurological techniques (called neuromarketing) that uses modern and sophisticated methods to study the brain and the people reactions to stimulus.

There are some spheres where market research can face ethical issues:

- Talking about the publics concerned, the researcher cannot use the research for other purposes (e.g. as a hidden tool to sell something). Also it is important to take care of sensitive publics (children of course, but also for example sick people if researching about commercial use of a medicine). The research institute has to keep exclusivity in a industry and cannot research for a direct competitor of a client. The people to be research have not to be *professionals* of surveys or focus groups (sometimes certain persons have converted this into an occupation). On the client side, it is important not to abuse the investigator (asking more and more information) and do not hide or fabricate risky data.
- Concerning the process. When designing a survey the agency has to be honest and not include unnecessary questions, oversize samples or manipulate scales. During the field work it is necessary to follow guidelines (of the sample plan) and do not invent answers. At the analysis phase all doubtful data has to be discharged and not used and the confidence intervals should not be manipulated. Also it is necessary to be careful with possible biases. Finally the agency has to be honest when presenting results and do not manipulate data even the client ask to do that.

As said previously in this chapter, ESOMAR, which is the worldwide Association for Market Researchers published in 1948 its first "International Code of Conduct on Market and Social Research". Some minor revisions have been made since then and in 1994 was issued the fourth edition (which is the valid until the moment). This code is based on these key fundamentals:

- Market researchers shall conform to all relevant national and international laws.
- Market researchers shall behave ethically and shall not do anything which might damage the reputation of market research.
- Market researchers shall take special care when carrying out research among children and young people.

- Respondents' cooperation is voluntary and must be based on adequate, and not misleading, information about the general purpose and nature of the project when their agreement to participate is being obtained and all such statements shall be honoured.
- The rights of respondents as private individuals shall be respected by market researchers and they shall not be harmed or adversely affected as the direct result of cooperating in a market research project.
- Market researchers shall never allow personal data they collect in a market research project to be used for any purpose other than market research.
- Market researchers shall ensure that projects and activities are designed, carried out, reported and documented accurately, transparently and objectively.
- Market researchers shall conform to the accepted principles of fair competition.

Other Spheres of Marketing Ethical Dilemma

Last (but not least) there are some other spheres in modern marketing that merit an ethical sight. Maybe the most important one is digital marketing and all that deals with spam, privacy and even the use of what is known as big data. Also e-commerce and the unfair delivery of goods that are not exactly the ones that are presented at the web page, but low quality versions. Public Relations and its relation with greenwashing, CSR and cause related Marketing is another field that needs a careful look into its practices.

Many spheres and behavior can be assessed and discussed under an ethical prism. Therefore, this chapter does not pretend to be a recipe book or a check list of good behavior or perfect decisions but tends to provide guidelines (based in examples and concrete situations) and criteria to act properly. This is why we do not consider closed and finished it if we do not give an overview of what is being done for improving the ethical education of future marketing managers.

TOOLS AND EDUCATION RESOURCES IN MARKETING ETHICS.

The Need for Ethic Education in Management Studies

All throughout this chapter we have seen that ethics is an abstract subject that can easily get overlooked in the high pressure world of business. Some companies treat ethical behavior as an obstacle and make only shallow efforts to behave responsibly. Others, on the contrary, has taken ethics as their motto. The only way to remain aware of the ethics of business decisions is to have a management team conformed of ethically minded business men and women and, for that purpose, an education in ethics is a must.

As we seen previously many prestigious business schools are now focusing their MBAs and postgraduates in humanism, ethical concerns rather in technical aspects. To this respect, there is a very interesting study by Franco (2011), form Loyola University, entitled "An Exploratory Study of the Curricular Integration of Ethics in Executive Mba Prog". His conclusions can be easily transferred to Marketing studies.

Other interesting topic deals with education. We have made a quick and therefore non exhaustive, search through the contents of many Universities' Master of Marketing curriculum. The webpage http://www.marketing-schools.org/ provide useful insights when searching for education in Marketing through the US but do not provide enough information on Ethics & Marketing full programs or contents and conveys to think that there is a lack of good teaching programs in this field. It is true that there are some Social Marketing and Responsibility Master but we are not talking about this anymore. We do not think it is a need for social marketing experts, that it is another professional field, but we are talking about marketing managers behavior: We think that every expert/professional in marketing must have the basic ethical rules to take good decisions at his/her job. In our search we have found also some examples of modules that talk about digital marketing ethics or other specific field, but nothing from a general, global perspective. So this should be another topic for further development: a good ethic in marketing education program to be included as a compulsory module at Master level.

An Outline for a Course in Marketing Ethics (Master Level)

As a conclusion of this chapter, it may be interested to have, at least as a draft a proposal for a course in Marketing ethics which put in practice all the topics written above and give some ideas, tools and resources for those teachers/program directors interested in include ethics in their courses or schools. It has been developed from our own teaching experience.

Objectives and Skills to Be Developed

The proposed course introduces students to the ethical foundations and the problems associated with the profession, as well as some management tools of CSR, especially those dedicated to Marketing as e.g. ethical branding or the value chain management. The aim of the course is twofold. On the one hand, this is to develop the student's ability to identify and analyze ethical problems in the various elements of a marketing strategy, with a view to proposing solutions. Furthermore, the student must understand what it means social responsibility of business and the basic tools for its implementation in a company are.

At the end of the course students will be able to:

- Apply correctly the modes of reasoning of ethics of duty, ethics of virtue, utilitarianism, and dialectic.
- Identify and analyze ethical issues in marketing strategies, proposing improvements.
- Understand the CSR as a necessary approach in business and marketing.
- Implement CSR management tools correctly.
- As instrumental skills they should perform in oral and written communication, troubleshooting, critical and self-critical thought and in listening, arguing and debating abilities.

Overview of Contents

The course content considers different topics: It starts reviewing the normative foundations of different ethical concepts that apply in solving the major problems of the profession (as this chapter do). It also analyzes the possible ethical dilemmas associated with the practice of marketing. Then CSR and its basics are introduced and finally are presented the basic management tools.

1. The ethical dimension of human existence. The specificity of ethical problems freedom in personal decision. The social dimension: morality and ethics.
2. Schools in ethical reasoning (Ethics of duty; Virtue ethics; Utilitarianism; Ethics of dialogue).

3. The ethical dimension of a marketing strategy: analysis and proposals. The 4ps.
4. Conceptual framework of CSR and the Stakeholder concept. The Business case vs. Society case. The role of policy makers and civil society in supporting CSR.
5. Management of CSR: Identification and relationship with stakeholders. Standards and labels. Ethical branding, fair pricing, trustful advertising and other tools.

Teaching Methods and Evaluation Methods and Criteria

We recognize the difficulties to elaborate a complete syllabus, given the space constraint and, which is more important, that everyone has his own way of doing things. Nevertheless, we share here some useful resources and tools that we have used at our courses. A regular 3 credits course should include, although not necessarily all at one time:

*   Lectures about the conceptual topics and expert conferences.
*   Readings (see a proposed list of books/papers below).
*   Individual reflection. We usually make students to prepare a case in which we find some ethical dilemma. We use role-play where one student is the firm and another represent the consumer (consumer union), and may another one (if needed) play the role of a third stakeholder as i.e. a charity or government's representative. The rest of the students should act as judges. Each student has to prepare his/her case and defend his/her position while the attendants have had to read previously a briefing about the case.
*   Video forums (see a proposed list of documentaries and movies below).
*   Group work. Students have to study the CSR strategy of a company, or launch a new brand/business with an ethical perspective.

The criteria for assessment the students' performance should be certainly linked to the objectives and has to reflect the acquisition of knowledge as well as the proposed skills. As this proposal is for a Master level we consider that, better than classical examination, the evaluation should comprise written essays about the readings and or the films saw; case analysis that include the preparation and in-class performance, where the capacity to argue and debate should be assessed and even not so orthodox methods as i.e, theatre representations (for example of the different ethical schools); wallpapers or posters to be presented in a mini-congress, with peer reviewers. Assistants to this mini congress and reviewers are the students, so they need to prepare a topic but should review one or two more.

Some Resources for Teaching an "Ethics in Marketing" Course

*   Kotler, Philip, Kartajaya Hermawan y Setiawan, Iwan (2010) *Marketing 3.0.* A basic book which present the evolution of marketing orientation, from product focused to societal concerns and/or consumer emotions and feelings. Is a good reading for understanding marketing dynamics and the essential adaptations to the societal changes that marketing has to challenge.
*   Guillén M. F. and Ontiveros, E. (2012) *Global Turning Points: Understanding the Challenges for Business in the 21st Century* .A book which presents in easy reading but profound way a good reflection on geopolitical change landscape, trade and financial interdependences, inequality, sustainable and climate change, all topics related with business and market performance.

- *The Jelly's Quality* http://www.puntodefuga.es/blog/?p=143 is a Spanish blog, written by two sociologists and markert researchers, where societal changes are seen as "jelly" (somehow remembering the "liquid society" that Z. Baumann described some years ago)
- *The Joneses* (2009) an American film written and directed by Derrick Borte which may provide a good debate about the excesses of marketing
- *Surplus, terrorized into being consumer* (2003) an Erik Gandini documentary about the evils of consumption society, narrated in the rythms and languages of this society. A very good tool tto provoke debate about anti-consumption and resistance methods
- *Supersize me* (2004) a classical film frorm Morgan Spurlock where himself experiments what happen to his body if it is only feed with junk food. Also useful to talk about the power of transnationals and about how this corporations do not want to see the problems they create and play hide-and seek with the consumer
- *My Stuff* a 2013 documentary film in which Petri Luukkainen a 26 year old director tells his own depression and crisis and how he gave up all his possessions and try to live in scarcity, deciding where happiness is.
- ICC/ESOMAR International Code On Market And Social Research https://www.esomar.org/uploads/public/knowledge-and-standards/codes-and-guidelines/ICCESOMAR_Code_English_.pdf
- AMA Statement Of Ethics https://www.ama.org/AboutAMA/Pages/Statement-of-Ethics.aspx
- Market Research Society https://www.mrs.org.uk/standards/code_of_conduct
- Code of Conduct of the Mobile Marketing Association http://www.mmaglobal.com/policies/code-of-conduct
- http://advertisingprinciples.com/ a page to learn how to do good advertising.
- Some good corporative codes of conduct as for example Starbucks http://www.starbucks.com/about-us/company-information/business-ethics-and-compliance

REFERENCES

Akaah, I. (1990). Attitudes of Marketing Professionals Toward Ethics in Marketing Research: A Cross-National Comparison. *Journal of Business Ethics*, *9*(9), 45–53. doi:10.1007/BF00382563

American Marketing Association. (2004). *AMA Statement of Ethics*. Retrieved December 2014 from https://archive.ama.org/Archive/AboutAMA/Pages/Statement%20of%20Ethics.aspx

Argandoña, A. (2004). ¿Por qué el marketing debe tener en cuenta la ética? *Harvard Deusto Marketing y ventas*, (62), 72-79.

Blackburn, S. (2001). *Sobre la bondad. Una breve introducción a la ética*. Barcelona: Paidos.

Brown, M. E., Trevino, L. K., & Harrison, D. A. (2005). Ethical leadership: A social learning theory perspective for construct development. *Organizational Behavior and Human Decision Processes*, *97*(2), 117–134. doi:10.1016/j.obhdp.2005.03.002

Casares, J. (2010, November-December). La ciencia económica, la diversión y la ética Aplicaciones generales al comercio y al consumo. *Distribución y Consumo*, 13-21.

Cortina, A. (1994). *Ética de la empresa: claves para una nueva cultura empresarial.* Madrid: Tecnos.

Cortina, A. (2002). *Por una ética del consumo.* Madrid: Taurus.

Ferrell, O. C., & Gresham, L. G. A. (1985). Contingency framework for understanding ethical decision making in marketing. *Journal of Marketing, 49*(3), 87–96. doi:10.2307/1251618

Franco, J. M. (2011). *An Exploratory Study of the Curricular Integration of Ethics in Executive MBA Programs.* Dissertations. Paper 149. Retrieved June 2015 from: http://ecommons.luc.edu/luc_diss/149

Gicquel, Y. (2007). *Le Marketing éthique.* Paris: Génies des Glaciers.

Grayson, K. (2014). *Morality and the Marketplace.* Retrieved July 2015 from http://jcr.oxfordjournals. org/page/Research_Curations/Morality_and_the_Marketplace?utm_source=Journal+of+Consumer+R esearch+-+July+21%2C+2015&utm_campaign=Constant+Contact&utm_medium=email

Hunt, S. D., & Vitell, S. J. (1986). A General Theory of Marketing Ethics. *Journal of Macromarketing, 6*(1), 5–16. doi:10.1177/027614678600600103

Joan Paulus, I. I. (1993). *Veritatis Splendor.* Retrieved November 2014 from http://w2.vatican.va/content/ john-paul-ii/es/encyclicals/documents/hf_jp-ii_enc_06081993_veritatis-splendor.html

Johnson, J.L. & Martin, K. L. (2008). A Framework for Ethical Conformity in Marketing. *Journal of Business Ethics, 80*(1), 103-109.

Kant, I. (1785). Fundamentación de la metafísica de las costumbres (M. Garcia, Ed. & Trans.). Madrid: Espasa-Calpe.

Kluver, J., Frazier, R., & Haidt, J. (2014). Behavioral ethics for Homo economicus, Homo heuristicus, and Homo duplex. *Organizational Behavior and Human Decision Processes, 123*(2), 150–158. doi:10.1016/j.obhdp.2013.12.004

Kotler, P., Kartajaya, H., & Setiawan, I. (2010). *Marketing 3.0.* John Wiley & Sons, Inc. doi:10.1002/9781118257883

Laczniak, G. R. (1983). Framework for Analyzing Marketing Ethics. *Journal of Macromarketing, 1*(1), 7–18. doi:10.1177/027614678300300103

McCarthy, E. J. (1960). *Basic Marketing, A Managerial Approach.* Homewood, IL: Richard D. Irwin. Retrieved February 2015 from http://babel.hathitrust.org/cgi/pt?id=inu.30000041584743;view=1up;seq=7

Schwalb, M. M. & Arrizabalaga, I. (2013). Dimensiones de la responsabilidad social del Marketing. *Revista Venezolana de Gerencia,* (63), 434-456.

Sirgy, M.J., Yu, G.B., Dong-Jin, L., Shuquin, W., & Ming-Wei, H. (2012). Does Marketing activity contribute to a society'swell-being? The role of economic efficiency. *Journal of Business Ethics, 107*(2), 91-102.

Smith, C. (1995). *Marketing Strategies for the Ethics Era.* Retrieved January 2015 from http://sloanreview.mit.edu/article/marketing-strategies-for-the-ethics-era/

Torres, F. (2007). *Cuestiones eticas en el Marketing.* Paper presented at VII Congreso Nacional e Internacional de Administracion "Management: visión prospectiva", Buenos Aires, Argentina.

Zollinger, M. (1993). Le concept de prix de référence dans le comportement du consommateur: D'une revue de la littérature à l'élaboration d'un modèle prix de réfé- rence-acceptabilité. *Recherche et Applications en Marketing, 8*(2), 61–77. doi:10.1177/076737019300800204

ENDNOTE

[1]   Nothing human is strange to me, as I am a Human Being.

Chapter 13
Teaching Peace and Marketing Education:
From Pieces to Peace

Maria Lai-Ling Lam
Point Loma Nazarene University, USA

ABSTRACT

This chapter presents a peace-centered process of teaching marketing that the author has implemented during 2002-2015 academic years with undergraduate and graduate business students in various market-ing courses at two Christian Universities in the United States. The peace-centered process is related to the development of a unified world view about human life in a culture of peace and culture of healing and the development of virtues in a marketing career. The chapter discusses (1) the manifestation of violence in marketing, (2) the concept of a peace-centered process of teaching marketing, (3) the responsibility of marketing educators, and (4) the seven pedagogical strategies for this approach.

INTRODUCTION

Peace is essential for the vibrancy of human beings and the fullness of happiness in our moral ecol-ogy which respects life and supports human development and community (Novak, 2004, Lam, 2015). Marketing activities that advocate social justice and sustainability are predicted to be the key trends in historical development of marketing practices (Kotler, 2007). Peace is a universal virtue that sustains good marketing practices and embraces much promise for guiding the behavior of marketers (William & Murphy, 1990; Murphy, 1999; Thompson, 2002). "Peace in its essence is a spiritual state with political, social and ethical expressions" (Danesh, 2006). Peace can be expressed in intrapersonal, interpersonal, and intergroup human relationships. In this chapter, peace is defined as "the harmony of all energies of life, their balance, and the recognition of all the opposites and conflicts" (Haring 1986:8). Peace is a process and will be shaped by a person's perspective about reality, human nature, and meanings of life. Our mindsets will affect how to frame the issues and create the possibility of having peaceful solu-tions (Lupovici, 2013). The new mindset about peace needs to be sustained and practiced in a culture of

DOI: 10.4018/978-1-4666-9784-3.ch013

peace and culture of healing with a peace-centered curriculum in education (Danesh, 2006). Teaching peace is strongly advocated to develop a better business environment and ecological sustainability in many countries' studies (Institute for Economics & Peace, 2015). Putting peace into the mind of people is one of the main focuses of the United Nations (United Nations Education, Scientific and Cultural Organization, 2015). Peace education is affirmed in the Universal Declaration of Human rights Article 26.2 (United Nation Human Right):

Education shall be directed to the full development of the human personality and to the strengthening of respect for human rights and fundamental freedoms. It shall promote understanding, tolerance and friendship among all nations, racial or religious groups, and shall further the activities of the United Nations for the maintenance of peace.

Harris and Synott (2002:4) state that peace education as 'teaching encounters" should draw out for people the (1) desire for peace, (2) non-violent alternatives for managing conflict; (3) and the skills for critical analysis of the structural arrangements that produce and legitimate injustice and inequality. Marketing education is defined as "a program designed to prepare secondary and postsecondary students to conduct the critical business functions associated with directing the flow of products and services from the producer to the consumer' (Association for Center and Technical Education, 2015). Do marketing educators just produce students to fulfill particular functions in the global digitalized market economy and continuously perpetuate social injustice in the system? Will these peace-building activities really be embraced in our existing competitive market? Does our marketing education really challenge the existing discourses or narratives that promote violence to human beings and nature? Do our marketing students cultivate the habits of life-long learning skills to examine themselves and their relationships with others? Is it possible to effectively teach peace in marketing education?

From my twenty one years' of experience with my business students in the United States and Hong Kong, I find that most students tend to follow cultural norms and achieve marketing objectives by stimulating materialistic or intense desires in their target customers. They accept the business reality as a battle field rather than a system for human flourishing. The consciousness of peace needs to be put into the students' mind set and our marketing curriculum in our pluralized, secularized, commoditized, digitalized global market economy. Students need more help in the development of becoming caring professionals as they are so distracted in their multitask reality and can easily compartmentalize their daily activities in the different realities without feeling any sense of responsibility to what they know. Carr (2008:221) said, "The more distracted we become, the less able we are to experience the subtlest, most distinctly human forms of empathy, compassion, and other emotions." Students' consciousness of themselves and others are found to be decreasing (Mirvis, 2008). The development of "multiple framing, reflective exploration of meaning, and practical reasoning" is not sufficiently covered in current business education (Waddock & Lozano, 2013). Through years of teaching and learning marketing, I assess more students are distracted and self-centered in the classrooms. I examine the common approach of teaching marketing is at best a piecemeal approach. Such an approach denies the inherent characteristic of wholeness of students and their calling. Students are trained to fulfill marketing functions[1] for the sake of organization objectives without being taught to treat people as sacred beings, and criticize self-deceptive practices in the field of marketing. I believe that it is a priority to guide my students through a broad range of classroom activities to understand how marketing relates to our human well-beings, discover who they are, to awaken their conscience, to aid them to use their conscience as their witness of the laws written on their heart, to assist them in developing awareness of certain virtues, to rouse their empathy toward others, to encourage them to commit to the highest Good with their free will and wise choices, and to lead them gradually to listen to God's voice as expressed through Scriptures.

In this chapter, I present a peace-centered process of teaching marketing that I have implemented during 2002-2015 academic years with my undergraduate and graduate business students in various marketing courses at two Christian Universities in the United States. My years of personal and professional study and reflective teaching have led me to develop this process. Peace comes from just relationships and needs the practices of empathy. I have years of research about human rights in higher education (Lam et. al., 2006) and have advocated empathy as another paradigm in the study of corporate social responsibility and sustainability (Cook & Lam, 2013; Lam, 2006—2015). This process affirms personhood through the practices of mindfulness and meditation (Eshelman et. al., 2012). This process needs educators and students to practice critical reflection skills and develop virtues together in a loving community. It is my contention that the process will equip my students to "take responsibility for fairly and honestly communicating a product's attributes and benefits while balancing the demand for exciting creativity and emotional enthusiasm within the nature of truthful relationships" between organizations and customers (Thompson, 2002), and to learn to be open to self-deceptive practices in their lives.

In the following segments of this chapter, I discuss (1) the manifestation of violence in marketing, (2) the concept of a peace-centered process of teaching marketing, (3) responsibility of marketing educators, and (4) the seven pedagogical strategies for this approach.

THE MANIFESTATION OF VIOLENCE IN TEACHING MARKETING

Traditional approaches to teaching marketing have overemphasized the rational decision-making process and objectified the knowledge presented in the textbooks without criticizing how the assumptions of human beings may violate the self-esteem and the social fabrics of humanity. Many marketing textbooks present ethics as a means to achieve organizational objectives and many successful marketing practices as a means to serve the interests of competent marketers rather than individual customers. Students are guided to reach organization goals "without being conscious of committing certain types of murder" as Ehrensal (2001) criticized business education. Marketing can be very harmful to the self-esteem of human beings when individuals are defined as subjects to be controlled by marketers and when human beings are treated as commodities through the social psychological process of domination of the firm over customers. The great tragedy is that "people begin to view themselves, and others, as commodities on the personality market" as Cheerier and Murray (2004) criticized marketing practices.

Rampel (2004) assessed that the conventional name of human beings as consumers in a market economy took away humanity element in our human relationships. The glorification of individual free choices and consumer sovereignty can expand the ego of an individual at the expense of the interdependent relationships among people in the exchange process. The notion of consumer as a summation of self-interested choices or as a king in the exchange process can dampen the social fabric of humanity. Harder (2003) analyzed that the notion of "self-interested choice" in individual economic decision- making can blind us to a realization that there were power imbalances among different groups of people in the world and that there is an embedded violence in the global market economy. A few powerful consumers dictate what is to be produced and even take away many people's security, esteem and choices when they are forced to be obedient to the global market rules.

The existing pervasive world view in marketing education is mainly a conflict-based perspective. War metaphors are frequently used to describe different marketing strategies and "The Art of War" written by the ancient Chinese strategist *Sun Tzu* is often quoted in the strategy classes. It is not surprising when students describe the business world as a dangerous, conflicted, and violent world by using the slogans, "dog eats dog or survival of the fittest." Students are more familiar with the conflict, violence, and destructive competition than the idea of coexistence and collaboration in market place. Power is sought to create order and order is illusively recognized as peace in a violent world when the order is to legitimate power differentials and structural inequalities. Lehman (2003:209-230) has criticized the acceptance of violence in our teaching:

When we accept the responsibility of teaching students to be realistic, we are implicitly granting the existing social order an inevitability that it does not to need to have....The so-called realistic approach is actually the attribution of inevitability and functionality—a quasi-ultimate validity—to structures and social norms that management are simply conventions that have been broadly accepted with a specific cultural context but that have no inherent inevitability or functionality. Put differently, my approach suggests the need to remind managers that in understanding business and management the only real world is the one we human through our own study and practice. And we can create a real world shaped by nonviolence.

Given the conventional norms of being violent in the market, the reality has seldom been challenged in marketing education. There is no critical learning "to perceive social, political, and economic contradictions and to take action against the oppressive elements of reality" (Freire & Macedo, 1995:381). Will the justification of existing violent practices in the business world deepen our self-centered behavior and increase the hegemony power of particular institutions or brands on our lives and community? What will the reality be like if it is based on a peace-oriented perspective? Should students acquire knowledge and skills to act on the new reality based on the development of human flourishing?

A PEACE-CENTERED PROCESS OF TEACHING MARKETING

This peace-centered process is related to the integrative theory of peace (ITP) proposed by Danesh (2006) and the development of virtues through practicing a peace-centered process in a learning community (MacIntyre, 1984). The virtues also sustain the practices and participants to sustain their unified lives through more knowledge of self and knowledge of peace. There are four prerequisites for peace education in the ITP theory: unity-based worldview, culture of healing, culture of peace and peace-oriented curriculum. The unity-based worldview is to change the mindset about the reality, humanity, and human relationships and purposes of life and cultivate the desire for peace. As I have taught in two Christian universities, I relied on traditional Christian resources to help students to connect their temporal selves with eternal truth and encourage them to develop virtues through their practices based on the vision of coexistence and collaborative reality in their professional careers. The culture of peace and culture of healing are generated through a loving community in the classroom and collaborative exercises in and outside the classroom. The structure of each institution may have developed certain ways of doing things which protect the existing power and marginalize the voice of the vulnerable. Educators may be hurt and need to be understanding healers in the process. Students may be hurt. Educators and students need to practice empathy and develop a culture that allows the seeds of peace-oriented marketing education to grow in a violent world. Thus, the peace-centered process of teaching marketing recognizes the wholeness of human beings and intentionally promotes a unified world view in a culture of peace and culture of healing and cultivates virtues through whole range of educational opportunities.

Unity-Based World View

In the peace-centered process of teaching marketing, the unified world view is to give meanings of human life in the understanding who God is and what we can become. It means that the unified world view is to affirm students' worth and their becoming in a living tradition. This view accepts the development process and the frailty of human beings. It also encourages participants to examine their lives and cultivate virtues from the perspective of a unitary life. "And the unity of a virtue in someone's life is intelligible only as a characteristics of a unitary life, a life that can be conceived and evaluated as a whole" (MacIntyre,1984:205). This view is different from existing culture about self-identity as the identity is being shaped by the existing conflict-based perspective. Students do not build their own worth in the streams of others' expectation, agenda, and judgment. The moral meaning of being human is interpreted in the context of Natural Law (i.e., human beings can aware that the laws written on our hearts cannot be denied and to know our self-destructive behavior when we suppress our conscience) (Aquinas, 1953; Budziszewski, 2003; Kreeft, 1994; Lewis, 1947), prevalent grace in the Wesleyan theology (Carver, 1993; Prince, 2004) and plain living in the Quaker tradition (Palmer 1983, 1989). We human beings are given to become Christ-like with God's grace. The practice of Quaker business people is a good example to illustrate how the unified world view guiding their decision. They acted on their beliefs and honored God through their daily lives and business. Their honesty and fair exchange business relationships earned their own niche in the business circles even the dominate principle of doing business was based on the principle of *caveat emptor* (Lehman, 2003:268).

Students are guided to affirm themselves as God's beloved children. "A healthy self-affirmation is an absolute requisite for authentic nonviolence" (Haring, 1986:68). When my students' consciences are awakened and their worth is affirmed as precious children of God, they will be inspired to explore other alternatives to deal with violence and know how to say "Yes" to peace-oriented choices and "No" to destructive competitive choices. They don't need to identify themselves with their anger and frustration in a world filled with confusion and fear. They are guided to discover their own identity and integrity through doing self-reflecting assignments, interacting with other students and mentors, and learning other people's feelings through role-playing assignments. They are asked to meditate on who they are and are challenged to understand the meaning of moral goodness in their written assignments and examinations. They are expected to learn that their professional marketing integrity does not come from strict adherence to codes of conduct of organizations or high moral standards but must come from each one's own personal identity given by God. Through their encounter experiences with their mentors, they are asked to find what hidden treasures they have and to affirm their own gifts from God. As they can affirm their wholeness, they learn to resist the temptation of being vehement to anyone who does not affirm their identities and they learn how to listen to the voices of adversaries who seem to be against them.

Students are guided to discern organization values and choose to work for some organization that matches their true selves. They also learn the importance of justice in human relationships through role-playing assignments. Thus, they gradually are helped to develop an enhanced capacity to make faithful commitments through their free will and their discernment. They learn to be grateful to God for their gifts and to rely on Divine power to resist temptation in the corporate world and their daily lives. As their inner light is recognized, they also develop their inner source of strength not to seek revenge when adversaries violate their God-given worth and especially help the adversaries to discover their own worth and inner strength. They are obedient to God in the context of gratitude and live as wounded healers in the world. Wolterstorff (2002:273) reminds us that "if we are true to who we are," we can "perform works of obedience as acts of gratitude." Ultimately, perhaps students may experience the transformation power of God in Christ, the Prince of Peace.

Culture of Peace

According to the definition by the United Nations (1997), a culture of peace is "a set of values, attitudes, traditions and customs, modes of behavior and ways of life that reflect and are directed towards respect for life, for human beings and their rights, the rejection of violence in all its forms, the recognition of the equal rights of men and women, the recognition of everyone to freedom of expression, opinion and information, attachment to the principles of democracy, freedom, justice, development for all, tolerance, solidarity, pluralism and acceptance of differences and understanding between nations, between ethnic, religious, cultural and other groups and between individuals." It seems that it is very easy to develop the culture of peace in our marketing classrooms. However, the complacency of students in Christian universities can be a stumbling block to create a culture of peace as our students nowadays can develop many alternatives to be alienated from those people whom they do not know. In a culture of confusion and fear, Christian students can easily be tempted to objectify others as particular groups and affirm their own values and identities much better than other groups. Christians do not know they also contribute to the injustices in the system when they try to objectify Christians' problems to other groups' problems. In my years of teaching at two Christian Universities, students tend to believe their personal ethical standards are much higher than the norms in the business world. They can easily consider themselves as martyrs if they are faithful. They don't understand the complexity of the environment in which corporate executives have to make decisions and how their choices are restricted by their own assumptions of reality. They don't understand how other people in other cultures have extended hospitality by being adapted to American ways of doing business and American language. Students need to know their own prejudices toward particular groups of people through sincere and thoughtful contacts while these contacts are based on equal power relationships. The culture of complacency of being Christians may be stumbling block for them to be open to others.

I deliberately create a trusting and loving community of learners. I must be very sensitive to students' feeling toward particular groups of people and facilitate them to expose our ignorance and misperceived selves. Students are provided opportunities to establish mutuality and positive dependence in a cooperative community (Johnson and Johnson, 2005). The process also addresses the power issues and the developmental process of human understanding and frailty of human beings. Students are guided to listen to the voice of others or collaborate with others they seldom do in their classroom assignments on equal power base. Students are guided to think what knowledge and actions need to be taken in a peaceful community.

Culture of Healing

Higher education environment definitely is not the same as war and post-war situations. Given the revolution in higher education, many institutions treat their staffs and professors as disposable commodities. These employees are in a continuous state of fear and mistrust. Given galaxy of information at the finger tips, some students do not have the patience to struggle with the questions and assignments for their own development. They have thousands of data points but do not know their destination. They do not exercise their brains to be excellent and consequently they deny their inner gifts and cheat themselves. According to the Natural Law, they have already known cheating is wrong. They attribute their cheating behavior to teachers. It needs reconciliation between teachers and students. Teachers need to know the students' fear and their tactics of transferring their negative feelings toward themselves to teachers. Teachers need to practice humility and love as they realize their limitations and their capacity of developing empathy toward their students. They need support from their social groups and discuss the issues coming from the peace-centered process of teaching in a trusting environment. Any manipulation of power in the social group will quickly destroy the possibilities of having a culture of reconciliation. Those who have power or perceived power in a hierarchical structure have to know how their desires for peace have been trapped by their fear of losing control and giving up their power in the reconciliation process. Those who are hurt will embrace their own God given dignity and refuse to use the abuse as their identities and develop better meanings in their lives.

A Well-Oriented Life through Acquired Virtues and Infused Virtues

Students are guided to awaken their deep conscience by reflecting on their previous experiences, to affirm their innate moral knowledge through sharing with other students, and to accept the Golden Rule in a peace-oriented process of marketing education. They also learn societal marketing and understand how marketing contributes to human flourishing and our moral ecology first before they learn the technical details. They can experience inner peace when they do not deny their innate moral knowledge. They have some awareness and some fleeting moments of attaining inner peace and peaceful relationships with others when they do not wrong others. They may have already known what is right or wrong but they have no courage to change their habits. It is important for teachers to cultivate a safe environment for them to examine how they deal with their cognitive dissonance and hopefully students can intuitively grasp that all good work must come from the primary principle of Natural Law, namely, "to do good and avoid evil." They know how to apply the basic principle in particular situations. They know how to develop their reasoning to prioritize their desires and to gain their practical wisdom through utilizing many good marketing practices and learning from excellent marketing professionals. This means that although trained marketing students can use their human ability to reason in making innate ethical knowledge more clearly known to themselves, they need to acquire virtues to make their reasoning more virtuous and to cultivate intellectual habits that "counsel, judge, and command those things that are for the sake of the end" (Aquinas, 1953: Summa Theologiae 1-2. 65.1). The end will be the good things that can flourish in human beings and can be known through our innate reasoning abilities.

When students have opportunities to have authentic encounters with some good marketers in their local communities, they will start to question why they have to tolerate those injustice practices and what knowledge they need to realize the vision of a peace world if they really value human flourishing in a community. Gradually they learn to discern what is good and evil and develop virtues of prudence.

They also know how to control themselves, not to perpetuate the existing injustice practices for their self-gratification, then they develop the virtues of temperance. They may have courage to challenge their own self-deceptive or cynical behavior. Thus, students are encouraged to acquire certain virtues through habitually practicing particular actions, and through witnessing and imitating good behavior in a community (Murphy, 1999). Acquired virtues (virtues such as prudence, temperance, fairness, courage) remain very important for the moral development of a whole person within the life of grace. They enumerate a set of ideals to which individuals aspire (Meara, Schmidt & Day, 1996), inspires a person to seek the ideals, and correlates with the principles of well-being of a community and the strength of character to flourish in a professional community (May, 1984). Using acquired virtues holds much promise for guiding the behavior of marketers (William & Murphy, 1990; Murphy, 1999; Thompson, 2002). It can provide a well-ordered life and a sense of peace.

The acquired virtues (such as prudence, temperance, fairness, and courage) are conditions for the reception and retention of a panoply of infused moral virtues (i.e., virtues given by God; these virtues are hope, faith, and love) (Ingis, 1999). This means that people are less likely to be self-indulgent and self-righteousness in their acquired virtues, but will realize that their acquired virtues depend on God's grace, not just on their efforts alone. The practices acquired virtues (i.e., virtues acquired by practice) will be better with the infused virtues (i.e., virtues given by God). Thus, acquired virtues prepare my students to be receptive to Divine Grace and to receive infused virtue when they can acknowledge the end of their actions is to be obedient to Divine Law and to be open to transcendence (Dell'Olio, 2003). From Aquinas' view, without infused virtues, my students cannot attain the state of peace.

When my students practice their human reasoning and learn to choose the best means to achieve their ends properly, they gradually learn how their choices resonate with their deep conscience and thus they acquire the virtue of prudence. They can use their innate reasoning to understand the Power behind the Moral Law and can eliminate any alternative that is against the Moral Law. The acknowledgement of the Power behind the Moral Law leads my students to realize the existence of God. When they are encouraged to acquire certain virtues and are exposed to Scriptures, they can realize that the achievement of the ultimate human good requires human effort and the influx of Divine grace. They are inspired to be open to transcendence in order for them to realize a state of peace. They can understand that they are participating in Divine goodness when they are exercising their innate abilities of moral reasoning. They can resolve many frantic moral dilemmas and arguments and can be delighted in following Divine Law as the Law leads them to proper virtues and to the attainment of peace as the book of Psalms describes:

Great peace have they which love thy law; and nothing shall offend them. (Psalm 119: 165)[2].

Mark the perfect man, and behold the upright: for the end of that man is peace. (Psalm 37:37).

RESPONSIBILITY OF A MARKETING EDUCATOR IN A PEACE-CENTERED PROCESS OF TEACHING

Any marketing educator practicing a peace-centered process of teaching must strive to exhibit peace in his or her teaching. He or she must be committed to a non-violent approach, act as a wounded healer, and model behavior that is obedient to God with gratitude. He or she must pay more attention to role models and self-transcendence. The whole being may be challenged by the students because a teacher's behavior will be examined in the light of ideals in the classroom. Thus, self-transcendence of educators would "imply to overcome defaults or claims grounding the necessity of business ethics courses" (Dion, 2000).

Marketing educators must affirm their own worth and embrace the unified world view they present to students. They acquire virtues through their calling as teachers and use their practices in their unified lives to inspire students to acquire certain virtues in their lives and professional careers. They respect their own identities and integrity in their teaching and avoid imposing only certain abstract goodness on themselves and students. Palmer (1998: 29) has commented, "A vocation that is not mine, no matter how externally valued, does violence to the self in the precise sense that it violates my identity and integrity on behalf of some abstract norms. When I violate myself, I invariably end up violating people I work with. How many teachers inflict their own pain on their students, the pain that comes from doing whatever was, or no longer is, their true work?"

Marketing educators must reflect on their lives and yearn to be men/women of peace. They must accept students' failure and fragility with compassion. They must respect their students' wholeness and must reflect on how the epistemology in marketing subjects may create violence in students' lives. Palmer (1983) reminded us how the objectification of our knowledge might keep our students from being transformed by the knowledge. It means that the way we lead students to know the subject matter may demoralize students' character if we are not sensitive to any hidden curriculum. We must give enough space for students to disclose themselves and reflect on ethical issues in their lives. We must lead students' life stories in connecting their life stories with the subject matter and create an atmosphere of peace in the classroom so that students can speak with truth and confidence. We must invite students to participate in a subject-centered culture and discipline ourselves and our students to listen for the voice of the Truth. When students are drawn by the revealed Truth, they can be guided to expose many self-deceptive practices in marketing. We can help them to appreciate their own gifts and guide them to use their innate abilities of reasoning to prioritize their lives for the higher end.

Marketing educators must take the risk of challenging students' prejudices and ignorance. We must have the courage to confront false reasoning if we hope to guide our students to listen to their deep conscience and to be truthful with themselves. We must be prepared to be challenged by angry students who do not want to be stretched or mentored to serve humanity. We must be patient with students' temporary cognitive dissonances as they can begin to re-orient their lives to God. We cultivate a positive environment for them discover and develop their self-disciplines to be peacemakers. We also have to take care of ourselves and patiently wait for God's work in these young people's lives. We need to discern and examine our assumption of our leaderships in the classroom. We need to practice self-care: being mindful in our daily lives and nurture relationships with others outside our work. We need to revisit our family of origin and know how our family history conditions us to frame peace in many situations. We need to know how to control our anger and anxiety in our jobs and find non-violent alternatives to deal with injustice in the structure. We learn how to be assertive for peace-making activities and learn not to take actions to reinforce our self-deceptive identities. We need to discern our directions and limitations through a community of peace-committed educators. We need accountable partners and develop capacities to define and maintain ourselves as "non-anxious presences" in an anxious world.

PEDAGOGICAL STRATEGIES

The peace-centered process of teaching marketing is designed to affirm students' wholeness, to lead students to be oriented to God, and to listen to their inner voice, voices of others, and the voice of God in a culture of peace and culture of healing. I expect my students to do good marketing activities and to have a life that is in harmony with God's will. I have adopted the process and designed appropriate pedagogical strategies as I taught marketing, marketing management and strategy, sales management, consumer behavior and marketing research to undergraduates and also marketing management to graduates during the 2001—2015 academic year.

The basic focus of my pedagogical strategies is facilitating the development of each student as a whole person. The key strategy is each student's reflection upon his or her identity and integrity through various activities grounded on the principles of collaborative learning, service learning, and mentor relationships. Supportive strategies are critical research, life stories' sharing, role playing, and Scriptures.

These activities can serve to awaken students' consciousness of themselves and others, experience peace in a community of learners, and examine their own assumptions about reality and human nature. They are guided to develop their own meanings of peace that will be manifested in themselves, interpersonal relationships, intergroup relationships, and even international relationships. The development of being committed to seek good in their professional practices is initiated by themselves, not being imposed by their teachers. They may realize how to frame some issues to create more opportunities for peaceful solutions in their lives. They will realize the promises of acquired virtues when they learn how to examine their intentions, attitudes and behaviors in these activities. They are asked to reflect their own moral development and changes. Hopefully, they develop life-long learning skills to examine themselves and become peace-makers. They will continue to bring innovative marketing practices that promote peace.

Self Reflection

Students are expected to reflect on their personal growth, discover possible opportunities for personal growth, see how their effort affects other people's lives, and experience their wholeness. They are guided to recognize that peace must come from integrating their multiple selves and minimizing the incongruence between the internal and external person. They are expected to examine how their compartmentalized-selves lose their own selves when they keep on being busier and quicker without any sense of who they are.

In their first assignment, undergraduates and graduates are led to discover who they are through reading articles, self-reflection, and self-projection (see Appendix 1, 2, 3). From their first assignment, most are inspired to cultivate virtues including integrity, fairness, trust, respect, and empathy. Most perceive themselves as people with high moral standards. Then we discuss character traits of their good friends and admired managers in order to help them to recognize that they have already known what constitutes their well being. They can recognize the quest of the good is quite similar to other students in the class. What their common desires can be used to promote a unified world view that respects life.

In their personal selling portfolio undergraduate students in sales management class are asked to explore their own identity and missions. They reflect on their life experiences and learn more about their calling in their career. As their professor, I would challenge their understanding of what virtue is and guide them to discover how they can resonate with some goodness in their hearts. I urge them to recognize their need to do good in order to maintain their God-given worth. The affirmation of God-given worth is to empower students not to use violence to protect their narrow definitions of self-identity shaped by current materialistic and commodity culture.

All my graduate students are employed adults and are generally more mature than undergraduates. Since they have had more in-depth experiences and opportunities for thought on their moral character and their future than undergraduate students; they can reflect the role of personal conscience, laws and corporate policies, supervisors' behavior, and market structure in their business decisions (see Appendix 3). Most affirm that personal conscience has played a significant role in their business decisions. They expect their companies' personnel to "walk their talk" and expect to be respected as dignified human beings. Many do not show strong faith in a company's written laws. Some even perceive that their personal ethical standards are much higher than that of their company. They are reluctant to practice their personal virtues when their company's focus is the bottom line. The utilitarian perspective of their company and the group decision-making process of many large companies discourages them from overtly practicing their virtues. I affirm their inclination to do good and lead them to discuss the literature about moral managers (Walton, 1988; Calian, 1992), the concept of Natural Law, and the concept of revenge conscience. They are asked to examine why inner peace is important to them and to explore potential problems when there is a great gap between their internal set of values and external actions. I encourage my students to reorient their life to God through a guided literature review (See Worthy, 1958; Walton, 1988; Calian, 1992; Drimmelen,1998; Calkins, 2000; William and Murphy, 1990; Vaill, 1996, 1998; Murphy, 1999; Wood, 1999; Alford & Naughton, 2000; Thompson, 2002). I encourage them to examine how bureaucratic procedures and group behavior take away their consciousness of their violence in their behavior when they use many meetings to legitimate their power and structural inequality. The fear among participants has been covered by those objectified process and documents.

I encourage my undergraduate and graduate students to reflect upon the meaning of abstraction of integrity, fairness, trust, respect and empathy in their professional careers and their sources of moral courage (i.e., to act in accordance with their basic values such as honesty with, fairness to, trust toward, respect for each other). Through the discussion and small group assignments (see Appendix 4), they are frequently reminded to examine any inconsistency among their virtuous attitude, their commitment to certain virtues, and any ways they may suppress their conscience. As I read their numerous self-reflection assignments and listen to their discussion in many collaborative settings, I am able to assist them in synthesizing their experience and in recognizing the need for wholeness or peace in their lives.

Collaborative Learning

All students are encouraged to consider and suggest solutions to a variety of business problems in many small group activities. They articulate their own moral reasoning, share their life stories, and participate in various role plays and peer group reviews. They learn to be accountable and experience the flow of positive energy when they practice being present in the midst of conflicts in some situations. They also learn how to support each other to grow and to develop better ability to create a community of learners, a sense of solidarity, and a more meaningful existence for everybody in the classroom. Thus, they can discover they learn more through collaboration rather than through competitive environment. Hopefully, each person's identity, conscience, creativity, autonomy, and responsibility is affirmed in a cooperative setting with an inclusive sense of stewardship.

A trusting and supportive learning community is extremely important for part-time graduate students who have more diversified experience and insights about life than undergraduates. The collaborative learning experience leads them to appreciate different perspectives, and know how to establish harmonious relationships among people in a learning community. They learn how to confront people with respect in the process of solving conflicts and to include people of different abilities. Hopefully, they learn how to affirm each one's worth in a culture of peace and healing.

Our undergraduate consumer behavior class discusses the child labor issues with students coming from different disciplines including political science, social work, and psychology. The experience can cultivate their empathy towards children's development, discover the universal rights of children, and exercise a more inclusive sense of stewardship in a global economy.

Service Learning

Undergraduate students in consumer behavior study the consumption behavior of disadvantaged groups such as the elderly, mental disabled people and ethnic minorities, and internalize the virtue of empathy toward others. In one project, students had to study residents and residents' family member about the quality of care in a nursing home. After the first field visits, many students expressed their sadness and fear about those aging residents even though they were under good care. They were afraid of not getting right information from these fragile aging residents. A few even complained about the difficulties of doing this project. I tried to ask students to tell their expectations about their behavior in the different stage of life spans. Many students could not imagine what their lives would be when they were eighty years old as they were now in the early twenties. They were facilitated to share their experience with aging people including their grandparents. Two students made fun about their grandparents' stupid behavior in the class. I tried to correct them while one student was so mad and wrote me a note about her anger toward seniors as her grandfather always abused her mother. I did not know I have hurt her when I told her to show respect to seniors even their behavior might not be up to your expectation of being educated people. When this student's grandfather passed away, we all wrote her a note. Students gradually overcome their reluctance to do this project as they were very surprised the senior residents welcomed them and cheered them whenever they did the field work in the second and third time. Later, students presented twice in the nursing home and were very impressed by the support from all participants in the nursing home. Some seniors had to lie on the beds and were in wheel-chairs as they came to listen my students' presentation. Students learned and showed their gratitude to these seniors. They told me the best part of their project was to have informal interactions with the residents. Students can develop a sense of connectedness between themselves and aging people through this nursing home project. They also broaden their horizons about aging people and examine their prejudice toward aging people. The peace-centered process is quite demanding as students were facilitated to develop a unified world view and practice culture of peace in several field trips, presentations, and reflections in the classes. If I used the existing conflict and competitive paradigms, I would quickly categorize these seniors to be in different groups according to their contributions to the business in the nursing home and develop different strategies to different segments. However, students had lost the opportunity to connect their lives with their subjects of study and to examine their prejudice against aging people. Through this peace-centered approaches, students also developed capacities to know how to communicate with aging seniors and were proud of collecting data from a group of seniors whom they never expected to encounter in their current experience. They also experienced how to develop better marketing solutions to seniors while they had empathy toward these people who had connections with their lives. They learned the skills of empathy toward seniors and in return knew how to serve them better. These skills also affected their own characters and made them not to follow the pattern of age-discrimination in the United States.

Graduate students and undergraduate students in marketing management are asked to serve the community through the development of a marketing plan for different profit and non-profit organizations in the local community. Through the service learning projects, students practice the concept of servant leadership and stewardship of resources in a community. They are expected to develop a pro-active attitude towards the solidarity of a community and to be inspired to seek the common good of a community with a sense of personal and communal growth. When they reflect their sense of feeling good in serving the community, they can discover their innate knowledge of a good community. The experience can inspire them to know how to be peacemakers in a community. Hopefully, they will change the house of fear to the house of love!

Critical Research

I believe that exposing falsehoods of our marketing practices can help students to be free of goal orientations and corporate controls which can do violence to our humanity. Through critical analysis of many companies' marketing practices, students learn to discern what kinds of organization culture enables them to flourish and to attain a state of peace. They also learn their peace is grounded in fulfilling their obligations, and being fair and honest in the exchange process.

Undergraduate students in marketing are required to do ethical marketing issue analysis and case studies. They are guided to learn the code of conducts proposed by the American Marketing Association and Consumer Bills of Rights. They are asked to use what they learn to judge whether some consumer ethics and business ethics scenarios to be morally acceptable or not (see Appendix 5). After they have made their individual decision, they were put in a group and had further discussion. I put their consensus on the board and let them to see how the group dynamics changed their judgment about different ethics scenarios and how the choices of each group are against other group's choices. These gave them opportunities to articulate their values among their choices and discover some shared values. Students tended to have better judgment in the consumer ethics scenario than business scenario as they had more personal experience about these practices. They showed more tolerance on business unethical behavior as they had already accepted this was business reality and did not want to challenge their perceived reality. I discussed with them these controversial cases and led them to reason why some practices were unacceptable from peace-centered perspective. I guided them to discover the sources of their reasoning and their logic of ethical reasoning. Some students were frustrated when I pointed out to them they violated the trusting relationships between companies and customers. In general, we experienced the flow of positive energy even though we were disagreement but we were engaged in the exercise. I also reinforced their learning and asked them to judge some scenarios in their test.

I show my undergraduate students in marketing a short video case about pricing decision of an Alzheimer drug and challenge them to think about what is good business and what is the meaning of "business is business." I also ask them whether pornography or child pornography is a good business. The discussion can create different levels of cognitive dissonance among students and push them to think why they care for the development of children but not for the development of adults. They also learn to recognize and identify the source of their inner cognitive dissonance. The process of reasoning will lead them to internalize the right practices and will guide them to do the right things in the future if they hope to have inner peace.

Undergraduate students in consumer behavior have to examine the deep root causes of child labor issues, the deceptive practices of companies that use child labor in the global supply chain, and the possibilities of a consumer boycott. Through discussion, their awareness of the child labor issue increases in their purchase behavior. They tend to read the purchasing tags on clothes more and make sure that they will not support child labor. In addition, they can see the positive contribution of child labor to a family's well-being and children's growth when they learn that children worked on farms in the past and recognize the problem of their classmates who grew up without any experience of doing household work. With this research, they can request companies to provide good working conditions for those children who must work to support their families. They also recognize the harmful effect to their beings when there are great discrepancies between their purchase behavior and their attitude toward child labor.

Graduate students are assigned to assess the changes in their working environment over the past five years and are expected to anticipate the possible changes in their work in the coming five years. They are oriented to learn how to guide their own learning, and to be prepared to sustain themselves through developing teams and to be able to renew their spirit in the dynamic and changing environment. They also have to assess their organization's missions and the moral standard of their supervisors. Through these assessments, they can come to realize that they are empowered by seeking peace and become the best versions of themselves in solitude and relationships.

Mentor Relationships

At the beginning of each course, students are encouraged to find mentors from whom they can learn virtues that they want to cultivate during the semester. Some good experienced marketing professionals are invited to be our guest speakers. In their presentations, they demonstrate the importance of integrating personal ethics and corporate ethics into their career. They model a life of peace to our students.

Students are inspired to connect their personal ethics and professional ethics with the corporate world. Undergraduate students in marketing and sales management are required to submit papers about their learning acquired from their mentors. Through the description of their mentors' job nature, spiritual challenge and character traits, they can relate their mentors' life stories to well-accepted moral values and principles in the business community. They can intuitively grasp what the good things they have to do in order to flourish in their career. Furthermore, their encounter with mentors can awaken their sense of who they are and their hidden idea of goodness in their hearts. Most students can have faith and hope in perfecting their souls in the corporate world through developing good work ethics.

Life Stories' Sharing

Undergraduates in marketing management and marketing have to share portions of their life stories with other classmates. The exercise helps them to remember their feelings of doing right things and the obstacles they met in doing right things. From the sharing, they can learn what are the common benefits and virtues for humanity. They also can review their worst learning situation and learn how to realize they can choose to move themselves from a victimized to a victorious situation. They experience peace when they have courage to do the right things.

Furthermore, graduate students are guided to yearn for a transcendent experience in their workplace by following Jesus in their spiritual path. I encourage my graduate students to share their life stories and their working experiences of being connected to Infinity by asking them to answer the following questions mainly created by Mitroff and Denton (1999):

1. Please list the top three things that give you the most meaning and purpose in your job.
2. Do you think that you are more able to show your intelligence than your emotions or feelings at your work? Explain your answer.
3. What are the basic values that guide you in making important decisions in your lives?
4. How often are you forced to compromise those values in making important decisions at your work? Why?
5. Have you ever had a strong spiritual experience at your work? What was this?
6. Have you ever cried or felt depressed by the nature of your job or your organization? Why?
7. Do you wish to be able to express and develop your complete self at work? Explain your wish.

When we listen to the strong spiritual experiences recalled from our work, we can feel the importance of nurturing our soul in our work and may be more willing to develop the courage to express ourselves in the corporate world. Through life stories' sharing, some students can experience spiritual strength when their professional decision is related to their personal conscience. In order for students not to treat their peak experience as their own idols of God, I have to guide them to focus on Jesus by quoting Peterson's (2003: 37) words:

There are a lot of people today who want spirituality without Jesus. But spirituality without Jesus degenerates into a sloppy subjectivism, tempting us to invent a way of life customized to accommodate aspiration, inspiration and "meaning" without the inconvenience of morals or personal sacrifice. A commitment to Jesus keeps spirituality in touch with God. And a concern for spirituality keeps Jesus in touch with us.

Some students affirm their Christian priorities in their work and some may try to make adjustments in their work through following Jesus in their lives. They can also learn how to reconcile the conflicts between their individual values and system values by developing support groups in their workplace, and even choosing jobs in which they can express their complete identity. Thus, they learn how to prepare themselves to be men and women of peace and to orient their lives to God.

Applying Scriptures in Managerial Decision Making Process

Students at a Christian College are expected to identify many Bible passages which relate to marketing themes and to pay more attention to the close relationships between faith and marketing in various courses at the undergraduate and graduate levels. Through various exercises of using Scriptures to justify their managerial decision-making process, my students are expected to develop a sense of moral compass in their minds and to know how to defend their world view or their life view biblically (Chewning, 2001). These exercises include three areas: ethical practices; marketing principles at work in the Book of Acts; and changing students' attitude toward work, stewardship, materialism, and poverty. They have to comprehend what the Scriptures indicate their behavior ought to be and think what changes they may need to make in order to fulfill the Divine commandment. Hopefully, in the future they will examine their lives with the Word of God.

Ethical Practices

My graduate students are encouraged to reflect on the ethical practices of their companies and to reflect on seven questions:

- Do you perceive that your company's formal system (codes of ethics and ethical policies) matches your supervisors' behavior? Why?
- Do you agree that your company's organization culture exerts more influence on your ethical behavior than written regulations? Why?
- Would you do what your supervisors do rather than follow policy? Why?
- Do you perceive that the code of ethics of your company significantly reduces unethical decision-making behavior? Why?
- Do you perceive that your company's reward system encourages unethical behavior? Why?
- Do you perceive that there is a low probability of being caught doing something unethical (with the stated result of dismissal)? Why?
- Do you think that your company has covenant relationships with the society? Do you think that your company has covenant relationships with the shareholders only? Why?

These questions help them to realize that most employees like to follow what supervisors do rather than what company policies say, and help the students to discover their reasons of not stopping evil in their work place. I ask some students to visualize their Divine Boss who is much bigger than their present boss. I encourage them to contribute to their system by exemplifying right actions through their personal modeling and to develop their strength from the support of spiritual mentors and friends.

After this exercise, I ask each of my students to meditate on one recent problem that bothers him or her and to write it down. Each student then reads a portion of the Scriptures which examines our intention, deception, integrity, presumption, and life orientation (see 'Food for Thought' in Appendix 6). Other students are to consider how these Scriptures can help them solve the problems. After we finish the reading, my students are asked their ways of handling their problems after being exposed to these Scriptures. A few admit being empowered through meditating upon these Scriptures, and their testimony may encourage other students to develop a habit of developing a personal relationship with God.

Marketing Principles at Work in the Book of Acts

Students are asked to discover the use of marketing principles (i.e., create customers' values through delivering right product with right price at right place to right target markets with right messages) in the Book of Acts in our senior Marketing course and graduate Marketing course (see Appendix 7). The exercise helps my students to understand the connection between various elements of marketing and principles of Christian faith, and to see the legitimacy and limitations of applying marketing principles in the contemporary church. We discuss the problem of commodification of the contemporary church and ways of reviving faith through proper marketing techniques. Some students coming from evangelical backgrounds feel discomfort in doing this assignment and are invited to examine their own faith system. They are challenged to rethink their assumptions about profaning God's Word in the business world and their wrong conscience of vocation calling in business.

Changing Students' Attitude toward Work, Stewardship, Materialism, and Poverty

My students are asked to read assigned Biblical passages related to work, stewardship, materialism, and poverty or economic injustice (see Appendix 8). In their assignments, undergraduates are requested to use their previous learning in their Philosophy, Faith and Ethics, and Christian Ethics courses in elaborating their own perspectives of work, stewardship, materialism and poverty. The objective is to help them to integrate their prior knowledge and to know how to connect to their Supreme Being through Scriptures. After the assignments, they are requested to examine their attitude toward creating wealth, managing people, possessing things, and empowering the poor through marketing activities. They are expected to respect human beings as sacred beings and seek for justice for the poor and the oppressed. They are also expected to understand the sacramental relationships between themselves and God's creation, and give up their control under God's providence. They are expected to see material things as part of God's creation and God's providence. For example, if they want to be good stewards, they should not feel guilty about using materials things, but they need to know how to make these materials things function properly according to the Divine principle. They are expected to be obedient to God in the context of gratitude.

My graduate students compare their attitude toward work, materialism, and stewardship with the biblical perspectives. They are guided to review some articles that apply biblical principles in work and stewardship (see Diddams, Surdyk, Daniels & Duzer 2004; Tinsley, 2002). They can understand how the idolatry of power or fear in their work place can destroy their personal relationship with God. They also can anticipate their inherent wholeness can be damaged in a quick pace and stressful working environment. Some can see how the concept of stewardship empowers them to be better leaders when they can submit themselves to God's will and practice humility. Hopefully, they can experience how their faith in Christ can give them moral courage, assurance and comfort in an uncertain and complex business environment.

CONCLUSION

Educators and students are living in a fast-paced fragmented world while we anticipate less and less time to appreciate simple things. There is not much time and energy to think about how the structure of the economic system creates our anxiety and how the framing of issues makes us impossible to develop peace relationships with ourselves, other human being, and nature. We need to practice being mindful and cultivate a desire for peace. We may develop new knowledge and action based on the collaborative and coexistence perspective.

It is my hope that my teaching of marketing will move from pieces to peace as I invite my students to seek peace and to receive promise of virtues development by advocating a unified world view that affirms our worth of lives in a culture of peace and healing. I equip students for peace through using Scriptures, models, self-reflection, dialogues, critical reasoning, collaboration, and service learning. Other educators in other tradition may use their rich resources to shape the students' desire for peace and to frame different issues for peace solutions.

As a marketing educator, I realize that it can be very demanding to use a peace-centered process of teaching marketing subjects. As my fellow marketing educators do, I have to finish a great amount of content material in a very short time including the assessment of students' content knowledge. However,

I must place high value on encouraging students to reflect upon being true to who they are and to seek a life of peace!

While there are difficulties and limitations in any approach, I am finding this peace-centered process of teaching marketing can facilitate students' becoming active moral agents and may reduce violence in our culture. I invite and encourage marketing educators to consider the possibilities of using the peace-center process in facilitating the development of students to have a life that is in harmony with God's will.

ACKNOWLEDGMENT

The essay is dedicated to my mentors who teach me how to practice peace-centered process: Dr. Frank Carver, Dr. Martha J.B. Cook, Dr. Georgia L. Eshelman, Dr. Pat Leslie, Dr. Herb Prince, and Dr. Peter B. Vaill. The author thanks the reviewer's comments and encouragement.

REFERENCES

Alford, H. J., & Naugton. (2001). Managing as if Faith mattered: Christian Social Principles in the modern organization. Notre Dame, IN: University of Notre Dame Press.

Aquinas, T. (1953). Summa theologiae (5 vols.). Ottawa: Harpell's Press.

Association for Center and Technical Education (ACTE). (n.d.). *What is marketing education?*. Retrieved 20 July 2015 https://www.acteonline.org/marketing_whatis/#.Va3JhmfJC1s

Budziszewski, J. (2003). *What We Can't Not Know*. Spence Publishing Company.

Calkins, M. (2000). Recovering Religion's Prophetic Voice for Business Ethics. *Journal of Business Ethics, 23*, 339–352. doi:10.1023/A:1005989824688

Carr, N. (2008). *The Shallows: What the internet is doing our brains*. New York: W.M. Norton & Company.

Carver, F. (1993). The essence of Wesleyanism. This essay was first delivered as a talk at "A Wesley Festival: Pilgrimage to Wholeness," a faculty chapel, Point Loma Nazarene College, February 19, 1993.

Cherrier, & Murray. (2004). The Sociology of Consumption: The Hidden Facet of Marketing. *Journal of Marketing Management*, 509-525.

Chewning, R. (2001). *A Dozen Styles of Biblical Integration: Assimilating the Mind of Christ*. Presentation at the Annual CBFA Conference.

Cook, M., & Lam, M. (2013). Empathy as a distinctive element in Christian business education. *Proceedings of the Christian Business Faculty Association Conference*.

Dell'Olio, A. J. (2003). *Foundations of Moral Selfhood: Aquinas on Divine Goodness and the Connection of the Virtues*. New York: Peter Lang Publishing, Inc.

Dion, M. (2000). Teaching Business Ethics, or the Challenge of A Socratic-Nietzschean Self-Transcendence for Teachers. *Teaching Business Ethics, 4*(3), 307–324. doi:10.1023/A:1009873711063

212

Drimmelen, R. (1998). *Faith in a global economy: A primer for Christians*. Geneva: WCC Publications.

Ehrensal, K. N. (2001). Training Capitalism's Foot Soldiers: The Hidden Curriculum of Undergraduate Business Education. In E. Margolis (Ed.), The Hidden Curriculum in Higher Education, (pp. 97-113). New York: Routledge.

Eshelman, G., Lam, M., & Cook, M. (2012). Three contributing factors to effective utilization of technology in management education and practice: Personhood, Mindfulness, and Meditation. *Journal of the North American Management Society, 6*, 24–34.

Freire, P., & Macedo, D. P. (1995). A dialogue: Culture, language, and race. *Harvard Educational Review, 65*(3), 377–403. doi:10.17763/haer.65.3.12g1923330p1xhj8

Harder, J. M. (2003). The Violence of Global Marketization. In J. D. Weaver & G. Biestecker-Mast (Eds.), Teaching Peace: Nonviolence and the Liberal Arts. Lanham, MD: Rowman & Littlefield Publishers, Inc.

Haring, B. (1986). *The Healing Power of Peace and Nonviolence*. Paulist Press.

Inglis, J. (1999). Aquinas's Replication of The Acquired Moral Virtues: Rethinking the Standard Philosophical Interpretation of Moral Virtues in Aquinas. *Journal of Religious Ethics, 27*(1), 3-27.

Institute for Economics & Peace. (2015). Retrieved 21 July 2015 from http://economicsandpeace.org/

Kerin, R., Berkowitz, E., Hartley, S., & Rudelius, W. (2003). Marketing (7th ed.). McGraw-Hill Companies, Inc.

Kotler, P. (2012). *Marketing*. Retrieved 22 July 2015 from: https://www.youtube.com/watch?v=sR-qL7QdVZQ

Kreeft, P. (1994). *C.S. Lewis for the Third Millennium: Six Essays on the Abolition of Man*. San Francisco: Ignatius Press.

Lam, A. L. H., Lam, M. L. L., & Lam, L. H. C. (2006). A Study of Human Rights Non-Government Organizations (NGOs) as Social Movement Organizations (SMOs) in Hong Kong, China: Implications for Higher Education. *The International Journal of the Humanities, 3*(9), 105–117.

Lam, M. L. L. (2007). A study of the transfer of corporate social responsibility from well-established foreign multinational enterprises to Chinese subsidiaries. In Controversies in international corporate responsibility. Pittsburgh, PA: Carnegie Mellon University.

Lam, M. L. L. (2008). Being innovative by doing good. In *Proceedings of Academy of Innovation and Entrepreneurship 2008*. Beijing, China: Tsinghua University.

Lam, M. L. L. (2009a). Beyond credibility of doing business in China: Strategies for improving corporate citizenship of foreign multinational Enterprises in China. *Journal of Business Ethics, 87*(S1), 137–146. doi:10.1007/s10551-008-9803-3

Lam, M. L. L. (2009b). Sustainable development and corporate social responsibility of multinational enterprises in China. In J. R. McIntyre, S. Ivanaj, & V. Ivanaj (Eds.), *Multinational Enterprises and the Challenge of Sustainable Development* (pp. 230–244). Cheltenham, UK: Edward Elgar. doi:10.4337/9781849802215.00023

Lam, M. L. L. (2010a). Political implications of the corporate social responsibility movement in China. *The Journal of International Business Research and Practice, 4*, 125–134.

Lam, M. L. L. (2010b). Managing corporate social responsibility as an innovation in China. In L. Al-Hakim & J. Chen (Eds.), *Innovation in Business and Enterprise: Technologies and Frameworks* (pp. 224–238). Hershey, PA: IGI Global. doi:10.4018/978-1-61520-643-8.ch015

Lam, M. L. L. (2010c). Beyond legal compliance: Toward better corporate citizenship of foreign multinational enterprises in China. *Journal of Biblical Integration in Business, 13*, 100–109.

Lam, M. L. L. (2010d). Sustainable development in a global market economy—A compassion-oriented approach. In *Proceedings of Christian Business Faculty Association Conference.*

Lam, M. L. L. (2011a). Becoming corporate social responsible foreign multinational enterprises in China. *The Journal of International Business Research and Practice, 5*, 47–61.

Lam, M. L. L. (2011b). Successful strategies for sustainability in China and the global market economy. *International Journal of Sustainable Development, 3*(1), 73–90.

Lam, M. L. L. (2011c). Becoming corporate social responsible foreign multinational enterprises in China. *The Journal of International Business Research and Practice, 5*, 47–61.

Lam, M. L. L. (2011d). Challenges of sustainable environmental programs of foreign multinational enterprises in China. *Management Research Review, 34*(11), 1153–1168. doi:10.1108/01409171111178729

Lam, M. L. L. (2012a). An alternative paradigm for managing sustainability in the global supply chain. *International Journal of Social Ecology and Sustainable Development, 3*(4), 1–12. doi:10.4018/jsesd.2012100101

Lam, M. L. L. (2012b). A best practice of corporate social responsibility: Going beyond words on a page and a check. Advances in Sociology Research, 13, 157-164.

Lam, M. L. L. (2012c). Corporate social responsibility movement in China: What can foreign corporations' corporate social responsibility programs in China do to universal values? In K. Wang (Ed.), *Dialogue among Cultures: Peace, Justice and Harmony* (pp. 221–234). Beijing, China: Foreign Language Press.

Lam, M. L. L. (2012d). Toward sustainability through innovation. In *Proceedings of Inaugural International Conference on Innovation and Entrepreneurship: Theory and practice relevant to China.* Wuhan, China.

Lam, M. L. L. (2013a). An educator as a contemplative practitioner in business education. *Journal of Higher Education Theory and Practices, 13*(2), 2013.

Lam, M. L. L. (2013b). Being Chinese: A reflective study of foreign multinational corporations' sustainable development and global talent programs in China. In *Proceedings of the NAMS (North American Management Society) of MBAA International Conference.*

Lam, M. L. L. (2013c). A Case Study of the Challenges of Sustainable Business Development in China. *The Journal of International Business Research and Practice, 7*, 2013.

Lam, M. L. L. (2013d). Sustaining and Extending Corporate Social Responsibility in China: One Company Initiative. The *Journal of International Business Research and Practice, 7*, 2013.

Lam, M. L. L. (2013e). Building Trust between American and Chinese Business Negotiators. In Dis(honesty) in Management: Manifestations and Consequences. Emerald Group Publishing Limited.

Lam, M. L. L. (2014a). Empathy as a major contributing factor to sustainable business development in China. In *Proceedings of the 2014 AIB-Midwest Conference*.

Lam, M. L. L. (2014b). Cultivate the habit of empathy in on-going sustainability research. In *Proceedings of the NAMS (North American Management Society) of MBAA International Conference*.

Lam, M. L. L. (2014c). Empathy as a Major Contributing Factor to Sustainability in the Global Supply Chain. In Khosrow-Pour (Ed.), Inventive Approaches for Technology Integration and Information Resources Management, (pp. 53-67). Hershey, PA: IGI Global Publications. doi:10.4018/978-1-4666-6256-8.ch002

Lam, M. L. L. (2014d). Empathy as a major contributing factor to sustainable business development in China. *The Journal of International Business Research and Practice, 8*, 2014.

Lam, M.L.L. (2014e). Harmonious Society' through Corporate Social Responsibility. *Journal of Public Affairs, 14*(2).

Lam, M. L. L. (2015). Improving moral ecology in a digitized global market economy through empathic practices. *Proceedings in the North American Management Society Conference*.

Lehman, G. A. (2003). The peaceful manager. In Nonviolence and the Liberal Arts, (pp. 266-274). Rowman & Littlefield Publishers, Inc.

Lewis, C. S. (1947). *The Abolition of Man*. New York: Macmillan.

Lupovici, A. (2013). Pacification: Toward a theory of the social construction of peace. *International Studies Review, 15*(2), 204–228. doi:10.1111/misr.12032

MacIntyre, A. (1984). *After Virtue*. Notre Dame: University of Notre Dame Press.

May, F. W. (1994). The Virtues in a Professional Setting. In *Readings in Christian Ethics: Theory and Method* (vol. 1, pp. 267-274). Academic Press.

McCracken, J., Martin, W., & Shaw, B. (1998). Virtue Ethics and the Parable of the Sadhu. *Journal of Business Ethics, 17*(1), 25–38. doi:10.1023/A:1017912300819

Meara, N. M., Schmidt, L. D., & Day, J. D. (1996). Principles and Virtues: A Foundation for Ethical Decisions, Policies, and Character. *The Counseling Psychologist, 24*(1), 4–77. doi:10.1177/0011000096241002

Mintz, S. M. (1996). Aristotelian Virtue and Business Ethics Education. *Journal of Business Ethics, 15*(8), 827–838. doi:10.1007/BF00381851

Mitroff, I. I., & Denton, E. A. (1999). A Study of Spirituality in the Workplace. *Sloan Management Review*, (Summer), 83–92.

Murphy, P. (1999). Character and Virtue Ethics in International Marketing: An Agenda for Managers, Researchers and Educators. *Journal of Business Ethics, 18*(1), 107–124. doi:10.1023/A:1006072413165

Palmer, P. J. (1983). *To Know as We are Known: Education As a Spiritual Journey*. Harper San Francisco: HarperCollins Publishers.

Palmer, P. J. (1989). *The Courage to Teach: Exploring the Inner Landscape of A Teacher's Life*. San Francisco: Jossey-Bass Publishers.

Peterson, E. H. (2003). Missing Ingredient: Why Spirituality Needs Jesus. *Christian Century (Chicago, Ill.)*, (March): 22, 30–33.

Prince, H. (2004). *A Wesleyan Way* (revised edition). San Diego, California: Point Loma Press.

Rampel, H. (2003). *A High Price for Abundant Living-The Story of Capitalism*. Waterloo, Ontario: Herald Press.

Samuel. (1992). Religious Roots and Business Practices: Vignettes from Life. In A Virtuous Life in Business: Stories of Courage and Integrity in the Corporate World (pp. 73-90). Academic Press.

Thompson, M. (2002). Marketing Virtue. *Business Ethics: An European Review*, *11*(4), 354–362. doi:10.1111/1467-8608.00295

United Nations. (2007). *Toward a Culture of Peace*. Retrieved 22 July 2015 from: http://www.un.org/en/ga/search/view_doc.asp?symbol=A/52/191&Lang=E

United Nations Education, Scientific and Cultural Organization (UNESCO). (2015). Retrieved 20 July 2015 from: http://en.unesco.org/about-us/introducing-unesco

United Nations Human Right. (2015). Retrieved 20 July 2015 from: http://www.ohchr.org/EN/UDHR/Pages/Introduction.aspx

Vaill, P. (1996). *Learning as a Way of Being: Strategies for Survival in a World of Permanent White Water*. San Francisco: Jossey-Bass Publishers.

Vaill, P. (1998). *Spirited leading and learning*. San Francisco: Jossey-Bass Publishers.

Wadlock, S., & Lozano, J. (2013). Developing more holistic management education: Lessons learned from two programs. *Academy of Management Learning & Education*, *12*(2), 265–284. doi:10.5465/amle.2012.0002

Walton, C. (1988). *The Moral Manager*. Ballinger Publishing Company.

Williams, O. F., & Murphy, P. E. (1990). The Ethics of Virtue: A Moral Theory for Marketing. *Journal of Macromarketing*, *10*(2), 19–29. doi:10.1177/027614679001000103

Winstanley, Clark & Lesson. (2002). Approaches to Child Labor in the Supply Chain. *Business Ethics: An European Review, 11*(3), 210-223.

Wolterstorff, N. (2002). *Educating for Life: Reflections on Christian Teaching and Learning* (G. G. Stronks & C. W. Joldersma, Eds.). Grand Rapids, MI: Baker Academic.

Wood, J. (1999). *Christians at Work: Not Business as Usual*. Scottsdale, PA: Herald Press.

Worthy, J. (1958). Religion and Its Role in the World of Business. *The Journal of Business*, *31*(4), 293–303. doi:10.1086/294216

ENDNOTES

[1] According to the American Marketing Association, marketing is the process of planning and executing the conception, pricing, promotion, and distribution of ideas, goods and services to create exchanges that satisfy individual and organization objectives (Kerin, Berkowitz, Hartley, Rudelius 2003:9).

[2] Bible verses are from the King James Version.

[3] Source of scenarios: Jim Fisher, David Taylor And Sam Fullerton (1999) "Attitudes toward consumer and business ethics among Canadian And new Zealand business students: An assessment of 28 scenarios," *Teaching Business Ethics 3:* 155–177, 1999. © 1999 Kluwer Academic Publishers. Printed in the Netherlands.

[4] Chewning, Richard C. and Delia Haak (2002), Integration Reinforced Through Apologetics: Two Case Illustrations. JBIB, 53-68.

[5] The version of Bible is New Revised Standard Version.

[6] Karns, G. (2002) Faith-Learning Integration Exercise: Marketing Principles in the Book of Acts, JBIB

[7] Surdyk, Lisa Klein (2002), "God's Economy: Teaching Students Key Biblical Principles", JBIB, 69-98.

APPENDIX 1: FIRST ASSIGNMENT OF BASIC MARKETING

The objective of the first assignment is to help us to reflect who we are and to be oriented to be wiser and more virtuous in the coming classes. Please go to www.Ohiolink.edu and to access these two articles

Article 1: Murphy, Patrick (1999), "Character and Virtue Ethics in International Marketing: An Agenda for Managers, Researchers and Educators." *Journal of Business Ethics* (18):107-124.
Article 2: Thompson, Mike (2002), "Marketing Virtue," *Business Ethics: An European Review*, Volume 11, Number 4,:354-362.

Each student has to submit a *Three* to *Four* page typed, double spaced *essay* and answer ALL questions.

1. What do you learn from these two articles? What ideas are related to moral character or virtues of decision makers? Why? (40%)
2. Will professional code of ethics (e.g. industry code of ethics, American Marketing Association code of ethics) improve ethical conduct in marketing activities? Why or Why not? (20%) (** Please read some examples of ethical codes: www.airforwarders.org/marapr98/stan.html. Standards of Conduct of the Air Forwarders Association, Alexandria, Virginia. www.isaca.org/standard/code2.htm. Code of Professional Ethics for the Information Systems Audit and Control Association, Rolling Meadows, Illinois. www.ncmpr.org/abo/ethics.html. Code of Ethics of the National Council for Marketing and Public Relations, Greeley, Colorado. Centre for the Study of Ethics in the Professions (www.iit.edu/departments/csep) contains hundred of codes of ethics online.)
3. Please describe the key characteristics of the most admired manager in your previous or present working organization. Please describe the key characteristics of the least admired manager in the organization. (10%)
4. What kinds of moral person would you like to be in the coming five years? What kind of organization would you like to work in the coming five years? What kinds of character traits or virtues do you need to cultivate if you like to be successful in your professional career in the coming five years? What kinds of character traits or virtues do you like to teach young generation? What are authentic moral truth in the relationships between an organization and customers? (Please consult career service officers, coacher, mentors or pastors in the church) (30%)

APPENDIX 2: CONSUMER BEHAVIOR FIRST ASSIGNMENT

The objective of the first assignment is to help us to reflect who we are and to be oriented to be wiser and more virtuous in the coming classes.
Each student has to submit a *Three* to *Four* page typed, double spaced *essay* and answer ALL questions.

1. What do you learn from the article? (Roy F. Baumeiste (2002), "Yielding to Temptation: Self Control Failure, Impulsive Purchasing, and Consumer Behavior" Journal of Consumer Research, Vol. 28, 670-676. What ideas are related to moral character or virtues of persons? Why? (20%)

2.	Please reflect what kinds of consumption experience make you happier and what are the reasons behind your happiness? For example, try to reflect what things you owned/disposed make you happier and then tell us why you feel happier. Try to reflect what good things you are seeking for in your life.

	Please explain how your regional, ethnic, religious, social class, age, gender and reference groups influences your consumer behavior and your ways of seeking happiness through consumption (20%)

3.	Please reflect one instance you feel meaningless in your life during or after your consumption. What is this? Why is the outcome out of your expectation? (10%)

4.	What is the relationships between materialistic value and well-being value? Is there any conflict between materialistic value and well-being value? Do you perceive that our life will be better as we have more things in our life? Do you think that what we own determines who we are? Please explain your rationale. (20%)

5.	Would you buy any product made by child labor? Would you try to stop to consume any Nike product when the company is found to have unethical business practices? Please explain your rationality? (10%)

6.	What are the characteristics of moral consumers? (10%)

7.	What kinds of moral person would you like to be in the coming five years? What kinds of virtues do you need to cultivate if you like to have good lives in the coming five years? What kinds of character traits or virtues do you like to teach young generation? (10%)

APPENDIX 3: FIRST ASSIGNMENT ON GRADUATE MARKETING MANAGEMENT AND STRATEGY

The objective of the first assignment is to help us to reflect who we are and to be oriented to be wiser and more virtuous in the coming classes. Our discussion will be more fruitful because of your work. Each student has to submit a FIVE to SIX page typed, double spaced essay and answer the following questions. Please contemplate your business practices and discover authentic moral truth in the marketing activities. You will be inspired if you read these reference articles listed in our first class. Please look up these articles through Malone Library Electronic Journal section.

1.	Do you perceive that you are doing marketing activities in your company? What is the relationship between your work and customers' satisfaction? Do you perceive that you are supported by a good system when you try to deliver best service to your customers? Why or why not? Explain your rational.

2.	Does your company have code of ethics statement? What are key virtues listed (e.g. integrity, honesty, trust) in the code of ethics statement? How do these virtues relate to customers' satisfaction? Do you have faith in the statement? Why or Why not? If your company does not have code of ethics statement, does your company have mission statement? Do you have faith in the mission statement? Why or Why not?

3.	Will professional code of ethics (e.g. industry code of ethics, American Marketing Association code of ethics) improve ethical conduct in marketing activities? Why or Why not?

4. Please describe the key characteristics of the most admired manager in your working organization. Please describe the key characteristics of the least admired manager in your organization. What kinds of character traits or virtues do you need to cultivate if you like to be successful in your organization? What kinds of character traits or virtues do you like to teach your colleagues?

5. Please think of particular decision you have made in your organization.
    a. What is the role of your personal conscience in your business decision making?
    b. What is the role of the law and corporate policy in framing your ethical business decision making?
    c. Does the marketplace exert its own ethics in your business? (Does market punish bad business practices?)
    d. What do your company's customers expect from your company? Is the "ethical gap" between your company's marketers and customers widening or narrowing? Is your company concerned about the differences in the ethical standard between marketers and customers? Why or why not?

6. What kind of moral person would you like to be in the coming five years? What kind of organization would you like to work in the coming five years? What are authentic moral truth in the relationships between an organization and customers?

APPENDIX 4: REFLECTION ASSIGNMENT

Please think about the following questions and think about *your practices in the course and the classroom*. You don't need to hand the sheet to me. The objective is to help you to reflect on your learning and prepare for your final paper.

1. What is the meaning of Integrity, Fairness, Trust, Respect, and Empathy to you? Please write it down clearly.

2. Do you have moral courage (i.e., to act in accordance with basic values such as honesty, respect for each other, fairness, trust)? What arc your problems?

3. Do you plan to cultivate some virtues in this course? What are these? What do you feel when you do not practice these virtues? Do you try to suppress your conscience by taking some defensive action? What mental activities do you need to keep your moral fitness?

4. Do you think that you have developed better abilities to create a community of learning, a sense of solidarity, and a more meaningful existence for everybody in the classroom? Why or why not?

APPENDIX 5: CONSUMER ETHICS AND BUSINESS ETHICS SCENARIO

Your Moral Reasoning of following customers ethics and business ethics scenarios. Please list scenarios are morally acceptable and morally unacceptable. Please write down your reasons.

A. List which scenarios are morally acceptable.
    Scenario_____
    Your Reason:_____

Scenario____

Your Reason:_____

Scenario____

Your Reason:_____

Scenario____

Your Reason:_____

Scenario____

Your Reason:_____

B.   List which scenarios are morally unacceptable

Scenario____ Your Reason:_____

Scenario____ Your Reason:_____

Scenario____ Your Reason:_____

Scenario____ Your Reason:_____

Scenario____ Your Reason:_____

Consumer Ethics Scenarios[3]

1.   A co-worker was given too much change from the shop assistant at the corner dairy and kept it.

2.   A friend had a fire at his apartment. In reporting the losses to the insurance company, your friend included items he never owned and inflated the value of items that were lost.

3.   You have seen other people misrepresent their age to take advantage of a senior citizen discount.

4.   You have seen other people misrepresent their children's ages to take advantage of a child's discount.

5.   A friend of yours finds an item that was obviously mismarked at a cheaper price. Rather than notifying the store, your friend purchased the product at the incorrect price.

6.   Some people will go to a retailer to get information on a specific product and then use this information to purchase this product from a less expensive source (i.e. a catalog).

7.   Some people will go to the same store repeatedly in order to take advantage of an offer which limits the amount that can be purchased per visit.

8.   Someone you know has sold a frequent flier ticket to a friend despite specific airline rules which prohibit such a sale.

9.   Through the grapevine, you hear that a neighbor returned a product to a store where it was not purchased.

10.   Someone went to purchase a television set and in order to get a better deal, told the salesperson that another retailer was selling the same set at much cheaper price. The retailer, without checking, matched the lower price.

11.   At the supermarket, the person in front of you redeems coupons for items that were not purchased.

12.   In order to sell an item at their garage sale, your neighbors exaggerated the item's quality.

13.   People you know have been less than truthful on surveys.

14.   Friends of yours have purchased clothing. After wearing the clothing, they see it at another shop for a substantially lower price. They return the original purchase and buy the clothing at the store offering the lower price.

Business Ethics Scenarios

15. A manufacturer agrees to supply a retailer with a desirable product. In return for a guarantee of a large initial purchase by the retailer, the manufacturer agrees not to sell to any other retailers within that trade area.

16. A retailer advertised a portable, name-branded color television for $199. When the customers arrived at the store, they found that the retailer had sold out of the bargain television. An attempt was then made to sell the customer a more expensive television.

17. Supply and demand dictate prices in the marketplace. After a recent hurricane in Florida and an earthquake in Los Angeles, many stores were closed. With the supply of many products down and demand up, many prices rose substantially. Prices on some products were three to eight times their normal price. Retailers argued that price is a function of economic conditions and refused to lower their prices.

18. A grocery chain has shops both in a wealthy suburb and a poor suburb with high incidence of crime. Insurance premiums, vandalism, and theft make it more expensive to operate in the poorer area. These expenses are passed on to the customers. As a result, customers in the poorer suburb pay more for identical products than their wealthier counterparts pay.

19. People have a great admiration for sports heroes. A marketer often uses these athletes to endorse products because of the belief that such an endorsement will increase the demand for those products.

20. A company has developed a new product which will render one of its old products obsolete. The company has a large inventory of the old products so it delays the introduction of the new technology until it has sold off the existing stock of the old product.

21. A manufacturer has a large stock of products which have been sold in Canada for several years. The government has recently ruled that the product is unsafe and required its recall from Canadian shops. Rather than discard the old product, it is exported and sold in countries which don't have such strict regulations on product safety. The manufacturer argues that this action is good for the company's shareholders and the Canadian economy.

22. A real estate agency sells a desirable house in a nice neighborhood. The agency does not put up a "SOLD" sign because they want people to continue to call. When potential buyers do call, they are informed that the house is sold and informed as to the availability of other houses listed by the agency.

23. A manufacturer does business in several countries. In allocating expenses to the various international operations, it is a common practice to assign higher costs in countries with high tax rates. As a result, the facilities that are located in low tax countries show larger profits. The net result is that the manufacturer reduces its total tax liability by "shifting" profits to low tax countries.

24. A Canadian doctor believes that a particular experimental pharmaceutical product could benefit some of his patients. The drug is illegal in Canada because it has not been certified by the government. It is legal and readily available in the United States. The doctor acquires a supply of the product in the US and smuggles it into Canada. He then distributes it to his patients.

25. A company advertises a 900 number for children to call and talk to Santa Claus. The call is ninety-nine cents a minute and the advertiser tells children to ask their parents before phoning Santa.

26. In order to hold down the costs of manufacturing a product, a company has shifted part of the production from Canada to a plant in Mexico. The lower labor cost results in lower prices to consumers.

27. A company advertises its product on television by giving the brand name of a competing product and indicating a particular issue where its product is considered to be superior to the competing product.

28. A retailer of men's and women's clothing raised its prices two weeks ago. Today, prices were dropped to their former level and the retailer is advertising its "sale" prices.

APPENDIX 6: FOOD FOR THOUGHT[4]

Intentions/Motives

I Corinthians 4:5[5] Therefore judge nothing before the appointed time; wait till the Lord comes. He will bring to light what is hidden in darkness and will expose the motives of men's hearts. At that time each will receive his praise from God.

II Corinthians 5:12 We are not trying to commend ourselves to you again, but are giving you an opportunity to take pride in us, so that you can answer those who take pride in what is seen rather than in what is in the heart.

Hebrews 4:13 Nothing in all creation is hidden from God's sight. Everything is uncovered and laid bare before the eyes of him to whom we must give account.

I Kings 8:39-40 then hear from heaven, your dwelling place. Forgive and act; deal with each man according to all he does, since you know his heart (for you alone know the hearts of all men), so that they will fear you all the time they live in the land you gave our fathers.

Psalm 139: 1-4 O Lord, you have searched me and you know me. You know when I sit and when I rise; you perceive my thoughts from afar. You discern my going out and my lying down; you are familiar with all my ways. Before a word is on my tongue you know it completely, O Lord.

Jeremiah 17:9-10 The heart is deceitful above all things and beyond cure. Who can understand it? 'I the Lord search the heart and examine the mind, to reward a man according to his conduct, according to what his deeds deserve.'

Deception/Falsehood

Job 36:4 Be assured that my words are not false; one perfect in knowledge is with you.

Psalm 5:6 You destroy those who tell lies; bloodthirsty and deceitful men the Lord abhors.

Psalm 12:2 Everyone lies to his neighbor; their flattering lips speak with deception.

Ephesians 4:25 Therefore each of you must put off falsehood and speak truthfully to his neighbor, for we are all members of one body.

Colossians 3:9 Do not lie to each other, since you have taken off your old self with its practices

Revelation 21:8 But the cowardly, the unbelieving, the vile, the murderers, the sexually immoral, those who practice magic arts, the idolaters and all liars--their place will be in the fiery lake of burning sulfur. This is the second death.

Integrity

Proverbs 19:1 Better a poor man whose walk is blameless than a fool whose lips are perverse.

Isaiah 33:15 He who walks righteously and speaks what is right, who rejects gain from extortion and keeps his hand from accepting bribes, who stops his ears against plots of murder and shuts his eyes against contemplating evil

Ezekiel 18:5-9 "Suppose there is a righteous man who does what is just and right. He does not eat at the mountain shrines or look to the idols of the house of Israel. He does not defile his neighbor's wife or lie with a woman during her period. He does not oppress anyone, but returns what he took in pledge for a loan. He does not commit robbery but gives his food to the hungry and provides clothing for the naked. He does not lend at usury or take excessive interest. He withholds his hand from doing wrong and judges fairly between man and man. He follows my decrees and faithfully keeps my laws. That man is righteous; he will surely live, declares the Sovereign Lord."

Luke 6:31 Do to others as you would have them do to you.

Luke 16:10 Whoever can be trusted with very little can also be trusted with much, and whoever is dishonest with very little will also be dishonest with much.

II Corinthians 4:2 Rather, we have renounced secret and shameful ways; we do not use deception, nor do we distort the word of God. On the contrary, by setting forth the truth plainly we commend ourselves to every man's conscience in the sight of God.

Presumption

Proverbs 13:10 Pride only breeds quarrels, but wisdom is found in those who take advice.

Proverbs 18:12-13 Before his downfall a man's heart is proud, but humility comes before honor. He who answers before listening—that is his folly and his shame.

James 4:13-16 Now listen, you who say, "Today or tomorrow we will go to this or that city, spend a year there, carry on business and make money." Why, you do not even know what will happen tomorrow. What is your life? You are a mist that appears for a little while and then vanishes. Instead, you ought to say, "If it is the Lord's will, we will live and do this or that." As it is, you boast and brag. All such boasting is evil.

II Peter 1:4-11 (v. 10) Through these he has given us his very great and precious promises, so that through them you may participate in the divine nature and escape the corruption in the world caused by evil desires. For this very reason, make every effort to add to your faith goodness; and to goodness, knowledge; and to knowledge, self-control; and to self-control, perseverance; and to perseverance, godliness; and to godliness, brotherly kindness; and to brotherly kindness, love. For if you possess these qualities in increasing measure, they will keep you from being ineffective and unproductive in your knowledge of our Lord Jesus Christ. But if anyone does not have them, he is nearsighted and blind, and has forgotten that he has been cleansed from his past sins. Therefore, my brothers, be all the more eager to make your calling and election sure. For if you do these things, you will never fall, and you will receive a rich welcome into the eternal kingdom of our Lord and Savior Jesus Christ.

Luke 12:18 Then he said, 'This is what I'll do. I will tear down my barns and build bigger ones, and there I will store all my grain and my goods.'

Seeking to Please God, Not Men

John 5:41-44 I do not accept praise from men, but I know you. I know that you do not have the love of God in your hearts. I have come in my Father's name, and you do not accept me; but if someone else comes in his own name, you will accept him. How can you believe if you accept praise from one another, yet make no effort to obtain the praise that comes from the only God?

Romans 2:29 No, a man is a Jew if he is one inwardly; and circumcision is circumcision of the heart, by the Spirit, not by the written code. Such a man's praise is not from men, but from God.

II Corinthians 10:18 For it is not the man who commends himself who is approved, but the man whom the Lord commends.

Hebrews 11:24-26 By faith Moses, when he had grown up, refused to be known as the son of Pharaoh's daughter. He chose to be mistreated along with the people of God rather than to enjoy the pleasures of sin for a short time. He regarded disgrace for the sake of Christ as of greater value than the treasures of Egypt, because he was looking ahead to his reward.

APPENDIX 7: MARKETING PRINCIPLES AT WORK IN THE BOOK OF ACTS[6]

The objective of the examination is to discuss the use of marketing by early church fathers and explore the legitimacy and moral limitations of using marketing principles to explain the growth of the early church. Please connect several key marketing principles when you study the Book of Acts

Each student has to submit a <u>seven to nine-page essays</u> and answer the following questions: Please support your reasoning with relevant scriptures.

1. What was the mission of the early church? What is the mission of today's church (See Mathew 28: 19-20; Luke 24: 45-49)
2. What was the Strength, Weakness, Opportunity, Threat of the early Church? (see Acts 2:5-12; 4:29-31; 6:11-14; 8:1-5; 9:15;13:44-47; 18:5-11; 19:23-27)
3. What was the church's primary goals? What was the core marketing strategies? (see Acts 1:8; 13:4; 13:14; 16:9-10; 17:16-23; 19:8-10.)
4. Who were the target markets of the early church? (see Acts 8:1-5; 10:1-3; 10:27-29; 10:34-48; 11:19-24; 13:4; 13:14; 16;9-10; 17:2-3; 20: 17-24; 23:11; 28:17-31)
5. What was the positioning of the early church compared to Judaism, Greco-Roman polytheism, and atheism? What values did the early church provided to people? (see Acts 4:12; 5:30-31)
6. What were these marketing mix? For example, what benefits did they get from accepting Christ and joining the church (product)? What price did they have to pay? What were the church's communication goals? What was the message? How was persuasion attempted? How did the church get its message out? How did the church make itself available to people (distribution)? (See Acts 2:29-41; 2: 46-47; 3:6-16; 4:12-21; 5:7-11; 5:19-20; 5:32; 5:42; 9:32; 15:22-29; 17:2-3; 17:16-32; 19:11-20; 28:17-31.)
7. What criteria were used to evaluate the church's effectiveness? How effective was the church's strategy? Why?
8. What lessons have you learned in the applying marketing principals in the Book of Acts? For example, is marketing inherently un-Christian or is there some legitimacy for it, even among Christians? Why? What are some limitations that should be put around it?

What lessons about contemporary church marketing efforts can be learned from this account of the establishment and spread of the early church? In what ways should church marketing differ from the marketing plans and activities for "secular" goods and services? Are relationships with God and with a local church best understood as exchange relationships?

APPENDIX 8:[7] BIBLICAL PERSPECTIVES ON WORK, STEWARDSHIP, POVERTY, MATERIALISM

1. **Biblical Perspectives on Work:** Read and reflect on Genesis 2:1-17, Genesis 3, Exodus 20:8-11, Exodus 16:23-30, Deuteronomy 5:12-15, Proverbs 10:4, Proverbs 23:4-5, Ecclesiastes 5:8-20, Mark 2:23-3:5, Hebrews 4:9-11, Colossians 3:22-4:1, and perhaps other passages we have discussed

about work and Sabbath rests. Answer the following questions, making reference to at least *three* of the specified bible passages.

   a.   What are the purposes of the Sabbath day observance? (10 points)
   b.   Why do people work? (10 points)
   c.   What are the benefits of working? (10 points)
   d.   Why is work hard sometimes? What is hard about the work you do?(10 points)
   e.   What brings you joy or satisfaction in the work you do? Explain. (10 points)
   f.   What values and attitudes should guide our work (for pay, at home, at school, etc.)? What does it mean in the Colossians 3 passage to work "for the Lord, not for men"? Explain. (10 points)
   g.   How are the biblical principles on work relevant to the life of a business profession? (40 points)

2. **Biblical Perspectives on Stewardship:** Read and reflect on Genesis 2, Exodus 16, Deuteronomy 8:6-18, Deuteronomy 15:1-15, Psalm 24:1-2, Matthew 6:19-34, and perhaps other passages we have discussed about stewardship. Answer the following questions, making reference to at least three of the specified bible passages.
   a.   What does it mean to be a steward? (10 points)
   b.   What Bible passages speak about God's ownership of all resources? (10)
   c.   Describe evidence from the Bible that God provides "enough" resources for people. (10)
   d.   How does God want people to use and care for God's resources? (10)
   e.   How are biblical perspectives on stewardship relevant to the work of a manager? (60 points)

3. **Biblical Perspectives on Poverty/Economic Injustice:** Read and reflect on Leviticus 25:1-43, Deuteronomy 15:1-15, Psalm 72, Proverbs 22:22-23, Isaiah 1:10-23, Acts 4:32-37, and perhaps other Bible passages we have discussed in class that deal with poverty or economic injustice. Answer the following questions, making reference to at least three of the specified Bible passages.
   a.   How do you define poverty? Explain.
   b.   What Bible passages indicate that God has a special concern for poor persons?
   c.   How are God's people expected to treat poor persons?
   d.   What are consumption behavior of the poor?
   e.   What are ways marketers can or do get in touch with poor persons?
   f.   How can we improve the life quality of the poor through marketing activities?
   g.   How are biblical perspectives on poverty relevant to your life or in our society today?

4. **Biblical Perspectives on Materialism:** Read and reflect on Proverbs 11:24-26, 23:4-5, and 30:7-9, Ecclesiastes 5:8-20, Matthew 6:19-34, Luke 12:13-21, Luke 19:1-10, Acts 4:32-37, 1 Timothy 6:6-19, and perhaps other passages we have discussed which deal with material wealth. Answer the following questions, making reference to at least three of the specific Bible passages.
   a.   In your view, in what ways do people store up treasure on earth?
   b.   In what ways can we store up treasure in heaven, do you think?
   c.   How does excessive worry about material possession affect people?
   d.   In what way(s) the love of money "a root of all kinds of evil" (1 Timothy 6:10)?
   e.   What is the proper attitude to have towards material wealth?
   f.   What responsibilities do people have in using their wealth?

g.   How do biblical perspectives on materialism relate to conspicuous consumption and impulsive consumption behavior?

h.   What are the relationships between biblical perspectives on materialism and moral complexity of consumption behavior ? (please refer to the articles, "Moral complexion of consumption," "Yielding to Temptation: Self-control failure, Impulsive Purchasing, and Consumer Behavior.")

i.   How are the biblical perspectives on materialism relevant to your life or society today?

Chapter 14
Promoting Effective Learning in Diverse Classrooms

Amir Manzoor
Bahria University, Pakistan

ABSTRACT

Cultural diversity in society, the workplace and classrooms is more or less is a global phenomenon. The multi-cultural classroom provides an opportunity for students from different cultures to bring their enormous range of experiences, knowledge, perspectives and insights to the learning – if the process is enabled. Many firms around the globe are expanding their businesses beyond domestic markets. These trends indicate that many individuals are likely to study or work in multicultural environments domestically and abroad. Research suggests that faculty and trainers adapt their teaching style and classroom policies to accommodate multicultural learners. Disconnections may arise, however, regarding the willingness to include these accommodations. This chapter explores various issues which faculty and students face regarding adjustments in teaching style, content, and policies to adapt to multicultural learners. Specific recommendations to meet the challenges of multicultural learning are also provided.

INTRODUCTION

According to Nahal (2005), a classroom where both faculty and students could benefit from each other's cultural experiences is the best classroom. Globalization is a reality for businesses and institutions of higher education. During 19090s, it was established that team compositions within organizations become more diverse and team diversity was expected to increase further in years to come (Triandis, Kurowski, & Gelfand, 1994). A concurrent trend of classrooms becoming more culturally diverse or multicultural is evident within universities in many developed western countries (such as Australia, the UK, Canada and the USA). The Association to Advance Collegiate Schools of Business (AACSB) stated that 5.1% (around 43,700) business schools undergraduates in the U.S. in 2009-2010 were international students. This number represented an increase of approximately 2% from 2005 (AACSB, 2011). The U.S. enrolled a record-breaking number of international students during the 2013-2014 school year, welcoming 886,052 undergraduates and graduate students at colleges and universities throughout the country. International

DOI: 10.4018/978-1-4666-9784-3.ch014

students from China, India and South Korea now represent roughly 50% of all international students in the U.S. (Haynie, 2014). The U.S. Bureau of Labor Statistics research showed that foreign-born workers increased from 14.8% in 2005 to 15.3% in 2006 (Bureau of Labor Statistics, 2007). In 2014, there were 25.7 million foreign-born persons in the U.S. labor force, comprising 16.5% of the total (Bureau of Labor Statistics, 2015). In 2007, international students represented approximately 17.3% (around 36,500 students) of the total population of Australian university students (IDP Education, 2010). In May of 2015, the total number of international students in Australian universities increased to approximately 63,000 (Department of Education and Training, 2015). In UK universities, in 2007-8, 15% of the total population of UK university students (around 341,795 students) were international students (UK Council for International Student Affairs, 2010). Around 18% of all students, in UK higher education came from other countries in 2012-13 (Gil, 2014). In 2008-9, 7% of total national undergraduate population in Canada comprised of international students (Association of Universities and Colleges of Canada, 2010). The number of international students in Canada has increased by 84% over the last decade, growing 22.8% from 2011 to 2013 and 11% from 2012 to 2013 (ICEF Monitor, 2014). In 2010, business faculties in these four countries had the highest percentage of international students (IDP Education, 2010; UK Council for International Student Affairs, 2010). In various business classes, students from diverse cultural backgrounds are required to participate in group projects and group-based assessment.

Many firms around the globe are expanding their businesses beyond domestic markets. Consequently, business schools and organizations overall are becoming increasingly multicultural. More and more individuals are expected to study or work in multicultural environments domestically and abroad as expatriates. Business savvy people are cognizant that employees can have multicultural experiences that are global in scope while remaining in their home country. Around the globe, we see an increasing number of international students on business programs in universities. These students belong to a diverse range of countries and for many of them English is not the first language. For these students, the experience of tertiary education at a foreign university is very different. This situation brings many challenges for the faculty teaching large classroom with a student body that comprises of both local and foreign students. It is anticipated that the existing cohort of domestic and international students will continue to grow in both size and diversity.

Countries around the world (such as UK, USA, Germany, and France) are internationalizing the tertiary education bringing more and more international students to the classrooms. This increasing mix of domestic and foreign students in the classrooms is beneficial for the host countries because foreign education is a big business. In USA, foreign education is the fifth largest services export (Marginson 2002). The communities in many of these preferred countries for foreign education are culturally diverse but the Anglo-American content of their tertiary education doesn't take into account this cultural diversity. Most institutions continue to provide mono-cultural higher education. Such system of higher education is not in a position to address the unique challenges of teaching and learning of large and culturally diverse classrooms.

Many international students are willing to adapt to the new learning styles of the host foreign countries. However, unfamiliarity with the process used to facilitate their learning is one big obstacle in their learning (Pincas, 2001). The classrooms of tertiary educational institutions in these host countries use a wide array of western teaching and learning strategies. These strategies (such as case analysis, group-based learning, critical analysis etc.) are based on the concept of active participation of students. Many international students are unfamiliar with this concept. Their expectations are largely founded on educational practices of their own countries which greatly vary from the educational practices in western countries. As a result, international students are unable to effectively take part in active learning and unable to learn whatever is offered to them.

Diverse classrooms can be beneficial due to many reasons. Besides providing an additional source of revenue for their host institutions, they are also a mean of sharing knowledge and perspectives that is essential for success in today's global business. These classrooms also offer numerous opportunities for intercultural understanding and skills development. Still, cultural engagement of various host foreign educational institutions is uni-directional where local students expect international students to adapt their culture and not vice versa (Marginson, 2002). Many overseas students spend time with the students who speak the same language or come from the same culture. As such they may learn about the business practices of their host countries but don't gain any practical insight. This uni-directional cultural engagement poses many implementation challenges for the faculty tasked with facilitating effective teaching and learning in diverse classrooms.

Effective teaching in a diverse classroom requires faculty to adapt their pedagogy to advance the learning of multicultural students (Clark & Stewart, 2009). Here the word 'multicultural' means a non-native learner, student, and the training participant, who is enrolled in business schools or working for organizations that engage in international business. Faculty and trainers may be inclined to make curricula and pedagogical changes used to teach multicultural learners. According to Ghemawat (2003) and Ghemawat (2008), the world is semi-globalized and semi-globalization acknowledges differences that exist between different countries. According to Ghemawat (2003) and Ghemawat (2008), cultural differences are distinctive rather than standardized for all countries. Business education should emphasize the significant differences that exist from one country to another. Business schools should examine their curriculum and systematically make changes to develop courses that integrate the notion of semi-globalization. This would encourage learners to take into account cultural differences specific to each country and ultimately to think globally.

Looking at this issue from an application perspective, Thatcher (2010) doesn't agree with the traditional definition of globalization provided by many contemporary theories of globalization. These theories define globalization as a significant amount of cultural blending, hybridization, Glocalization, and cross-border flow of rhetorical and cultural patterns with geopolitical borders relatively meaningless. According to Thatcher, the relevance of geo-political borders in globalization cannot be discounted. Multicultural learning is challenging and cultural fluency is not simply produced by language fluency (Beamer, 1992; St. Amant, 2002; Thrush, 1993). The flow of the learning, both from and to the instructor and student, also sets up a complex dynamic. Ghemewat (2008) emphasized that business school faculty who teaches multicultural learners is in a unique position to enrich the educational experience of all. Ghemewat (2008) argues that in order to do so faculty need to gain invaluable information and knowledge about the home country and culture of multicultural learners.

Integration of globalization into the curriculum is equally challenging. As Beamer and Varner (2008) pointed out that "in the past, many business majors and practitioners immersed in questions of financial forecasting, market studies, and management models did not examine the culture and the way it affects business" (p. ix). Ghemewat (2008) conducted a mixed method study that examined 77 highly rated US colleges and universities to ascertain the extent to which business schools integrated globalization into the content of courses in the graduate curriculum. The focus of the study was on business strategy courses that used the case study methodology to teaching MBA classes. Ghemewat (2008) found that 33% of the business strategy courses did not utilize cases set outside of the USA. Approximately 21% of the cases used featured businesses in Europe or Israel. According to Ghemawat (2008), the lack of focus on cross-cultural differences in business courses is due to two reasons. First the faculty lacks motivation to change the course content. Second, faculty are not convinced that significant differences exist across different countries. This suggests that the inclination of business faculty to teach or integrate cross-cultural content is important.

Faculty may be receptive to adapt their courses or teaching style to include a multicultural component. They can be made more approachable if they are provided training to do so. Clarke and Stewart (2009) described a training program designed and implemented at Xaiver University for business faculty. This program was designed to enhance faculty understanding of the best practices for multicultural learning and incorporation of these practices into their pedagogy. Faculty responded to the program. As Clark and Stewart, (2009) noted that after examining the unspoken assumptions of their communication behaviors in and out of the classroom and reconsidering his classroom pedagogies through the eyes of students they felt committed to keeping up to date on trends in multiculturalism, so that their classes are responsive to the increasing diversity of students in the increasingly global business environment.

Woods et al., (2006) used data collected from the focus groups to develop a program meant to enhance the teaching skills of faculty who taught in multicultural classrooms. Improving the teaching competencies of the faculty served as the basis for an intensive training workshop for faculty and trainers. As Thatcher (2010) pointed out "global scholars must avoid using approaches that implicitly espouse U.S. or western cultural values, most notably individualism" (p. 6). Many researchers (Northedge, 2003; Witte, Sequeira, & Fonteyne, 2003) agree to understand this concept and its link to the creation of training programs for faculty to encourage faculty members to be cognizant of the way they teach in multicultural classrooms. A by-product of the training was to improve teacher-student interactions for international and domestic students. According to Cardon (2010), faculty and trainers "inevitably face the challenge of providing cross-cultural experiences in the classroom, and students are eager to have real exposure to other cultures" (p. 150).

Scott (2010) cited the example of teaching exercises about ethnocentrism and noted that "despite many claims that such activities are valuable, there are relatively few sources that mention specific exercises that might be incorporated into classrooms" (p. 82). Woods et al. (2006) noted multiple limitations of training and supporting resources aimed at addressing specific challenges faced by instructors in multicultural classrooms. Woods et al. (2006) noted that these training and supporting resources were developed to focus on different challenges such as non-participation of students from non-English speaking countries in classroom discussions, problems faced by faculty in grading written assignments submitted by students whose first language is not English, problems faced by faculty to apply concepts and examples that are framed within the cultural and business context of countries other than the U.S, and problems faced by faculty trying to engage students whose were not used to apply critical thinking or an analytical approach to learning.

According to Rhinesmith (1993), the dynamics of the global mindset emphasize a "predisposition to see the world in a particular way that sets boundaries and provides explanations for why things are the way they are, while at the same times establishing guidance for ways in which we should behave…a mindset is a filter through which we look at the world" (p. 24). Furthermore, Rhinesmith (1993) advocated that people with global mindsets "drive for the bigger, boarder picture, accept life as a balance of contradictory forces that are to be appreciated, pondered, and managed, trust process rather than structure to deal with the unexpected, value diversity and multicultural teamwork and play as the basic forum within which they accomplish their personal, professional, and organizational objectives, flow with change as opportunity and are comfortable with surprises and ambiguity, and continuously seek to be open to themselves and others by rethinking boundaries, finding new meanings, and changing their direction and behavior."(pp. 25-26).

Describing the importance of the global mindset, Gupta and Govindarajan (2002) describes it as "one that combines an openness to and awareness of diversity across cultures and markets with the propensity and ability to synthesis across this diversity" (p. 117). Hitt, Javidan, and Steers (2007) emphasized a global mindset and understanding of "a complex web of global interdependencies" (p. 2). Ghemawat (2011) argues that "global success requires that companies appreciate diversity and distance rather than seek to eliminate them" (p. 92). According to Dyer and Tarimcilar (2011), business educators are exploring "ways to increase the global IQ of their MBA students" (p. 47).

A culturally diverse classroom has students with multiple learning styles and preferences. With increasing cultural diversity in the classrooms, a fresh look is needed on the teaching and learning practices of the faculty to tailor them to the specific needs of culturally diverse classrooms. This is equally important due to the growing importance of the concept of globally responsible citizens. A globally responsible citizen is the one who has the knowledge, skills, attitudes and values required to succeed in the present global society. (Brownlie, 2001). The objective of this chapter is to explore the issues of diverse learning from the 'best practice' perspective and offer ideas to improve the teaching and learning in culturally diverse classrooms.

BENEFITS AND ISSUES OF DIVERSE CLASSROOMS

According to Levin (2005), a culturally diverse classroom in an institution of higher education provides students learning opportunities to assess, process and react to unfamiliar values and ideas. Such experience is highly regarded in the workplace both at the time of fresh employment or promotion. This positive regard for the value of multicultural class experience seems reciprocal. In a study of MBA students at two leading UK business schools, Robinson (2006) found that students regarded multicultural group work experience as good preparation for real-world multicultural organizations. According to Fowler, Gudmundsson, and Whicker (2006), group work in a culturally diverse classroom results in increased creativity in group decision making. Levin (2005) points out that group work provides better preparation for students to work in multicultural organizations. To reap the benefits of culturally diverse classrooms, cultural awareness among students is needed. Academicians need to identify and explore that attitudes that can facilitate effective group work. A structured approach to group process is needed that give students opportunity to develop intercultural skills. The faculty needs to define learning objectives that promote multicultural group work and align these learning objectives with their teaching and assessment methodologies.

Many issues can limit the effectiveness of diverse classrooms. While team-based learning theory provides guidance on improving the effectiveness of group work in management education, it is only possible if good team processes are in place (Michaelson, Peterson, & Sweet, 2009). Diverse multicultural classrooms can also intensify the level of difficulty in managing task-oriented groups (Strauss & U, 2007). Multicultural group work brings many challenges such as different learning attitudes and expectations, (Barker, Troth & Mak, 2002; Zepke & Leach, 2007; Nguyen, Terlouw, & Pilot, 2008), different cultural learning styles (i.e. passive vs. participative) (Nguyen et al., 2008; Holmes, 2004). According to Currie (2007), the issue of contrasting cultural learning styles can isolate those students who lack the ability to make their voice heard. Another problem is that group work outcomes and processes have different cultural expectations (Nguyen et al., 2008; Napier & Gershenfeld, 2004; Write & Drewery, 2006). Differing levels of language proficiencies are another problem where the first-language students are strongly positioned as compared with second-language foreign students (Holmes, 2004; Strauss & U, 2007). This issue may give rise to non-participation by the foreign students because they feel inferior (Nguyen et al., 2008). Many scholars (Triandis, 1971; Ajzen & Fishbein, 1980; Nesdale, 2000) have also identified learners attitude towards cultural differences as an issue and the importance of this issue has been established by other researchers as well (Bennett, 1986; Woods, 2004). According to Bennett (1986) and Woods (2004), for effective cross-cultural interactions, attentions should be paid to increasing levels of intercultural sensitivity and respect. Many researchers (Leiba-O'Sullivan, 1999; Oudenhoven, Zee, & Kooten, 2001; Oudenhoven, Mol, & Zee, 2003) have also identified personality as an issue for multicultural interactions. Personality, in a multicultural context, include attributes such as: emotional stability, extraversion, agreeableness, openness to experience and conscientiousness (Norman, 1963); cultural empathy, open-mindedness, emotional stability, social initiative and flexibility (Oudenhoven, Zee, & Kooten, 2001); and patience (Bishop et al., 2004; Woods, 2004).

Therefore, there exist a range of issues that need to be addressed for effective teaching and learning to occur in culturally diverse classrooms. All these issues may not be relevant in all situations. These issues include:

- **Personal Issues:** Personal issues arise because diverse classroom have students from many countries. These students may suffer from cultural shocks, home sickness, and stress.
- **Language Issues:** These issue are diverse and can range from common limited ability of foreign language to difficulties in understanding specific language/concepts. For faculty, these language challenges are important because of their direct impact on choice of words particularly the use of colloquial language. Faculty also face difficulty in understanding whether student problem is the language or inability. Contextual issues can make the language issues worse. A western faculty member teaching the concept of democracy actually refers to the western concept of democracy. This concept may differ from country to country. When foreign students are asked to write about democracy, they write according to the context of their home country.
- **Teaching and Learning Issues:** These issues arise because foreign students need more faculty time and preferably face-to-face contact to understand and learn why they couldn't in limited interactions/discussions in class. Although mixing of international and domestic students would provide integration it can also create free-riding problem where foreign students try to take advantage of domestic students. This problem is especially significant at undergraduate level. At post graduate level, foreign students are a resource of knowledge and experience to add professionally and culturally to the group. These foreign students are important because the emphasis of business education programs is to develop graduates with skills to manage global businesses. There could be another issue. Foreign students may not challenge the information given and rather try to find the right answer. This is because these students were trained in their home countries as the recipient of learning and not the active learners. They may have been trained to accept the teacher's "truth". Some cultures have very high regard for teachers and as such students do not challenge what they teacher says. It is also possible that students were not trained for critical analysis, oral presentations, participation, and debate skills in their home countries. These students may expect that the teacher will know the right answer and all they have to do is learn from it. As a result,

these students could face an expectation gap that should be filled by the faculty so that these foreign students are clear what is expected from them.

- **Support and Professional Development Issues:** Foreign students need support, both academically and socially, so that they don't feel isolated. Faculty should play an active role to guide foreign students about the student support services available. Foreign students also need more focused support for their professional development.

- **Group Dynamics and Individual Ability Issues:** Language difficulties and time pressures can make multicultural group work difficult. Faculty need patience and a sound strategy to overcome these difficulties. Some foreign students may lack language ability and appropriate academic foundation necessary to effectively participate in multicultural groups. Faculty should spot these lack of skills and come up with some strategies to overcome these shortcoming of students.

- **Contextual Knowledge Issues:** Foreign students many a times lack contextual knowledge and this can cause significant problems in both teaching and assessment. Both faculty and students may have problems in understanding each other. This lack of contextual knowledge by foreign students can restrict faculty's ability to cover the curriculum and increase the level of participation and discussion that occurs. Faculty is required to make repetitions and provide more explanations. Faculty also needs to be careful with respect to the choice of words and often are restrained to lowest level of student. Many a time, foreign students are passive learners and in order make them active learners faculty need to carefully choose learning resources and assessment strategies.

- **Attitudinal Issues:** In multicultural diverse classrooms, students need to respect each other's cultures. This respect is the basis for effective intercultural interactions. According to Woods 92004), respect for cultural others and their culture is vital to effective cross-cultural interactions. According to Trompenaars and Woolliams (2003), respect is the inner realization that individuals may interpret the same event or object differently, depending on their inner cultural perspective. As an attitude, cultural respect may vary based individual experiences and understanding. Cultural respect should be an outcome of the effective multicultural group work and teaching to increase intercultural understanding. As an attitude, cultural respect is difficult to develop in an isolated course in a university program. However, university courses can help develop this attitude through implementation of modules. Faculty can also model these attributed to help develop students' attitudes.

- **Personality Issues:** One important personality issue for effective multicultural interactions is patience towards other cultures. While this issue is not highlighted in western research literature but its importance in intercultural interactions is evident (Woods, 2004). People also need to open to the ideas of people belonging to different cultures in order develop effective multicultural interactions. Due to relative permanency of these two personality attributes, it is important for faculty to design courses in such a way that students develop these two personality attributes. Faculty support and guidance is required while students develop these two traits. In some cases, faculty may need to opt for alternative processes and assessment methods if some students are not able to change their personality. This is because forcing students to change their personality might work counterproductively.

- **Skills Issues:** Effective multicultural interactions require team work which is both a process and a skill. Being a good listener and building relationships are important. Faculty needs to select explicit group process interventions by discussing with students the type of activities and processes they feel could foster group work. The students and faculty should be clear about the effectiveness of the selected activities and processes for group work. It is important that students should be empowered to use these processes so that they could use them at their own in the future.

- **Knowledge Issues:** Students vary in their knowledge and understanding of different cultures and their attributes (norms, practices, values, communication styles etc.). This knowledge can help students in their preparation for effective multicultural group work and for work in global organizations. Faculty needs to understand that this knowledge is best gained when students learn from each other.

STRATEGIES FOR EFFECTIVE LEARNING IN DIVERSE CLASSROOMS

Now that we know the various issues involved in teaching diverse classroom, we need to identify teaching and learning strategies that can be used to encourage students' active participation and success in these classrooms. Following are some suggested strategies. It is important that these strategies should be employed right from the beginning of the course so that any difficulties of students coping up with these strategies could be identified earlier.

Avoid Stereotyping

It is important that both faculty and students should not stereotype each other with respect to knowledge, abilities, or perceived differences. It is very difficult to judge someone from his appearance.

Help and Support

Students should be encouraged to ask for help in case they face any difficulties in getting things done or settling in the new culture. Faculty should make efforts to know the interests of the students and develop teaching material that is relevant to all the students. Most foreign students use the knowledge gained in their home countries to learn new things. Faculty should accept that promote dialogue among domestic and foreign students where they seek knowledge of each other's culture and country. More specifically, students should discover how different things occur in their cultures. In these discussions, faculty should provide a context in which this discussion should be carried out and also ensure that every student has a shared understanding. Faculty should also provide students with handouts of things being discussed, along with a glossary of terms, in case sufficient time is not available to faculty to explain the context.

Make Explicit the Benefits of Diversity

To encourage multicultural interactions, it is imperative that students know the benefits of cultural diversity in interactions. This is faculty's responsibility to explain students why different activities of a course are important and what are the intended objective of different activities. Domestic students may be impatient with students who are not fluent in their home language. These students should be explained why their participation is important.

Good Classroom Communication

Many foreign students struggle to learn new language. As such, it is a good communication practice for faculty and domestic students to not use any jargon and slang words. This will help all students. Faculty should encourage students become active and genuine listeners and be patient to give everybody their due opportunity to express themselves. Faculty should prepare written material so that foreign students struggling to understand verbal discussions could be facilitated. Students can then clearly understand the instructions and effectively learn and participate in the classroom. In a discussion, faculty should share among students the feedback from different groups. This could also help them establish credibility of their answers. This would facilitate groups interrelate their ideas. It is best if this feedback is shared in writing. Students should be given appropriate time to work out answer of any question. Small work groups are often produce better results. In small groups, participants get enough time for interaction, sharing their thoughts, and manage any language issues. Faculty should also provide feedback to these small groups so they are better prepared when they work in large groups. To facilitate those having language problems, faculty should related the issue being discussed to some specific place in the textbook. This would help student establish the context.

Clear Instructions

Faculty should clearly explain the process of any participative activity and why it is important. In case of a group activity, there should be some clear questions to be answered. More specific requirements boost self-confidence of students and increase their willingness to participate.

Clear Expectations

Setting clear expectation would help faculty match their expectations with students' expectations. Faculty should clearly explain the assessment methodology. A clear marking scheme would help students learn from their mistakes and clearly understand what is expected from them. Any requirements of academic dishonesty (such as plagiarism) should be clearly explained.

Recognition of Age and Experience

The foreign students at post graduate levels not only provide another cultural perspective but also a source of professional experience and knowledge. As such, faculty should employ strategies to effectively utilize their knowledge and experience for the benefit of the whole class. To help these students, faculty should provide appropriate written material with glossary of terms. An audio book could be of great help. It is important because many times students understand the word when they read it but don't understand it when they hear it.

Use of Activities

Discussion groups around important content work well. A 'getting to know you activity' can help break the ice and encourage integration between different groups.

PRACTICAL/MANAGERIAL IMPLICATIONS AND RECOMMENDATIONS

Students can have a strong inclination to adjust semantics regarding verbal and written explanation, avoid using country-specific colloquialisms and idioms, and using international examples. There could be a sharp contrast to course content adjustments, which most faculty members may not incline to do so. A caution here is that some learners in the global training setting may actually request that faculty utilizes local idioms, such as the whole nine yards. This sports reference does not have world application, so it is likely that learners would want to be aware of it, since this and other idioms, particularly those related to sports, are frequently used in U.S. business contexts

Teaching process flexibility among faculty is a complex dynamic. Although some faculty may be prepared to be flexible, many may not incline to adjust assignments, in-class activities, or team assignments/ length of examinations. This limited flexibility could link to a disinclination for content adjustment, too. Faculty could use technology themselves and may allow its use during instruction and even in examinations. Faculty may also be inclined to adjust their communication behaviors (including rapport, feedback, and non-verbal communication). Faculty may adopt their actions so as to not be seen as behaving inappropriately.

For global instructional issues, such as being open to ambiguity and modifying expectations faculty should show a significant inclination to adjust. In this regard, the satisfaction level of training received to prepare teachers for multicultural student populations is important. Additional research may clarify the thrust of this need, including the challenges involved. Clarification might also indicate the type of training support that faculty desire.

The variation in adaptation and the inclination to do so may highlight unevenness in the pedagogical application of a multicultural perspective. This could specifically be dependent on the individual faculty member. There could be several possible interpretations of this. Some faculty adapt because they wish to reach their audiences effectively while others may have personal experience with traveling abroad where they experienced first-hand the need for cultural adaption. Conversely, some faculty may be threatened by what they do not understand. Faculty may erroneously believe that the Western way is the only successful method. The faculty may also mistakenly expect that their students will work only in a domestic environment. Inclination could be impacted by the instructional model itself. If faculty know the student's language, it could create a persuasive communication and cultural understanding. In a typical university business school classroom with 20-30 students from multiple cultures, it could be very helpful.

Multicultural training should be incorporated into the faculty development process with particular focus on the complexity surrounding norms, values, and beliefs that students carry with them to the classroom. The preparation could include expectations regarding communication patterns, behaviors, relationships, and other dynamics, with the intent to prepare teachers for the dynamics of diverse class sessions, especially when there is a high population of multicultural students.

The challenge is to encourage faculty to develop the attitudes and skills to implement the strategies mentioned, and to recognize that this will assist not only their students but also make their jobs more fulfilling. In light of the strong representation of international students in both undergraduate and postgraduate university courses in many countries, the higher education context provides students and staff with a unique opportunity to foster a cross-cultural awareness, appreciation and understanding of diverse peoples and environments.

Development of cultural respect and cultural empathy may be regarded as major attitudinal factors in effective multicultural group work. To realize the benefits of multicultural group work, therefore, faculty need to be aware of these attitudes and nurture them where possible. Some students may not have personality attributes of patience and openness that are important in making multicultural group work succeed. Alternative teaching methods may be required for these students. It may be necessary in future course offerings to make the implicit processes of group development more explicit.

FUTURE RESEARCH DIRECTIONS

One area that needs further investigation is to evaluate whether students apply the multicultural group work skills and knowledge learned in courses to other group work projects in other courses and in their careers. This is particularly relevant for students who may work in job roles where the skills, attitudes and cultural awareness are relevant to professional practice. Additional research should be conducted regarding the current application of global mindset competencies and how these competencies can be transported into teaching in multicultural classrooms. Concurrent with the preparation, further research should be conducted regarding the willingness of faculty to adopt the expectations. Additional research is needed to explore how the relevant attitudes of respect for the culture of others can be enhanced in the university classroom. Another area for further research is the development of students' personality traits such as patience and openness. Research is needed to explore how students lacking these two key personality traits can still effectively participate in multicultural interactions.

CONCLUSION

The full potential of active learning environment is still to be realized in many tertiary institutions. This chapter discusses how faculty can ensure that students avail the opportunities to improve their intercultural skills and to become globally responsible citizens who have the required knowledge, skills, attitudes and values to work in a world characterized by global complexity and mobility. Multicultural group work is a successful strategy for increasing intercultural competence among students. In particular, the potential benefits include greater preparation for the multicultural and global orientations of today's organizations; creative problem-solving; creative decision-making; and greater understanding of the cultural values and norms of the students in the group and the class.

This chapter contributes to the understanding of adaptation that faculty makes with respect to various aspects of the course content, pedagogical methods, and their own behaviors when teaching courses with a high population of multicultural students. This chapter will hopefully advance an extensive examination regarding teaching style and classroom policies as well as other specific types of adaptations faculty could make to enhance the experiences of learners in multicultural classrooms.

REFERENCES

Ajzen, I., & Fishbein, M. (1980). *Understanding attitudes and predicting social behavior.* Englewood Cliffs, NJ: Prentice-Hall.

Association of Universities and Colleges of Canada. (2010). *Quick facts.* Retrieved from http://www.aucc.ca/

Barker, M., Troth, A., & Mak, A. (2002). Transition to a new academic context: Intercultural skills training for international students. In J. Seale, & D. Roebuck (Eds.), *Envisioning practice-implementing change: Proceedings of the International Conference on Post-Compulsory Education and Training* (pp. 90-96). Brisbane, Australia: Australian Academic Press.

Beamer, L. (1992). Learning intercultural communication competence. *Journal of Business Communication, 29*(3), 285–303. doi:10.1177/002194369202900306

Beamer, L., & Varner, I. (2008). *Intercultural Communication in the Global Workplace* (4th ed.). New York: McGraw-Hill Irvin.

Brownlie, A. (2001). *Citizenship education: The global dimension: Guidance for Key Stages 3 and 4.* London: Development Education Association.

Bureau of Labor Statistics. (2007, April 25). *Foreign-born workers: Labor force characteristics in 2006.* Washington, DC: U.S. Department of Labor. Retrieved from http://www.bls.gov/cps/

Bureau of Labor Statistics. (2015, May 21). *Labor Force Characteristics of Foreign-born Workers Summary.* Retrieved from http://www.bls.gov/news.release/forbrn.nr0.htm

Cardon, P. (2010, June). Using films to learn about the nature of cross-cultural stereotypes in intercultural business communication courses. *Business Communication Quarterly, 73*(2), 150–165. doi:10.1177/1080569910365724

Clarke, T., & Stewart, J. (2009, Summer). Reflections on exhibiting multicultural fluency in the modern classroom. *Business Review (Federal Reserve Bank of Philadelphia), 12*(2), 114–121.

Currie, G. (2007). "Beyond our imagination": The voice of international students on the MBA. *Management Learning, 38*(5), 539–556. doi:10.1177/1350507607083206

Department of Education and Training. (2015, May). *International Student Data 2015.* Retrieved from https://internationaleducation.gov.au/research/International-Student-Data/Pages/InternationalStudentData2015.aspx

Dyer, R., & Tarimcilar, M. M. (2011, May/June). What's your global IQ? *BizEd, X*(2), 46–53.

Education, I. D. P. (2010). *International students in higher education.* Retrieved from http://www.idp.com

Fowler, J. L., Gudmundsson, A. J., & Whicker, L. M. (2006). *Groups work! A guide for working in groups.* Bowen Hills, Australia: Australian Academic Press.

Ghemawat, P. (2003, March). Semiglobalization and international business strategy. *Journal of International Business Studies, 34*(2), 138–152. doi:10.1057/palgrave.jibs.8400013

Ghemawat, P. (2008). The globalization of business education: Through the lens of semiglobalization. *Journal of Management Development, 27*(4), 391–414. doi:10.1108/02621710810866741

Ghemawat, P. (2011, May). The cosmopolitan corporation. *Harvard Business Review, 89*(5), 92–99.

Gil, N. (2014, October 13). *International students in the UK: who are they really?* Retrieved from http://www.theguardian.com/education/2014/oct/13/-sp-international-students-in-the-uk-who-are-they

Gupta, A., & Govindarajan, V. (2002, February). Cultivating a global mindset. *The Academy of Management Executive, 16*(1), 116–126. doi:10.5465/AME.2002.6640211

Haynie, D. (2014, November 17). *Number of International College Students Continues to Climb.* Retrieved from http://www.usnews.com/education/best-colleges/articles/2014/11/17/number-of-international-college-students-continues-to-climb

Hitt, M., Javidan, M., & Steers, R. (2007). The global mindset: An introduction. In M. Javidan, R. Steers, & M. Hitt (Eds.), *The global mindset.* San Diego, CA: JAI Press. doi:10.1016/S1571-5027(07)19001-X

Holmes, P. (2004). Negotiating differences in learning and intercultural communication. *Business Communication Quarterly, 67*(3), 294–307. doi:10.1177/1080569904268141

Leiba-O'Sullivan, S. (1999). The distinction between stable and dynamic cross-cultural competencies: Implications for expatriate trainability. *Journal of International Business Studies, 30*(4), 709–725. doi:10.1057/palgrave.jibs.8490835

Levin, P. (2005). *Successful teamwork.* New York: McGraw-Hill Education.

Marginson, S. (2002). The phenomenal rise of international degrees down under lucrative lessons for US institutions? *Change: The Magazine of Higher Learning, 34*(3), 34–43. doi:10.1080/00091380209601854

Michaelson, L., Peterson, T., & Sweet, M. (2009). Building learning teams: The key to harnessing the power of small groups in management education. In S. J. Armstrong & C. V. Fukami (Eds.), *The SAGE handbook of management learning, education and development* (pp. 325–343). Thousand Oaks, CA: Sage. doi:10.4135/9780857021038.n17

Monitor, I. C. E. F. (2014, November 25). *Record-high international enrolment in Canada in 2013; many students plan to stay.* Retrieved from http://monitor.icef.com/2014/11/record-high-international-enrolment-canada-2013-many-students-plan-stay/

Nahal, A. (2005). Cultural collisions. *Diverse Issues in Higher Education, 22*(20), 41.

Napier, R. W., & Gershenfeld, M. K. (2004). *Groups: Theory and experience.* Boston, MA: Houghton Mifflin.

Nesdale, D. (2000, December). *Children's ethnic prejudice: A comparison of approaches.* Paper presented at the Transcending Boundaries Conference, Brisbane, Australia.

Nguyen, P.-M., Terlouw, C., & Pilot, A. (2008). Culturally appropriate pedagogy: The case of group learning in a Confucian heritage culture context. *Intercultural Education, 17*(1), 1–20. doi:10.1080/14675980500502172

Norman, W. T. (1963). Toward an adequate taxonomy of personality attributes: Replicated factor structure in peer nomination personality ratings. *Journal of Abnormal and Social Psychology, 66*(6), 574–583. doi:10.1037/h0040291 PMID:13938947

Northedge, A. (2003). Rethinking teaching in the context of diversity. *Teaching in Higher Education, 8*(1), 17–32. doi:10.1080/1356251032000052302

Pincas, A. (2001). Culture, cognition and communication in global education. *Distance Education, 22*(1), 30–51. doi:10.1080/0158791010220103

Rhinesmith, S. (1993). *A manager's guide to globalization.* Alexandria, VA: American Society for Training and Development/Irwin.

Robinson, S. (2006). Reflecting on the "international group working experience": A study of two MBA programmes. *International Journal of Management Education, 5*(2), 3–14.

Scott, J. B. (2010, December). Intercultural rhetoric in the technical communication curriculum: A review of the literature. *Rhetoric. Professional Communication and Globalization, 1*(1), 77–90.

Strauss, P., & U, A. (2007). Group assessments: Dilemmas facing lecturers in multicultural tertiary classrooms. *Higher Education Research & Development, 26*(2), 147–161. doi:10.1080/07294360701310789

Thatcher, B. (2010, December). Editor's introduction to first edition: Eight needed developments and eight critical contexts for global inquiry. *Rhetoric, Professional Communication and Globalization, 1*(1), 1-34.

Thrush, E. (1993). Bridging the gaps: Technical communication in an international and multicultural society. *Technical Communication Quarterly, 16*(2), 139–174.

Triandis, H. C. (1971). *Attitude and attitude change.* New York: Wiley.

Trompenaars, F., & Woolliams, P. (2003). *Business across cultures.* Chichester, UK: Capstone Publishing.

UK Council for International Student Affairs. (2010). *Higher education statistics.* Retrieved from http://www.ukcisa.org.uk

van Oudenhoven, J. P., Mol, S., & van der Zee, K. (2003). Study of the adjustment of Western expatriates in Taiwan ROC with the multicultural personality questionnaire. *Asian Journal of Social Psychology, 6*(2), 159–170. doi:10.1111/1467-839X.t01-1-00018

van Oudenhoven, J. P., van der Zee, K. I., & van Kooten, M. (2001). Successful adaptation strategies according to expatriates. *International Journal of Intercultural Relations, 25*(5), 467–482. doi:10.1016/S0147-1767(01)00018-9

Witte, A. E., Sequeira, I., & Fonteyne, C. (2003). Internationalizing the assessment criteria to build cross-cultural competency: American and Chinese educational encounters. *Journal of Teaching in International Business, 14*(4), 61–78. doi:10.1300/J066v14n04_04

Woods, P. R. (2004, July). *A framework for evaluating cross-cultural management performance.* Paper presented at the International Federation of Academies of Management (IFSAM) VII World Congress, Goteborg, Sweden.

Woods, P. R., Jordan, P. J., Loudoun, R., Troth, A. C., & Kerr, D. (2006). Effective Teaching in the Multicultural Business Classroom. *Journal of Teaching in International Business, 17*(4), 27–47. doi:10.1300/J066v17n04_03

Write, N. S., & Drewery, G. P. (2006). Forming cohesion in culturally heterogeneous teams: Differences in Japanese, Pacific Islander and Anglo experiences. *Cross Cultural Management: An International Journal, 13*(1), 43–54. doi:10.1108/13527600610643475

Zepke, N., & Leach, L. (2007). Implementing student outcomes in higher education: New Zealand teachers' views on teaching students from diverse backgrounds. *Teaching in Higher Education, 12*(5), 655–668. doi:10.1080/13562510701596190

ADDITIONAL READING

Beal, D. J., Cohen, R., Burke, M. J., & McLendon, C. L. (2003). Cohesion and performance in groups: A meta-analytic clarification of construct relations. *The Journal of Applied Psychology, 88*(6), 989–1004. doi:10.1037/0021-9010.88.6.989 PMID:14640811

Biggs, J. B. (2011). *Teaching for quality learning at university: What the student does.* UK: McGraw-Hill Education.

Chapdelaine, R. F., & Alexitch, L. R. (2004). Social skills difficulty: Model of culture shock for international graduate students. *Journal of College Student Development, 45*(2), 167–185. doi:10.1353/csd.2004.0021

De Vita, G. (2000). Inclusive approaches to effective communication and active participation in the multicultural classroom. *Active Learning in Higher Education, 1*(2), 168–180. doi:10.1177/1469787400001002006

Gardenswartz, L., Rowe, A., Digh, P., & Bennett, M. J. (2003). *The global diversity desk reference: Managing an international workforce.* San Francisco, CA: Pfeiffer.

Higgins, P., & Li, L. (2008). Fostering the appropriate learning environment? British and Chinese students' experiences of undertaking an organisational-based cross-cultural group work project in a London university. *International Journal of Management Education, 7*(3), 57–68.

Peelo, M., & Luxon, T. (2007). Designing embedded courses to support international students' cultural and academic adjustment in the UK. *Journal of Further and Higher Education, 31*(1), 65–76. doi:10.1080/03098770601167930

Watson, W. E., Kumar, K., & Michaelsen, L. K. (1993). Cultural diversity's impact on interaction process and performance: Comparing homogeneous and diverse task groups. *Academy of Management Journal, 36*(3), 590–602. doi:10.2307/256593

KEY TERMS AND DEFINITIONS

Cultural Diversity: It refers to the existence of a variety of cultural or ethnic groups within a society.

Ethnicity: An ethnic group is a group that has a distinct culture of its own.

Global Citizen: A global citizen is a person who places their identity with a global community above their identity as a citizen of a particular nation or place.

Group Work: It is a form of collaborative learning that involves students working collaboratively on set tasks.

Multicultural Training: It is training imparted to individuals to embrace consideration of diversity regarding issues such as race, ethnicity, gender, sexual orientation, disability etc.

Multicultural: It is a term which describes the cultural and ethnic diversity of a society.

Professional Development: It refers to a wide variety of specialized training, formal education, or advanced professional learning intended to help individuals improve their professional knowledge, competence, skill, and effectiveness.

Tertiary Education: It refers to any type of education pursued beyond the high school level.

Chapter 15
Logistic Issues in Introducing Remote Learning Devices:
Case Study

Amiram Porath
AmiPorCon Ltd., Israel

ABSTRACT

Educational organizations have to face logistic hurdle when introducing remote learning using mobile devices. Unlike the introduction of a new textbook, the introduction of e-learning into educational environment requires adaptation, on the physical as well as the human infrastructure levels. The case study below describe such a move in a regional high school in Israel and presents the major logistic question the move presented to the school and other interested parties. The answers may differ from country to country but the questions seem to be more generalize, and therefore should at least be considered when preparing for the move. The paper ends with some of the lessons learnt, and recommendations for the future.

INTRODUCTION

Normally when dealing with the introduction of remote or electronic learning the issues discussed are pedagogic in nature and relate to topics involving the learning experience, improved learning, the role of the teachers and even to some extent relate to the cost of the change (Twigg, 2003; Garrison and Vaugham, 2007).

The educational models dealing with the use of new technologies cannot be separated from general models of learning. The models of technology use in learning those as Siemens has shown (2004), require us to adapt the learning process to the technology as it changes the learning process as it has changed our daily lives. These models (Siemens, 2005) are ever changing and require constant monitoring to better understand the way they change.

The use of social networks has created communities of learning, and neither their impact on the learning process nor their importance for the learning experience can be ignored (Arbaugh, 2008), moreover, it requires constant watching for developments and new emerging models (Garrison, 2009).

DOI: 10.4018/978-1-4666-9784-3.ch015

To order the analysis of the status of technology in education we shall make use of their impact on three types of interactions involved in the learning process, as described by Anderson (2003): Student – Teacher; student – student; and student-Material. It is mostly related to that last interaction that we aim the discussion in this chapter. However, our focus will not be the pedagogic issues related to remote learning, but rather the logistics involved in making the move from the old method of teaching using textbooks, and frontal teaching in the classroom, to using tablets as remote learning device in the classroom and on-line. To illustrate some of the aspects involved a case study will be presented below.

Unlike the old hard copy books used for study from high school and up to the top of the academic world, the new technologies used for remote or distance learning seem to hold new challenges.

The hardcopy books, were inflexible in the aspect of updating, which could be done only by issuing a new version, which was both costly and time consuming. The new technologies seem to be more flexible, easier to update even during the courses and therefore seem to offer better information, better updated, with a potential to focus on interest areas of the students and teachers.

However, the new technologies involving both hardware and software seem to offer new challenges. The hardware needs to be compatible with the software used for the learning process, its platform requires adaptation to the applications popping up regularly all the time, there is demand to make the learning material adaptable to the platform and the applications regularly.

However, the complexity is bigger than can be envisaged in a single glance. The structured education system from high school and upwards, requires that the teaching material be compatible with the system approved curriculum. That is done by two parallel means: the authority approving the education organization degrees and courses requires that the teaching be compatible with predetermined approved curriculum, so as to create a unity of degrees and diplomas. Further to that there are regular state, regional, international exams that determine the grades of the students and these refer to a specific set of knowledge, predetermined as part of the study plan, and therefore enforcing the specifically approved curriculum on all student.

It is therefore evident, that while the platforms (hardware and software) seem to offer more flexibility in the study plan, it is so only for private un-regulated courses and teaching systems. Otherwise the degree awarding authority, if not the teaching organization by itself, are responsible to inflexibility in the teaching environment that supersedes any technological inflexibility caused in the hardcopy version of learning books by their technology.

Any degree awarding system would require the teachers or the teaching organization to at least supply the curriculum of the course or degree program, including reading material, topics to be covered etc. and in many cases would also at least in the preliminary stages, require also a monitoring period to determine the level of teaching and availability of material to the students.

Therefore when dealing with the remote learning technology the flexibility allowed by the technology regarding the teaching material is negated by the inflexibility resulting from the regulation in the education system, except in the unregulated sectors, which are not part of the official degree awarding education system.

While the above seems to be clear enough and perhaps requires some changes to the regulation in order to allow for more flexibility, there are logistic issues that seem to come up specifically for the new technologies. These issues will be presented below via a test case and discussed later on.

REGIONAL SCHOOL REMOTE LEARNING CASE

Background

In the academic year of 2012 it was decided in a high school at the middle of the Sharon area in Israel to replace the text books with electronic books, and in order to allow for more flexibility the decision was to focus not on eBooks platforms alone, but rather to use tablets in order to enjoy the additional benefits of teaching applications and connectivity of the platform. The actual start of the project as far as the students and parents (an most teachers) were concerned was in December of 2012, about four months after the start of he school year. The beginning was small, some 100 students in three classes and about 16 teachers participated in the initial stage. But already on September 2013, the following school year, the entire age group, some 285 students and 50-60 teachers were involved in the project. This year, since September 2014 700 students in three age groups and about 100 teachers are involved.

This rapid growth rate presented some logistic issues of the move as well as pedagogue challenges. The rapid growth requiring at the same time organization on the one hand and training of stuff and students on the other made the issues even more challenging. Augmenting the problems presented before the school, most of the training had to be done during the school year while the teachers were also teaching. While there was a limited possibility to train the teachers at least partially during the vacation time, it was not possible to do so with the student. Luckily the students seem to take to the new technology faster than the teachers, and their adaptation rate was faster.

Immediately two problems presented themselves, the first was a requirement to keep the alternative of the hardcopy books for the students unwilling to make the transit to electronic learning. This problem was actually a little bit more complex as it require the regulatory approval of the eBooks to be used, and verification of their compatibility with the hardcopy books either already at the school or available for purchase. This problem of course had to be translated to budgetary issues and to a time question regarding the date of approval relevant to the starting date of the school year. It is important to recall that sue to the nature of the system requiring that both students and teachers be trained and ready to sue the system by the start of the new-year, otherwise, if starting the year with the hardcopy books, brings the usefulness of the move to eBooks into question.

The second was a decision required regarding weather to allow the students to select their own devices, or to centrally purchase the platform and licenses, and distribute it to the students. This is more than a mere question of budgeting the cost. Doing the selection for the students as was recently demonstrated by such a decision by the municipality of Jerusalem purchasing over 4,000 units for students in its territory, entails responsibility for the selection, as well as warranty regarding good function of the devices. Purchasing the devices and loaning them to the students means that the organization has to set a maintenance and support unit as statistically from several hundred units, every once in a while there a need for maintenance. Allowing the students to deal with the selection and purchase by themselves, would mean higher purchasing costs, as the advantage of purchasing large quantities would be dissipated by the selection of different makes, and therefore would increase parents objection to the move, as well as creating a significant compatibility problem for the teachers and the organization.

In our case, as the school would not set a central maintenance unit, it allowed the students to make the selection, but negotiated preferred deals for a short list of platforms from which the students and teachers could select their favorite. This smart compromise seemed to solve the maintenance issue (each student or teacher is responsible for his own device), and managed to achieve some reduction in cost by creating centralized purchasing, which helped reduce parents objection to the move. However, this still left a major issue to overcome, and that is to solve the compatibility of the platforms and the teacher training in using the applications and in solving platform issues for the students.

285 students as mentioned above, in eighth and ninth grade started the new-year, with nearly all of them 96% of them using platforms that were divided approximately 75% iPads, and the rest using other marks. The teachers were supplied with Asus tablets following a screening as to the optimal platform regarding adaptability to the software and pricing.

The teachers were offered training before the beginning of the year, and were accompanied by remote learning experts from the board of education during the year assisting in the introduction of new application and in the usage of their devices as well as the other devices in use by the students.

One has to bear in mind that 4% of the students elected to use their right and remain with the hardcopy textbooks, which required the teachers to teach in a classes with several platforms, not all electronic. In an interview with the headmaster, it is a matter of policy to allow that election to students in the future and that would require the adaptation to continue. This has not been the case in other schools that have made a parallel move later on.

The teachers' responses also varied. In a general way the younger teachers while being apprehensive regarding the use of unfamiliar platforms were quick to make use of the training and on-going support and guidance and therefore were quicker also to adapt to the change and embrace it. Some even declared that they felt they were being upgraded themselves as teachers due to the move. The older teachers were slower to adapt and make use of the support and therefore had more difficulties in getting used to the new platforms. The headmaster reports that About 60 teachers of the 100 participating currently, came in the afternoon for instruction on the topics (their own time), and have adopted the technology. Generally judging from the level of activity, at least 33% of the teachers write content regularly and are "deep", another 33% write occasionally and the rest are trying to avoid writing content as much as possible using the platforms as electronic books only. This presents a deeper level of involvement and seems to be very encouraging as it also signals that teachers view the move as a paramagnet change and most try to adapt to it. They understand that this is here to stay. In a more quantified approach, 800 new content pieces (lessons) additional reading material and application were created by the teachers in these three years and more are still being created.

Was the Move Successful?

The move has been monitored by an annual survey among the students measuring usage parameters (hours used at school and outside), effectively regarding the learning process (estimation by the children), time spent at the break outside and with friends compared to working with the tablet, social interaction and more (Sofer, Kahan & Livneh, 2014).

However, on the teacher side there are two other indicators regarding the level of interest and commitment of the teachers. The first and probably most telling is the number of teaching pieces created by the teachers locally. The second item is the number of teachers taking active part in the off hour training sessions organized for them by the school and the ministry of education. Although encouraged to participate by the ministry recognizing their participation towards bonuses in the salary (the training itself was not enough to gain the bonus, only part of it).

The Main Logistic Challenges

There were several logistic challenges that the school faced and still faces today regarding the move towards the electronic platforms. They can be grouped into the following categories:

1. Infrastructure

In order to allow such large groups to access the internet simultaneously while maintaining an acceptable rate of communication, one that would allow the classes to function continuously without prolonged waiting periods, the communication system in the school had to be upgraded. As long as the teachers were using the platforms as electronic books, the load was not a problem, but in anticipation of specially prepared material, connection to different sites during the classes, usage of video and other learning possibilities and applications the system had to be augmented. The infrastructure presented two challenges, the first was a cost challenge and the second was a technological design issue that required a rare specialty. About 150,000 (c.a. 35,000US$) were invested in the system m which was designed by a father of one the students, an expert in the field. The Ministry of education supported the cost and allocated funds for the system maintenance and upkeep. This according to the headmaster was the real challenge as without a seamless connection the acceptance of the platforms would have been slower. The school was also required to add another permanent position, of a network technician that maintains the network and gives support when needed.

2. Devices

Based on the ministry of education policy of "Bring Your Own Device" (Education, 2015), requiring the students to have, a permanent device to be used for the learning experience. There are currently two alternatives which the policy allows, one is to have the devices purchased centrally by the school /municipality, and the second to allow for the children to select their own devices and bring them to school. The first alternative allows for cost reduction as well as making sure that all the equipment is compatible and therefore eases also the training of the teachers. However, this creates a dependence on the municipality / school which is then expected to take responsibility over the equipment and therefore increases the logistic burden on the school. The second alternative while being less cumbersome for the school / municipality, may reduce the take up on the side of the students (some parents may from economic reasons decline to purchase the device), and also if there is no enforcement of a single platform, as if each one buys their own they may elect different marks, increases the complexity of operation and compatibility for the teachers. In our case the second alternative was preferred resulting in the division of platforms as mentioned above. The school also keeps several devices as reserve for loan to children temporary without devices (device forgotten at home, in repair etc.).

The BYOD policy was adopted by the ministry of education after consideration of issues such as internet safety, familiarity with the device and the accumulation of the knowledge on the platform. Additionally, the Ministry feels that the responsibility to bring the device and carry it around, maintaining its functionality is an important educational message. It teaches responsibility in regard to the education. It also encourages the student to develop its own shortcuts and databanks, as the student knows they will be therefore for the future, thus further encouraging investment in the learning process and creativity in preparing the material and background for the learning (education, 2015).

Another aspect, which may become more important in the future would be the updating of the platforms, especially in families with several children.

3. Teacher Training

In the case of introducing the new platforms, the teachers had to be trained in the following activities:

Familiarity with Their Own Platforms

At least part of the teachers have not had any experience with tablets of any kind before the introduction of the system into the school. While all have been computer proficient the specific use of mobile devices for educational purposes and not as a social communication, or document preparation tool was new to many. In any case the teachers level of proficiency at least with their own devices had to be brought to the highest possible level so as to allow them to function regularly and without support in the classroom. In order to ease that issue the teachers were all given the same platform, an Asus tablet, and were given training courses after hours, consisting of familiarity with the device as well as using it for educational purposes (see below). The selection of a single platform was made in order to reduce the complexity of the training, as well as to allow the teachers also to support each other in real time. As the critical point seemed to be to have the teachers perform as well with the devices as they used to do before without.

Familiarity with the Students' Platforms

Part of the training was also given regarding mainly the differences between the teachers' platform and the most common other platforms. The main idea was that if the student had a problem in the class they would tend to approach the teacher first and therefore it would be best if the teacher had some idea how to support the student. This however, was deemed less important than the first point above, as the students usually become proficient with their platforms quicker than most teachers, and also tended to seek other students with the same platform for help, while the teachers, could only train in a limited number of platforms due to time and technical capabilities constraints. One of the lessons the headmaster reported were learnt, was that it would have been better to select the same platform as the majority of the students, as the application the teachers wrote would have been more easily compatible with most of the class.

Familiarity with the Concept and Possibilities of the New Platforms for Teaching

Since the applications and possibilities of remote learning were not evident to most of the teachers involved in the move, specific training sessions were prepared for the teachers involved in the move after hours and in preparation for the move, concentrated days were planned. The teachers could elect whether they wanted to take part in the training and about 60% took advantage of it. Even more so availed themselves of the on-going remote learning guidance during the school year, approaching the remote learning guide supplied by the ministry in support of the move.

All this effort was required as the intention was to allow the teachers to have the tools to create their own material and move beyond the use of the platforms as electronic books. The full intent was to allow them the ability to create interactive, web-based learning material and use the applications offered to enhance the learning experience, allow for group-work, and design the lessons around the applications running on the platform. That required a higher level of proficiency and the ability to comprehend and deal with the concepts of remote learning. The resulting over 800 different learning items created by the teachers is a testimonial to the level of adoption of that general concept. It is here that the selection of the teachers' platforms presented some problems, as not all platforms presented the resulting applications in the same way, and the teachers found themselves working on a platform that did not represent the platform most of their students were using. This require some adaptation on the teachers side in the classroom.

4. Student Training

The student training was done "on the go" that is to say that the students were expected to follow the instructions of the teachers. However, it soon proved to be less of a problem for the students who very quickly became used to the platforms and learnt to operate them quite efficiently. Minor problem arose when students were using the reserve platforms in the class, in cases when they used to have a different platform as their own device. Here, both teachers' support, and colleagues' support were important.

Lessons Learnt

Monitoring System

Before the move to the new platforms was initiated the need for a monitoring system was recognized. The school has entered a monitoring project with the school of education at Tel Aviv University, and each year towards the end of the school year, a survey regarding the levels of satisfaction, social networking, spending the break time in class or out etc., is made and the answers analyzed and published.

The importance of the system is not only to allow the school to learn from its own experience, but rather to allow the results to be compared and applied to other schools either undergoing similar changes or considering them.

Lessons for the Future

The reasons for making the move were important to the direction of the concept and the resulting decisions charactering the school and the move.

The approach here was pedagogically different, (e.g. Other schools wanted just to reduce the weight of the student's bag, they managed to eliminate the books completely, by prohibiting the use of hardcopy books) to allow each to being their own device and for some the device was the hardcopy, as long as the learning experience became richer for the bulk of the students and new ways of learning were opened, the school was ready to support the move. However, the school allows for those who do not want to adopt the new technologies, to remain with the hardcopy books, and according to the headmaster, this will continue until all the students are using the electronic platforms regularly. As he said in an interview "There is no rush". That approach allowed also to reduce some of the apprehension and objection to the move from the parents side, and also as the teacher support (time a specific teacher sends with a specific class is reduce in junior high and in high school, the hardcopy books are also an issue of self assurance and confidence.

The investment in the network infrastructure is important for the success of the move both from the student's side and as a result also from the teacher's side. Normal waiting times for uploads and for audio/visual application to function continuously was very important in encouraging teachers to create their own teaching material. This allows for layered books and additional applications to be used. This investment should be made with a view towards the entire school making use of the system as an upgrade would be very costly. Here the help from the ministry was augmented by clever design' allowing for the same quality wireless service over all the school buildings.

It is important to select the platforms following a professional evaluation of each platform, and if in the case of central supply of platforms for the teachers, it is bet to select the most preferred platform of the students. This will increase the ease of use of the new material created by the teachers, as well as increasing the assistance they can give the students at the early stages. That evaluation should include parameters such as speed, cash memory, application compatibility and more.

Discussion

The case study presented above illustrates some of the problems incurred in the move to electronic and remote learning platforms. It is important to remember, that while most of the teachers are still not "WebNatives", and therefore require some training in the new platforms, that this should be part of the introduction of such a move into an educational organization.

The new networking and enhancing the learning experience utilizing the new systems require additional training for those who grew up and learnt the older pedagogical methodologies, which while they have not changed, require some adaptation to the new possibilities technology offers today. While this investment in the human aspect of the teaching infrastructure is important and long term, it is not the only one required.

It is important to recall that the schools we use today were not designed to house such system and that the investment in infrastructure, physical infrastructure s also long term and required for maximizing the potential benefit from such a move. This not just a question of cost, but also of conceptual design and as the results may impact many years to come, enough attention is required.

The selection of the platforms and the methodology for acquiring the individual student device may vary from place to place, but it is important to make sure that all the devices used are compatible and that the school environment can manage the different devices, and give them the designed support. It is best if the teachers in the classroom can give immediate support to each student at the beginning of the year, and the ability to acquire at least some proficiency with different platforms should be considered regarding the device policy formulated.

As this discussion hopefully demonstrated while the pedagogical aspects of remote learning m ay encompass a world of knowledge, the move towards a remote system is also a question in logistics and should be considered as such. The solution of the logistics issues here is the enabler of the pedagogical activity. As such it is different than most logistic questions in the school and therefore require special attention both inside the organization and by other entities involved, such as the ministry for education and the municipality.

REFERENCES

Anderson, T. (2003). Getting the mix right again: An updated and theoretical rationale for interaction. *The International Review of Research in Open and Distributed Learning, V4(2).*

Arbaugh, J. B. (2008). Does the community of inquiry framework predict outcomes in online MBA courses? *The International Review of Research in Open and Distributed Learning, V9(2).*

Education. (2015). Retrieved 24.05.2015 from http://sites.education.gov.il/cloud/home/tikshuv/Pages/Byod.aspx

Garrison, D. R., & Vaughan, N. (2007). *Blended learning in higher education.* CA, USA: Jossey-Bass. doi:10.1002/9781118269558

Garrison, R. D. (2009). Implications of online learning for the conceptual development and practice of distance education. *International Journal of E-Learning & Distance Education, 23*(2), 93–104.

Siemens, G. (2004a). *A learning theory for the digital age.* Elearnspace: everything learning. Downloaded April 10 2015.

Siemens, G. (2004b). *Connectivism: Learning as network-creation.* Elearnspace: everything learning. Downloaded April 10 2015

Sofer, T., Kahan, T., & Livneh, E. (2014). *Estimating the use of tablets for learning: Results of student's survey at the Ben-Gurion education center (Heb) working paper.* Tel Aviv University.

Twigg, C. A. (2003). Improving learning and reducing costs: New models for online learning. *EDUCAUSE Review, 38*(5), 29–38.

Compilation of References

AACSB International. (n.d.). *Standard 9: Curriculum content is appropriate to general expectations for the degree program type and learning goals*. Retrieved June 26, 2015 from http://www.aacsb.edu/en/accreditation/standards/2013-business/learning-and-teaching/standard9/

Achtenhagen, S. H. (1979). Letter from the editor. *Journal of Marketing Education, 1*(1), 2–2. doi:10.1177/027347537900100101

Ackerman, D. S., Gross, B. L., & Perner, L. (2003). Instructor, Student, and Employer Perceptions on Preparing Marketing Students for Changing Business Landscapes. *Journal of Marketing Education, 25*(1), 46–56. doi:10.1177/0273475302250572

AdAge. (2014, January 13). *How the Marine Corps enlists Big Data for recruitment efforts: The USMC has worked closely with JWT Atlanta for around 65 years*. Retrieved January 3, 2015 from http://adage.com/article/datadriven-marketing/marine-corps-enlists-big-data-recruitment/291009/

Adams, J. Q., & Welsch, J. R. (2009). Multiculturalism: The Manifest Destiny of the U.S.A.: An Interview with Ronald Takaki. *Multicultural Perspectives, 11*(4), 227–231. doi:10.1080/15210960903475522

Ajzen, I., & Fishbein, M. (1980). *Understanding attitudes and predicting social behavior*. Englewood Cliffs, NJ: Prentice-Hall.

Akaah, I. (1990). Attitudes of Marketing Professionals Toward Ethics in Marketing Research: A Cross-National Comparison. *Journal of Business Ethics, 9*(9), 45–53. doi:10.1007/BF00382563

Alderson, W., & Cox, R. (1948). Towards a theory of marketing. *Journal of Marketing, 13*(2), 137–152. doi:10.2307/1246823

Alford, H. J., & Naugton. (2001). Managing as if Faith mattered: Christian Social Principles in the modern organization. Notre Dame, IN: University of Notre Dame Press.

Alon, I., Jaffe, E., & Vianelli, D. (2013). *Global marketing: contemporary theory, practice, and cases*. New York, NY: McGraw-Hill/Irwin.

Alvaro, M. (2006, Feb 22). Deal sought for Ecuador flower exports. *Wall Street Journal*. Retrieved from http://search.proquest.com/docview/398970029

AMA. (2009). Available at http://www.marketingpower.com/Pages/default.aspx

American Marketing Association. (2004). *AMA Statement of Ethics*. Retrieved December 2014 from https://archive.ama.org/Archive/AboutAMA/Pages/Statement%20of%20Ethics.aspx

Anderson, T. & Dron, J (2011). Three generations of distance learning education pedagogy. *The International Review of Research in Open and Distributed Learning*.

Anderson, T. (2003). Getting the mix right again: An updated and theoretical rationale for interaction. *The International Review of Research in Open and Distributed Learning, 4*(2).

Andrew, M., & Erik, B. (2012, October). The management revolution. *Harvard Business Review, 90*(10), 60–68. PMID:23074865

Andrews, J., & Higson, H. (2008). Graduate Employability, "Soft Skills" Versus "Hard" Business Knowledge: A European Study. *Higher Education in Europe, 33*(4), 411–422. doi:10.1080/03797720802522627

Annand, D. (2007). Re-organizing universities for the information age. *International Review of Research in Open and Distance Learning, 8*(3). Retrieved from http://www.irrodl.org/index.php/irrodl/article/view/372/952

Anon. (2011). *Learning Theory, Teaching Higher-Order Thinking*. Teach for America. Retrieved from http://teachingasleadership.org/sites/default/files/Related-Readings/LT_Ch5_2011.pdf

Aquinas, T. (1953). Summa theologiae (5 vols.). Ottawa: Harpell's Press.

Aquino, J. (2012, January). 5 hot marketing trends: Customer strategists must step up their engagement efforts as mobile's mercury rises. *CRM Magazine, 16*, 20.

Arbaugh, J. B. (2008). Does the community of inquiry framework predict outcomes in online MBA courses? *The International Review of Research in Open and Distributed Learning, 9*(2).

Ardley, B. (2006). Situated learning and marketing: Moving beyond the rational technical thought cage. *Marketing Intelligence & Planning, 24*(3), 202–217. doi:10.1108/02634500610665682

Argandoña, A. (2004). ¿Por qué el marketing debe tener en cuenta la ética? *Harvard Deusto Marketing y ventas,* (62), 72-79.

Armstrong, G., & Kotler, P. (2013). *Marketing: an introduction*. Boston, MA: Prentice Hall.

Arum, R., & Roksa, J. (2011). *Academically adrift: Limited learning on college campuses*. Chicago, IL: University of Chicago Press.

Association for Center and Technical Education (ACTE). (n.d.). *What is marketing education?.* Retrieved 20 July 2015 https://www.acteonline.org/marketing_whatis/#.Va3JhmfJC1s

Association of Universities and Colleges of Canada. (2010). *Quick facts*. Retrieved from http://www.aucc.ca/

Atkinson, R. C., & Blanpied, W. A. (2008). Research universities: Core of the US science and technology system. *Technology in Society, 30*(1), 30–48. doi:10.1016/j.techsoc.2007.10.004

Authers, J. (2013, December 8). The changing face of the MBA curriculum. *FT.Com.* Retrieved March 1, 2015 from http://www.ft.com/cms/s/2/b52b57d8-5d07-11e3-81bd-00144feabdc0.html#axzz3RGW3FcND

Ayob, M. A., & Yaakub, F. N. (2000), *Development of Graduate Education in Malaysia: Prospect for Internationalization.* Paper presented at the 2000 ASAIHL Seminar on University and Society: New Dimensions for the Next Century held at Naresuan University, Phitsanulok, Thailand. Available at: http://mahdzan.com/papers/thaipaper00/

Baack, D., Harris, E., & Baack, D. (2013). *International marketing*. Thousand Oaks, CA: Sage.

Bacellar, F. C. T., & Ikeda, A. A. (2011). Evolução do ensino de marketing: Um breve histórico. *Organizações & Sociedade, 18*(58), 487–511. doi:10.1590/S1984-92302011000300008

Bacon, D., Paul, P., Johnson, C., & Conley, T. (2008). Improving Writing Through the Marketing Curriculum: A Longitudinal Study. *Journal of Marketing Education, 30*(3), 217–225. doi:10.1177/0273475308322643

Baker, G. & Henson, D. (2010). Promoting employability skills development in a research-intensive university. *Education + Training, 52*(1), 62-75. doi: 10.1108/00400911011017681

Baker, M. J. (2013). Michael J. Baker: Reflections on a career in marketing. *Journal of Historical Research in Marketing, 5*(2), 223–230. doi:10.1108/17557501311316842

Baker, S., & Holt, S. (2004). Making marketers accountable:a failure of marketing education? *Marketing Intelligence & Planning, 22*(5), 557–567. doi:10.1108/02634500410551932

Ballve, M. (2014, October 22). Mobile, social, and big data: The convergence of the internet's three defining trends. *Business Insider*. Retrieved June 26, 2015 from http://www.businessinsider.com/mobile-and-social-drive-big-data-industry-2014-2019

Barker, M., Troth, A., & Mak, A. (2002). Transition to a new academic context: Intercultural skills training for international students. In J. Seale, & D. Roebuck (Eds.), *Envisioning practice-implementing change:Proceedings of the International Conference on Post-Compulsory Education and Training* (pp. 90-96). Brisbane, Australia: Australian Academic Press.

Barker, B. (2014). Employability skills: Maintaining relevance in marketing education. *The Marketing Review, 134*(1), 29–48. doi:10.1362/146934714X13948909473149

Barnes, B. E. (1996). Introducing introductory advertising student to the World Wide Web. *Journal of Advertising Education, 1*(1), 5–12.

Barnett, R., Parry, G., & Coate, K. (2010, August 25). *Conceptualising curriculum change*. San Diego, CA: Academic Press.

Barnett, S. T., Dascher, P. E., & Nicholson, C. Y. (2004). Can School Oversight Adequately Assess Department Outcomes? A Study of Marketing Curriculum Content. *Journal of Education for Business, 79*(3), 157–162. doi:10.3200/JOEB.79.3.157-162

Beamer, L. (1992). Learning intercultural communication competence. *Journal of Business Communication, 29*(3), 285–303. doi:10.1177/002194369202900306

Beamer, L., & Varner, I. (2008). *Intercultural Communication in the Global Workplace* (4th ed.). New York: McGraw-Hill Irvin.

Beard, F. K., & Tarpening, D. (2001, Spring). Teaching TV advertising creative using digital video on the desktop. *Journal of Advertising Education, 5*(1), 24–33.

Beggs, J. M. (2011). Seamless Integration of Ethics. *Marketing Education Review, 21*(1), 49–56. doi:10.2753/MER1052-8008210107

Bel, S., & Churchill, C. (2012). Using insurance to drive trade. *International Trade Forum*, (1), 24-26.

Bell, J., & Cornelius, M. (2013). *Underdeveloped: A National Study of Challenges Facing Nonprofit Fundraising*. San Francisco, CA: CompassPoint Nonprofit Services & the Evelyn and Walter Haas, Jr. Fund.

Bell, M. P. (2007). *Diversity in organizations*. Mason, OH: Thomason South-Western.

Bennis, W., & O'Toole, J. (2005). How business schools lost their way. *Harvard Business Review, 83*(5), 96–104. PMID:15929407

Beqiri, M. S., Chase, N. M., & Bishka, A. (2010). Online course delivery: An empirical investigation of factors affecting student satisfaction. *Journal of Education for Business, 85*(2), 95–100. doi:10.1080/08832320903258527

Berkeley, L. (2009). Media education and new technology: A case study of major curriculum change within a university media degree. *Journal of Media Practice, 10*(2-3), 185–197. doi:10.1386/jmpr.10.2-3.185_1

Berman, B., & Evans, J. (2013). *Retail management: a strategic approach*. Boston: Pearson.

Beroggi, G. E. G. (2001). Visual-interactive decision modeling (VIDEMO) in policy management: Bridging the gap between analytic and conceptual decision modeling. *European Journal of Operational Research, 128*(2), 338–350. doi:10.1016/S0377-2217(00)00076-X

Bestall, C. (Producer and Director) & Mandela, N. (Performer). (2010). *The 16th man*. [Motion picture]. United States; 30 for 30 ESPN Films.

Bigelow, J. D. (2004). Using problem-based learning to develop skills in solving unstructured problems. *Journal of Management Education, 28*(5), 591–609. doi:10.1177/1052562903257310

Bjørkquist, C. (2008). Continuity and Change in Stakeholder Influence Reflections on Elaboration of Stakeholder Regimes. *Reflecting Education, 4*(2), 24–38.

Blackburn, S. (2001). *Sobre la bondad. Una breve introducción a la ética*. Barcelona: Paidos.

Blythe, J., & Megicks, P. (2010). *Marketing planning: strategy, environment and context*. Harlow, UK: Financial Times / Prentice Hall.

Boddy, C. R. (2007). Academia marketing myopia and the cult of the PhD. *Marketing Intelligence & Planning, 25*(3), 217–228. doi:10.1108/02634500710747734

Bok, D. C. (2006). *Our underachieving colleges: A candid look at how much students learn and why they should be learning more*. Princeton, NJ: Princeton University Press.

Bonilla-Silva, E. (2006). *Racism without racists: color-blind racism and the persistence of racial inequality in the United States*. Lanham, MD: Rowman & Littlefield.

Boone, L. E., & Kurtz, D. L. (2011). *Contemporary marketing*. Mason, OH: South-Western/Cengage.

Booth, J. (2005). Prospering with juggernauts: Implementing excellent customer service. *Control, 31*(1), 23.

Borin, N., & Metcalf, L. (2010). Integrating Sustainability Into the Marketing Curriculum: Learning Activities That Facilitate Sustainable Marketing Practices. *Journal of Marketing Education, 32*(2), 140–154. doi:10.1177/0273475309360156

Borneo Post. (2009, May 21). Govt. to help 4,000 graduates land jobs. *Borneo Post*, pp. 1-2.

Bowen, H. R. (1953). *Social responsibilities of the businessman*. New York: Harper.

boyd, D., & Crawford, K. (2012). Critical questions for big data. *Information, Communication & Society, 15*(5), 662-679.

Breen, J. (2014). Exploring criticality in management education through action learning. *Action Learning Research and Practice, 11*(1), 4–24. doi:10.1080/14767333.2013.874328

Brennan, R. (2004). Should we worry about an "academic-practitioner divide" in marketing? *Marketing Intelligence & Planning, 22*(5), 492–500. doi:10.1108/02634500410551879

Brennan, R. (2009). Using case studies in university-level marketing education. *Marketing Intelligence & Planning, 27*(4), 467–473. doi:10.1108/02634500910964038

Brennan, R. (2014). Reflecting on experiential learning in marketing education. *The Marketing Review, 14*(1), 97–108. doi:10.1362/146934714X13948909473266

Brennan, R., & Ankers, P. (2004). In search of relevance: Is there an academic-practitioner divide in business-to-business marketing? *Marketing Intelligence & Planning*, *22*(5), 511–519. doi:10.1108/02634500410551897

Brooks, D. D., & Althouse, R. C. (Eds.). (2007). *Diversity and social justice in college sports: Sport management and the student athlete*. Morgantown, WV: Fitness Information Technology.

Brown, B., Chui, M., & Manyika, J. (2012, May). Are you ready for the era of big data? *Intermedia*, *40*, 28–33.

Brownlie, A. (2001). *Citizenship education: The global dimension: Guidance for Key Stages 3 and 4*. London: Development Education Association.

Brown, M. E., Trevino, L. K., & Harrison, D. A. (2005). Ethical leadership: A social learning theory perspective for construct development. *Organizational Behavior and Human Decision Processes*, *97*(2), 117–134. doi:10.1016/j.obhdp.2005.03.002

Brown, S. L., & Eisenhardt, K. M. (1998). *Competing on the edge*. Harvard College.

Budziszewski, J. (2003). *What We Can't Not Know*. Spence Publishing Company.

Bureau of Labor Statistics. (2007, April 25). *Foreign-born workers: Labor force characteristics in 2006*. Washington, DC: U.S. Department of Labor. Retrieved from http://www.bls.gov/cps/

Bureau of Labor Statistics. (2015, May 21). *Labor Force Characteristics of Foreign-born Workers Summary*. Retrieved from http://www.bls.gov/news.release/forbrn.nr0.htm

Burger, K. J., & Schmidt, S. L. (1987). Integrating Information Management Skills into the Marketing Curriculum: An Example Using the Marketing Research Course. *Journal of Marketing Education*, *9*(1), 12–18. doi:10.1177/027347538700900103

Burki, R., Elsasser, H., & Abegg, B. (2003). Climate change and winter sports: environmental and economic threats. *5th World Conference on Sport and Environment*.

Burns, D. (2011). MBA Marketing Curriculum for the 21st Century. *Journal of Marketing*. doi:10.1300/J050v10n02

Butler, D. D. (2007). Planning your own funeral: A helpful pedagogical tool. *Marketing Education Review*, *17*(1), 95–100. doi:10.1080/10528008.2007.11488993

Byrd, K. (2014). *Bringing the five practices to life*. Retrieved from http://www.leadershipchallenge.com/leaders-section-articles-stories-detail/bringing-the-five-practices-to-life-kenya-jesuit-commons-kareena-byrd.aspx

Cadwallader, S., Atwong, C., & Lebard, A. (2013). Proposing Community-Based Learning in the Marketing Curriculum. *Marketing Education Review*, *23*(2), 137–150. doi:10.2753/MER1052-8008230203

Calkins, M. (2000). Recovering Religion's Prophetic Voice for Business Ethics. *Journal of Business Ethics*, *23*, 339–352. doi:10.1023/A:1005989824688

Camangian, P. R. (2015). Teach Like Lives Depend on It: Agitate, Arouse, and Inspire. *Urban Education*, *50*(4), 424–453. doi:10.1177/0042085913514591

Čančer, V. (2012). Teaching creative problem solving methods to undergraduate economics and business students. *Journal of Further and Higher Education*, *38*(4), 485–500. doi:10.1080/0309877X.2012.726968

Capelo, C., & Dias, J. F. (2009). A feedback learning and mental models perspective on strategic decision making. *Educational Technology Research and Development*, *57*(5), 629–644. doi:10.1007/s11423-009-9123-z

Caravella, M., Ekachai, D., Jaeger, C., & Zahay, D. (2009, Spring). Web 2.0 opportunities and challenges for advertising educators. *Journal of Advertising Education*, *13*(1), 58–63.

Cardon, P. (2010, June). Using films to learn about the nature of cross-cultural stereotypes in intercultural business communication courses. *Business Communication Quarterly, 73*(2), 150–165. doi:10.1177/1080569910365724

Carlton Associates, Inc. (n.d.). *Is your agency ready for big data?* Chagrin Falls, OH: Carlton Associated Incorporated.

Carr, N. (2008). *The Shallows: What the internet is doing our brains.* New York: W.M. Norton & Company.

Carver, F. (1993). The essence of Wesleyanism. This essay was first delivered as a talk at "A Wesley Festival: Pilgrimage to Wholeness," a faculty chapel, Point Loma Nazarene College, February 19, 1993.

Casares, J. (2010, November-December). La ciencia económica, la diversión y la ética Aplicaciones generales al comercio y al consumo. *Distribución y Consumo,* 13-21.

Catterall, M., Maclaran, P., & Stevens, L. (2002). Critical reflection in the marketing curriculum. *Journal of Marketing Education, 24*(3), 184–192. doi:10.1177/0273475302238041

Census, U. S. (2015). *U.S. and World Population Clock.* United States Census Bureau. Retrieved from http://www.census.gov/popclock/

Central Intelligence Agency. (2015). *The World Factbook.* Central Intelligence Agency. Retrieved from https://www.cia.gov/library/publications/the-world-factbook/

Chambers, R. (1983). *Rural development: putting the last first.* London: Longman.

Charities Aid Foundation. (2012). *World Giving Index 2012.* Retrieved January 26, 2015, from http://www.cafonline.org/PDF/WorldGivingIndex2012WEB.pdf

Chaturvedi, A. (2015, February 5). Big data embedded into marketing curriculum at B-schools: Niraj dawar, ivey business school. *The Economic Times of India.* Retrieved January 10, 2015 from http://articles.economictimes.indiatimes.com/2015-02-03/news/58751790_1_big-data-customers- tilt.

Chen, H., Chiang, R. H. L., & Storey, V. C. (2010). Business intelligence research. *Management Information Systems Quarterly, 34*(1), 201–203.

Chen, H., Chiang, R. H. L., & Storey, V. C. (2012, December). Business intelligence and analytics: From big data to big impact. *Management Information Systems Quarterly, 36*(4), 1165–1188.

Chennamaneni, P. R., Lala, V., & Srivastava, P., Goutam, & Chakraborty. (2011, Spring). Teaching consumer analytics in advertising and IMC courses: Opportunities and challenges. *Journal of Advertising Education, 15*(1), 52–58.

Cherrier, & Murray. (2004). The Sociology of Consumption: The Hidden Facet of Marketing. *Journal of Marketing Management,* 509-525.

Chewning, R. (2001). *A Dozen Styles of Biblical Integration: Assimilating the Mind of Christ.* Presentation at the Annual CBFA Conference.

Christensen, C. M., & van Bever, C. (2014). The capitalist's dilemma. *Harvard Business Review,* (June): 61–68.

Chrysler, M. (2011). Japanese auto industry faces somber market. *WardsAuto.Com.* Retrieved from http://search.proquest.com/docview/926925346

CIM. (2009). Available at http://www.cim.co.uk/resources/understandingmarket/definitionmkting.aspx

Cinta, R., Beatty, M., & Faustino-Pulliam, V. (2012). Lessons from the Field: Teaching a Completely Online "Global Business" Course to African Refugees in Northern Kenya and Malawi. *Jesuit Higher Education Journal, 1*(1), 144–147.

Clarke, P., Gray, D., & Mearman, A. (2006). The marketing curriculum and educational aims: Towards a professional education? *Marketing Intelligence & Planning*, *24*(3), 189–201. doi:10.1108/02634500610665673

Clarke, T., & Stewart, J. (2009, Summer). Reflections on exhibiting multicultural fluency in the modern classroom. *Business Review (Federal Reserve Bank of Philadelphia)*, *12*(2), 114–121.

Clinebell, S. K., & Clinebell, J. M. (2008). The tension in business education between academic rigor and real-world relevance: The role of executive professors. *Academy of Management Learning & Education*, *7*(1), 99–107. doi:10.5465/AMLE.2008.31413867

Cloud Standards Customer Council. (2013, June). *Convergence of social, mobile and cloud: 7 steps to ensure success.* Retrieved March 1, 2015 from http://www.cloud-council.org/ Convergence_of_Cloud_Social_Mobile_Final.pdf

Clow, K., & Baack, D. (2010). *Marketing management: a customer-oriented approach.* Thousand Oaks, CA: Sage.

Columbia Business School. (2013, August 28). *Press release, Columbia Business School unveils redesigned core curriculum for first-year MBA students.* Retrieved January 10, 2015 from http://www8.gsb.columbia.edu/newsroom/newsn/2450/columbia-business-school-unveils-redesigned-core-curriculum-for-first-year-mba-students

Commons, J. Higher Education at the Margins. (2014). *About Us.* Retrieved from http://www.jc-hem.org

Commons, J.Higher Education at the Margins. (2015). Retrieved from http://alumni.jc-hem.org/story?TN=PROJECT-20150220014952

Connolly, D. (2012). Why b-schools should teach business intelligence. *Bloomsberg Businessweek.* Retrieved from http://www.businessweek.com/articles/2012-04-23/why-b-schools-should-teach-business-intelligence

Conway, M., & Vasseur, G. (2009). The new imperative for business schools. *Business Intelligence Journal*, *14*(3), 13–17.

Cook, M., & Lam, M. (2013). Empathy as a distinctive element in Christian business education.*Proceedings of the Christian Business Faculty Association Conference.*

Cortina, A. (1994). *Ética de la empresa: claves para una nueva cultura empresarial.* Madrid: Tecnos.

Cortina, A. (2002). *Por una ética del consumo.* Madrid: Taurus.

Cox, S., & Taylor, J. (2006). The Impact of a Business School on Regional Economic Development: A Case Study. *Local Economy*, *21*(2), 117–135. doi:10.1080/02690940600608069

Crenshaw, K. W. (1989). *Demarginalizing the Intersection of Race and Sex: A Black Feminist Theory and Antiracist Politics.* University Chicago Law Forum 139.

Cunningham, A. C. (1999). Commentary: Confessions of a reflective practitioner: meeting the challenges of marketing's destruction. *European Journal of Marketing*, *33*(7/8), 685–697. doi:10.1108/03090569910274311

Cunningham, G. B. (2011). *Diversity in sport organizations.* Scottsdale, AZ: Holcomb Hathaway.

Currie, G. (2007). "Beyond our imagination": The voice of international students on the MBA. *Management Learning*, *38*(5), 539–556. doi:10.1177/1350507607083206

Dai, J., Huang, J., Huang, S., Liu, Y., & Sun, Y. (2012). The hadoop stack: New paradigm for big data storage and processing. *Intel Technology Journal*, *16*(4), 92–110.

Davenport, T. H. (2013). Analytics 3.0. *Harvard Business Review.* Retrieved from https://hbr.org/2013/12/analytics-30

Davenport, T. H. (2013). *Enterprise analytics: Optimize performance, process, and decisions through big data*. Upper Saddle River, NJ: FT Press.

Davenport, T. H. (2013, December). Analytics 3.0. *Harvard Business Review*, 64–72.

Davis, K. (1967). Understanding the social responsibility puzzle: What does the businessman owe to society? *Business Horizons*, *10*(4), 45–50. doi:10.1016/0007-6813(67)90007-9

Dell'Olio, A. J. (2003). *Foundations of Moral Selfhood: Aquinas on Divine Goodness and the Connection of the Virtues*. New York: Peter Lang Publishing, Inc.

Delong, D., & McDermott, M. (2013). Current perceptions, prominence and prevalence of sustainability in the marketing curriculum. *The Marketing Management Journal*, *23*(3), 101–116.

Delor, J., Al Mufti, I., Amagi, I., Carneiro, R., Chung, F., Geremek, B., & Nanzhao, Z. (1996). *Learning the treasure within: Report to UNESCO of the International Commission on Education for the Twenty-first Century* (pp. 1–46). Paris: UNESCO publishing.

DeMera, J. (2014). 2014 is the year of digital marketing analytics: What it means for your company. *Forbes*, *5*(June). Retrieved from http://www.forbes.com/sites/jaysondemers/2014/02/10/2014-is-the-year-of-digital-marketing-analytics-what-it-means-for-your-company/

Dennis, J. (2014). Designing relevant marketing curriculum: The state of the nation. *The Marketing Review*, *14*(1), 49–66. doi:10.1362/146934714X13948909473185

Department of Education and Training. (2015, May). *International Student Data2015*. Retrieved from https://internationaleducation.gov.au/research/International-Student-Data/Pages/InternationalStudentData2015.aspx

Deshpande, R., & Webster, F. E. Jr. (1989). Organization Culture and Marketing: Defining the Research Agenda. *Journal of Marketing*, *53*(1), 3–15. doi:10.2307/1251521

DEST. (2002). Employability skills for the future. A report by the Australian Chamber of Commerce and Industry and the Business Council of Australia for the Department of Education, Science and Training, Canberra.

Dickinson, J. R. (2002). A need to revamp textbook presentations of price elasticity. *Journal of Marketing Education*, *24*(2), 143–149. doi:10.1177/027753024002007

Dion, M. (2000). Teaching Business Ethics, or the Challenge of A Socratic-Nietzschean Self-Transcendence for Teachers. *Teaching Business Ethics*, *4*(3), 307–324. doi:10.1023/A:1009873711063

Ditch the silos: Data integration is key tech need in 2013. (2013, Spring). *Chief Marketer*, 17.

Done, A. (1979). Matching the Marketing Curriculum To Market Needs. *Journal of Marketing Education*, *1*(1), 4–12. doi:10.1177/027347537900100103

Drimmelen, R. (1998). *Faith in a global economy: A primer for Christians*. Geneva: WCC Publications.

Drucker, P. (1984). The New Meaning of Corporate Social Responsibility. *California Management Review*, *26*(2), 53–63. doi:10.2307/41165066

Drucker, P. F. (1954). *The Practice of Management*. New York, NY: Collins. (reprinted 2006)

Dugar, A. (2012, Summer). Case study Rebranding: Yes or no? *Journal of Brand Strategy*, *1*(2), 149–163.

Dyer, R., & Tarimcilar, M. M. (2011, May/June). What's your global IQ? *BizEd*, *X*(2), 46–53.

Eckman, A. (2010, Spring). It's not new to them: Using ning.Com to enhance student engagement in the study of social web marketing and web 2.0 direct response methods. *Journal of Advertising Education, 14*(1), 15–19.

Economist. (2010). *The other oil spill.* Retrieved 10 April 2015 from http://www.economist.com/node/16423833

Education, I. D. P. (2010). *International students in higher education.* Retrieved from http://www.idp.com

Education. (2015). Retrieved 24.05.2015 from http://sites.education.gov.il/cloud/home/tikshuv/Pages/Byod.aspx

Ehrensal, K. N. (2001). Training Capitalism's Foot Soldiers: The Hidden Curriculum of Undergraduate Business Education. In E. Margolis (Ed.), The Hidden Curriculum in Higher Education, (pp. 97-113). New York: Routledge.

Ejolt. (2012). *Unilever and how to greenwash tropical devastations.* Retrieved 10 April 2015 from: http://www.ejolt.org/2012/09/unilever-and-how-to-greenwash-tropical-devastations/

Elbeck, M., & Bacon, D. (2015). Toward Universal Definitions for Direct and Indirect Assessment. *Journal of Education for Business, 90*(5), 278–283. doi:10.1080/08832323.2015.1034064

Elbeck, M., & Vander Schee, B. (2014). Global benchmarking of marketing doctoral program faculty and institutions by subarea. *Journal of Marketing Education, 36*(1), 45–61. doi:10.1177/0273475313514234

Elbeck, M., Williams, R., Peters, C. O., & Frankforter, S. (2009). What marketing educators look for when adopting a principles of marketing textbook. *Marketing Education Review, 19*(2), 49–62. doi:10.1080/10528008.2009.11489074

Equal Employment Opportunity Commission. (2014). *Charge Statistics FY 1997-FY 2013.* Retrieved from www.eeoc.gov/stats/charges.html

Eshelman, G., Lam, M., & Cook, M. (2012). Three contributing factors to effective utilization of technology in management education and practice: Personhood, Mindfulness, and Meditation. *Journal of the North American Management Society, 6*, 24–34.

ESPN.com. (2014, October 18). *Shamil Tarpischev fined, banned year.* Retrieved from: espn.go.com/tennis/story/_/id/11718876/Russian-tennis-federation-president-shamil-tarpischev-sanctioned-serena-venus-williams-gender-comments

Esteves, J., & Curto, J. (2013). A risk and benefits behavioral model to assess intention to adopt big data. *Journal of Intelligence Studies in Business, 3*(3), 37–46.

Everett, R. F. (2014). A crack in the foundation: Why SWOT might be less than effective in market sensing analysis. *Journal of Marketing and Management, 1*(1), 58–78.

Fan, S., Lau, R. Y. K., & Zhao, J. L. (2015, March). Demystifying big data analytics for business intelligence through the lens of marketing mix. *Big Data Research, 2*(1), 28–31. doi:10.1016/j.bdr.2015.02.006

Fechheimer, M., Webber, K., & Kleiber, P. B. (2011). How well do undergraduate research programs promote engagement and success of students? *CBE Life Sciences Education, 10*(2), 156–163. doi:10.1187/cbe.10-10-0130 PMID:21633064

Ferrell, O. C., & Gresham, L. G. A. (1985). Contingency framework for understanding ethical decision making in marketing. *Journal of Marketing, 49*(3), 87–96. doi:10.2307/1251618

Ferrell, O. C., & Hartline, M. (2011). *Marketing strategy.* Mason, OH: South-Western/Cengage.

Ferrell, O. C., & Keig, D. L. (2013). The Marketing Ethics Course: Current State and Future Directions. *Journal of Marketing Education, 35*(2), 119–128. doi:10.1177/0273475313491498

Financial Times. (2015). *Global MBA Ranking 2015.* The Financial Times Ltd. Retrieved from http://rankings.ft.com/businessschoolrankings/global-mba-ranking-2015

Finch, D., Nadeau, J., & O'Reilly, N. (2012). The Future of Marketing Education: A Practitioner's Perspective. *Journal of Marketing Education, 35*(1), 54–67. doi:10.1177/0273475312465091

Finn, A. (1985). Consumer Behavior Textbooks: A Comparative Review. *Journal of Marketing Education, 7*(3), 46–54. doi:10.1177/027347538500700308

Fong, J. (2013). Preparing Marketing for the Future: Strategic Marketing Challenges for Continuing Education. *New Directions for Adult and Continuing Education*, (140). doi:10.1002/ace.20077

Fowler, J. L., Gudmundsson, A. J., & Whicker, L. M. (2006). *Groups work! A guide for working in groups*. Bowen Hills, Australia: Australian Academic Press.

Franco, J. M. (2011). *An Exploratory Study of the Curricular Integration of Ethics in Executive MBA Programs*. Dissertations. Paper 149. Retrieved June 2015 from: http://ecommons.luc.edu/luc_diss/149

Frederick, W. C. (1960). The growing concern over business responsibility. *California Management Review, 2*(4), 52–61. doi:10.2307/41165405

Freire, P., & Macedo, D. P. (1995). A dialogue: Culture, language, and race. *Harvard Educational Review, 65*(3), 377–403. doi:10.17763/haer.65.3.12g1923330p1xhj8

Friedman, L. (2013). *Big data little data new data*. Presentation at Consumer Intelligence Conference.

Friedman, M. (1970, September 13). The social responsibility of a business is to increase its profits. *The New York Times Magazine*.

Friedman, M. (1962). *Capitalism and Freedom*. Chicago: University of Chicago Press.

Fulgoni, G. (2013, December). Big data: Friend or foe of digital advertising? Five ways marketers should use digital big data to their advantage. *Journal of Advertising Research, 53*(4), 372–376. doi:10.2501/JAR-53-4-372-376

Fung, A., & Wright, E. O. (2001). Deepening Democracy: Innovations in Empowered Participatory Governance. *Politics & Society, 19*(1), 5–41. doi:10.1177/0032329201029001002

Garneau, J. P., & Brennan, R. (1999). *New relevance in the marketing curriculum: stakeholder perceptions of the effectiveness of marketing education*. Paper presented at the Academy of Marketing Annual Conference, Stirling.

Garrison, D. R., & Vaughan, N. (2007). *Blended learning in higher education*. Jossey-Bass. doi:10.1002/9781118269558

Garrison, R. D. (2009). Implications of online learning for the conceptual development and practice of distance education. *International Journal of E-Learning & Distance Education, 23*(2), 93–104.

Gartner. (2012, October 22). *Gartner says Big Data creates big jobs: 4.4 million IT jobs globally to support Big Data by 2015*. Retrieved January 15, 2015 from http://www.gartner.com/newsroom/id/2207915

Gary, M. S., & Wood, R. (2001). Mental models, decision rules, and performance heterogeneity. *Strategic Management Journal, 32*(6), 569–594. doi:10.1002/smj.899

Geography. (2013). In *Merriam-Webster Collegiate Dictionary*. Retrieved March 28, 2013, from http://www.merriam-webster.com/dictionary/geography

Geography. (2013). In *OED Online*. Oxford University Press. Retrieved March 28, 2013, from http://www.oed.com/view/Entry/77757

Ghemawat, P. (2003, March). Semiglobalization and international business strategy. *Journal of International Business Studies, 34*(2), 138–152. doi:10.1057/palgrave.jibs.8400013

Ghemawat, P. (2008). The globalization of business education: Through the lens of semiglobalization. *Journal of Management Development, 27*(4), 391–414. doi:10.1108/02621710810866741

Ghemawat, P. (2011, May). The cosmopolitan corporation. *Harvard Business Review, 89*(5), 92–99.

Gibson-Sweet, M., Brennan, R., Foy, A., Lynch, J., & Rudolph, P. (2010). Key issues in marketing education: The marketing educators' view. *Marketing Intelligence & Planning, 28*(7), 931–943. doi:10.1108/02634501011086508

Gicquel, Y. (2007). *Le Marketing éthique*. Paris: Génies des Glaciers.

Gil, N. (2014, October 13). *International students in the UK: who are they really?* Retrieved from http://www.theguardian.com/education/2014/oct/13/-sp-international-students-in-the-uk-who-are-they

Gillespie, K., & Hennessey, H. (2011). *Global marketing*. Mason, OH: South-Western/Cengage.

Glass, R., & Callahan, S. (2014). *The big data-driven business: How to use big data to win customers, beat competitors, and boost profits*. Hoboken, NJ: Wiley.

Glen, R., Suciu, C., & Baughn, C. (2014). The need for design thinking in business schools. *Academy of Management Learning & Education, 13*(4), 653–667. doi:10.5465/amle.2012.0308

Global Fund. (2010). *(PRODUCT)RED generates landmark US$150 million*. Retrieved January 26, 2015, from http://www.theglobalfund.org/en/mediacenter/newsreleases/2010-06-01_PRODUCT_RED_generates_landmark_USD_150_million_for_the_Global_Fund/

Global skills shortage in marketing analytics remedied by Teradata University Network. (2014). Retrieved from http://online.wsj.com/article/PR-CO-20140812-908039.html

Gopaldas, A. (2013). Intersectionality 101. *Journal of Public Policy & Marketing, 32*(Special Issue), 90–94. doi:10.1509/jppm.12.044

Graduating from an email service provider to marketing automation. (2013). Marketo, Inc. Retrieved from http://www.marketo.com

Gray, B. J., Ottesen, G. G., Bell, J., Chapman, C., & Whiten, J. (2007). What are the essential capabilities of marketers? A comparative study of managers', academics' and students' perceptions. *Journal of Marketing Intelligence and Planning, 25*(3), 271–295. doi:10.1108/02634500710747789

Gray, D. M., Peltier, J. W., & Schibrowsky, J. (2012). The Journal of Marketing Education: Past, Present, and Future. *Journal of Marketing Education, 34*(3), 217–237. doi:10.1177/0273475312458676

Grayson, K. (2014). *Morality and the Marketplace*. Retrieved July 2015 from http://jcr.oxfordjournals.org/page/Research_Curations/Morality_and_the_Marketplace?utm_source=Journal+of+Consumer+Research+-+July+21%2C+2015&utm_campaign=Constant+Contact&utm_medium=email

Greene, S., & Boa, Y. (2009). Addressing AACSB global and technology requirements: Exploratory assessment of a marketing management mssignment. *Journal of Teaching in International Business, 29*(4), 272–292. doi:10.1080/08975930903405043

Greengard, S. (2012, August). Advertising gets personal. *Communications of the ACM, 55*(8), 18–20.

Greensmith, J. (2002). Trends in Fundraising and Giving by International NGOs. *Global Policy Forum*. Retrieved January 26, 2015, from https://www.globalpolicy.org/component/content/article/176/31462.html

Grewal, D., & Levy, M. (2012). *Marketing*. New York, NY: McGraw-Hill/Irwin.

Griffith, D. A., & Hoppner, J. J. (2013). Global marketing managers. *International Marketing Review*, *30*(1), 21–41. doi:10.1108/02651331311298555

Gross, S. T. (2012, July 5). The new millennial values. *Forbes*. Retrieved January 1, 2015 from http://www.forbes.com/sites/prospernow/2012/07/05/the-new-millennial-values/

Guan, J., & Knottnerus, J. D. (2006). Chinatown Under Siege: Community Protest and Structural Ritualization Theory. *Humboldt Journal of Social Relations*, *30*(1), 5–52.

Gupta, A., & Govindarajan, V. (2002, February). Cultivating a global mindset. *The Academy of Management Executive*, *16*(1), 116–126. doi:10.5465/AME.2002.6640211

Hamilton, L. C., Rohall, D. E., Brown, B. C., Hayward, G. F., & Keim, B. D. (2003). Warming winters and New Hampshire's lost ski areas: An integrated case study. *The International Journal of Sociology and Social Policy*, *23*(10), 52–73. doi:10.1108/01443330310790309

Harder, J. M. (2003). The Violence of Global Marketization. In J. D. Weaver & G. Biestecker-Mast (Eds.), Teaching Peace: Nonviolence and the Liberal Arts. Lanham, MD: Rowman & Littlefield Publishers, Inc.

Haring, B. (1986). *The Healing Power of Peace and Nonviolence*. Paulist Press.

Harrigan, P., & Hulbert, B. (2011). How Can Marketing Academics Serve Marketing Practice? The New Marketing DNA as a Model for Marketing Education. *Journal of Marketing Education*, *33*(3), 253–272. doi:10.1177/0273475311420234

Hart, C., Stachow, G. B., Farrell, A. M., & Reed, G. (2007). Employer perceptions of skills gaps in retail: Issues and implications for UK retailers. *International Journal of Retail & Distribution Management*, *35*(4), 271–288. doi:10.1108/09590550710736201

Hart, S. L. (1995). A natural-resource-based view of the firm. *Academy of Management Review*, *20*(4), 986–1014.

Harvey, L. (2000). New realities: The relationship between higher education and employment. *Tertiary Education and Management*, *6*(1), 3–17. doi:10.1080/13583883.2000.9967007

Hayat, S. A. (2014). Indonesian global expansion: A case study. *International Journal of Global Business*, *7*(2), 9–32.

Haynie, D. (2014, November 17). *Number of International College Students Continues to Climb*. Retrieved from http://www.usnews.com/education/best-colleges/articles/2014/11/17/number-of-international-college-students-continues-to-climb

Hayward, G. (1999). Sun-burned. *Airman*, *43*(10), 46–48.

Hazan, E., & Banfi, F. (2013, August). *Leveraging big data to optimize digital Marketing*. McKinsey & Company. Retrieved January 13, 2015 from http://www.mckinsey.com/client_service/marketing_and_sales/latest_thinking/leveraging_big_data_to_optimize_digital_marketing

Hendrick, D. (2014, December 11). 6 ways big data will shape online marketing in 2015. *Forbes.com*. Retrieved June 26, 2015 from http://www.forbes.com/sites/drewhendricks/2014/2012/2011/2016-ways-big-data-will-shape-online-marketing-in-2015/

Herring, C. (2009). Does Diversity Pay? Race, Gender, and the Business Case for Diversity. *American Sociological Review*, *74*(2), 208–224. doi:10.1177/000312240907400203

Hill, N. (1967). *Think and Grow Rich*. Dutton, Penguin Books.

Hill, T., & Westbrook, R. (1997). SWOT analysis: It's time for a product recall. *Long Range Planning*, *30*(1), 46–52. doi:10.1016/S0024-6301(96)00095-7

Hing, J. (2013). *Brittney Griner's Nike contract is just the latest of her barrier-breaking moves*. Retrieved from http://colorlines.com/archives/2013/06/brittney_griners_gender-bending_nike_contract_just_the_latest_of_her_barrier-breaking_moves.html

Hitt, M., Javidan, M., & Steers, R. (2007). The global mindset: An introduction. In M. Javidan, R. Steers, & M. Hitt (Eds.), *The global mindset*. San Diego, CA: JAI Press. doi:10.1016/S1571-5027(07)19001-X

Hoelzel, M. (2014, September 25). The social media advertising report: Growth forecasts, market trends, and the rise of mobile. *Business Insider*. Retrieved January 5, 2015 from http://www.businessinsider.com/social-media-advertising-spending-growth-2014-2019

Hofstede Centre. (2015). *Country Comparisons*. The Hofstede Centre. Retrieved from http://geert-hofstede.com/countries.html

Holian, R. (2004). The practice of management education in Australian universities. *Management Decision, 42*(3/4), 396-405. Retrieved on January 6, 2006 from: www.emeraldinsight.com/0025-1747.htm

Hollensen, S. (2011). *Global marketing: a decision-oriented approach*. Harlow, UK: Financial Times / Prentice Hall.

Holmes, P. (2004). Negotiating differences in learning and intercultural communication. *Business Communication Quarterly, 67*(3), 294–307. doi:10.1177/1080569904268141

Hopkins, C., Raymond, M. A., & Carlson, L. (2011). Educating Students to Give Them a Sustainable Competitive Advantage. *Journal of Marketing Education, 33*(3), 337–347. doi:10.1177/0273475311420241

Hoskisson, R., Eden, L., Lau, C., & Wright, M. (2000). Strategy in emerging economies. *Academy of Management Journal, 43*(3), 249–267. doi:10.2307/1556394

Howard, D. G., & Ryans, J. K. J. Jr. (1993). What role should marketing theory play in marketing education: A cross-national comparison of marketing educators. *Asia Pacific Journal of Marketing and Logistics, 5*(2), 29–43. doi:10.1108/eb010249

Howard, D. G., Savins, D. M., Howell, W., & Ryans, J. K. J. (1991). The evolution of marketing theory in the United States and Europe. *European Journal of Marketing, 25*(2), 7–16. doi:10.1108/03090569110145150

Hubbard, R., & Armstrong, J. S. (2006). Why we don't really know what statistical significance means: Implications for educators. *Journal of Marketing Education, 28*(2), 114–120. doi:10.1177/0273475306288399

Hudson, B. (1986). Landscape as resource for national development: A Caribbean view. *Geography (Sheffield, England), 71*(2), 116–121.

Hughey, M. W. (2014). White backlash in the 'post-racial' United States. *Ethnic and Racial Studies, 37*(5), 721–730. doi:10.1080/01419870.2014.886710

Hunt, S. D. (2002). Marketing as a profession: On closing stakeholder gaps. *European Journal of Marketing, 36*(3), 305–312. doi:10.1108/03090560210417138

Hunt, S. D., & Vitell, S. J. (1986). A General Theory of Marketing Ethics. *Journal of Macromarketing, 6*(1), 5–16. doi:10.1177/027614678600600103

Hutt, M. D., & Speh, T. W. (2007). Undergraduate Education: The Implications of Cross-Functional, Relationships in Business Marketing–The Skills of High-Performing Managers. *Journal of Business-To-Business Marketing, 14*(1), 75–94. doi:10.1300/J033v14n01_08

IBM. (2009). *The new voice of the CIO: Insights from the global chief information officer study*. Retrieved from http://www-304.ibm.com/businesscenter/cpe/download0/183490/NM_CIO_Study.pdf

IEG LLC. (2015). *Sponsorship Spending Report: Where the Dollars are going and Trends for 2015*. Retrieved from www.sponsorship.com/Resources/Sponsorship-SpendingReport--Where-The-Dollars-Are.aspx

Ignatius, A. (2012, October). Big Data for Skeptics. *Harvard Business Review*. Retrieved January 5, 2015 from https://hbr.org/2012/10/big-data-for-skeptics

Inglis, J. (1999). Aquinas's Replication of The Acquired Moral Virtues: Rethinking the Standard Philosophical Interpretation of Moral Virtues in Aquinas. *Journal of Religious Ethics*, *27*(1), 3-27.

Innes, R. (2004). *Reconstructing undergraduate education: Using learning science to design effective courses*. Mahwah, NJ: Lawrence Erlbaum Associates.

Institute for Economics & Peace. (2015). Retrieved 21 July 2015 from http://economicsandpeace.org/

Institute of International Education. (2014). *Report on International Educational Exchange*. Institute of International Education, 2014 Open Doors Presentation, November 17. Retrieved from http://www.iie.org/Research-and-Publications/Open-Doors

Intelligence in harmony: How an integrated analytics model is driving retail success. (2012, February). Oracle Whitepaper.

ITBusinessEdge. (n.d.). Big Data is creating big jobs: 4.4 million bBy 2015. *ITBusinessEdge*. Retrieved January 5, 2015 from http://www.itbusinessedge.com/slideshows/big-data-is-creating-big-jobs-4.4-million-by-2015.html

Jansen, T., Chioncel, N., & Dekkers, H. (2006). Social Cohesion and Integration: Learning Active Citizenship. *British Journal of Sociology of Education*, *27*(2), 189–205. doi:10.1080/01425690600556305

Joan Paulus, I. I. (1993). *Veritatis Splendor*. Retrieved November 2014 from http://w2.vatican.va/content/john-paul-ii/es/encyclicals/documents/hf_jp-ii_enc_06081993_veritatis-splendor.html

Johansson, J. (2009). *Global marketing: foreign entry, local marketing, & global management*. Boston, MA: McGraw-Hill Irwin.

Johnson, J.L. & Martin, K. L. (2008). A Framework for Ethical Conformity in Marketing. *Journal of Business Ethics*, *80*(1), 103-109.

Jones, T. M. (1980). Corporate social responsibility revisited, redefined. *California Management Review*, *22*(3), 59–67. doi:10.2307/41164877

Kagaari, J. R. K. (2007). Evaluation of the effects of vocational choice and practical training on students' employability. *Journal of European Industrial Training*, *31*(6), 449–471. doi:10.1108/03090590710772640

Kalamas, M., Mitchell, T., & Lester, D. (2009, Spring). Modeling social media use: Bridging the gap in higher education. *Journal of Advertising Education*, *13*(1), 44–57.

Kalantzis, M., & Cope, M. (2015). Didactic. *New Learning*. Retrieved from http://newlearningonline.com/learning-by-design/glossary/didactic

Kant, I. (1785). Fundamentación de la metafísica de las costumbres (M. Garcia, Ed. & Trans.). Madrid: Espasa-Calpe.

Karakaya, F., & Yannopoulos, P. (2010). Defensive strategy framework in global markets: A mental models approach. *European Journal of Marketing*, *44*(7/8), 1077–1100. doi:10.1108/03090561011047535

Kaye, K. (2014, August 20). Get a hands on education at Ad Age Data Conference 2014: Two days of practical and entertaining insights in New York this October. *AdAge.com*. Retrieved January 3, 2015 from http://adage.com/article/datadriven-marketing/hands-education-ad-age-data-conference-2014/294635/

Kaye, K. (2015, January 20). IAB survey: Marketers using a hodge-podge of data-tech tools trade group's study showed marketers use upwards of 12 systems. *AdAge.com*. Retrieved January 4, 2015 from http://adage.com/article/datadriven-marketing/iab-surveys-marketing-execs-data-tech/296653/

Kaye, K. (2013, August19). Big data. *Advertising Age, 84*, 14. PMID:24229463

Keesing, R. M. (1974). Theories of Culture. *Annual Review of Anthropology, 3*(1), 73–97. doi:10.1146/annurev.an.03.100174.000445

Kennedy, E. J., Lawton, L., & Walker, E. (2001). The Case for Using Live Cases: Shifting the Paradigm in Marketing Education. *Journal of Marketing Education, 23*(2), 145–151. doi:10.1177/0273475301232008

Kerin, R., Berkowitz, E., Hartley, S., & Rudelius, W. (2003). Marketing (7th ed.). McGraw-Hill Companies, Inc.

Kerin, R., & Peterson, R. (2013). *Strategic marketing problems: cases and comments*. Boston, MA: Pearson.

Khon Thai Monitor. (2012). *Research Report sponsored by the Khon Thai Foundation*. Bangkok, Thailand: Khon Thai Foundation.

Kim, H. J., Pelaez, A., & Winston, E. R. (2013, April). *Experiencing big data analytics: Analyzing social media data in financial sector as a case study*. Paper presented at the 2013 Northeast Decision Sciences Institute Annual Meeting Proceedings, New York, NY.

Kim, Y., & Patel, S. (2012, Fall). Teaching advertising media planning in a changing media landscape. *Journal of Advertising Education, 16*(2), 15–26.

Kirpalani, N., & College, L. I. M. (2009). *Developing Entrepreneurial Self-Efficacy in Marketing Students by Using Simulation-Based Pedagogy*. Society for Marketing Advances Proceedings.

Kluver, J., Frazier, R., & Haidt, J. (2014). Behavioral ethics for Homo economicus, Homo heuristicus, and Homo duplex. *Organizational Behavior and Human Decision Processes, 123*(2), 150–158. doi:10.1016/j.obhdp.2013.12.004

Knoppers, A., & McDonald, M. (10, August 2010). Scholarship on Gender and Sport. *Sex Roles and Beyond, 63*(5-6), 311-323. Retrieved from www.ncbi.nlm.nih.gov/pmc/articles/PMC2928920/

Korr, C. P. (2013, December 6). Mandela used sport's power. *USA Today*.

Kotler, P. (2012). *Marketing*. Retrieved 22 July 2015 from: https://www.youtube.com/watch?v=sR-qL7QdVZQ

Kotler, P., & Armstrong, G. (2008). *Principles of Marketing* (12th ed.). Prentice Hall.

Kotler, P., & Armstrong, G. (2013). *Principles of marketing*. Boston, MA: Pearson.

Kotler, P., Kartajaya, H., & Setiawan, I. (2010). *Marketing 3.0*. John Wiley & Sons, Inc. doi:10.1002/9781118257883

Kotler, P., & Keller, K. (2012). *Marketing management*. Upper Saddle River, NJ: Prentice Hall.

Kreeft, P. (1994). *C.S. Lewis for the Third Millennium: Six Essays on the Abolition of Man*. San Francisco: Ignatius Press.

Kroeber, A.L. & Kluckhohn, C. (1952). Culture: A critical review of concepts and definitions. *Papers of the Peabody Museum, 47*(1a).

Kumar, R., & Usunier, J.-C. (2001). Management education in a globalizing world: Lessons from French experience. *Management Learning, 32*(3), 363–391. doi:10.1177/1350507601323005

Kurthakoti, R., Boostrom, R. E., Summey, J. H., & Campbell, D. (2013). Enhancing Classroom Effectiveness Through Social Networking Tools. *Marketing Education Review, 23*(3), 251–264. doi:10.2753/MER1052-8008230304

Laclede, A. (2013, August 6). *JRS intern reports. Independent Catholic News.* Retrieved from http://www.indcatholic-news.com/news.php

Laczniak, G. R. (1983). Framework for Analyzing Marketing Ethics. *Journal of Macromarketing, 1*(1), 7–18. doi:10.1177/027614678300300103

LaFleur, E. K., Babin, L. A., & Burnthorne, L. T. (2009). Assurance of Learning for Principles of Marketing Students: A Longitudinal Study of a Course-Embedded Direct Assessment. *Journal of Marketing Education, 31*(3), 131–141. doi:10.1177/0273475309335242

Lam, M. L. L. (2007). A study of the transfer of corporate social responsibility from well-established foreign multinational enterprises to Chinese subsidiaries. In Controversies in international corporate responsibility. Pittsburgh, PA: Carnegie Mellon University.

Lam, M. L. L. (2012b). A best practice of corporate social responsibility: Going beyond words on a page and a check. Advances in Sociology Research, 13, 157-164.

Lam, M. L. L. (2013b). Being Chinese: A reflective study of foreign multinational corporations' sustainable development and global talent programs in China. In *Proceedings of the NAMS (North American Management Society) of MBAA International Conference.*

Lam, M. L. L. (2013e). Building Trust between American and Chinese Business Negotiators. In Dis(honesty) in Management: Manifestations and Consequences. Emerald Group Publishing Limited.

Lam, M. L. L. (2014b). Cultivate the habit of empathy in on-going sustainability research. In *Proceedings of the NAMS (North American Management Society) of MBAA International Conference.*

Lam, M. L. L. (2014c). Empathy as a Major Contributing Factor to Sustainability in the Global Supply Chain. In Khosrow-Pour (Ed.), Inventive Approaches for Technology Integration and Information Resources Management, (pp. 53-67). Hershey, PA: IGI Global Publications. doi:10.4018/978-1-4666-6256-8.ch002

Lam, M.L.L. (2014e). Harmonious Society' through Corporate Social Responsibility. *Journal of Public Affairs, 14*(2).

Lam, A. L. H., Lam, M. L. L., & Lam, L. H. C. (2006). A Study of Human Rights Non-Government Organizations (NGOs) as Social Movement Organizations (SMOs) in Hong Kong, China: Implications for Higher Education. *The International Journal of the Humanities, 3*(9), 105–117.

Lamb, C. W., Hair, J. F., & McDaniel, C. (2014). *MKTG 7.* Mason, OH: South-Western/Cengage.

Lam, M. L. L. (2008). Being innovative by doing good. In *Proceedings of Academy of Innovation and Entrepreneurship 2008.* Beijing, China: Tsinghua University.

Lam, M. L. L. (2009a). Beyond credibility of doing business in China: Strategies for improving corporate citizenship of foreign multinational Enterprises in China. *Journal of Business Ethics, 87*(S1), 137–146. doi:10.1007/s10551-008-9803-3

Lam, M. L. L. (2009b). Sustainable development and corporate social responsibility of multinational enterprises in China. In J. R. McIntyre, S. Ivanaj, & V. Ivanaj (Eds.), *Multinational Enterprises and the Challenge of Sustainable Development* (pp. 230–244). Cheltenham, UK: Edward Elgar. doi:10.4337/9781849802215.00023

Lam, M. L. L. (2010a). Political implications of the corporate social responsibility movement in China. *The Journal of International Business Research and Practice, 4*, 125–134.

Lam, M. L. L. (2010b). Managing corporate social responsibility as an innovation in China. In L. Al-Hakim & J. Chen (Eds.), *Innovation in Business and Enterprise: Technologies and Frameworks* (pp. 224–238). Hershey, PA: IGI Global. doi:10.4018/978-1-61520-643-8.ch015

Lam, M. L. L. (2010c). Beyond legal compliance: Toward better corporate citizenship of foreign multinational enterprises in China. *Journal of Biblical Integration in Business, 13*, 100–109.

Lam, M. L. L. (2010d). Sustainable development in a global market economy—A compassion-oriented approach. In *Proceedings of Christian Business Faculty Association Conference.*

Lam, M. L. L. (2011a). Becoming corporate social responsible foreign multinational enterprises in China. *The Journal of International Business Research and Practice, 5*, 47–61.

Lam, M. L. L. (2011b). Successful strategies for sustainability in China and the global market economy. *International Journal of Sustainable Development, 3*(1), 73–90.

Lam, M. L. L. (2011d). Challenges of sustainable environmental programs of foreign multinational enterprises in China. *Management Research Review, 34*(11), 1153–1168. doi:10.1108/01409171111178729

Lam, M. L. L. (2012a). An alternative paradigm for managing sustainability in the global supply chain. *International Journal of Social Ecology and Sustainable Development, 3*(4), 1–12. doi:10.4018/jsesd.2012100101

Lam, M. L. L. (2012c). Corporate social responsibility movement in China: What can foreign corporations' corporate social responsibility programs in China do to universal values? In K. Wang (Ed.), *Dialogue among Cultures: Peace, Justice and Harmony* (pp. 221–234). Beijing, China: Foreign Language Press.

Lam, M. L. L. (2012d). Toward sustainability through innovation. In *Proceedings of Inaugural International Conference on Innovation and Entrepreneurship: Theory and practice relevant to China.* Wuhan, China.

Lam, M. L. L. (2013a). An educator as a contemplative practitioner in business education. *Journal of Higher Education Theory and Practices, 13*(2), 2013.

Lam, M. L. L. (2013c). A Case Study of the Challenges of Sustainable Business Development in China. *The Journal of International Business Research and Practice, 7*, 2013.

Lam, M. L. L. (2013d). Sustaining and Extending Corporate Social Responsibility in China: One Company Initiative. The*Journal of International Business Research and Practice, 7*, 2013.

Lam, M. L. L. (2014a). Empathy as a major contributing factor to sustainable business development in China. In *Proceedings of the 2014 AIB-Midwest Conference.*

Lam, M. L. L. (2014d). Empathy as a major contributing factor to sustainable business development in China. *The Journal of International Business Research and Practice, 8*, 2014.

Lam, M. L. L. (2015). Improving moral ecology in a digitized global market economy through empathic practices. *Proceedings in the North American Management Society Conference.*

Laney, D. (2001). *3d data management: Controlling data volume, velocity and variety.* Retrieved January 4, 2015 from http://blogs.gartner.com/doug-laney/files/2012/01/ad949-3D-Data-Management- Controlling-Data-Volume-Velocity-and-Variety.pdf

Lee, M. H., Ling, L. A., Muniapan, B., & Gregory, M. L. (2011). General enterprising tendency (GET) and recommendations to boost entrepreneurship education in Sarawak. *International Journal of Asian Business and Information Management, 2*(1), 32–47. doi:10.4018/jabim.2011010103

Lehman, G. A. (2003). The peaceful manager. In Nonviolence and the Liberal Arts, (pp. 266-274). Rowman & Littlefield Publishers, Inc.

Leiba-O'Sullivan, S. (1999). The distinction between stable and dynamic cross-cultural competencies: Implications for expatriate trainability. *Journal of International Business Studies, 30*(4), 709–725. doi:10.1057/palgrave.jibs.8490835

Leite, D., Santiago, R., Sarrico, C., Leite, C., & Polidori, M. (2006). Students' perceptions on the influence of institutional evaluation on universities. *Assessment & Evaluation in Higher Education, 31*(6), 625–638. doi:10.1080/02602930600760264

Lester, D. H. (2012, January). Social media: Changing advertising education. *Online Journal of Communication and Media Technologies, 2*(1), 116–125.

Lester, R. (1999). *Stagg's University: The rise, decline, and fall of big time football at Chicago.* Chicago, IL: University of Illinois Press.

Levin, P. (2005). *Successful teamwork.* New York: McGraw-Hill Education.

Levitt, T. (1958). The dangers of social responsibility. *Harvard Business Review, 36,* 41–50.

Levy, M., & Weitz, B. (2012). *Retailing management.* New York, NY: McGraw-Hill/Irwin.

Lewis, C. S. (1947). *The Abolition of Man.* New York: Macmillan.

Lewis, R. D. (1996). *When Cultures Collide: Leading Across Cultures.* Nicholas Brealey International.

Liang, N., & Wang, J. (2004). Implicit mental models in teaching cases: An empirical study of popular MBA cases in the United States and China. *Academy of Management Learning & Education, 3*(4), 397–413. doi:10.5465/AMLE.2004.15112545

Lim, M., & Svensson, P. (2013). Embedding critique in the university: A new role for critical marketing education? *Journal of Applied Research in Higher Education, 5*(1), 32–47. doi:10.1108/17581181311310252

Ling, L. A., Gregory, M. L., & Muniapan, B. (2010). Marketing education in Sarawak: Some issues and challenges from the employers' perspectives. *Int. J. Education Economics and Development, 1*(3), 227–242. doi:10.1504/IJEED.2010.032876

Lockwood, P., Marshall, T. C., & Sadler, P. (2005). Promoting success or preventing failure: Social comparisons across cultures. *Personality and Social Psychology Bulletin, 31,* 379–394. doi:10.1177/0146167204271598 PMID:15657453

Longenecker, C. O., & Ariss, S. S. (2002). Creating competitive advantage through effective management education. *Journal of Management Development, 21*(9), 640–654. doi:10.1108/02621710210441649

Luftman, J., & Ben-Zvi, T. (2010). Key issues for IT executives 2009: Difficult economy's impact on IT. *MIS Quarterly Executive, 9*(1), 49–59.

Lupovici, A. (2013). Pacification: Toward a theory of the social construction of peace. *International Studies Review, 15*(2), 204–228. doi:10.1111/misr.12032

Lyons, T. S. (2002). *The Entrepreneurial League System: Transforming Your Community's Economy through Enterprise Development.* The Appalachian Regional Commission Washington.

MacIntyre, A. (1984). *After Virtue.* Notre Dame: University of Notre Dame Press.

Mackay, H. (1988). *Swim with the sharks without being eaten alive.* Mackay, USA: Harvey B.

Mackay, H. (1990). *Beware the naked man who offers you hi shirt*. Mackay, USA: Harvey B.

Mahrt, M., & Scharkow, M. (2012). The value of big data in digital media research. *Journal of Broadcasting & Electronic Media, 57*(1), 20–33. doi:10.1080/08838151.2012.761700

Maignan, I., & Lukas, B. A. (1997). Entry mode decisions: The role of managers' mental models. *Journal of Global Marketing, 10*(4), 7–23. doi:10.1300/J042v10n04_02

Mainardes, E., Alves, H., & Raposo, M. (2010). An Exploratory Research on the Stakeholders of a University. *Journal of Management and Strategy, 1*(1), 76–88. doi:10.5430/jms.v1n1p76

Mainardes, E., Alves, H., & Raposo, M. (2013). Identifying stakeholders in a Portuguese university : A case study. *Revista de Educación, 362*, 429–457. doi:10.4438/1988-592X-RE-2012-362-167

Manyika, J., Chui, M., Brown, B., Bughin, J., Dobbs, R., Roxburgh, C., & Byers, A. H. (2011, May). *Big data: The next frontier for innovation, competition, and productivity*. McKinsey Global Institute (MGI). Retrieved January 1, 2015 from http://www.mckinsey.com/insights/business_technology/big_data_the_next_frontier_for_innovation

Manyika, J., Chui, M., Brown, B., Bughin, J., Dobbs, R., Roxburgh, C., & Hung Byers, A. (2011). *Big data: The next frontier for innovation, competition, and productivity*. McKinsey Global Institute. Retrieved from http://wwwmckinsey.com/Insights?MGI/Research?Technology_and_Innovation/Big-data_The_next_frontier_for_innovation

Marginson, S. (2002). The phenomenal rise of international degrees down under lucrative lessons for US institutions? *Change: The Magazine of Higher Learning, 34*(3), 34–43. doi:10.1080/00091380209601854

Marshall, J. (2013, September 25). The advertising industry has a big crush on Big Data. *DigiDay*. Retrieved March 1, 2015 from http://digiday.com/platforms/dstillery-advertising-data-crush/

Marshall, G. W., Lassk, F. G., Kennedy, K. N., & Goolsby, J. R. (1996). Integrating Quality Improvement Tenets into the Marketing Curriculum. *Journal of Marketing Education, 18*(2), 28–38. doi:10.1177/027347539601800204

Marshall, T. H. (1950). *Citizenship and Social Class and Other Essays*. Cambridge: University of Cambridge Press.

Martin, D. G. (2002, Spring). In search of the golden mean: Impact of computer mediated technologies on the media planning course. *Journal of Advertising Education, 6*(1), 25–35.

Maske, M. (2009). *NFL Extends Rooney Rule to Encourage Hiring of Minorities in Front Offices*. Retrieved from http://www.washingtonpost.com/wp-dyn/content/article/2009/06/15/AR2009061502806.html

Maslen, G. (2012). Worldwide student numbers forecast to double by 2025. *University World News*. Retrieved from http://www.universityworldnews.com/article.php?story=20120216105739999

Mason, G., Williams, G., & Cranmer, S. (2009). Employability skills initiatives in higher education: What effects do they have on graduate labour market outcomes? *Education Economics, 17*(1), 1–30. doi:10.1080/09645290802028315

Maxwell, J. A. (1996). *Qualitative research design*. London: Sage Publication.

May, F. W. (1994). The Virtues in a Professional Setting. In *Readings in Christian Ethics: Theory and Method* (vol. 1, pp. 267-274). Academic Press.

McAfee, A., & Brynjolfsson, E. (2012, October). Big data: The management revolution. *Harvard Business Review*, 59–68. PMID:23074865

McCarthy, E. J. (1960). *Basic Marketing, A Managerial Approach*. Homewood, IL: Richard D. Irwin. Retrieved February 2015 from http://babel.hathitrust.org/cgi/pt?id=inu.30000041584743;view=1up;seq=7

McCracken, J., Martin, W., & Shaw, B. (1998). Virtue Ethics and the Parable of the Sadhu. *Journal of Business Ethics*, *17*(1), 25–38. doi:10.1023/A:1017912300819

McGuire, J. (1963). *Business and Society.* New York, NY: McGraw-Hill.

McLelland, L. (2012). *By 2017 the CMO will spend more on IT than the CIO.* Gartner Webinar. Retrieved from http://my.gartner.com/portal/server.pt?open=512&objID=202&mode=2&PageID=5553&resid=1871515

McMillan, S. J., Sheehan, K. B., & Frazier, C. (2001, Fall). What the real world really wants: An analysis of advertising employment ads. *Journal of Advertising Education*, *5*(2), 9–21.

Meara, N. M., Schmidt, L. D., & Day, J. D. (1996). Principles and Virtues: A Foundation for Ethical Decisions, Policies, and Character. *The Counseling Psychologist*, *24*(1), 4–77. doi:10.1177/0011000096241002

Menon, A., Bharadwaj, S. G., Adidam, P. T., & Edison, S. W. (1999). Antecedents and consequences of marketing strategy making: A model and a test. *Journal of Marketing*, *63*(2), 18–40. doi:10.2307/1251943

Meyers, E. J. (2010). *Gender and sexual diversity in schools.* Springer. doi:10.1007/978-90-481-8559-7

Michaelson, L., Peterson, T., & Sweet, M. (2009). Building learning teams: The key to harnessing the power of small groups in management education. In S. J. Armstrong & C. V. Fukami (Eds.), *The SAGE handbook of management learning, education and development* (pp. 325–343). Thousand Oaks, CA: Sage. doi:10.4135/9780857021038.n17

Miller, F. (1985). Integrating the Personal Computer into the Marketing Curriculum: A Programmatic Outline. *Journal of Marketing Education*, *7*(3), 7–11. doi:10.1177/027347538500700302

Miller, F. L., Holmes, T. L., & Mangold, W. G. (2007). Integrating Geographic Information Systems (GIS) into the Marketing Curriculum. *Marketing Education Review*, *17*(3), 49–63. doi:10.1080/10528008.2007.11489013

Minelli, M., Chambers, M., & Dhiraj, A. (2013, January). *Big data, big analytics: Emerging business intelligence and analytic trends for today's businesses.* Hoboken, NJ: John Wiley & Sons.

Mintz, S. M. (1996). Aristotelian Virtue and Business Ethics Education. *Journal of Business Ethics*, *15*(8), 827–838. doi:10.1007/BF00381851

Minzesheimer, B. (2008, August 14). How Mandela won over a nation. *USA Today*.

Mitroff, I. I., & Denton, E. A. (1999). A Study of Spirituality in the Workplace. *Sloan Management Review*, (Summer), 83–92.

Monitor, I. C. E. F. (2014, November 25). *Record-high international enrolment in Canada in 2013; many students plan to stay.* Retrieved from http://monitor.icef.com/2014/11/record-high-international-enrolment-canada-2013-many-students-plan-stay/

Mooradian, T., Matzler, K., & Ring, L. (2012). *Strategic marketing.* Boston, MA: Pearson Prentice Hall.

Mortimer, K. P., & Sathre, C. O. (2007). The art and politics of academic governance: Relations among boards, presidents, and faculty. Westport, CT: Praeger Publishers.

Moskal, P., Ellis, T., & Keon, T. (2008). Summary of assessment in higher education and the management of student-learning data. *Academy of Management Learning & Education*, *7*(2), 269–278. doi:10.5465/AMLE.2008.32712624

Muniapan, B. (2015). The Bhagavad-Gita and Business Ethics: A Leadership Perspective. Asian Business and Management Practices: Trends and Global Considerations: Trends and Global Considerations.

Muniapan, B. (2005). *HRM Education: The Role of Malaysian Universities and Institution of Higher Learning. In Invent and Innovate* (pp. 344–346). Kuala Lumpur: Genuine Circuit.

Muniapan, B. (2008). Perspectives and Reflections on Management Education in Malaysia. *International Journal of Management in Education, 2*(1), 77–87. doi:10.1504/IJMIE.2008.016232

Muniapan, B. (2014). *The Roots of Indian Corporate Social Responsibility (CSR) Practice from a Vedantic Perspective. In Corporate Social Responsibility in Asia* (pp. 19–34). Springer International Publishing.

Muniapan, B., & Rajantheran, M. (2011). Ethics (business ethics) from Thirukurral and its Relevance for Contemporary Business Leadership in the Indian Context. *International Journal of Indian Culture and Business Management, 4*(4), 453–471. doi:10.1504/IJICBM.2011.040961

Muniapan, B., & Raj, S. J. (2014). Corporate Social Responsibility Communication from the Vedantic, Dharmic and Karmic Perspectives. In *Communicating Corporate Social Responsibility: Perspectives and Practice. Emerald Group Publishing Limited.*

Murphy, C. (2012). Why P&G CIO is quadrupling analytics expertise. *Information Week, 16*(February). Retrieved from http://www.informationweek.com/news/global-cio-interviews/232601003

Murphy, P. (1999). Character and Virtue Ethics in International Marketing: An Agenda for Managers, Researchers and Educators. *Journal of Business Ethics, 18*(1), 107–124. doi:10.1023/A:1006072413165

Nadkarni, S. (2003). Instructional methods and mental models of students: An empirical investigation. *Academy of Management Learning & Education, 2*(4), 335–351. doi:10.5465/AMLE.2003.11901953

Nahal, A. (2005). Cultural collisions. *Diverse Issues in Higher Education, 22*(20), 41.

Napier, R. W., & Gershenfeld, M. K. (2004). *Groups: Theory and experience.* Boston, MA: Houghton Mifflin.

Narayandas, N., Rangan, V. K., & Zaltman, G. (1998). The pedagogy of executive education in business markets. *Journal of Business-To-Business Marketing, 5*(1/2), 41–64. doi:10.1300/J033v05n01_05

National Center for Education Statistics. (2013). *Digest of Education Statistics.* National Center for Education Statistics. Table 105.20. Retrieved from http://nces.ed.gov/programs/digest/d13/tables/dt13_105.20.asp

National Research Council. (1987). *Education and Learning to Think.* National Research Council Committee on Research in Mathematics, Science, and Technology Education.

Nature. (2013). In *OED Online.* Oxford University Press. Retrieved March 28, 2013, from http://www.oed.com/view/Entry/125353?rskey=LWvDsZ

Nesamoney, D. (2015). *Personalized digital advertising: How data and technology are transforming how we market.* Old Tappan, NJ: Pearson Education, Inc.

Nesdale, D. (2000, December). *Children's ethnic prejudice: A comparison of approaches.* Paper presented at the Transcending Boundaries Conference, Brisbane, Australia.

Ng, E., & Bloemraad, I. (2015). A SWOT analysis of multiculturalism in Canada, Europe, Mauritius, and South Korea. *The American Behavioral Scientist, 59*(6), 619–636. doi:10.1177/0002764214566500

Nguyen, P.-M., Terlouw, C., & Pilot, A. (2008). Culturally appropriate pedagogy: The case of group learning in a Confucian heritage culture context. *Intercultural Education, 17*(1), 1–20. doi:10.1080/14675980500502172

Nicholls, J., Hair, J. F., Ragland, C. B., & Schimmel, K. E. (2013). Ethics, Corporate Social Responsibility, and Sustainability Education in AACSB Undergraduate and Graduate Marketing Curricula: A Benchmark Study. *Journal of Marketing Education, 35*(2), 129–140. doi:10.1177/0273475313489557

Nobel Prize. (2014). Grameen Bank – Facts. *Nobel Prize.* Retrieved January 26, 2015, from http://www.nobelprize.org/nobel_prizes/peace/laureates/2006/grameen-facts.html

Norman, W. T. (1963). Toward an adequate taxonomy of personality attributes: Replicated factor structure in peer nomination personality ratings. *Journal of Abnormal and Social Psychology, 66*(6), 574–583. doi:10.1037/h0040291 PMID:13938947

Northedge, A. (2003). Rethinking teaching in the context of diversity. *Teaching in Higher Education, 8*(1), 17–32. doi:10.1080/1356251032000052302

November, P. (2004). Seven reasons why Marketing Practitioners should ignore Marketing Academic Research. *Journal of Marketing Research, 12*(1991), 39–50. doi:10.1016/S1441-3582(04)70096-8

Nuttavuthisit, K. (2008). *Yaowawit School Kapong.* Kellogg School Case 5-308-500.

Nuttavuthisit, K., Jindahra, P., & Prasanpanich, P. (2015). Participatory Community Development: Evidence from Thailand. *Community Development Journal: An International Forum, 50*(1), 55–70. doi:10.1093/cdj/bsu002

Nye, J. (2004). *Soft Power: The Means to Success in World Politics.* New York: Public Affairs.

O'Donoghue, J., & Maguire, T. (2005). The individual learner, employability and the workplace: A reappraisal of relationships and prophecies. *Journal of European Industrial Training, 29*(6), 436–446. doi:10.1108/03090590510610236

O'Leary, D. E. (2013, December). Exploiting big data from mobile device sensor-based apps: Challenges and benefits. *MIS Quarterly Executive, 12*(4), 179–187.

Oliver, S. L., & Hyun, E. (2011). Comprehensive curriculum reform in higher education: Collaborative engagement of faculty and administrators. *Journal of Case Studies in Education,* 1-20.

Orihuela, R., & Bass, D. (2015, June 4). Help wanted: Black belts in data. *Bloomberg Businessweek.* Retrieved June 26, 2015 from http://www.bloomberg.com/news/articles/2015-2006-2004/help-wanted-black-belts-in-data

Ormrod, R. P., Henneberg, S., & O'Shaughnessy, N. (2013). Political marketing: Theory and concepts. *Sage (Atlanta, Ga.).*

Orton-Jones, C. (2008). Bloom and bust. *Financial Management,* (Feb): 18–21.

Palmer, P. J. (1983). *To Know as We are Known: Education As a Spiritual Journey.* Harper San Francisco: HarperCollins Publishers.

Palmer, P. J. (1989). *The Courage to Teach: Exploring the Inner Landscape of A Teacher's Life.* San Francisco: Jossey-Bass Publishers.

Palmunen, L.-M., Pelto, E., Paalumäki, A., & Lainema, T. (2013). Formation of novice business students' mental models through simulation gaming. *Simulation & Gaming, 44*(6), 846–868. doi:10.1177/1046878113513532

Panagiotou, G., & Wijen, R. (2005). The telescopic observations framework: An attainable strategic tool. *Marketing Intelligence & Planning, 23*(2), 155–171. doi:10.1108/02634500510589912

Parasuraman, B., Satrya, A., Abdullah, M. M., Hamid, F., Muniapan, B., & Rathakrishnan, B. (2009, July). Analyzing the Relationship Between Unions and Joint Consultation Committee: Case studies of Malaysian and Indonesian Postal Industries. *International Journal of Business and Society, 10*(1), 41–58.

Patrizio, A. (2015, March 23). 4 ways to beat the big data talent shortage. *Network World.* Retrieved June 26, 2015 from http://www.networkworld.com/article/2897617/big-data-business-intelligence/2897614-ways-to-beat-the-big-data-talent-shortage.html

Pattison, W. D. (1964). The four traditions of geography. *The Journal of Geography, 63*(5), 211–216. doi:10.1080/00221346408985265

Patton, M. Q. (2002). *Qualitative research and evaluation methods* (3rd ed.). Thousand Oaks, CA: Sage Publications.

Pearson, P. G. (2014, June 27-30). *Putting the learner at the center: Just saying 'digital' is not enough.* Paper presented at the ACBSP 2014 Annual Conference: Teaching Excellence and Teaching Excellence Global Business Education Concurrent Sessions, Chicago, IL.

Peltier, J. W., Hay, A., & Drago, W. (2005). The Reflective Learning Continuum: Reflecting on Reflection. *Journal of Marketing Education, 27*(3), 250–263. doi:10.1177/0273475305279657

Peltier, J. W., Hay, A., & Drago, W. (2006). Reflecting on reflection: Scale extension and a comparison of undergraduate business students in the United States and the United Kingdom. *Journal of Marketing Education, 28*(1), 5–16. doi:10.1177/0273475305279658

Peltier, J. W., & Scovotti, C. (2010). Enhancing entrepreneurial marketing education: The student perspective. *Journal of Small Business and Enterprise Development, 17*(4), 514–536. doi:10.1108/14626001011088705

Pestonjee, D. D., Spillan, J. E., Song, H., & Virzi, N. D. (2010). A Comparative Analysis of Curriculum in International Marketing and Business Between Peruvian and Guatemalan University Students. *Journal of Teaching in International Business, 21*(4), 282–306. doi:10.1080/08975930.2010.526027

Peters, T. J. (1993). Liberation management. Pan books Ltd.

Peterson, E. H. (2003). Missing Ingredient: Why Spirituality Needs Jesus. *Christian Century (Chicago, Ill.),* (March): 22, 30–33.

Peters, T. J. (1994). *The Tom Peters Seminar.* Excel.

Peters, T. J., & Waterman, R. H. (1982). *In search of excellence: Lessons from America's best-run companies.* New York: Harper & Row.

Petkus, E. (2007). Enhancing the relevance and value of marketing curriculum outcomes to a liberal arts education. *Journal of Marketing Education, 29*(1), 39–51. doi:10.1177/0273475306297384

Pettey, C., & Goasduff, O. (2011). *Gartner executive programs worldwide survey of more than 2,000 CIOs identifies cloud computer as top technology priority for CIOs in 2011.* Stamford, CT: Gartner Research.

Pew Research Center. (2008). *U.S. Population Projections: 2005-2050.* Washington, DC: Author.

Pfeffer, J., & Fong, C. (2002). The end of business schools? Less success than meets the eye. *Academy of Management Learning & Education, 1*(1), 78–95. doi:10.5465/AMLE.2002.7373679

Pfeffer, J., & Fong, C. T. (2004). The Business School 'Business': Some Lessons from the US Experience. *Journal of Management Studies, 41*(8), 1501–1520. doi:10.1111/j.1467-6486.2004.00484.x

Philip, N. (March 14, 2014). *The impact of big data on the digital advertising industry.* Mountain View, CA: Qubole Data Service. Retrieved January 3, 2015 from http://www.qubole.com/blog/big-data/big-data-advertising-case-study/

Pickton, D. W., & Wright, S. (1998). What's SWOT in strategic analysis? *Strategic Change, 7*(2), 101–109. doi:10.1002/(SICI)1099-1697(199803/04)7:2<101::AID-JSC332>3.0.CO;2-6

Piercy, N. (1992). *Market-led strategic change*. Oxford, UK: Butterworth-Heineman.

Piercy, N. F. (2002). Research in marketing: Teasing with trivia or risking relevance? *European Journal of Marketing, 36*(3), 350–363. doi:10.1108/03090560210417165

Pincas, A. (2001). Culture, cognition and communication in global education. *Distance Education, 22*(1), 30–51. doi:10.1080/0158791010220103

Pollack, C. (2014, September 29). It's not big data, it's the big idea, stupid. *AdAge*. Retrieved January 2, 105 from http://adage.com/article/advertising-week-2014/big-data-big-idea-stupid/295199/

Pollack, B. L., & Lilly, B. (2008). Gaining Confidence And Competence Through Experiential Assignments: An Exploration Of Student Self-Efficacy And Spectrum Of Inquiry. *Marketing Education Review, 18*(2), 55–66. doi:10.1080/10528008.2008.11489039

Porter, M. E. (1980). *Competitive Strategy*. The Free Press.

Porter, M. E. (1985). *Competitive Advantage*. The Free Press.

Prayukvong, P., & Olsen, M. (2009). *Research paper on Promoting Corporate Social Responsibility in Thailand and the Role of Volunteerism*. The NETWORK of NGO and Business Partnerships for Sustainable Development, commissioned by UNDP.

Price, C. (2014, September 2). Attracting the right audience with big data insights. *The Telegraph*. Retrieved January 2, 2015 from http://www.telegraph.co.uk/sponsored/technology/4g- mobile/engaging-customers/11070094/attract-right-audience-big-data.html

Prince, H. (2004). *A Wesleyan Way* (revised edition). San Diego, California: Point Loma Press.

Purushottam, N. (2013). Sustainability and marketing education: Emerging research themes. In *Vision 2020: Innovation, Development Sustainability, and Economic Growth - Proceedings of the 21st International Business Information Management Association Conference, IBIMA 2013* (Vol. 2, pp. 600–605).

PWC. (2015, February). *Data driven: What students need to succeed in a rapidly changing business world*. Retrieved June 26, 2015 from http://www.pwc.com/us/en/faculty-resource/assets/pwc-data-driven-paper-feb2015.pdf

Pyle, J. L., & Forrant, R. (2002). *Globalization, universities and sustainable human development*. Cornwall: MPG Books Ltd. doi:10.4337/9781843767398

Quesenberry, K. A., Saewitz, D., & Kantrowitz, S. (2014, Spring). Blogging in the classroom: Using wordpress blogs with buddy press plugin as a learning tool by. *Journal of Advertising Education, 18*(2), 5–17.

Rampel, H. (2003). *A High Price for Abundant Living-The Story of Capitalism*. Waterloo, Ontario: Herald Press.

Rapp, S., & Collins, T. L. (1987). Maximarketing. McGraw-Hill USA.

Read, B., & Bentz, B. (2011, Sep 29). Preparing for the panama canal. *Journal of Commerce*. Retrieved from http://search.proquest.com/docview/894806986

Rhinesmith, S. (1993). *A manager's guide to globalization*. Alexandria, VA: American Society for Training and Development/Irwin.

Rigg, J. (1991). Grass-roots development in rural Thailand: A lost cause? *World Development*, *19*(2/3), 199–211. doi:10.1016/0305-750X(91)90255-G

Rimer, E. (1996). Discrimination in Major League Baseball: Hiring Standards for Major League Managers, 1975-1994. *Journal of Sport and Social Issues*, *20*(2), 118–133. doi:10.1177/019372396020002002

Robbs, B. (2010, Fall). Preparing young creatives for an interactive world: How possible is it? *Journal of Advertising Education*, *14*(2), 7–14.

Robinson, J. L. (1976). A new look at the four traditions of geography. *The Journal of Geography*, *75*(9), 520–530. doi:10.1080/00221347608980845

Robinson, S. (2006). Reflecting on the "international group working experience": A study of two MBA programmes. *International Journal of Management Education*, *5*(2), 3–14.

Rosa, J. A. (2012). Marketing education for the next four billion challenges and innovations. *Journal of Marketing Education*, *34*(1), 44–54. doi:10.1177/0273475311430802

Rosenbloom, B. (2013). *Marketing channels: a management view*. Cincinnati, OH: South-Western/Cengage.

Roy, A., & Macchiette, B. (2005). Debating the Issues: A Tool for Augmenting Critical Thinking Skills of Marketing Students. *Journal of Marketing Education*, *27*(3), 264–276. doi:10.1177/0273475305280533

Roy, D. P., & Tennessee, M. (2006). *Enhancing Marketing Curriculum Through Experiential Education*. Marketing Management Association.

Sampson, S. D., & Betters-reed, B. L. (2008). Assurance of Learning and Outcomes Assessment: A Case Study of Assessment of a Marketing Curriculum. *Marketing Education Review*, *18*(3), 25–36. doi:10.1080/10528008.2008.11489045

Samuel. (1992). Religious Roots and Business Practices: Vignettes from Life. In A Virtuous Life in Business: Stories of Courage and Integrity in the Corporate World (pp. 73-90). Academic Press.

Sawyer, R. D. (1994). *Sun Tzu: the art of war*. Boulder, CO: Westview Press, Inc.

Schiller, S., Goodrich, K., & Gupta, P. (2013). Let Them Play! Active Learning in a Virtual World. *Information Systems Management*, *30*(1), 50–62. doi:10.1080/10580530.2013.739891

Schlee, R., & Harich, K. (2010). Knowledge and Skill Requirements for Marketing Jobs in the 21st Century. *Journal of Marketing Education*, *32*(3), 341–352. doi:10.1177/0273475310380881

Schultz, D. E. (2014, May). *Why Big Data is so difficult. Marketing News*. American Marketing Association. Retrieved January 2, 2015 from https://www.ama.org/publications/MarketingNews/Pages/why-big-data-so-difficult.aspx

Schwalb, M. M. & Arrizabalaga, I. (2013). Dimensiones de la responsabilidad social del Marketing. *Revista Venezolana de Gerencia*, (63), 434-456.

Scottish Executive. (2004). A Smart, Successful Scotland - Strategic direction to the Enterprise Networks and an enterprise strategy for Scotland. Author.

Scott, J. B. (2010, December). Intercultural rhetoric in the technical communication curriculum: A review of the literature. *Rhetoric. Professional Communication and Globalization*, *1*(1), 77–90.

Scovotti, C., & Jones, S. K. (2011, Spring). From Web 2.0 to Web 3.0: Implications for advertising courses. *Journal of Advertising Education*, *15*(1), 6–15.

Sharp, A. M., Register, C. A., & Grimes, P. W. (2013). *Economics of social issues*. New York: McGraw-Hill.

Sheth, J. N. (2011). Impact of emerging markets on marketing: Rethinking existing perspectives and practices. *Journal of Marketing, 75*(4), 166–182. doi:10.1509/jmkg.75.4.166

Sheth, J. N., Gardner, D. M., & Garrett, D. E. (1988). *Marketing theory: Evolution and evaluation.* New York, NY: John Wiley & Sons.

Shuptrine, F. K., & Lichtenstein, D. R. (1985). Measuring readability levels of undergraduate marketing textbooks. *Journal of Marketing Education, 7*(3), 38–45. doi:10.1177/027347538500700307

Shuptrine, F. K., & Willenborg, J. F. (1998). Job experience for marketing graduates – implications for university education. *Marketing Education Review, 8*(1), 1–11. doi:10.1080/10528008.1998.11488614

Siemens, G. (2004). *A learning theory for the digital age.* Elearnspace: everything learning. Downloaded April 10 2015.

Siemens, G. (2004). *Connectivism: Learning as network-creation.* Retrieved 9 April 2015 from https://www.youtube.com/watch?v=EvIJfUySmY0

Siemens, G. (2004a). *A learning theory for the digital age.* Elearnspace: everything learning. Downloaded April 10 2015.

Siemens, G. (2004b). *Connectivism: Learning as network-creation.* Elearnspace: everything learning. Downloaded April 10 2015

Simonite, T. (2013, February 5). AT&T brings online ad targeting tactics to TV commercials. *MIT Technology Review.* Retrieved June 26, 2015 from http://www.technologyreview.com/news/510186/att-brings-online-ad-targeting-tactics-to-tv-commercials/

Singer, A. (2013). Analytics = Most Desirable Skill (And Largest Talent Gap) for 2014. *The Future Buzz.* Retrieved from http://thefuturebuzz.com/2013/12/04/analytics-most-desirable-skill-and-largest-talent-gap-for-2014/

Sircar, S. (2009). Business intelligence in the business curriculum. *Communications of the Association for Information Systems, 24*(17), 289–302.

Sirgy, M.J., Yu, G.B., Dong-Jin, L., Shuquin, W., & Ming-Wei, H. (2012). Does Marketing activity contribute to a society'swell-being? The role of economic efficiency. *Journal of Business Ethics, 107*(2), 91-102.

Smith, C. (1995). *Marketing Strategies for the Ethics Era.* Retrieved January 2015 from http://sloanreview.mit.edu/article/marketing-strategies-for-the-ethics-era/

Smith, J. N. (2010). Sci-fi supply chain innovations. *World Trade, WT 100, 23*(5), 50-50.

Smith, B. (2010). Gazelle, lion, hyena, vulture, and worm: A teaching metaphor on competition between early and late market entrants. *Marketing Education Review, 20*(1), 9–16. doi:10.2753/MER1052-8008200102

Smith, E., & Hattery, A. (2011). Race Relations Theories: Implications for Sport Management. *Journal of Sport Management, 25,* 107–117.

Smith, G. F. (2014). Assessing business student thinking skills. *Journal of Management Education, 38*(3), 384–411. doi:10.1177/1052562913489028

Smith, W. L., Schallenkamp, K., & Eichholz, D. E. (2007). Entrepreneurial skills assessment: An exploratory study. *International Journal of Management and Enterprise Development, 4*(2), 179–201. doi:10.1504/IJMED.2007.011791

Soare, L. (2012, March 22). The rise of Big Data in higher education. *EDUCAUSE BRIEF: Spotlight on Analytics Series.* Retrieved January 4, 2015 from https://net.educause.edu/ir/library/pdf/LIVE1208s.pdf

Sofer, T., Kahan, T., & Livneh, E. (2014). *Estimating the use of tablets for learning: Results of student's survey at the Ben-Gurion education center (Heb) working paper*. Tel Aviv University.

Solomon, M., Marshall, G., & Stuart, E. (2012). *Marketing: real people, real choices*. Boston, MA: Prentice Hall.

Southgate, N. (2006). The academic-practitioner divide: Finding time to make a difference. *Marketing Intelligence & Planning*, *24*(6), 547–551. doi:10.1108/02634500610701645

Spector, S., Chard, C., Mallen, C., & Hyatt, C. (2012). Socially constructed environmental issues and sport: A content analysis of ski resort environmental communications. *Sport Management Review*, *15*(4), 416–433. doi:10.1016/j.smr.2012.04.003

Spiro, R. L., Kossack, S., & Kossack, E. (1981). The introductory marketing text: An examination of readability. *Journal of Marketing Education*, *3*(2), 41–51. doi:10.1177/027347538100300209

Stanaland, A. J. S., Helm, A. E., & Kinney, L. (2009, Spring). Bridging the gap in IMC education: Where the academy is falling short? *Journal of Advertising Education*, *13*(1), 38–43.

Stark, J. S., & Lattuca, L. R. (1997). *Shaping the college curriculum: Academic plans in action*. Needham Heights, MA: Allyn and Bacon.

State of the industry research series: Big data in consumer goods. (2012). Whitepaper, Edgell Knowledge Network. Retrieved from www.eknresearch.com

Stevens, G. E. (2000). The art of running a business school in the new millennium: A dean's perspective. *S.A.M. Advanced Management Journal*, *65*(3), 21–28.

Stock, K. (2013). *Nike's Big Gay-Marketing Coup*. Retrieved from https://www.google.com/webhp?sourceid=chrome-instant&ion=1&espv=2&ie=UTF-8#q=nike%27s%20big%20gay-marketing%20coup

Stoddart, M. C. (2012). *Making meaning out of mountains: the political ecology of skiing*. UBC Press.

Stommel, J. (2014). *Critical digital pedagogy*. Retrieved from http://www.hybridpedagogy.com/journal/critical-digital-pedagogy-definition

Strauss, V. (2013). *Nelson Mandela on the Power of Education*. Retrieved from http://www.washingtonpost.com/blogs/answer-sheet/wp/2013/12/05/nelson-mandelas-famous-quote-on-education

Strauss, P., & U, A. (2007). Group assessments: Dilemmas facing lecturers in multicultural tertiary classrooms. *Higher Education Research & Development*, *26*(2), 147–161. doi:10.1080/07294360701310789

Stringfellow, L., Ennis, S., Brennan, R., & Harker, M. J. (2006). Mind the gap: The relevance of marketing education to marketing practice. *Marketing Intelligence & Planning*, *24*(3), 245–256. doi:10.1108/02634500610665718

Stura, C., & Lepadatu, D. (2014). The Black Box of Diversity in Sports Teams: Converging Factors and Theoretical Explorations. *International Journal of Sport and Society*, *4*(2), 47–56.

Tan, A. M. (2002). *Malaysian Private Higher Education: Globalization, Privatization, Transformation and Marketplaces*. London: Asean Academic Press.

Tay, A. (1995). Management's perceptions on MBA graduates in Malaysia. *Journal of Management Development*, *20*(3), 258-274. Available at http://www.emerald-library.com/ft

Taylor, R. L., & Brodowsky, G. H. (2012). Integrating Cross-Cultural Marketing Research Training in International Business Education Programs: It's Time, and Here's Why and How. *Journal of Teaching in International Business*, *23*(2), 145–172. doi:10.1080/08975930.2012.718706

Teer, H. B., Teer, F. P., & Kruck, S. E. (2007). A Study of the Database Marketing Course in AACSB Accredited Business Schools. *Journal of Marketing Education, 29*(3), 245–253. doi:10.1177/0273475307306891

Teradata 2015 global data-driven marketing survey: Progressing toward true individualization. (2015). Teradata, Inc. Retrieved from http://www.teradatauniversitynetwork.com/assetmanagement/DownloadAsset.aspx?ID=204376de-2dfd-4201-9352-5c06a8c73a1f&version=c2fbe4de34304ae08b724028f5dacec41.pdf

Thailand Development Research Institute. (2005). Bangkok: Economic Impact of Tsunami on Thailand.

Thanki, R. (1999). How do we know the value of higher education to regional development? *Regional Studies, 33*(1), 84–89.

Thatcher, B. (2010, December). Editor's introduction to first edition: Eight needed developments and eight critical contexts for global inquiry. *Rhetoric, Professional Communication and Globalization, 1*(1), 1-34.

The Economist. (2014, December). *Africa rising.* Retrieved from http://www.economist.com/news/special-report/21572377-african-lives-have-already-greatly-improved-over-past-decade-says-oliver-august

The rise of the marketer: Driving engagement, experience and revenue. (2015). The Economist Intelligence Unit. Retrieved from http://futureofmarketing.eiu.com/briefing/EIU_MARKETO_Marketer_WEB.pdf

Thompson, M. (2002). Marketing Virtue. *Business Ethics: An European Review, 11*(4), 354–362. doi:10.1111/1467-8608.00295

Thrush, E. (1993). Bridging the gaps: Technical communication in an international and multicultural society. *Technical Communication Quarterly, 16*(2), 139–174.

TIME. (2014, August 25). Ice Bucket Challenge Nears $80 Millions Mark. *TIME.* Retrieved January 26, 2015, from http://time.com/3173833/als-ice-bucket-challenge-fundraising-total/

Title IX of the Education Amendments Act of 1972, 20 U.S.C.A. § 1681, et seq., on June 23, 1972.

Titus, P. (2007). Applied Creativity: The Creative Marketing Breakthrough Model. *Journal of Marketing Education, 29*(3), 262–272. doi:10.1177/0273475307307600

Torres, F. (2007). *Cuestiones eticas en el Marketing.* Paper presented at VII Congreso Nacional e Internacional de Administracion "Management: visión prospectiva", Buenos Aires, Argentina.

Tregear, A., Dobson, S., Brennan, M., & Kuznesof, S. (2010). Critically divided?: How marketing educators perceive undergraduate programmes in the UK. *European Journal of Marketing, 44*(1/2), 66–86. doi:10.1108/03090561011008619

Triana, M. D. C., & García, M. F. (2009). Valuing Diversity: A Group-value Approach to Understanding the Importance of Organizational Efforts to Support Diversity. *Journal of Organizational Behavior, 30*(7), 941–962. doi:10.1002/job.598

Triandis, H. C. (1971). *Attitude and attitude change.* New York: Wiley.

Trompenaars, F., & Woolliams, P. (2003). *Business across cultures.* Chichester, UK: Capstone Publishing.

Tryce, S.A. & Smith, B. (2015). A Mock Debate on the Washington Redskins Brand: Fostering Critical Thinking and Cultural Sensitivity Among Sport Business Students. *Sport Management Education Journal, 9,* 1-10. 10.1123/SMEJ.2013-0016

Tryce, S. A., & Brooks, S. N. (2010). "Ain't I a Woman?": Black Women and Title IX. *Journal for the Study of Sports and Athletes in Education, 4*(3), 243–255. doi:10.1179/ssa.2010.4.3.243

TUN KPI Summary. (2015). Presentation at April TUN board meeting. Minutes from Board Meeting.

Turban, E., Sharda, R., Dursun, D., & King, D. (2010). *Busness intelligence: A managerial approach* (2nd ed.). Upper Saddle River, NJ: Pearson Prentice Hall.

Twigg, C. A. (2003). Improving learning and reducing costs: New models for online learning. *EDUCAUSE Review*, *38*(5), 29–38.

Tymon, A. (2013). The student perspective on employability. *Studies in Higher Education*, *38*(6), 841–856. doi:10.10 80/03075079.2011.604408

U.S. Department of Education. (2013). *Digest of Education Statistics, 2012*. National Center for Education Statistics. (NCES 2014-015), Chapter 2. Retrieved from https://nces.ed.gov/fastfacts/display.asp?id=84

Ueltschy, L. C. (2001). An Exploratory Study of Integrating Interactive Technology into the Marketing Curriculum. *Journal of Marketing Education*, *23*(1), 63–72. doi:10.1177/0273475301231008

UK Council for International Student Affairs. (2010). *Higher education statistics*. Retrieved from http://www.ukcisa.org.uk

Ulfarsson, G. F., & Unger, E. A. (2011). Impacts and responses of Icelandic aviation to the 2010 Eyjafjallajokull volcanic eruption case study. *Transportation Research Record*, *2214*, 144–151. doi:10.3141/2214-18

UNICEF. (2014). *Private Fundraising and Partnerships. 2013 Annual Report*. Retrieved January 26, 2015, from http://www.unicef.org/about/annualreport/files/Private_Fundraising_and_Partnerships_AR_2013.pdf

United Nations Education, Scientific and Cultural Organization (UNESCO). (2015). Retrieved 20 July 2015 from: http://en.unesco.org/about-us/introducing-unesco

United Nations Human Right. (2015). Retrieved 20 July 2015 from: http://www.ohchr.org/EN/UDHR/Pages/Introduction.aspx

United Nations. (2007). *Toward a Culture of Peace*. Retrieved 22 July 2015 from: http://www.un.org/en/ga/search/view_doc.asp?symbol=A/52/191&Lang=E

United States Department of Education. (1997). *Title IX: 25 Years of Progress*. Retrieved from: www2.ed.gov/pubs/Title IX/index.html

United States Department of Justice. (n.d.). *Title IX Legal Manual*. Retrieved from www.justice.gov/crt/about/cor/coord/ixlegal.php

Vaill, P. (1996). *Learning as a Way of Being: Strategies for Survival in a World of Permanent White Water*. San Francisco: Jossey-Bass Publishers.

Vaill, P. (1998). *Spirited leading and learning*. San Francisco: Jossey-Bass Publishers.

Valentin, E. (2006). Away with SWOT analysis: Use defensive/offensive evaluation instead. *Journal of Applied Business Research*, *21*(2), 91–104.

Van Doren, D. C., & Smith, D. B. (1999). Scenario planning: A new approach to teaching marketing strategy. *Journal of Marketing Education*, *21*(2), 146–155. doi:10.1177/0273475399212008

van Oudenhoven, J. P., Mol, S., & van der Zee, K. (2003). Study of the adjustment of Western expatriates in Taiwan ROC with the multicultural personality questionnaire. *Asian Journal of Social Psychology*, *6*(2), 159–170. doi:10.1111/1467-839X.t01-1-00018

van Oudenhoven, J. P., van der Zee, K. I., & van Kooten, M. (2001). Successful adaptation strategies according to expatriates. *International Journal of Intercultural Relations*, *25*(5), 467–482. doi:10.1016/S0147-1767(01)00018-9

Vansteenkiste, M., Lens, W., & Deci, E. L. (2006). Intrinsic versus Extrinsic Goal Contents in Self-determination Theory: Another Look at the Quality of Academic Motivation. *Educational Psychologist, 41*(1), 19–31. doi:10.1207/s15326985ep4101_4

Vichit-Vadakan, J. (2002). Part One: The Country Report. In Investing In Ourselves: Giving and Fund Raising in Thailand (pp. 3-27). Manila: Asian Development Bank.

Vogel, D., Zhou, H., & Hu, D. (2015, March). Special issue on computation, business, and health science. *Big Data Research, 2*(1), 1. doi:10.1016/j.bdr.2015.03.002

Von der Heidt, T., & Quazi, A. (2013). Enhancing learning-centeredness in marketing principles curriculum.[AMJ]. *Australasian Marketing Journal, 21*(4), 250–258. doi:10.1016/j.ausmj.2013.08.005

Waddock, S., & Lozano, J. M. (2013). Developing more holistic management education: Lessons learned from two programs. *Academy of Management Learning & Education, 12*(2), 265–284. doi:10.5465/amle.2012.0002

Walker, I., Tsarenko, Y., Wagstaff, P., Powell, I., Steel, M., & Brace-Govan, J. (2009). The Development of Competent Marketing Professionals. *Journal of Marketing Education, 31*(3), 253–263. doi:10.1177/0273475309345197

Walton, C. (1988). *The Moral Manager*. Ballinger Publishing Company.

Wang, T.-H., Chiu, M.-H., Lin, J.-W., & Chou, C.-C. (2013). Diagnosing students' mental models via the web-based mental models diagnosis system. *British Journal of Educational Technology, 44*(2), E49–E48. doi:10.1111/j.1467-8535.2012.01328.x

Warren, H. (1992). Implementing holistic education in marketing courses. *Marketing Education Review, 2*(2), 21–24. doi:10.1080/10528008.1992.11488361

Watson, H. J. (2008). Business schools need to change what they teach. *Business Intelligence Journal, 13*(4), 407.

Watson, H. J., & Marjanovic, O. (2013). Big data: The fourth data management generation. *Business Intelligence Journal, 18*(3), 4–8.

Webometrics. (2015). *Countries arranged by Number of Universities in Top Ranks*. Webometrics. Retrieved from http://www.webometrics.info/en/node/54

Weinrauch, J. D. (2005). An Exploratory Use of Musical Metaphors to Enhance Student Learning. *Journal of Marketing Education, 27*(2), 109–121. doi:10.1177/0273475304273353

Wellman, N. (2010). Relating the curriculum to marketing competence: A conceptual framework. *The Marketing Review, 10*(2), 119–134. doi:10.1362/146934710X505735

Wenger, E. (1998). *Communities of practice: Learning, meaning, and identity*. Cambridge University Press. doi:10.1017/CBO9780511803932

Wildemeersch, D., Jansen, T., Vandenabeele, J., & Jans, M. (1998). Social Learning: A New Perspective on Learning in Participatory Systems. *Studies in Continuing Education, 20*(2), 251–265. doi:10.1080/0158037980200210

Williams, G. F. (1994). Another disaster, another market crisis. *American Agent & Broker, 66*(2), 18–18.

Williams, O. F., & Murphy, P. E. (1990). The Ethics of Virtue: A Moral Theory for Marketing. *Journal of Macromarketing, 10*(2), 19–29. doi:10.1177/027614679001000103

Wilson, E. (1998). Commentary on: 'The pedagogy of executive education in business markets'. *Journal of Business-to-Business Marketing, 5*(1-2), 65-70.

Winstanley, Clark & Lesson. (2002). Approaches to Child Labor in the Supply Chain. *Business Ethics: An European Review, 11*(3), 210-223.

Witkowski, T. H. (1989). History's Place in the Marketing Curriculum. *Journal of Marketing Education, 11*(2), 54–57. doi:10.1177/027347538901100209

Witte, A. E., Sequeira, I., & Fonteyne, C. (2003). Internationalizing the assessment criteria to build cross-cultural competency: American and Chinese educational encounters. *Journal of Teaching in International Business, 14*(4), 61–78. doi:10.1300/J066v14n04_04

Wixom, B., Ariyachandra, T., Goul, M., Gray, P., Kulkarni, U., & Phillips-Wren, G. (2011). The current state of business intelligence in academia. *Communications of the Association for Information Systems, 29*(16), 299–312.

Wolterstorff, N. (2002). *Educating for Life: Reflections on Christian Teaching and Learning* (G. G. Stronks & C. W. Joldersma, Eds.). Grand Rapids, MI: Baker Academic.

Wood, J. (1999). *Christians at Work: Not Business as Usual.* Scottsdale, PA: Herald Press.

Woods, P. R. (2004, July). *A framework for evaluating cross-cultural management performance.* Paper presented at the International Federation of Academies of Management (IFSAM) VII World Congress, Goteborg, Sweden.

Woods, P. R., Jordan, P. J., Loudoun, R., Troth, A. C., & Kerr, D. (2006). Effective Teaching in the Multicultural Business Classroom. *Journal of Teaching in International Business, 17*(4), 27–47. doi:10.1300/J066v17n04_03

Wordsman, E. (2014, December 14). Journalism schools add courses in sports, emerging technology. *American Journalism Review.* Retrieved January 4, 2015 from http://ajr.org/2014/12/18/journalism-schools-add-courses-sports-emerging-technology/

World Bank. (2000). *Higher education in developing countries: Peril and promise.* Washington, DC: The International Bank for Reconstruction and Development, World Bank.

Worthy, J. (1958). Religion and Its Role in the World of Business. *The Journal of Business, 31*(4), 293–303. doi:10.1086/294216

Write, N. S., & Drewery, G. P. (2006). Forming cohesion in culturally heterogeneous teams: Differences in Japanese, Pacific Islander and Anglo experiences. *Cross Cultural Management: An International Journal, 13*(1), 43–54. doi:10.1108/13527600610643475

Xu, Y., & Yang, Y. (2010). Student learning in business simulation: An empirical investigation. *Journal of Education for Business, 85*(4), 223–228. doi:10.1080/08832320903449469

Yüksel, İ., & Dağdeviren, M. (2007). Using the analytic network process (ANP) in a SWOT analysis – A case study for a textile firm. *Information Sciences, 177*(16), 3364–3382. doi:10.1016/j.ins.2007.01.001

Zepke, N., & Leach, L. (2007). Implementing student outcomes in higher education: New Zealand teachers' views on teaching students from diverse backgrounds. *Teaching in Higher Education, 12*(5), 655–668. doi:10.1080/13562510701596190

Zollinger, M. (1993). Le concept de prix de référence dans le comportement du consommateur: D'une revue de la littérature à l'élaboration d'un modèle prix de réfé- rence-acceptabilité. *Recherche et Applications en Marketing, 8*(2), 61–77. doi:10.1177/076737019300800204

About the Contributors

Brent Smith is Associate Professor of Marketing, Interim Associate Director of the Pedro Arrupe Center for Business Ethics, and Director of Fellowships at Saint Joseph's University in Philadelphia, PA. His areas of expertise include marketing strategy, marketing ethics, marketing analytics, global business, and cross-cultural engagement. He has developed several teaching innovations, including the "Five Creatures Lesson," a novel paradigm for competing effectively in business and industry. Dr. Smith's research focuses on the role of culture in marketing ethics, marketing channels, sales management, and leadership. His work appears in various scholarly outlets, such as *Psychology & Marketing, Journal of Business Ethics, Journal of Marketing Channels, Advances in International Management, Marketing Education Review*, and *Journal of Business-to-Business Marketing*.

Amiram Porath is an expert at innovation. He published his first book in 2010 regarding collaborative research between industry and public research organizations. He published several chapters in other books as well as co-edited special issues and written several articles. He advises the Chief Scientist of Israel regarding collaborative research programs. He also advises other public bodies with a focus on environmental technologies. He has been an evaluator of European research programs since FP7 regarding bringing new firms and technologies to the market.

* * *

Mirjeta Beqiri, PhD, has been teaching in the School of Business Administration at Gonzaga University, USA, since 2002, where she is currently an Associate Professor of Statistics and Operations Management (2009). She was an Adjunct Faculty of Quantitative Methods (Ph.D.) at Universiteti "Aleksandër Moisiu", Durrës, Albania (2012-2013) and University of New York, Tirana (2008). During 1993-1994, as well as 1997-1998, Dr. Beqiri taught at the Faculty of Economy, Universiteti i Shkodrës "Luigj Gurakuqi", Albania, and chaired the Department of Management (1998). She has published articles in several academic journals and is a frequent participant in national and international conferences and symposiums. She has co-authored with Dr. Will Terpening and Sarah Schwering, MBA, Statistical Analysis for Business and Economics: Concepts and Practices (2013) and has contributed as a reviewer of scientific journals, such as Decision Sciences Institute Proceedings, International Journal of Production Research, International Journal of the Academic Business World, and The Asia-Pacific Education Researcher, as well as academic textbooks, such as: Business Statistics and Supply Chain Management. In recognition of her research and teaching excellence, Dr. Beqiri has earned many awards, including: "Outstanding MBA Professor of the Year" by Graduate Students Association, Gonzaga University (2007,

2009, 2010, 2012, and 2013); "Best Paper Award" by Academic Business World International Conference for "Business Ethics Education: The Service Quality Perspective" co-authored with Drs. Kurpis & Helgeson (2007); "Jepson Fellowship" award for distinguished research (2007, 2008 and 2009) by the School of Business Administration, Gonzaga University; "Exemplary Faculty Award" (2013) by Gonzaga University; "Shkodra University Gratitude Award" (2013) by the Senate of Universiteti i Shkodrës "Luigj Gurakuqi" for "Distinguished contribution in the establishment, sustainment and advancement of the Faculty of Economy"; and Loeken SBA Vision and Values Award (2014) by the School of Business Administration, Gonzaga University. She completed her undergraduate studies in Statistics (1988) at Universiteti i Tiranës, Albania, and her MBA (1996) and PhD in Operations Management (2005) at Southern Illinois University, Carbondale, USA.

David J. Burns, DBA (1987, Kent State University) is Professor of Marketing, Kennesaw State University. He has co-authored several books, published over 100 journal articles and book chapters, and presented over 200 papers. His research interests include retail location and atmospherics, ethics, and consumer culture. His teaching interests include retailing and other consumer-based areas, including Marketing and the Consumer Culture and Neuromarketing.

Paulo Duarte is professor of marketing at the Business and Economics Department and head of the Master in Marketing at University of Beira Interior, Portugal. Prior to receiving his Ph.D. in Management at the University of Beira Interior, he held a senior marketing position in a fast moving consumer goods distribution company. Academically, has been doing research in the fields of consumer behaviour, student satisfaction, brand management and online marketing having published articles on these topics. He is also member of the editorial board of several international journals.

Matt Elbeck earned his PhD in Business Administration from Cardiff University, U.K., and has taught undergraduate and graduate business students at universities in the United States, United Kingdom, Canada, and Saudi Arabia. Matt's scholarship in marketing education and personal marketing has been published various journals including the Journal of Marketing Education, Journal for Advancement of Marketing Education, Marketing Education Review, Journal of Education for Business, e-Journal of Business Education & Scholarship of Teaching and Journal of Higher Education Policy and Management. Matt has won various awards including an American Marketing Association summer educator's conference marketing education track paper award and is presently editor, Journal for Advancement of Marketing Education. Matt spent one year outside academe as Director of Programs and Strategy for IT Centre, U.K., and has consulted for corporations including Orange-KPN, American Psychiatric Association, Price Waterhouse, Lloyds Bank PLC, Canadian Red Cross and Unilever.

Ana Estima is an adjunct professor of marketing at the Institute for Accounting and Administration of the University of Aveiro and holds a PhD in Marketing and strategy, from a joint program among the Universities of Minho, Aveiro and Beira Interior - Portugal.

Vivian Faustino-Pulliam has been teaching Marketing and Economics at University of San Francisco's School of Management since 2009. She is also an affiliate faculty at Regis university teaching Global Business and was a former professor of Marketing at Ateneo de Manila University's Graduate School of Business. Vivian has over 18 years of marketing management experience in the financial industry (Asia

Pacific and North America) and took a sabbatical from her last post as Vice-President for Marketing of a major British bank to pursue her passion in teaching. Her research and advocacy work deals primarily with higher education for those underrepresented and marginalized communities. This cause brought her to focus her volunteer work to Jesuit Commons: Higher Education at the Margins (JC:HEM). Currently, Vivian is the lead faculty for JC:HEM Global Markets course and is teaching Global Business and Introduction to Economics courses. Vivian developed the online curriculum for two of JC:HEM's courses: Marketing and Family Economics.

Carlos Ballesteros Garcia has over 20 years of teaching in the area of Marketing and Consumer Behavior. He has taught social marketing and nonprofit marketing strategies for NGOs, Ethics of marketing in various Graduate programs such as doctoral courses, seminars and workshops both in Spain (UNED, UCM, Mondragón) and in France (ESC-Poitiers), Sweden (Univ. Boras), Colombia (Univ. of North), China (Guangzhou Univ.) and Mexico (ITESM). He is a volunteer faculty (on-line) for Global Markets course for Regis University (USA) offered in collaboration with JC: HEM (Jesuit Commons: Higher Education in the Margins).

Margaret L. Gregory is a Lecturer in Marketing at Universiti Teknologi MARA (UiTM), Malaysia (Sarawak Campus) in Kota Samarahan. Previously she taught Marketing at the School of Business & Design, Swinburne University of Technology (Sarawak Campus) in Kuching. Her research interests are in the areas of Marketing Communications, Marketing Education and Service Innovation. She holds a BBA (Marketing & Management) from Oklahoma University, USA and MBA from University Utara Malaysia.

Yowei Kang, PhD, is Assistant Professor at Degree Program of Creative Industries and Digital Films, Kainan University, Taiwan. His research interests focus on digital game research, technology and rhetoric, composition pedagogy using digital game technology, and teaching English as a second language (ESL).

Maria Lai-ling Lam is a Professor of Marketing at Point Loma Nazarene University, San Diego, California since 2014. She has taught a variety of marketing and organizational behavior courses at Malone University, Canton, Ohio during 2001 to 2014. She is well-known for adopting integrated experiential learning pedagogy into her undergraduate and graduate courses. Over the years, she has facilitated her students to serve more than 50 profit and non-profit organizations. She holds a PhD in marketing and organization behavior from George Washington University, a MA degree in Religion Studies focusing on Christianity and Chinese religions, a MBA degree in Marketing and International Business, and a BBA degree in Marketing from the Chinese University of Hong Kong. She has published one book and more than 70 peer-reviewed journal articles, book chapters and proceedings published in refereed academic and professional outlets. She has presented extensively at national and international conferences. Her research interests are corporate social responsibility, cross-cultural negotiation, and business education. She is a fellow of International Academy of Intercultural Research, a member of the editorial review board of business journals and several professional organizations. She received the Distinguished Faculty Award in Scholarship and Creative Expression at Malone University in 2011. Her joint paper with Dr. Georgia Eshelman and Dr. Martha Cook titled "Three contributing factors to effective utilization of technology in management education and practice: Personhood, mindfulness, and meditation" and her paper, "An alternative paradigm of managing sustainability in the global supply chain" have won distinguished paper and the best research paper award respectively in the national conferences.

Edith Lim Ai Ling is a Lecturer in Marketing at the School of Business & Design, Swinburne University of Technology Sarawak Campus in Kuching. She had previously taught at Curtin University of Technology, Sarawak Campus in Miri. Edith holds a B.Com (Commercial Law) from Curtin University of Technology in Perth, Western Australia and MBA (Marketing) from University of Southern Queensland. Her research areas of interest are in the area of Marketing Education, Human Behavior and Product Modification.

Amir Manzoor holds a bachelor's degree in engineering from NED University, Karachi, an MBA from Lahore University of Management Sciences (LUMS), and an MBA from Bangor University, United Kingdom. He has many years of diverse professional and teaching experience working at many renowned national and internal organizations and higher education institutions. His research interests include electronic commerce and technology applications in business. He is a member of Chartered Banker Institute of UK and Project Management Institute, USA.

Balakrishnan Muniapan is a specialist in HRM and is currently with Wawasan Open University in Penang. He has previously held Senior Lecturer positions at Swinburne University of Technology, Curtin University of Technology, and BIMC in Beijing (China). Dr. Bala was recently conferred the "Best Professor in HRM" award at the World Education Congress, Asia's Education Excellence Award 2014 in Singapore. He has also been a Visiting Professor in HRM for universities and management institutes in the Philippines, Vietnam and India. In academia, Dr. Bala has published over fifty research papers and articles in several international journals, conference proceedings, and book chapters. As a HRM speaker, Dr. Bala is frequently honored as an invited speaker on people management issues at numerous national and international conferences and seminars in several countries within Asia, Australia, Africa and Europe As a HRM trainer and consultant, Dr. Bala has vast experience in conducting training and consultancy programs in HRM and have contributed tremendously towards HRM effectiveness for more than hundred organizations within Malaysia and in Asia.

Krittinee Nuttavuthisit is a full-time faculty member who teaches courses in consumption and marketing and postmodern consumer research. She is a scholar of the King Anandamahidol Foundation in Thailand. She received her PhD in Marketing from the Kellogg School of Management, Northwestern University. In 2009, Dr. Krittinee received Sasin Teacher of the Year Award followed by Chulalongkorn's Award for Teaching Excellence. She received Sasin Teacher of the Year Award again in 2011 and 2012 and Chulalongkorn's Award in 2013. Dr. Krittinee's research interests are in consumer experience and postmodern marketing. Her work has appeared in several leading journals such as Business Horizon, Journal of Consumer Research, Journal of Consumer Psychology, Journal of Retailing, and Journal of Contemporary Ethnography. Moreover, Dr. Krittinee has also served as the consultant and advisor for primary companies in businesses such as retailing, gem and jewelry, banking, hospitality, and tourism.

Dulce Saldaña is assistant professor at Tecnologico de Monterrey, Campus Querétaro. Has over 8 years of teaching in Marketing and Consumer Behaviour area. She is member of the Research Group "Consumption Scene" from Universidad Pontificia Comillas. Her current research projects explore the acculturation of bicultural families (mexican-spaniards) living in Madrid, Spain. The main contribution is to interpret the meanings of traditions, culture and customs in other country in three different moments as leisure, daily and traditional holidays. Ethnography and the Grounded Theory were the basis for that research. Now her research is focused on ethical, responsible and ecological consumption in Mexico using qualitative methodologies as ethnographics. She is interested in transformative consumer research.Her research has been published in journals and congresses as Association for Consumer Research. She is personal volunter in differents ONG helping them with marketing strategies. She has coordinated more than 20 groups of students involved with ONG'S marketing projects.

Camille Schuster, PhD, from The Ohio State University is currently a Full Professor of Marketing and International Business at California State University San Marcos and President of Global Collaborations, Inc. She founded and is past Chair of the Marketing Option Advisory Board, a member of the Management Information Systems Advisory Board, a member of the Executive Committee of the Teradata University Network Advisory Board, a member of RetailWire.com Braintrust, a member of the Global Supply Chain Advisory Board at California State University San Marcos and a member of the San Diego Imperial Valley District Export Council. Dr. Schuster, has conducted seminars and worked with over 60 companies in more than 20 countries around the world. Dr. Schuster has published two e-Books entitled New Ways of Working Together: Collaboration Within and Between Companies and New Ways of Working Together: Organizational and Employee Change with GettothePointBooks.com. Dr. Schuster co-authored two books with Michael Copeland, retired human resources manager with Procter & Gamble, Global Business Practices: Adapting for Success and Global Business: Planning for Sales and Negotiations. She has co-authored a book entitled, The Consumer . . . Or Else! with Don Dufek, retired senior vice president and officer of The Kroger Company. The Rise of Consumer Power: Adopting the Right Marketing Communication Strategies, was published in Singapore. Dr. Schuster has authored over 30 articles in professional and academic publications. Dr. Schuster has also taught at Xavier University, Arizona State University, Garvin School of International Business (Thunderbird), Virginia Polytechnic Institute and State University, and Indiana University Northwest.

Stephanie A. Tryce received a JD from Temple University School of Law. She is currently an Assistant Professor at Saint Joseph's University teaching sport business classes. She began teaching as a Lecturer in the Mark H. McCormack Sport Management Department at the University of Massachusetts-Amherst, and has taught in the Legal Studies and Business Ethics Department of The Wharton School of the University of Pennsylvania and the Sport Management Department at the University of Delaware. Professor Tryce's research interests are at the intersection of sport, law and social justice. Most recently Professor Tryce co-authored an article titled, "Mock Debate on the Washington Redskins Brand – Fostering Critical Thinking and Cultural Sensitivity in Sport Business Students," which appeared in the Spring 2015 edition of the Sport Management Education Journal.

Homer Warren (DBA, Kent State University with a major concentration in urban economics and minor in marketing). He is an Associate Professor of Marketing at Youngstown State University. Over his 30 years in the marketing department he has taught many undergraduate and graduate marketing courses, concentrating mostly on consumer behavior, strategic marketing management, and social responsibility. His recent research publications concern creative thinking methodologies in teaching marketing courses, (dis)empowerment issues relative to consumerism, and retail store atmospherics. He is currently undertaking research concerning consumer and producer consciousness.

Kenneth C. C. Yang is a Professor at the Department of Communication. His research focuses on new media and advertising, consumer behavior in East Asia, impacts of new media in Asia.

Index

Become an IRMA Member

Members of the **Information Resources Management Association (IRMA)** understand the importance of community within their field of study. The Information Resources Management Association is an ideal venue through which professionals, students, and academicians can convene and share the latest industry innovations and scholarly research that is changing the field of information science and technology. Become a member today and enjoy the benefits of membership as well as the opportunity to collaborate and network with fellow experts in the field.

IRMA Membership Benefits:

- **One FREE Journal Subscription**

- **30% Off Additional Journal Subscriptions**

- **20% Off Book Purchases**

- Updates on the latest events and research on Information Resources Management through the IRMA-L listserv.

- Updates on new open access and downloadable content added to Research IRM.

- A copy of the Information Technology Management Newsletter twice a year.

- A certificate of membership.

IRMA Membership $195

Scan code to visit irma-international.org and begin by selecting your free journal subscription.

Membership is good for one full year.

CPSIA information can be obtained at www.ICGtesting.com
Printed in the USA
BVOW04*2011140316

440298BV00007B/48/P